Robert A. Geffner, PhD
Peter G. Jaffe, PhD
Marlies Sudermann, PhD
Editors

Children Exposed to Domestic Violence: Current Issues in Research, Intervention, Prevention, and Policy Development

Children Exposed to Domestic Violence: Current Issues in Research, Intervention, Prevention, and Policy Development has been co-published simultaneously as *Journal of Aggression, Maltreatment & Trauma,* Volume 3, Number 1 (#5) 2000.

Pre-publication
REVIEWS,
COMMENTARIES,
EVALUATIONS . . .

"**T**his text will be a welcome addition to the resource library of every professional whose career encompasses issues of children's mental health, well-being and best interest.

I strongly recommend this helpful and stimulating text."

The Honorable Justice
Grant A. Campbell
Justice of the Ontario Superior Court of Justice, Family Court, Canada

HMTP

The Haworth Maltreatment & Trauma Press
An Imprint of The Haworth Press, Inc.

Children Exposed to Domestic Violence: Current Issues in Research, Intervention, Prevention, and Policy Development

Children Exposed to Domestic Violence: Current Issues in Research, Intervention, Prevention, and Policy Development has been co-published simultaneously as *Journal of Aggression, Maltreatment & Trauma,* Volume 3, Number 1 (#5) 2000.

The *Journal of Aggression, Maltreatment & Trauma* Monographic "Separates"

Below is a list of "separates," which in serials librarianship means a special issue simultaneously published as a special journal issue or double-issue *and* as a "separate" hardbound monograph. (This is a format which we also call a "DocuSerial.")

"Separates" are published because specialized libraries or professionals may wish to purchase a specific thematic issue by itself in a format which can be separately cataloged and shelved, as opposed to purchasing the journal on an on-going basis. Faculty members may also more easily consider a "separate" for classroom adoption.

"Separates" are carefully classified separately with the major book jobbers so that the journal tie-in can be noted on new book order slips to avoid duplicate purchasing.

You may wish to visit Haworth's website at . . .

http://www.haworthpressinc.com

. . . to search our online catalog for complete tables of contents of these separates and related publications.

You may also call 1-800-HAWORTH (outside US/Canada: 607-722-5857), or Fax 1-800-895-0582 (outside US/Canada: 607-771-0012), or e-mail at:

getinfo@haworthpressinc.com

Children Exposed to Domestic Violence: Current Issues in Research, Intervention, Prevention, and Policy Development

Robert A. Geffner, PhD
Peter G. Jaffe, PhD
Marlies Sudermann, PhD
Editors

Children Exposed to Domestic Violence: Current Issues in Research, Intervention, Prevention, and Policy Development has been co-published simultaneously as *Journal of Aggression, Maltreatment & Trauma,* Volume 3, Number 1 (#5) 2000.

HMTP

The Haworth Maltreatment & Trauma Press
An Imprint of
The Haworth Press, Inc.
New York • London • Oxford

Published by

The Haworth Maltreatment & Trauma Press, 10 Alice Street, Binghamton, NY 13904-1580 USA

The Haworth Maltreatment & Trauma Press is an imprint of The Haworth Press, Inc., 10 Alice Street, Binghamton, NY 13904-1580 USA.

Children Exposed to Domestic Violence: Current Issues in Research, Intervention, Prevention, and Policy Development has been co-published simultaneously as *Journal of Aggression, Maltreatment & Trauma* ™, Volume 3, Number 1 (#5) 2000.

Cover design by Thomas J. Mayshock Jr.

Library of Congress Cataloging-in-Publication Data

Children exposed to domestic violence : current issues in research, intervention, prevention, and policy development / Robert A. Geffner, Peter G. Jaffe, Marlies Sudermann, editors.
    p. cm.
    "Has been co-published simultaneously as Journal of aggression, maltreatment & trauma, volume 3, number 1 (#5) 2000."
    Includes bibliographical references and index.
    ISBN 0-7890-0785-1 (alk. paper)–ISBN 0-7890-0820-3 (alk. paper)
    1. Abused children. 2. Abused children–Services for. 3. Children and violence. 4. Family violence–Prevention. 5. Victims of family violence–Services for. I. Geffner, Robert. II. Jaffe, Peter G. III. Sudermann, Marlies. IV. Journal of aggression, maltreatment & trauma.
HV6626.5 .C555 2000
362.76–dc21
                                                       00-035034

INDEXING & ABSTRACTING

Contributions to this publication are selectively indexed or abstracted in print, electronic, online, or CD-ROM version(s) of the reference tools and information services listed below. This list is current as of the copyright date of this publication. See the end of this section for additional notes.

- *BUBL Information Service, an Internet-based Information Service for the UK higher education community <URL: http://bubl.ac.uk/>*

- *Cambridge Scientific Abstracts*

- *caredata CD: the social & community care database*

- *Child Development Abstracts & Bibliography*

- *CNPIEC Reference Guide: Chinese National Directory of Foreign Periodicals*

- *Criminal Justice Abstracts*

- *EMBASE/Excerpta Medical Secondary Publishing Division*

- *Family Studies Database (online and CD/ROM)*

- *FINDEX www.publist.com*

- *Index to Periodical Articles Related to Law*

- *Mental Health Abstracts (online through DIALOG)*

- *National Clearinghouse on Child Abuse & Neglect Information*

- *PASCAL, c/o Institute de L'Information Scientifique et Technique*

- *Psychiatric Rehabilitation Journal*

- *Published International Literature on Traumatic Stress (The PILOTS Database)*

- *Referativnyi Zhurnal*

- *Social Services Abstracts www.csa.com*

(continued)

Special Bibliographic Notes related to special journal issues
(separates) and indexing/abstracting:

- indexing/abstracting services in this list will also cover material in any "separate" that is co-published simultaneously with Haworth's special thematic journal issue or DocuSerial. Indexing/abstracting usually covers material at the article/chapter level.
- monographic co-editions are intended for either non-subscribers or libraries which intend to purchase a second copy for their circulating collections.
- monographic co-editions are reported to all jobbers/wholesalers/approval plans. The source journal is listed as the "series" to assist the prevention of duplicate purchasing in the same manner utilized for books-in-series.
- to facilitate user/access services all indexing/abstracting services are encouraged to utilize the co-indexing entry note indicated at the bottom of the first page of each article/chapter/contribution.
- this is intended to assist a library user of any reference tool (whether print, electronic, online, or CD-ROM) to locate the monographic version if the library has purchased this version but not a subscription to the source journal.
- individual articles/chapters in any Haworth publication are also available through the Haworth Document Delivery Service (HDDS).

Children Exposed to Domestic Violence: Current Issues in Research, Intervention, Prevention, and Policy Development

CONTENTS

POLICY DEVELOPMENT AND INTERNATIONAL ISSUES

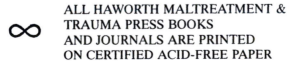

ABOUT THE EDITORS

Robert A. Geffner, PhD, ABPN, is Founder and President of the Family Violence and Sexual Assault Institute in Fort Worth, TX and San Diego, CA. Dr. Geffner is licensed in California and Texas as a Psychologist and as a Marriage and Family Therapist. His most recent books are *Children Exposed to Marital Violence* (with G. Holden and E. Jouriles), *Ending Spouse/Partner Abuse* (with C. Mantooth) and *Violence and Sexual Abuse at Home* (with S. Sorenson and P. Love). He is the editor of several international professional journals and a book program concerning maltreatment, trauma and interpersonal aggression for The Haworth Maltreatment & Trauma Press. He is Former Professor of Psychology at the University of Texas at Tyler, and is currently Clinical Research Professor of Psychology at the California School of Professional Psychology, San Diego. He directed a large private practice mental health clinic in Texas for 15 years, and continues to do consulting, training and forensic practice. He was a founding member and former President of the Board of the East Texas Crisis Center and Shelter for battered women and their children.

Peter G. Jaffe, PhD, is Executive Director of the London Family Court Clinic; member of the Clinical Adjunct Faculty for the Departments of Psychology and Psychiatry at the University of Western Ontario; former chair of the Board of Directors of the Battered Women's Advocacy Centre; member of the Advisory Committee to the Chief of Police of the London Police Service; and Chairperson of the Board of Directors for the Centre for Research on Violence Against Women and Children. He gives addresses and presentations of over 50 workshops a year on violence to audiences including teachers, students, lawyers, judges, police, doctors, clergy and various community groups. Dr. Jaffe is the recipient of many awards and grants; author of numerous research articles, and co-author of two books dealing with child witnesses to family violence entitled: *Children of Battered Women* (Sage, 1990), and *Ending the Cycle of Violence* (Sage, 1995).

Marlies Sudermann, PhD, CPsych, received her doctorate in psychology from Queen's University in Kingston, Canada and is currently Psychologist with the Thames Valley District School Board, and Adjunct Clinical Professor at the University of Western Ontario Department of Psychology in London, Ontario. She has developed and evaluated school-based prevention and early intervention programmes for violence and woman abuse.

DEDICATION

RG – – To Ellen who has been there through the good and the difficult for so many years, and to all of those victims and survivors of family violence who have taught me about the importance of this work and the need for change.

PJ – – To Nicole and Conny who have taught me about male privilege for over half a century

MS – – To Anna Sudermann who taught me about the importance of women's writings

ABOUT THE CONTRIBUTORS

Nicholas Bala, BA, LLB, LLM, is Professor of Law, Queen's University, Kingston, Ontario, Canada. He specializes in Family and Children's Law, including legal issues related to child abuse, domestic violence, youth offending and the definition of the family.

Sandra K. Beeman, PhD, is Assistant Professor in Social Work and Faculty Associate at the Minnesota Center Against Violence and Abuse, University of Minnesota. She has conducted research and published in the areas of child maltreatment, family violence, kinship foster care, and collaboration between child protection and battered women's services.

Helene Berman, PhD, RN, is a faculty member at the University of Western Ontario, School of Nursing. Prior to pursuing a career in nursing, education, and research, she received a Bachelor's Degree in Anthroplogy from the University of Wisconsin. She presently holds a nationally-funded research scientist award and is the recipient of several major research grants. Her research is community-based, primarily qualitative, and includes a focus on children who have witnessed violence in and out of the home, the impact of woman abuse on family health promotion processes among single mothers and their children, and the interrelationships between culture, health, and violence. She is currently a principal investigator on a national project focusing on violence prevention and the "girl child."

Corina Brown, MA, is a doctoral student in clinical psychology at Simon Fraser University. Her research interests include the study of parent-child relationships as buffers against the effects of stress on children.

Ruth Busch, JD, is Associate Professor in the Law School at the University of Waikato. She has published extensively on judicial discourses of domestic violence and has a special interest in the effects of domestic violence on children and the implications for custody and access decision-making.

Rose Catallo, MES, is affiliated with York University, Toronto, Canada. Ms. Catallo's research within the Faculty of Environmental Studies focused on urban planning and women's safety. She is currently employed with an international research firm conducting market potential studies.

Donald G. Dutton received his PhD in Social Psychology from the University of Toronto. From 1979 to the present, he has served as a therapist in the Assaultive Husband's Project, a court-mandated treatment program for men convicted of wife assault. Dutton has served as an expert witness in civil trials involving domestic abuse and in criminal trials involving family violence, including his work for the prosecution in the O. J. Simpson trial. He is currently Professor of Psychology at the University of British Columbia.

Carole Echlin, BSW, MSW, is a Family Services Social Worker for the Children's Aid Society of London and Middlesex. She was recently seconded by the provincial government to assist in piloting a Child Welfare Competency Based Training Program for child welfare social workers. Her interest in woman abuse and the impact that it has on children dates back to the early 80s. Since then she has written about woman abuse, run numerous group programs for children, co-facilitated many workshops for professionals, and more recently helped design, along with Bina Osthoff (woman's advocate), a group program for women who have been mandated by the court to attend a woman abuse counselling program. This new project is a significant and important step in working collaboratively with women's advocates.

Jeffrey L. Edleson, PhD, is Professor of Social Work and Director of the Minnesota Center Against Violence and Abuse at the University of Minnesota. He is actively involved in international research, training, and technical assistance in the effort to end violence against women, and the author of numerous publications on family violence. He is also the Director of Research and Evaluation for the Domestic Abuse Project in Minneapolis.

John W. Fantuzzo, PhD, is the Diana Riklis Professor of Education in the School, Community, and Child Clinical Psychology program and the program in Policy Research Evaluation and Measurement at the University of Pennsylvania. His research and grant experience have focused primarily on the design, implementation, and evaluation of school- and community-based assessment and prevention strategies for vulnerable, low-income children and families in high-risk urban environments.

Anne Fedorowicz, MA, is a doctoral student in clinical psychology at Simon Fraser University. Her research interests include the assessment of children's coping and the study of resiliency in maltreated children.

Colleen Friend, MSSA, has been a Child Protective Service worker and supervisor. Currently she teaches in a social work/child welfare training program in the UCLA Department of Social Welfare, Los Angeles, CA.

Robert A. Geffner, PhD, ABPN, is Founder and President of the Family Violence and Sexual Assault Institute in Fort Worth, TX and San Diego, CA. Dr. Geffner is licensed in California and Texas as a Psychologist and as a Marriage and Family Therapist. His most recent books are *Children Exposed to Marital Violence* (with G. Holden and E. Jouriles), *Ending Spouse/Partner Abuse* (with C. Mantooth) and *Violence and Sexual Abuse at Home* (with S. Sorenson and P. Love). He is the editor of several international professional journals and a book program concerning maltreatment, trauma, and interpersonal aggression for The Haworth Maltreatment & Trauma Press. He is Former Professor of Psychology at the University of Texas at Tyler, and is currently Clinical Research Professor of Psychology at the California School of Professional Psychology, San Diego.

Richard J. Gelles, PhD, holds The Joanne and Raymond Welsh Chair of Child Welfare and Family Violence in the School of Social Work, at the University of Pennsylvania, Philadelphia, PA 19104.

Sandra A. Graham-Bermann, PhD, is Associate Professor of Psychology and Women's Studies at the University of Michigan. She has been studying the effects of family violence on children's functioning and intervention in family violence.

N. Zoe Hilton, PhD, is Research Psychologist at the Mental Health Centre, Penetanguishene, Ontario. Her current research concerns violence among teenagers, program evaluation, and risk prediction.

Joyce Ho, MA, is a graduate student in the Doctoral Program in Clinical Psychology at the University of Denver. Her research interests include posttraumatic stress response in children exposed to interparental violence and other forms of abuse, and the mental health of ethnic minority populations.

Peter G. Jaffe, PhD, is Executive Director of the London Family Court Clinic; member of the Clinical Adjunct Faculty for the Departments of Psychology and Psychiatry at the University of Western Ontario; former chair of the Board of Directors of the Battered Women's Advocacy Centre; member of the Advisory Committee to the Chief of Police of the London Police Service; and Chairperson of the Board of Directors for the Centre for Research on Violence Against Women and Children. He gives addresses and presentations of over 50 workshops a year on violence to audiences including teachers, students, lawyers, judges, police, doctors, clergy and various community groups. Dr. Jaffe is the recipient of many awards and grants; author of numerous research articles, and co-author of two books dealing with child witnesses to family violence entitled: *Children of Battered Women* (Sage, 1990), and *Ending the Cycle of Violence* (Sage, 1995).

Ernest N. Jouriles, PhD, is Associate Professor of Psychology at the University of Houston. Dr. Jouriles received his BA from Indiana University at Bloomington and his PhD from the State University of New York at Stony Brook. He has published numerous scientific articles in the areas of marital conflict, domestic violence, child maltreatment, and child adjustment. Dr. Jouriles also directs programs at Shelter-Outreach-Solutions, and he is Co-Director of Project SUPPORT, a program for women and children departing from battered women's shelters.

Patricia K. Kerig, PhD, is Associate Professor at James Madison University and a staff psychologist at the Shenandoah Valley Child Development Clinic. Her research focuses on the search for protective factors for children exposed to interparental conflict and violence.

Peter Lehmann, DSW, is a clinical member and approved supervisor, American Association for Marriage and Family Therapy. He is on the faculty with the School of Social Work, UTA, Arlington, TX as well as a trainer with the Child Protective Services Training Institute, Houston, TX.

Nancy K. D. Lemon, JD, is Lecturer in Domestic Violence Law at Boalt Hall School of Law, University of California, Berkeley, CA since 1988. Ms. Lemon is an attorney, writer, expert witness, trainer, legislative advocate, and consultant specializing in domestic violence legal issues since 1979.

Alytia A. Levendosky, PhD, is Assistant Professor in the Department of Psychology at Michigan State University. She received her PhD from the University of Michigan and has been studying the effects of domestic violence on parenting for about seven years.

Susan Loosely is currently Coordinator of the Community Group Treatment Programme, and was formerly children's advocate at Women's Community House, a shelter for abused women and their children in London, Ontario. Susan took a leading role in the development of a video, *Make a Difference*, outlining the impact of witnessing violence on children and is the principal author of a new group treatment manual for child witnesses of woman abuse.

Larry Marshall, MSW, is currently Intake Supervisor with Children's Aid Society of London and Middlesex, Supervisor of the Community Group Treatment Programme and Chair of the Children's Subcommittee of the London Coordinating Committee to End Woman Abuse. He is also Lecturer at the School of Social Work, King's College, London, Ontario. He was a leader in developing a video, *Make a Difference*, outlining the impact of witnessing violence on children and a new manual on group treatment for child witnesses of woman abuse.

Renee McDonald, PhD, is Assistant Research Professor of Psychology at the University of Houston. Dr. McDonald received her BA and her PhD from the University of Houston. She is an active researcher in the areas of marital violence, child adjustment, and child maltreatment. Dr. McDonald is also very active in planning, implementing, and evaluating shelter programs at Shelter-Outreach-Solutions. She is Co-Director of Project SUPPORT, a program for women and children departing from battered women's shelters.

Timothy Moore, PhD, CPsych, is Associate Professor of Psychology and Chair, Department of Psychology, Glendon College, York University, Toronto, Canada. Professor Moore's research interests include: child psychopathology, mother-child dynamics, and forensic interviewing.

Megan J. Noone, MSED, is working on her doctorate in School, Community, and Clinical Child Psychology at the University of Pennsylvania. Her professional and research interests include young children's exposure to violence, the impact of exposure on development, and strategies for early identification and intervention.

Bina Osthoff, SSW, is Program Manager, London Battered Women's Advocacy Centre. She has advocated for women seeking safety for themselves and their children for approximately eight years and is a member of the London Coordinating Committee to End Woman Abuse. She has also recently presented to the panel of experts on child protection issues and to the special joint committee on child custody and access. These are government initiatives.

Debra J. Pepler, PhD, CPsych, is Professor of Psychology and Director of the LaMarsh Centre for Research on Violence and Conflict Resolution, York University, Toronto, Canada. Dr. Pepler's research interests include: the development of aggression, bullying and victimization, girls' aggression, family violence, and peer relations.

Stephanie Rabenstein, MSC, is a clinical member and approved supervisor, American Association for Marriage and Family Therapy. She is a child and family therapist with Madame Vanier Children's Services, London, Ontario as well, and provides training and consultation to various children's mental health workers across Ontario.

Neville Robertson, MSocSc, DipPsych in Community Psychology, is Senior Lecturer in the Department of Psychology at the University of Waikato. His research focuses on institutional and community responses to violence against women and children and includes studies of policing, custody and access decision-making, and the effectiveness of protection orders.

B. B. Robbie Rossman, PhD, is Senior Clinical Professor in the Psychology Department at the University of Denver and Adjunct Clinical Instructor with the University of Colorado Health Sciences Center. Her research interests include children's reactions to stressful and traumatic experiences, including witnessing interparental violence.

Nanette S. Stephens, PhD, is Assistant Research Professor of Psychology at the University of Houston. Dr. Stephens received her BA from the University of Texas and her PhD from the University of Houston. Dr. Stephens is Co-Director of Project SUPPORT, a program for women and children departing from battered women's shelters.

Marlies Sudermann, PhD, received her doctorate in psychology from Queen's University in Kingston, Canada and is currently Psychologist with the Thames Valley District School Board, and Adjunct Clinical Professor at the University of Western Ontario Department of Psychology in London, Ontario. She has developed school-based prevention and early intervention programmes for violence and woman abuse, including: *A.S.A.B.: A School-Based Anti-Violence Programme*, and *No to Bullying: Early Intervention in Youth Crime*.

Michelle Warren, MA, is a doctoral student in clinical psychology at Simon Fraser University. Her research focuses on PTSD and defense mechanisms in children and youth exposed to violence and maltreatment.

INTRODUCTION

Emerging Issues for Children Exposed to Domestic Violence

Peter G. Jaffe
Marlies Sudermann
Robert Geffner

SUMMARY. The significant trauma caused by domestic violence has become more widely known in recent years as research and conferences focus on this area. The effect on the children exposed to such situations in their own home is an emerging issue. This article discusses the importance of expanding the research, interventions, and prevention programs concerning children exposed to domestic violence, and emphasizes the need for innovative and updated policies in this field. Current theoretical perspectives, intervention techniques and approaches that appear to be successful in dealing with the issues and trauma, prevention programs that have been implemented in the United States and Canada, and recent legal and policy changes regarding these issues are presented in this book. The present article introduces the issues, and describes the articles in this volume. *[Article copies available for a fee from*

Address correspondence to: Peter G. Jaffe, PhD, London Family Court Clinic, Inc., 200-254 Pall Mall Street, London, Ontario N6A 5P6, Canada.

[Haworth co-indexing entry note]: "Emerging Issues for Children Exposed to Domestic Violence." Jaffe, Peter G., Marlies Sudermann, and Robert Geffner. Co-published simultaneously in *Journal of Aggression, Maltreatment & Trauma* (The Haworth Maltreatment & Trauma Press, an imprint of The Haworth Press, Inc.) Vol. 3, No. 1 (#5), 2000, pp. 1-7; and: *Children Exposed to Domestic Violence: Current Issues in Research, Intervention, Prevention, and Policy Development* (ed: Robert A. Geffner, Peter G. Jaffe, and Marlies Sudermann) The Haworth Maltreatment & Trauma Press, an imprint of The Haworth Press, Inc., 2000, pp. 1-7. Single or multiple copies of this article are available for a fee from The Haworth Document Delivery Service [1-800-342-9678, 9:00 a.m. - 5:00 p.m. (EST). E-mail address: getinfo@haworthpressinc.com].

The Haworth Document Delivery Service: 1-800-342-9678. E-mail address: getinfo@haworthpressinc.com <Website: http://www.haworthpressinc.com>]

KEYWORDS. Domestic violence, children of battered women, spouse abuse, child maltreatment, psychological abuse

Over the past decade there has been a dramatic increase in research and interventions with children exposed to domestic violence. Before the 1990s there were few references to the plight of these children in contrast to issues such as sexual abuse and woman abuse. In this decade there have been major international conferences that focused on children exposed to domestic violence that have demonstrated tremendous interest by front-line professionals in human services as well as social scientists. Two major edited books have captured some of the advances in this field (Peled, Jaffe & Edleson, 1995; Holden, Geffner & Jouriles, 1998).

In 1992, the Domestic Abuse Project in Minneapolis hosted a conference on children exposed to violence that drew about 300 participants from across the world. In 1996, the Family Violence and Sexual Assault Institute together with the University of Texas in Austin, also had about 300 participants in a similar conference. The following year in London, Ontario, Canada, almost 800 people attended an international conference on children exposed to violence hosted by the London Family Court Clinic and the Family Violence and Sexual Assault Institute. Almost every US state and Canadian province was represented as well as seven countries around the world. In 1998, the Family Violence and Sexual Assault Institute, in conjunction with YWCA Domestic Violence Institute of San Diego County and the San Diego Domestic Violence Council, expanded the participants to 1,100 in San Diego, California. This included people from the United States, Canada, Mexico, and seven other countries. What has been apparent throughout these conferences is how this topic attracts such a diverse audience of children's advocates, women's advocates, researchers, clinicians and people from a cross section of systems including justice, education, social service, mental health, and health.

The present volume is a testament to the growth and development in this field. The number of important research questions raised have multiplied. Innovative programs and improved collaboration among different human services have spread across North America. Policy makers and legislators have challenged the field to find practical solutions to the many needs posed by abused women and their children. The articles that follow outline the leading-edge thinking about these areas. To focus on each area we have divided the volume into three major sections: theoretical and research issues; intervention and prevention strategies; and policy development from an international perspective.

In Article 1, Fantuzzo and his colleagues make a compelling argument for the importance of partnerships between the domestic violence front-line workers and researchers at universities. He offers important perspectives on how these partnerships can be mutually beneficial. Professor Fantuzzo emphasizes the challenges of moving from the comforts of the ivory tower into real world problems and crises experienced by abused women and their children. Good research that is appropriately disseminated can raise the profile of domestic violence and assist in fund-raising and program development.

In Article 2, Levendosky and Graham-Bermann address the thorny issues of parenting in abused women. Because abused women are often revictimized by the child protection and family law systems, there is a need for better research and a clearer analysis of their parenting abilities. Both these researchers have developed extensive community collaboration to work with abused mothers and provide a context for the many issues and problems presented.

Pepler and her colleagues address the diverse effects of exposure to domestic violence on children in Article 3. A central point is the need to assess all areas of children's adjustment (family, school, community) as well as different relationships that may be problematic (mother-child, father-child, siblings). Dr. Pepler suggests that interventions need to be specifically tailored for individual children according to assessment findings in these areas. That is, a one size fits all approach is unlikely to be successful. As an example, an evaluation of a peer counseling group is presented as a strategy that impacts anxiety and depression but falls short with other measures.

In Article 4, Dutton has outlined the results of a quarter century of research on men who batter by reminding the reader of the crucial link between exposure to violence in childhood and adult marital behavior. Dutton's analysis extends beyond the modeling effects of such violence and instead draws attention to the shaping of the abusive personality by the trauma of the violence. Dutton suggests a model in which these childhood traumas create insecure attachment and a life-long sense of shame. The article is a sobering reminder of the long-term effects of growing up with violence and the horrendous costs in human suffering in subsequent generations.

The following article by Mohr and Fantuzzo expands the analysis of social development and personality structure to examine the role of physiology. These authors rightly claim that physiological factors are often ignored in understanding domestic violence and yet may play a central role. Their ideas are reinforced by the work of Perry (1998), who has written extensively on the impact of trauma on brain development in infants. These neurological changes predict increased emotional arousal and sensitivity demonstrated by more severe anxiety and rage reactions in later years. As with Perry's work,

Mohr and Fantuzzo look for more complex models of violence that combine environmental and physiological variables.

In Article 6, Rossman and Ho address the current research that links exposure to violence to post traumatic stress disorder. The original research in this field focused on children's emotional and behavioral problems after being exposed to domestic violence without a clear conceptualization of these adjustment difficulties as trauma symptoms. Rossman and Ho provide a good theoretical foundation to examine trauma in the context of adaptation to stress as well as more extreme posttraumatic stress disorder (PTSD) reactions. Their data suggests some consistency in re-experiencing symptoms (e.g., intrusive thoughts) in children exposed to violence. The authors provide a helpful analysis of the overlap between PTSD symptoms and a diagnosis of Attention Deficit Hyperactivity Disorder (ADHD) in children which could easily lead to improper assessment and treatment.

The research section ends with a compelling article by Berman on the value of narrative approaches by examining children of war in comparison to children of battered women. The children's perspectives would inspire advocacy in anyone not convinced about the human suffering in war zones. Berman demonstrates the profound trauma symptoms including the "erosion of basic assumptions about the expected order of things." The contrast to children of battered women who may have never experienced peace provides an interesting analysis.

Thus, the first section of this volume provides an overview of the complexity of the research questions in regard to children exposed to family violence. The question is no longer simply, are children affected by the violence, but rather, in what ways are boys and girls at different stages of development affected in different spheres of their functioning, and what are the significant risk and protective factors that predict short-term and long-term sequelae of this traumatic experience? Berman's article is an important reminder that children may be exposed to violence in places other than their homes which may significantly shape their development. It will be important to continue to link the family violence literature to other forms of violence within countries and even neighborhoods.

The second section of this book deals with promising intervention and prevention strategies on behalf of children exposed to family violence. Sudermann, Marshall, and Loosely review a group counseling program for children and adolescents exposed to woman abuse in Article 8. The authors provide an extremely helpful evaluation tool to assess the impact of the group on the children and teens involved. This questionnaire is well-structured and founded on the needs of children who are exposed to domestic violence. Given the widespread utilization of this approach, practitioners are encouraged to utilize the questionnaire to evaluate their own groups.

Article 9 provides an excellent overview of the challenges faced by shelter staff in providing services for the children who accompany their mother to find refuge. The fact that children are often in crisis at a time when their principal caretaker is unavailable because of the physical and psychological consequence of the violence places special demands on child care staff. Stephens, McDonald and Jouriles raise important questions about the outcome of different interventions. They remind us that not all interventions are beneficial and there may be unintended negative consequences in some circumstances.

Kerig, Fedorowicz, Brown and Warren offer a thorough account of assessment and treatment issues for PTSD in children exposed to family violence in Article 10. They emphasize the importance of a proper diagnosis which was reinforced by Rossman and Ho in Article 6. Kerig and her colleagues stress the importance of safety plans as a starting point in children's healing from the trauma. The specific strategies in helping children cope with trauma symptoms are valuable for clinicians to review.

In Article 11, Rabenstein and Lehmann present an innovative treatment model for children exposed to violence. The model is described in a comprehensive fashion that involves working with mothers and children together. The authors articulate the pro-feminist principles behind their work which ensure that the "family" approach will not become a breeding ground for "victim blaming" and the perpetrators of the violence will be held accountable for their behavior. Rabenstein and Lehmann provide convincing arguments for the value in this approach. This article also details a number of helpful activities to encourage open discussion of feelings and family secrets.

Article 12 outlines a major problem of failed collaboration in the field of domestic violence. Echlin and Osthoff suggest ways to improve the relationship between children's advocates working with the child protection agencies and women's advocates working in shelters and community services. The authors outline a common set of dilemmas and assumptions that can be used to build a better understanding among advocates and the development of new protocols. Examples of how to collaborate at a variety of levels are reviewed and an innovative group program is suggested as a fresh approach to this issue.

The final article in this section by Hilton will stimulate the readers' ideas about the benefits of primary prevention programs in schools, addressing domestic violence. Hilton's data raises questions about the assumptions that negative attitudes underline violence within intimate relationships. She argues that prevention programs should focus on the development of social skills and healthy relationships rather than just challenging attitudes and raising awareness. Hilton demonstrates that some awareness programs may even create a backlash and force boys to take on even more negative attitudes. In these circumstances, more intensive programs need to be developed for at-risk students and programs have to be developed to recognize gender differences.

This section provides exciting examples of progress in the field of children exposed to violence. Different intervention models that can be adapted by social service, mental health and educational settings are thoroughly reviewed. The importance of evaluation is underlined and practical strategies are offered. Echlin and Osthoff leave us with the challenge of finding better ways to collaborate among different agencies, especially these services advocating the safety of women and children in their homes. Hilton promises some hope for prevention programs if we can teach how to have "healthy relationships."

The third and last section of this volume examines policy and legislative implications of the growing body of literature on the impact of exposure to violence on children. In Article 14, Gelles explores the dilemma in the child welfare system of family preservation programs being promoted without a full appreciation of safety factors for mothers and children. Gelles is able to put this controversy within a historical context of a swinging pendulum that is moved by tragedies created by natural parents or the state. He offers a helpful conclusion to the debate by focusing on risk factors and making more conscious decisions on the impact of different cut-off points.

In Article 15, Friend reviews all the clinical and research data that should convince child protection workers that domestic violence should be one of their central concerns. She highlights a number of new programs that bring together the expertise of the domestic violence and child protection fields into common training programs, protocols and policies. Friend details a major training initiative by the UCLA School of Social Work to train large groups of child protection workers (CPS) on domestic violence. The training utilizes specific approaches to help reduce the perceived threat of CPS workers for abused mothers and encourages a higher level of safety planning and empowerment for clients. The article concludes with some of the ongoing challenges in this field that include excessive caseloads that are often a "disincentive to discovering information" about domestic violence.

The next three articles provide an international perspective on how child custody laws and court decisions are being changed by the realities of domestic violence. Article 16 by Ruth Busch and Neville Robertson summarizes major developments in New Zealand's child custody laws. After a major tragedy in that country that led to a major judicial inquiry, new legislation was developed that clearly recognizes the impact of domestic violence on victims and child witnesses. The legislation recognizes that batterers should not have care and control of the children and safety has to be a priority. Among the innovations described is the ability of the courts to order counseling for victims, perpetrators of violence, and child witnesses.

In Article 17, Bala describes the Canadian experience. A number of court decisions are reviewed which recognize the impact of exposure to violence on children in determining custody and access arrangements. After a thorough literature review, Bala argues for a differential approach by the courts to recognize the varying nature and severity of domestic violence. He concludes by suggesting important legal remedies and resources that are required by communities to respond more effectively to this issue.

Lemon reviews the US experience in child custody cases involving domestic violence in Article 18. Although there are clear public statements by the US Congress, American Bar Association, and the National Council of Juvenile and Family Court Judges, about presumptions that abusive husbands should not have custody of their children, there is still tremendous variation in court decisions across the states. Lemon indicates that there is a serious lag between good legislation and the training or resources to help operationalize the change at the local level. Controversial cases such as the O. J. Simpson child custody trial and appeal, are reviewed to illustrate these points.

The final article by Beeman and Edleson indicates the divisions among different service systems that hamper coordinated services for abused women and their children. The results of focus groups of child and women's advocates provide an excellent analysis of the major roadblocks that prevent advocates from working together. Solutions are outlined that include cross-training, improved communication and consultation and protocols for more integrated services. Beeman and Edleson leave the reader with hope that these gaps can be bridged in very practical ways.

This final section of the book exemplifies the serious challenges we face in the field as we move from research to practice to new policy development and legislation. There are some who will argue that the research is not well enough developed to leave us confident in our intervention and prevention strategies, let alone changing systems or laws. However, in the front lines, there is an urgent need to make safety a priority and banish approaches that revictimize abused women and their children. This ongoing tension will hopefully produce better research that is grounded in finding practical solutions to ending the violence for abused women and their children. Given the growth of these developments in the past decade, the early part of the new Millennium is likely to bring significant breakthroughs in this field. Hopefully, this will lead to better and more comprehensive policies and procedures to identify and intervene quickly when domestic violence has occurred, and then to a profound reduction in the numbers of adults and children who are victimized in their own home.

REFERENCES

Holden, G. W., Geffner, R. & Jouriles, E. N. (1998). *Children exposed to marital violence: Theory, research and applied issues.* Washington, DC: American Psychological Association.

Peled, E., Jaffe, P. G. & Edleson, J. L. (1995). *Ending the cycle of violence: Community responses to children of battered women.* Thousand Oaks, CA: Sage Publications.

Perry, B. D. (1997). Neurodevelopmental factors in the "cycle of violence." In J. D. Osofsky (Ed), *Children in a violent society* (pp. 1-13). New York, NY: Guilford Press.

THEORETICAL
AND RESEARCH ISSUES

Making the *Invisible* Victims
of Violence Against Women
Visible Through
University/Community Partnerships

John W. Fantuzzo
Wanda K. Mohr
Megan J. Noone

This research project was supported in part by a grant received from the U.S. Department of Health and Human Services' Head Start Bureau.

A special thanks goes to our collaborators at the City of Philadelphia Police Department: Deputy Commissioner Richard Zappile and the Domestic Violence and Victim Assistance Units. Additionally, we are grateful to Head Start: Director Rosemary Mazzatenta and her Head Start staff. This outstanding group of law enforcement professionals and educators have made notable contributions to the ongoing research efforts.

Address correspondence to: John W. Fantuzzo, Graduate School of Education, University of Pennsylvania, 3700 Walnut Street, Philadelphia, PA 19104-6216.

[Haworth co-indexing entry note]: "Making the *Invisible* Victims of Violence Against Women Visible Through University/Community Partnerships." Fantuzzo, John W., Wanda K. Mohr, and Megan J. Noone. Co-published simultaneously in *Journal of Aggression, Maltreatment & Trauma* (The Haworth Maltreatment & Trauma Press, an imprint of The Haworth Press, Inc.) Vol. 3, No. 1 (#5), 2000, pp. 9-23; and: *Children Exposed to Domestic Violence: Current Issues in Research, Intervention, Prevention, and Policy Development* (ed: Robert A. Geffner, Peter G. Jaffe, and Marlies Sudermann) The Haworth Maltreatment & Trauma Press, an imprint of The Haworth Press, Inc., 2000, pp. 9-23. Single or multiple copies of this article are available for a fee from The Haworth Document Delivery Service [1-800-342-9678, 9:00 a.m. - 5:00 p.m. (EST). E-mail address: getinfo@haworthpressinc.com].

9

SUMMARY. The absence of scientifically credible information about the nature and extent of children exposed to abuse of their mothers is an impediment to effective intervention and prevention efforts. This article proposes a research agenda based upon guiding principles of a public health surveillance model. Three major principles are presented and applied to this social problem. Additionally, a concrete example of the application of these principles is drawn from an ongoing university/community partnership in Philadelphia. *[Article copies available for a fee from The Haworth Document Delivery Service: 1-800-342-9678. E-mail address: getinfo@haworthpressinc.com <Website: http://www.haworthpressinc.com>]*

KEYWORDS. Domestic violence, children, prevalence, interagency collaboration, community-based assessment and intervention, police involvement

Violence against women by intimate partners has become a widely recognized social problem. More than one million women in the US are violently assaulted by an intimate, with national estimates ranging from 9.2 to 220 assaults per 1,000 women (National Research Council, 1996). Furthermore, studies consistently show that young women with limited financial resources are at increased risk for violent assault (Bachman & Saltzman, 1995; National Research Council, 1996). However, these young, vulnerable women are not the only victims of this national problem. Children of battered women are the nation's *invisible* victims of domestic violence (Osofsky, 1995).

Children who witness maternal assaults are indirect, yet vulnerable victims as well. They are faced with feelings of fear for themselves and their loved ones, a sense of powerlessness, and a host of emotional and behavioral problems (Hughes & Fantuzzo, 1994). Furthermore, children of battered women are at increased risk for being direct victims of abuse themselves (McCloskey, Figueredo, & Koss, 1995).

This "invisibility" is comprehensive. Professional and societal attention to these children is relatively recent and sadly inadequate. Although concern about battered women has been growing for nearly three decades, their children did not appear in the research literature until the 1980s, and then only with indirect, unscientific speculation. Children exposed to domestic violence are overridingly absent in public policy and in relevant documents such as the yearbook of the Children's Defense Fund (Children's Defense Fund, 1996), the report of the US Attorney General's Task Force on Domestic Violence (US Attorney General, 1984), and the National Crime Victimization Survey conducted by the National Institute of Justice (Bachman & Saltzman, 1995). Currently, few laws exist to protect children who are exposed to domestic violence. Therefore, no organized reporting mechanism exists to provide data to inform intervention and prevention efforts for these vulnerable children.

One reason children exposed to domestic violence have remained invisible to researchers, educators, and policy makers is the absence of scientifically credible information about the nature and scope of the problem (Osofsky, 1995). A careful inspection of our existing knowledge base regarding the impact of witnessing family violence reveals several fundamental flaws that affect both the internal and external validity of the data. Internal validity has been jeopardized, in part, by an overdependence on certain data collection methods for the independent variable, that is, the child's exposure to interparental violence. Much of our information about children's exposure comes from retrospective reports of female victims in shelter residence, anonymous telephone surveys, or retrospective accounts from adult survivors of interparental violence (Fantuzzo & Lindquist, 1989; Spaccarelli, Sandler & Roosa, 1994; Straus & Gelles, 1986). These data have serious shortcomings. Reports obtained from women in crisis or from anonymous telephone calls may be affected by confounding variables. For example, women in crisis who are seeking shelter may fear that their responses could impact the services they receive. Women who are surveyed over the telephone may inaccurately report levels of domestic violence due to issues of mistrust or privacy. Tomkins, Mohamed, Steinman and Macolini (1994) demonstrated problems with the accuracy of maternal report in these conditions. They found that although most agencies working with domestic violence cases asked if the female victim's child had witnessed the abuse, victims tended not to report the effects of the battering on their children, and agency staff tended not to report these experiences to protective services.

The over-reliance on shelter or crisis samples has also been criticized as a threat to the external validity of our knowledge base. Since shelter samples are believed to be only the tip of the iceberg, it is unknown how representative they are of the entire population of battered women and their children (Fantuzzo, DePaola, Lambert, Martino, Anderson, & Sutton, 1991; Spaccarelli et al., 1994). The assessment of children's psychological adjustment in unique settings, like shelters, may be associated with factors particular to the setting. For example, uprooting children from their home, separating them from their father, or having them experience their mother under conditions of great stress related to leaving home abruptly may contribute significantly to assessment results (Spaccarelli et al., 1994). Fantuzzo and his colleagues provide empirical evidence of this potential confound (Fantuzzo et al., 1991). They found that children who were living with their mothers in temporary domestic violence shelters evidenced significantly higher levels of psychological distress and different types of distress than carefully matched children who were exposed to the same level and type of violence but were living at home.

One of the primary explanations for the existence of these serious critiques of our knowledge base is that we have failed to give adequate attention to the most basic aspects of this research area. Because of an urgency to understand the consequences, researchers have made too many assumptions about the child's exposure to family violence. It is difficult to explore the impact of an event on child development without a true understanding of what that event is. A fundamental element of such an understanding is knowledge of the incidence and prevalence of the event. Currently, our understanding of the incidence and prevalence of children exposed to family violence is almost non-existent.

The most frequently cited incidence estimate is that "at least 3.3 million children yearly are at risk of exposure to parental violence" (Carlson, 1984). This estimate is truly more of a "factoid" than it is a fact (Gelles, 1997). In other words, it is a completely inadequate figure that has prevented authentic inquiry about the incidence and prevalence of exposure.

There are several reasons why the accuracy of this statistic is questionable. First, the figure is derived from the First National Family Violence Survey (Straus, Gelles, & Steinmetz, 1980) conducted more than 20 years ago. Second, the estimate is based on a number of limiting assumptions. For example, it excluded children under the age of three and families in which the mother and abusive father were divorced. Third, although the Survey inquired whether a child between the ages of 3 and 17 was present in the home, there were no direct questions about whether the child was exposed in any way to the violence (Gelles, 1997).

Therefore, to build a knowledge base that will accurately inform intervention and prevention efforts for the entire population of children exposed to maternal violence, we must first seek to understand the incidence and prevalence of this problem. An understanding of the scope of the problem will give us a basis to examine more precisely the manifold ways that children are exposed to this family violence and the unique ways that these types of exposure impact child development (see Figure 1). The purpose of this article is to propose a research agenda to investigate the nature and scope of this problem using a public health surveillance conceptual framework to guide inquiry. This framework and its guiding principles will be presented as well as a concrete application of this model to a large urban center.

PUBLIC HEALTH SURVEILLANCE MODEL

The public health surveillance model provides a relevant comprehensive framework to investigate the incidence and prevalence of children's exposure to maternal abuse. Public health surveillance is a discipline dedicated to the systematic, scientific assessment of the health of a population or community

FIGURE 1. Display of the Importance of Incidence/Prevalence and Taxonomy of Exposure Research to the Developmental Consequences and Intervention Investigations

Children Exposed to Family Violence

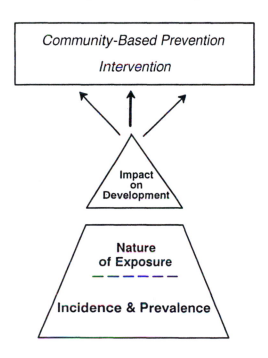

(Teutch, 1994). Tracking major threats to the public well-being is the corner-stone of these health assessments that result in information about the incidence and prevalence of the epidemic. One such threat is violence. Current leaders in the fields of public health and criminology are highlighting the need to attend to violence as a public health priority (Koop & Lundberg, 1992). In fact, because of the alarming numbers of individuals affected, violence has been identified by some scholars as the largest public health problem currently facing the United States (Rosenberg, O'Carroll, & Powell, 1992). A high proportion of violent incidents are committed within the confines of the family, particularly when women are the primary victims (Bachman & Saltzman, 1995; Rosenberg et al., 1992). Therefore, *family* violence specifically is an important issue to be placed under surveillance. It is essential, however, to avoid the oversight that characterized the field of family violence for many years. In using the public health surveillance model to track the epidemic of family violence in our country, the children exposed to the violence must be included in the incidence and prevalence figures obtained.

The public health surveillance model is grounded in three important principles that guide inquiry into issues of incidence and prevalence of child exposure to maternal abuse: (a) the definition and substantiation of the community-wide problem, (b) the representativeness of the population being monitored in the community, and (c) the collaboration among authorized community investigators and scientists (Cates & Williamson, 1994; Teutch, 1994). These principles interact to guide the establishment of scientifically sound methods for collecting information.

The first principle highlights the importance of implementing criteria for valid and consistent data. A clear definition of maternal abuse and the capacity to substantiate both violent incidents in the community and children's exposure to these incidents are critical to public health surveillance and scientific study. If these criteria are not met, we are left with a body of formless information based on hearsay and imprecise recollection. However, although validity and consistent definitions are necessary criteria in creating an agenda to document the incidence and prevalence of exposure to maternal abuse, they are not sufficient.

As the second principle suggests, data must be collected in a way that reaches the largest, most representative group of children possible in the community that is being studied without sacrificing the ability to substantiate or validate the reports of violence and levels of exposure. As discussed earlier, an exclusive focus on small subsamples of children exposed to domestic violence (such as shelter populations) threatens the ability to generalize information learned to the entire population of children exposed. Therefore, researchers must identify means of accessing the most comprehensive pool of substantiated cases of maternal abuse to develop an effective surveillance system. Researchers need to explore current community capacities to gather relevant information and examine existing national research databases to inform a credible surveillance system.

Balancing the ideals set forth in the first two principles is impossible without adherence to the third principle: building partnerships and collaborations between authorized community investigators and researchers. Effective partnerships can provide researchers with access to existing representative databases already equipped with working definitions for maternal abuse and natural substantiation processes. In turn, using resources otherwise unavailable to community agencies, the existing investigation systems can be enhanced both to facilitate the established mission of the agency and to accommodate a rigorous research agenda. This mutually beneficial, minimally intrusive process helps to ensure that the surveillance system established will be easily maintained, and therefore will survive an ongoing tracking effort.

The effectiveness of the public health surveillance model in monitoring issues of violence and children has already been demonstrated in the field of child abuse and neglect. Mandated reporting of child maltreatment to child protective services (CPS) across the country has established the capacity to document and track large numbers of children who have been abused or neglected. Within CPS agencies, specific case definitions of the different forms of maltreatment have been developed in conjunction with the research community. These definitions enable researchers to collect standardized, consistent data sets that can be compared across sites. CPS is also the official agency charged to investigate and substantiate reports of child maltreatment, providing a natural mechanism for validation of the data. Although it is true that not all maltreated children come to the attention of CPS agencies, these agencies constitute the largest, most representative source of investigated and substantiated cases of abuse or neglect. *The Third National Incidence Study of Child Abuse and Neglect* (NIS-3) (Sedlak & Broadhurst, 1996) provides an illustration of the third public health surveillance principle: NIS-3 researchers partnered with CPS agencies across the country to establish the most comprehensive documentation of the current national incidence of child maltreatment. The investigation of these data provides findings that can be used by CPS agencies to improve their surveillance capacity.

In applying the public health surveillance principles to children exposed to maternal abuse, it is helpful to borrow the analogy of an iceberg described in the final report of the NIS-3 (Sedlak & Broadhurst, 1996). Figure 2 illustrates this iceberg, and a parallel iceberg that represents the universe of exposed children. It is clear from this illustration that the only level of children exposed to maternal assault currently visible to researchers and other professionals are those in domestic violence shelters. While these children are certainly in need of services, they represent only a very small, unrepresentative percentage of the universe of children exposed. Using the field of child maltreatment as a model, a parallel investigative agency to CPS must be identified. The community agency currently authorized to investigate and to intervene when women are assaulted in their homes is the police department.

Domestic abuse is a crime as well as a public health problem. Recent criminal codes have been revised to broaden the categories of activities that are considered domestic abuse and to strengthen the authority of police officers to intervene in violent or potentially violent situations. All states have passed some form of domestic violence legislation providing civil as well as criminal penalties for acts of violence within the home. Most states also have laws allowing police to make warrantless arrests, that is, arresting batterers on probable cause without actually witnessing abuse. In addition, all but five states have laws that require that health practitioners report suspected physical abuse to the police (Hyman, Schillinger, & Lo, 1995). In Pennsylvania, this

FIGURE 2. Pictorial Display of the Analogous Relationship Between Child Protective Service Agencies and Child Maltreatment Research and the Police Department and Child Exposure to Family Violence Research

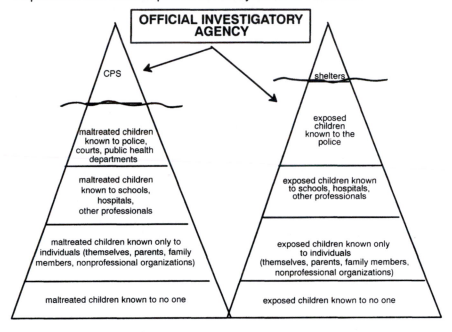

legislation is called the Protection from Abuse Act and it designates the police department of each municipal corporation as the official law enforcement agency under this act. The act also provides for mandatory reporting of all domestic violence incidents to a statewide registry (Commonwealth of Pennsylvania, 1995). The police department, therefore, represents an existing agency, parallel to CPS, that has the potential to serve as a public health surveillance system for children exposed to maternal assault. What researchers need to do is form partnerships with police departments and take steps to actualize this potential.

There are a few notable examples of university/police department partnerships that have been established in small to moderately sized urban areas to protect children from the effects of community and family violence. In New Orleans, researchers from the Louisiana State University have developed a program to study the impact of violence on children in conjunction with one of the police districts with the highest level of violence in the city. Among its various features, this program contains an educational component for police officers that is designed to enhance police awareness of the invisible child victims of domestic violence and link those children to services (Osofsky, 1995). In addition, the Yale Child Study Center's Program on Child Development and Community Policing started in 1990 is one of the first programs to link the police with the mental health community. This program is based on the assumption that police officers have the most immediate and sustained contact with victims of community violence. The Yale initiative in New Haven is designed to optimize and expand the police officer's role by developing partnerships between the police department and community and mental health resources (Marans, 1995).

A UNIVERSITY/POLICE DEPARTMENT PARTNERSHIP FOR THE CHILDREN OF PHILADELPHIA

Faced with the lack of clear, epidemiological data to inform issues of magnitude, an interdisciplinary research team from the University of Pennsylvania, including psychologists, statisticians, and psychiatric nurses, designed a research agenda guided by public health surveillance principles. The following describes the initial development phases of this research endeavor.

Phase One: Identifying the Issues

The first phase involved identifying existing national data sets that could increase our understanding of the problem of children exposed to maternal assault. One such data set comes from the National Institute of Justice's Spouse Assault Replication Program (SARP). The SARP project was a series of randomized experiments in seven major US cities, conducted to evaluate the effectiveness of arrest in reducing recidivism of spousal assault (see Garner, Fagen, & Maxwell, 1995 for a summary and critical review). Fantuzzo and Boruch conducted secondary analyses of these citywide data sets to find information about patterns of children's exposure to substantiated female assaults (Fantuzzo, Boruch, Beriama, Atkins, & Marcus, 1997). Analyses addressed four major questions: (a) Are children disproportionately represented in households with substantiated cases of abuse of adult female? (b) Are young children below the age of six years old disproportionately present in households in which domestic violence occurs? (c) Do these households involve a disproportional level of developmental risk factors for children? (d) In domestic violence households with children, to what degree are children involved in the violent incident? Of the seven cities included in the SARP project, data were available on the following five cities to address these questions: Miami, Atlanta, Milwaukee, Omaha, and Charlotte.

In response to these questions, the research team found the following: First, children were disproportionately present in households where there was a substantiated incident of adult female assault, and young children were disproportionately represented among these witnessing children. Second, family violence households included high levels of additional major developmental risk factors including poverty, single-female household, and low educational level of principle care provider. Furthermore, the youngest children in these households were most likely to experience the added instability of multiple incidents of maternal abuse and parental substance abuse. Third, a sizable number of children in these violent households appeared to be involved in multiple ways in the abuse incident by: (a) either literally calling for help, (b) being identified as a precipitant cause of the dispute that led to violence, or (c) being physically abused by the perpetrator. These findings indicate that children in family violence households are not just "witnessing" a tragedy; they are involved in various ways in the violent incident. Overall, the data suggest that those children who are most dependent on their caregivers are most vulnerable to being exposed to serious violence between them.

Phase Two: Partnership Development

The next phase involved forging a partnership with strategic community institutions to design a public health surveillance system for the children of Philadelphia. To accomplish this goal, the research team sought the cooperation of the City of Philadelphia's Police Department and the Office of Early Childhood Education in the School District of Philadelphia. We learned from the SARP data that police officers are not only among the first to have contact with children on the scene of a violent domestic dispute, they are also able to help investigators identify households with children present.

Early childhood education programs like Head Start, that specifically target low-income, urban children and families, are essential for two reasons: First, according to the research, they are serving the most vulnerable families; and second, they have many resources as well as talented staff and parents to contribute to the development of victim services. Because prior research conducted by Fantuzzo has established substantial partnership links with the District's Head Start program (Fantuzzo, Stevenson, Weiss, Hampton, & Noone, 1997), the team devoted efforts to initiating a partnership with the Domestic Violence and Victim Assistance Units of the Police Department.

We were pleased to find that the Domestic Violence Unit of the Southwest Division of the Police Department was very receptive to working with researchers to make the invisible child victims in Philadelphia more visible and more likely to receive victim services. Based on the success of initial meetings with the Southwest Division, the Deputy Commissioner of Police Operations invited the researchers to consider ways to expand the partnership to include all Domestic Violence (DOM) units and the Victim Assistance (VA) units in the city. He presented the team with his vision of a citywide Police/Mental

Health Partnership. In pursuit of this vision, he offered full cooperation of the Police Department to the Penn research team.

The first partnership effort with the DOM and VA units was to conduct a citywide needs assessment to identify ways to enhance the units' effectiveness and responsiveness to victims (women and children). After meeting with selected members of DOM and VA units to elicit their expertise and knowledge of the system, the team generated a questionnaire. These questionnaires were distributed to all DOM and VA officers across units and 99% were returned for analysis. Findings corroborated the invisibility of children in the system, the need for comprehensive victim services, and the recognition that interagency collaboration was the best hope for a coordinated citywide effort. Feedback from the officers and detectives also reflected their deep and sincere concern about the vulnerability of children in domestic disputes.

The needs assessment process revealed another issue of primary concern to the domestic violence officers, detectives, and victim assistance officers: the need for improved communication systems. Enhancing the capacity to gather and record information in a standardized, computerized database was the essential first step in refining communication. This need for a database provided an opportunity to facilitate the existing operations of the domestic violence units while advancing the research agenda, by building a surveillance system to reach children exposed to maternal assault. Currently we are working with the Deputy Commissioner and representatives for the DOM and VA units to develop a computerized database for all domestic violence cases, as well as new police incident forms that will record information regarding the presence of child witnesses. Plans are underway to develop these data tracking methods in the Southwest Division and ultimately to consider city-wide application.

Once the database and new incident forms are operating in the Southwest Division, the research team will then have the capability to test the reliability and validity of the public health surveillance system. The first step in this process involves studying the "pipeline" or flow of domestic violence cases through the police department. Figure 3 provides an example of a tree diagram designed to illustrate the central information that will be collected to this end. Each incident report filed within the Southwest Division during the study period will be recorded in the computerized database. These cases will then be classified according to the nature of the incident. The action taken on all domestic incidents will be carefully tracked and recorded. Information about child witnesses obtained from the new incident report forms will also be recorded in the pipeline study, as indicated by the encircled C's in Figure 3.

The second step in evaluating the scientific rigor of the surveillance system involves implementing active "reliability checks" into the pipeline study. The first such checkpoint occurs at the very top of the tree diagram in

FIGURE 3. Illustration of a Route to Identify Children Exposed to Family Violence via a Pipeline of Police Investigations of Domestic Disturbance

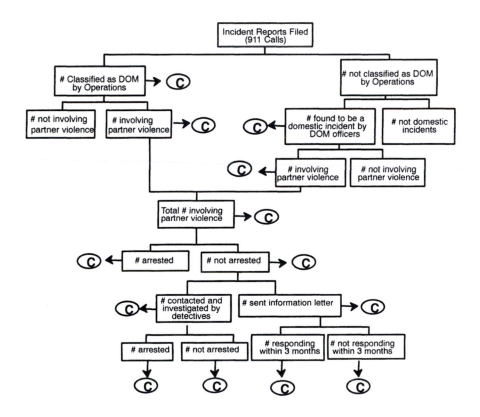

Figure 3. This will be conducted by the DOM officers who currently read each incident report to identify cases inaccurately coded as not domestic. These data will allow the research team to calculate a "hit rate" indicating the reliability of the current police operations in classifying domestic incidents. Additionally, the reliability of data about children exposed to domestic violence will be assessed by calling a random selection of homes, offering victim services, and verifying the presence of children. Researcher "ride-alongs" with police officers will also be conducted to evaluate the integrity of the data being collected. The completion of a pipeline study with reliability checks will provide rich information about the quality of a surveillance system involving the police department to track children exposed to maternal assault.

Although partnership with the police department is central in reaching children exposed to maternal abuse, one agency cannot reach all children. For this reason, the Penn research team has forged additional community linkages with other agencies that serve large numbers of vulnerable children: the Pre-Kindergarten Head Start Program of the School District of Philadelphia, and the Department of Human Services, the Child Protective Service agency for the City of Philadelphia. We are currently conducting a federally funded project that capitalizes on and combines these partnerships to further understand the needs of children exposed to violence. The goal of the project, entitled "Safety First: Identification and Enhancement of Factors that Protect Head Start Children from the Ill Effects of Community and Family Violence," is to identify and cultivate strengths in one of the leading Head Start programs in the country to respond to the needs of vulnerable children. The objectives of the "Safety First" project include:

- To establish an open dialogue with Head Start parents on violence and safety;
- To co-construct research methods with Head Start partners;
- To assess the impact of violence on Head Start children;
- To investigate protective factors and resiliency;
- To translate research findings into Head Start-based intervention;
- To assess the effects of violence and the stability of protective factors across the transition to kindergarten.

We are very excited about the potential that these initial partnership activities have for contributing to our understanding of a serious threat to the well-being of vulnerable children exposed to the abuse of their mother. Partnership with strategic community agencies provides the capacity: (a) to study the incidence and prevalence of child exposure to domestic violence, (b) to learn about what ways children are exposed, (c) to improve the scientific rigor of our knowledge base, and (d) to contribute to enhanced city services for vulnerable children. As we surface children who are now invisible, we open the door for future research with a population in which the exposure to this violence is substantiated by a front line professional. We also produce information to inform early intervention for these children, who might otherwise "fall through the cracks." Moreover, the vision of linkages with other agency databases makes possible the longitudinal study of developmental consequences across multiple domains of child functioning. For example, linking the police database with the School District's database affords an opportunity to track these children and potentially investigate and intervene when we see that they are evidencing adjustment problems. As we work to build linkages among the University of Pennsylvania, the City of Philadelphia Police Department, School District of Philadelphia, and Department of Human Services, we appreciate how our partnerships are enriched by the unique strengths that each partner brings to making invisible victims of domestic violence visible.

REFERENCES

Bachman, R., & Saltzman, L. E. (1995). *Bureau of Justice Statistics special report: Violence against women: Estimates from the redesigned survey.* Washington, DC: US Department of Justice.

Carlson, B. E. (1984). Children's observations of interparental violence. In A. R. Roberts (Ed.), *Battered women and their families* (pp. 147-167). New York: Springer.

Cates, W., Jr., & Williamson, G. D. (1994). Descriptive epidemiology: Analyzing and interpreting surveillance data. In S. M. Teutsh & R. E. Churchill (Eds.), *Principles and practice of public health surveillance* (pp. 96-135). New York: Oxford University Press.

Children's Defense Fund (1996). *The state of America's children.* Washington, DC: Children's Defense Fund.

Commonwealth of Pennsylvania (1995). Protection from Abuse Act 23 Pa.C.S. 6101-6118. In *Stalking and domestic violence manual* (pp. 149-162). Harrisburg, PA: Author.

Fantuzzo, J., Boruch, R., Beriama, A., Atkins, M., & Marcus, S. (1997). Domestic violence and children: Prevalence and risk in five major US cities. *Journal of the American Academy of Child & Adolescent Psychiatry, 36,* 116-122.

Fantuzzo, J. W., & Lindquist, C. U. (1989). The effects of observing conjugal violence on children: A review and analysis of research methodology. *Journal of Family Violence, 4,* 77-94.

Fantuzzo, J. W., DePaola, L. M., Lambert, L., Martino, T., Anderson, G., & Sutton, S. (1991). Effects of interparental violence on the adjustment and competencies of young children. *Journal of Consulting and Clinical Psychology, 59,* 258-265.

Fantuzzo, J., Stevenson, H., Weiss, A., Hampton, V., & Noone, M. (1997). A partnership-directed school-based intervention for child physical abuse and neglect: Beyond mandatory reporting. *School Psychology Review, 26,* 298-313.

Garner, J., Fagen, J., & Maxwell, C. (1995). Published findings from the spouse assault replication program: A critical review. *Journal of Quantitative Criminology, 11,* 3-28.

Gelles, R. J. (1997, June). *International trends in community responses to children exposed to domestic violence: Awareness, policy, and program development.* Keynote panel presented at the 2nd International Conference on Children Exposed to Family Violence, London, Canada.

Hughes, H., & Fantuzzo, J. (1994). Family violence: Child victims. In M. Hersen, R. Ammerman, & L. Sisson (Eds.), *Handbook of aggressive and destructive behavior in psychiatric patients* (pp. 135-150). New York: Plenum.

Hyman, A., Schiller, D., & Lo, B. (1995). Laws mandating reporting of domestic violence. *Journal of the American Medical Association, 22,* 1781-1787.

Koop, C. E., & Lundberg, G. D. (1992). Violence in America: A public health emergency. *Journal of the American Medical Association, 267,* 3075-3076.

Marans, S. (1995). *The police mental health partnership: A community based response to urban violence.* New Haven: Yale University Press.

McCloskey, L. A., Figueredo, A. J., & Koss, M. P. (1995). The effects of systemic family violence on children's mental health. *Child Development, 66,* 1239-1261.

National Research Council (1996). *Understanding violence against women*. Washington, DC: National Academy Press.

Osofsky, J. D. (1995). The effects of exposure to violence on young children. *American Psychologist, 50*, 782-788.

Rosenberg, M. L., O'Carroll, P. W., & Powell, K. E. (1992). Let's be clear: Violence is a public health problem. *Journal of the American Medical Association, 267*, 3071-3072.

Sedlak, A. J., & Broadhurst, D. D. (1996). *Third national incidence study of child abuse and neglect: Final report*. Washington, D.C.: US Department of Health and Human Services.

Spaccarelli, S., Sandler, I. N., & Roosa, M. (1994). History of spouse violence against mother: Correlated risks and unique effects in child mental health. *Journal of Family Violence, 9*, 79-98.

Straus, M. A., & Gelles, R. J. (1986). Societal change and change in family violence from 1975 to 1985 as revealed by two national surveys. *Journal of Marriage and the Family, 48*, 465-479.

Straus, M. A., Gelles, R. J., & Steinmetz, S. K. (1980). *Behind closed doors: Violence in the American family*. Garden City: Doubleday.

Teutch, S. M. (1994). Considerations in planning a surveillance system. In S. M. Teutsch & R. E. Churchill (Eds.), *Principles and practice of public health surveillance* (pp. 31-82). New York: Oxford University Press.

Tomkins, A. J., Mohamed, S., Steinman, M, & Macolini, R. M. (1994). The plight of children who witness woman battering: Psychological knowledge and policy implications. *Law & Psychology Review, 18*, 137-187.

U. S. Attorney General (1984). *Attorney General's Task Force on family violence: Final report*. Washington, DC.

Trauma and Parenting in Battered Women: An Addition to an Ecological Model of Parenting

Alytia A. Levendosky
Sandra A. Graham-Bermann

SUMMARY. While research has documented the harmful effects of domestic violence on women and children, little attention has been paid to the effects on women's ability to parent in this dangerous environment. This paper examines theoretical perspectives on the effects of domestic violence on parenting and proposes an ecologically-based model which can be used to inform research on parenting and treatment of battered mothers. Trauma theory and traumatic bonding are integrated into the ecological model of parenting in battered women. *[Article copies available for a fee from The Haworth Document Delivery Service: 1-800-342-9678. E-mail address: getinfo@haworthpressinc.com <Website: http://www.haworthpressinc.com>]*

KEYWORDS. Domestic violence, ecological theory, parenting, trauma theory

If I didn't have a violent husband, I would be happier, enjoy my children more, and we would be easier together.

Address correspondence to: Alytia A. Levendosky, Department of Psychology, Michigan State University, E. Lansing, MI 48824.

[Haworth co-indexing entry note]: "Trauma and Parenting in Battered Women: An Addition to an Ecological Model of Parenting." Levendosky, Alytia A., and Sandra A. Graham-Bermann. Co-published simultaneously in *Journal of Aggression, Maltreatment & Trauma* (The Haworth Maltreatment & Trauma Press, an imprint of The Haworth Press, Inc.) Vol. 3, No. 1 (#5), 2000, pp. 25-35; and: *Children Exposed to Domestic Violence: Current Issues in Research, Intervention, Prevention, and Policy Development* (ed: Robert A. Geffner, Peter G. Jaffe, and Marlies Sudermann) The Haworth Maltreatment & Trauma Press, an imprint of The Haworth Press, Inc., 2000, pp. 25-35. Single or multiple copies of this article are available for a fee from The Haworth Document Delivery Service [1-800-342-9678, 9:00 a.m. - 5:00 p.m. (EST). E-mail address: getinfo@haworthpressinc.com].

I feel like I would be and could have been a loving, high-quality parent in many aspects of my child's upbringing, including cognitive, emotional, social, and physical development, if I'd had a helpful, support-. ive, and cooperative spouse. I sacrificed too much due to the pressures of my marriage.

I had a hard time learning how to love my daughter because I didn't love her father since he was so emotionally abusive.

These are quotes from an interview study of battered mothers (Levendosky, Lynch, & Graham-Bermann, 1998). They demonstrate women's feelings that the abuse they were experiencing had very much affected their abilities to parent. While research has documented the harmful effects of domestic violence on women and children (e.g., Graham-Bermann, 1998; McCloskey, Figueredo, & Koss, 1995; Saunders, 1994; Sternberg et al., 1993), relatively little attention has been paid to the effects of the violence on women's ability to parent in this type of dangerous environment. Studies examining the effects of domestic violence on parenting have not consistently incorporated an understanding of the effects of the mother's mental health on her parenting. This article briefly reviews the few studies of the effects of battering on the parenting of battered women, as well as research on the traumatic effects of domestic violence on women. Next, we adapt Belsky's (1984) model of parenting to the circumstances of parenting under the stress of woman abuse. Specifically, we propose that trauma be incorporated into an ecologically-based model of parenting. Finally, suggestions are made for future research and interventions with battered women who are mothers.

In 1984 Belsky proposed an ecological model in which parenting is described as existing in a buffered system, such that deficits in one area in the model can be buffered by strengths in another area. He proposed three types of factors that could influence parenting by providing either risk or protection, including (1) contextual variables such as work, social network and marital relations, (2) ontogenic variables, such as a parent's developmental history, personality, and (3) child characteristics. This model has been studied with a number of normal and high-risk populations since Belsky first proposed it (Cicchetti & Howes, 1991; Conger et al., 1993; Huston, McLoyd, & Garcia Coll, 1994). Support has been found for many of the linkages described in his model (Belsky & Vondra, 1989). In this paper, however, we argue that the traumatic effects of domestic violence on women's mental health should be added to the ecological model as a mediator of the effect of violence on women's parenting.

PARENTING IN THE CONTEXT OF DOMESTIC VIOLENCE

A few studies have examined the impact of domestic violence on parenting (Holden & Ritchie, 1991; Holden, Stein, Ritchie, Harris, & Jouriles, 1998; Levendosky & Graham-Bermann, 1998a, 1998b; McCloskey et al., 1995; Sullivan et al., 1997; Wolfe et al., 1985). While the results are somewhat mixed, in general, researchers report that psychological and physical abuse of women by their partners affects parenting stress and parenting behaviors.

Four studies found that maternal parenting stress was higher in domestic violence families than comparable, but nonviolent families (Holden & Ritchie, 1991; Holden et al., 1998; Levendosky & Graham-Bermann, 1998a; Wolfe et al., 1985). Holden and Ritchie (1991), Holden et al. (1998), and Levendosky and Graham-Bermann (1998a) measured maternal stress as the self-report of experienced parenting stress in mothers of school-age children. In contrast, Wolfe and colleagues (1985) used an ecological framework in designing their maternal stress variable. Here, maternal stress was comprised of maternal physical and emotional health, negative life events, and sociodemographic variables. While these are two distinct ways of defining maternal stress, both were positively related to the experience of domestic violence.

Some research has found no effect of battering on women's parenting behaviors. When Holden and Ritchie (1991) measured the parenting variables of reasoning, physical affection, punishment, and a composite of negative child-rearing behavior, they found no differences between battered and comparison women. Sullivan and colleagues (1997) also found that the severity of domestic violence was not related to battered mothers' parenting stress, discipline strategies, or to their physical and emotional availability to the children.

In contrast, other studies have shown differences in parenting behaviors between battered women and nonbattered women. McCloskey, Figueredo, and Koss (1995) measured parenting style as well as maternal warmth in families of 6-12 year-old children. While they did not directly report on their findings on parenting style, they did note that violent families had lower levels of maternal warmth. The Holden et al. (1998) study had mixed results for the effects of domestic violence on parenting. In comparison with nonbattered mothers, in this study, battered mothers were more physically aggressive and used more corporal punishment with their 2-8 year-old children. However, these mothers were not less warm or emotionally available.

Holden et al. (1998) also report on a longitudinal study of parenting in 50 battered women over six months after leaving their abusive partners. (Eighteen of the women did not return for the second data collection.) With this caveat, however, there was a significant decrease in maternal aggression towards the child after six months. These results suggest that the stress of woman abuse may directly affect the amount of aggression a mother perpetrates towards her own child. This is in contrast to viewing maternal aggression as a stable aspect of the woman's parenting.

In the only study to date that incorporated trauma symptoms as predictors of parenting, Levendosky and Graham-Bermann (1998b) used an ecological model to propose that the effects of domestic violence on the parenting of 120 school-age children were mediated by maternal psychological functioning. Significant relations were found between the severity and frequency of physical and psychological abuse and women's trauma symptoms, and between trauma symptoms and parental warmth, control, and effectiveness. Specifically, increased trauma symptoms were associated with decreased warmth, control, and effectiveness.

A major limitation of the above studies is that the parenting data were collected using self-report measures. The one exception to this is the Holden group's (1998) study that incorporated a few observational measures of parenting in their design. It will be important for future studies of parenting with this population to have multiple sources of information about parenting processes, including the use of observational methods. It is also clear from these studies that most of them performed a simple test of two groups in comparing parenting, i.e., was parenting different in the battered women than in the nonbattered women? To date, the mechanism through which domestic violence affects parenting has not been examined. In this article we propose that the psychological trauma of the battered woman is an important mechanism through which domestic violence affects parenting. A review of the theories and research about trauma and battered women reveals some of these potential influences.

TRAUMA AND BATTERED WOMEN

Both theory and research have indicated that most battered women are traumatized by the abuse that they experience. Herman (1992a, b) argued that many battered women suffer from a complex traumatic syndrome that is similar to the diagnosis of post-traumatic stress disorder in the Diagnostic and Statistical Manual IV (American Psychiatric Association, 1994). Yet Herman includes additional symptoms due to the chronic nature of the trauma. Some of these symptoms are depression, idealization of the perpetrator, and dissociation. While arguing that battered women suffer characterological changes in personality that leave them vulnerable to harm, Herman emphasized the perpetrator's actions, rather than the woman's premorbid psychological functioning, in accounting for these changes (Herman, 1992a). She noted that some perpetrators attempt to gain control over the woman's body through deprivation of sleep, food, or shelter. In doing so, the perpetrator then becomes the potential source of solace when he grants small indulgences. Herman reported that this particular dynamic greatly diminishes the woman's ability to initiate action (Herman, 1992a).

Trauma perpetrated by another person, as opposed to experiencing severe illness or natural disasters, is simultaneously a psychological, physiological, and relational event. Herman (1992a, b) theorized that trauma overwhelms the person's ego capacities to understand what has happened. The person's most fundamental assumptions about the safety of the world and trust in the relationship with the perpetrator are undermined as the woman does not know how to assimilate this into her cognitive experience (Herman, 1992b). In addition, her normal capacity to contain her emotions is overwhelmed by the flood of painful feelings that accompany what is considered to be such a devastating betrayal (van der Kolk, 1987). In reaction to these overwhelming emotions, the trauma victim may become emotionally numb.

Physiologically, a trauma victim's capacities to react to save herself is thwarted and proves meaningless, as the normal physiological reactions to stress (such as hyperarousal), may repeat themselves in an altered and exaggerated form, even after the trauma is over. These physiological responses have been linked to changes in the hypothalamic-pituitary-adrenal axis and associated neurotransmitters (Charney, Deutch, Krystal, Southwick, & Davis, 1993; van der Kolk, Greenberg, Boyd, & Krystal, 1985; van der Kolk, 1987). Most trauma survivors have a poor tolerance for stress and may react with aggression or withdrawal in response to even minor stimuli. Trauma may cause a person to lose the ability to modulate arousal, probably due to the effects of the trauma on serotonin levels (van der Kolk, 1994).

Relationally, battered women (and victims of other types of interpersonal trauma) may experience traumatic bonding. Kuleshynk (1984) was first to describe the Stockholm Syndrome, where bonding to one's captor was interpreted as taking place in order to ensure survival in life-threatening situations. Kuleshynk developed this concept after a bank kidnapping in the 1970s in Sweden, in which a kidnap victim married her captor after he was released. He attempted to understand the nature of the bonding between victim and captor during long periods of stress and deprivation. This theory of traumatic bonding was then proposed by Graham and Rawlings (1991) to explain the seemingly illogical actions of battered women. They extended the traumatic bonding concept by arguing that bonding to an abusive partner is one survival strategy used by battered women.

Graham and Rawlings (1991) hypothesized that as the batterer traumatizes the woman by threatening her physical and/or psychological survival, she comes to see him as a captor. Then, due to her subsequent isolation and her abuser's small kindnesses, she must turn to him alone for any nurturance and sustenance. In this closed system, she learns to keep him happy so that he will let her live. However, in doing so, the woman unconsciously takes on his perspective on the world. Another significant aspect of this dynamic is her denial of the abuse and denial of rage at the abuser; this defensive process is critical for her ability to keep the abuser happy and to remain alive. Leaving the abuser is difficult because it means losing the only relationship now available to her, and losing the sense of identity that she has developed now through the eyes of the abuser (Graham & Rawlings, 1991). While this theory is intriguing, it has not yet been empirically tested. In addition, the universal claims to traumatic bonding in battered women do not adequately explain the experience of many women who are able to leave the abuser after either one or many violent episodes.

Dutton and Painter (1981; 1995) also wrote about the traumatic bonding that develops in abusive relationships. They argued that trauma symptoms, self-esteem deficits, and traumatic attachment develop both through the power differential in the relationship, and the intermittency and unpredictability of the abuse (Dutton & Painter, 1981). In an empirical investigation of this theory, they interviewed 75 battered women and found some evidence to support their suppositions (Dutton & Painter, 1993). Specifically, the women reported high rates of trauma symptoms, low self-esteem, and high levels of attachment to the batterer. In addition, more than half of the variance in these effects was accounted for by the intermittency of the abuse, the power differential in the relationship, the severity of physical abuse, and the presence of emotional abuse.

After the immediate trauma, most survivors begin a long process of recovery, that includes an assimilation of the trauma into their personal schema of their world. During this time survivors frequently use denial, minimization, and behavioral self-blame in their attempts to cope (Janoff-Bulman, 1979; Janoff-Bulman, 1992). Janoff-Bulman hypothesized that denial and minimization allow the survivor to integrate the new overwhelming experience of the trauma slowly so that she does not again become overwhelmed. Self-blame allows the survivor to feel that she does have some control over her world, and if she does things differently next time, this will not happen again (Janoff-Bulman & Wortman, 1977; Janoff-Bulman, 1979; Kushner, Riggs, Foa, & Miller, 1992; Terr, 1990). During this process, intrusive memories, dreams, and thoughts about the trauma may reawaken the terror and hyperarousal that she once felt during the traumatic incident. Many survivors, therefore, often appear to oscillate between states of overwhelming emotions and emotional numbing (van der Kolk, 1994). Trauma survivors also may become physiologically addicted to the hyperarousal state (van der Kolk et al., 1985). Some theorists suggest that this physiological addiction explains why trauma survivors remain in traumatic situations over an extended period of time (Janoff-Bulman, 1992; van der Kolk, 1994).

These reactions are common to most survivors of interpersonal trauma and the road to recovery is long and hard. However, women who live in violent homes may never have the chance to recover while they remain in these environments. Many of the women experience trauma and the resulting psychological and physiological reactions to trauma over and over again (Herman, 1992a). Due to the prolonged, unpredictable, and repetitive nature of domestic violence, persistent affective, cognitive, and even personality changes may occur (van der Kolk, 1987). Herman (1992a,b) describes these changes in her proposed new diagnosis of complex post-traumatic stress disorder. The changes include alterations in affect regulation (e.g., alternating explosive and inhibited anger), alterations in consciousness (e.g., dissociation), and alterations in self-perceptions (e.g., shame and self-blame). Dissociation of affect from cognition, clinically noted as a prominent symptom in many trauma survivors (Davies & Frawley, 1994), may make a woman less alarmed by future abuse towards herself or others, including her children.

Research on trauma symptoms in battered women has generally focused on the DSM criteria for PTSD. Herman's complex post-traumatic stress disorder has not yet been studied in this population. The prevalence of post-traumatic stress disorder, as defined by the DSM criteria, in battered women is high, ranging from 40% to 84% (Astin, Ogland-Hand, Coleman, & Foy, 1995; Gleason, 1993; Houskamp & Foy, 1991; Kemp, Rawlings, & Green, 1991; Kemp, Green, Hovanitz, & Rawlings, 1995; Vitanza et al., 1995). A number of factors have been found to significantly predict PTSD symptoms in battered women, including severity of violence, recency of last abusive episode, history of childhood sexual abuse, experiencing other negative life events, and use of disengagement coping strategies in dealing with the abuse (Astin, Lawrence, & Foy, 1993; Kemp et al., 1995). Several protective factors have also been identified, including social support and intrinsic religiosity (Astin, Lawrence, & Foy, 1993).

TRAUMA AND PARENTING IN BATTERED WOMEN

Thus, based on a number of studies, it is clear that many, if not most, battered women are psychologically traumatized by the violence they experience. This article makes the argument that the psychological trauma may be an important factor influencing the parenting behaviors of these women. Two possible outcomes for parenting will be hypothesized. The first possible outcome is that of no apparent change in parental functioning. Here, it may be the case that some battered women step up their attentional focus in order to compensate for the deficits experienced in such chronic and traumatic circumstances. In this explanatory process, the mother may be able to achieve consistency in parenting despite the trauma in her life. For example, she can read and regulate her emotions well, can become attuned to her child as needed, and can manage her worry without unduly burdening her child–all this in addition to coping with the violence in her life. However, given the ongoing, chronic nature of the trauma in many abused women's relationships, and the escalating nature of such violence, it is unclear whether efficacy in parenting can be consistently maintained over long periods of time under these deleterious circumstances without some cost. It should be kept in mind that parenting for battered women includes making up for and attempting to correct the malparenting of the batterer who has exposed the children to the violence and abuse of their mother, among other problems (Levendosky, Lynch, & Graham-Bermann, 1998). The costs to the woman of this type of extraordinary, compensatory effort have yet to be determined and taken into account.

The second possible outcome is that the physiological and psychological reactions of alternating states of hyperarousal and numbing associated with trauma could serve to diminish the mother's ability to maintain adequate functioning, including her parenting capacities. That is, some battered women may have parenting that oscillates between periods of being disengaged or withdrawn, angry, or warm and loving, as they attempt to respond to the violence, to their internal traumatized state, and to the external demands of parenting. Their undermined trust in loved ones (coupled with the abuser's isolation tactics) may cause them to withdraw from their friends and family, furthering their social isolation, or to be overprotective and hypervigilant about their children, restricting their normal growth towards independence. Either way, whether parenting is diminished or is compensated for with extraordinary effort, it is hypothesized here that the process of parenting children in the face of domestic violence is influenced by the traumatic effects experienced by the mother.

The other risk and protective factors in the ecological model of parenting as described by Belsky (1984), including social support, work, and personality factors, would remain important in determining parenting behaviors in these women. These factors may be crucial to explaining which women are at-risk for stress in parenting and which are able to maintain parental competence as abused women. For example, women who have high levels of social support and low levels of depression would be expected to have more resilient parenting, regardless of trauma symptoms, compared with women with low levels of social support and high levels of depression.

Research, assessment and interventions must be careful not to pathologize further the women who have suffered from domestic violence. Rather, we need to learn more about the ways that their functioning may be inhibited, stressed, or damaged by the battering. Current research on parenting in the context of domestic violence tends to be atheoretical and does not examine mediating factors. We argue that trauma may be one of the important mediating variables. Trauma symptoms may be operationalized, and tested as a mediator through which domestic violence affects parenting. Specific protective and vulnerability factors for the effects of trauma on parenting may also be tested.

Intervention programs that take into account the traumatic effects of woman abuse on parenting can be designed. A number of parenting support programs already exist. However, few parenting support and empowerment groups focus attention on identifying aspects of trauma and addressing how trauma affects parenting. Further, the costs to the woman of maintaining high quality and resilient parenting in the face of domestic violence should be addressed. In this way, parenting programs can be designed that both enhance protective factors and reduce the risk factors associated with parenting for battered women.

REFERENCES

American Psychiatric Association (1994). *Diagnostic and statistical manual of mental disorders IV.* Washington, DC: APA.

Astin, M. C., Lawrence, K. J., & Foy, D. W. (1993). Posttraumatic stress disorder among battered women: Risk and resiliency factors. *Violence and Victims, 8* (1), 17-28.

Astin, M. C., Ogland-Hand, S. M., Coleman, E. M., & Foy, D. W. (1995). Posttraumatic stress disorder and childhood abuse in battered women: Comparisons with maritally distressed women. *Journal of Consulting and Clinical Psychology, 63* (2), 308-312.

Baumrind, D. (1967). Child care practices anteceding 3 patterns of preschool behavior. *Genetic Psychology Monographs, 75,* 43-88.

Baumrind, D. (1971). Current patterns of parental authority. *Developmental Psychology Monographs, 4* (1, Pt. 2).

Baumrind, D. (1973). The development of instrumental competence through socialization. In A. Pick (Ed.). *Minnesota Symposium of Child Psychology,* Vol. 7. Minneapolis: University of Minnesota Press.

Baumrind, D. (1991). The influence of parenting style on adolescent competence and substance use. *Journal of Early Adolescence, 11,* 56-95.

Belsky, J. (1980). Child maltreatment: An ecological integration. *American Psychologist, 35,* 320-335.

Belsky, J. & Vondra, J. (1989). Lessons from child abuse: The determinants of parenting. In D. Cicchetti & V. Carlson (Eds.). *Child maltreatment: Theory and research on the causes and consequences of child abuse and neglect.* Cambridge: Cambridge Univ. Press.

Bronfenbrenner, U. (1977). Toward an experimental ecology of human development. *American Psychologist, 32,* 513-531.

Bronfenbrenner, U. (1979). *The ecology of human development.* Cambridge, MA: Harvard University Press.

Burgess, R. (1978). Child abuse: A behavioral analysis. In B. Lakey & A. Kazdin (Eds.). *Advances in child clinical psychology.* New York: Plenum Press.

Burgess, A.W. & Holstrum, L. (1974). Rape trauma syndrome. *American Journal of Psychiatry, 131*, 981-986.

Charney, D. S., Deutch, A. Y., Krystal, J. H., Southwick, S. M., & Davis, M. (1993). Psychobiological mechanisms of post-traumatic stress disorder. *Archives of General Psychiatry, 50*, 294-305.

Cicchetti, D. & Howes, P. W. (1991). Developmental psychopathology in the context of the family: Illustrations from the study of child maltreatment. *Canadian Journal of Behavioural Sciences, 23*, 257-281.

Conger, R. D., Conger, K. J., Elder, G. H., Lorenz, F. O., Simons, R. L., & Whitbeck, L. B. (1993). Family economic stress and adjustment of early adolescent girls. *Developmental Psychology, 29*, 206-219.

Davies, J. M. & Frawley, M. G. (1994). *Treating the adult survivor of childhood sexual abuse: A psychoanalytic perspective.* New York: Basic Books.

Dutton, D. G. & Painter, S. (1981). Traumatic bonding: The development of emotional attachment in battered women and other relationships of intermittent abuse. *Victimology, 6*, 139-155.

Dutton, D. G. & Painter, S. (1993). The battered woman syndrome: Effects of severity and intermittency of abuse. *American Journal of Orthopsychiatry, 63*, 614-622.

Dutton, D. G. (1995). *The domestic assault of women: Psychological and criminal justice perspectives.* Vancouver, BC: UBC Press.

Gleason, W. J. (1993). Mental disorders in battered women. *Violence and Victims, 8* (1), 53-68.

Graham, D. L. R. & Rawlings, E. I. (1991). Bonding with abusive dating partners: Dynamics of Stockholm Syndrome. In B. Levy (Ed.). *Dating violence: Young women in danger.* Seattle: Seal Press.

Graham-Bermann, S. A. (1998). The impact of woman abuse on children's social development, in G. W. Holden, R. Geffner, & E. N. Jouriles (Eds.). *Children and marital violence: Theory, research, and intervention.* Washington, DC: APA Books, 21-54.

Herman, J. L. (1992a). Complex PTSD: A syndrome in survivors of prolonged and repeated trauma. *Journal of Traumatic Stress, 5*, 377-391.

Herman, J. L. (1992b). *Trauma and recovery.* New York: Basic Books.

Holden, G. W. & Ritchie, K. L. (1991). Linking extreme marital discord, child rearing, and child behavior problems: Evidence from battered women. *Child Development, 62*, 311-327.

Holden, G. W., Stein, J. D., Ritchie, K. L., Harris, S. D., & Jouriles, E. N. (1998). Parenting behaviors and beliefs of battered women. In G.W. Holden, R. Geffner, & E. N. Jouriles (Eds.). *Children exposed to marital violence: Theory, research, and applied issues.* Washington, DC: APA.

Houskamp, B. M. & Foy, D. W. (1991). The assessment of posttraumatic stress disorder in battered women. *Journal of Interpersonal Violence, 6*, 367-375.

Huston, A. C., McLoyd, V., & Garcia Coll, C. (Eds.) (1994). Children and poverty [Special Issue], *Child Development, 60*, 838-845.

Janoff-Bulman, R. & Wortman, C. B. (1977). Attributions of blame and coping in the "Real World": Severe accident victims react to their lot. *Journal of Personality and Social Psychology, 35,* 351-363.

Janoff-Bulman, R. (1979). Characterological versus behavioral self-blame: Inquiries into depression and rape. *Journal of Personality and Social Psychology, 37,* 1798-1809.

Kemp, A., Green, B. L., Hovanitz, C., & Rawlings, E. I. (1995). Incidence and correlates of posttraumatic stress disorder in battered women. *Journal of Interpersonal Violence, 10* (1), 43-55.

Kemp, A., Rawlings, E. I., & Green, B. L. (1991). Post-traumatic stress disorder in battered women: A shelter sample. *Journal of Traumatic Stress, 4,* 137-148.

Kuleshnyk, I. (1984). The Stockholm Syndrome: Toward an understanding. *Social Action and the Law, 10,* 37-42.

Kurdek, L. A. & Fine, M. A. (1994). Family acceptance and family control as predictors of adjustment in young adolescents: Linear, curvilinear, or interactive effects? *Child Development, 65,* 1137-1146.

Kushner, M. G., Riggs, D. S., Foa, E. B., & Miller, S. M. (1992). Perceived controllability and the development of posttraumatic stress disorder (PTSD) in crime victims. *Behavioral Research and Therapy, 31,* 105-110.

Levendosky, A. A. & Graham-Bermann, S. A. (1998a). The moderating effects of parenting stress in woman-abusing families. *Journal of Interpersonal Violence, 13* (3), 383-397.

Levendosky, A. A. & Graham-Bermann, S. A. (1998b). *Parenting in battered women: The effects of domestic violence on women and their children.* Under review.

McCloskey, L. A., Figueredo, A. J., & Koss, M. P. (1995). The effects of systemic family violence on children's mental health. *Child Development, 66,* 1239-1261.

Saunders, D. G. (1994). Post-traumatic stress symptoms profiles of battered women: A comparison of survivors in two settings. *Violence and Victims, 9,* 31-44.

Terr, L. (1990). *Too scared to cry.* New York: Basic Books.

Van der Kolk, B. A. (1987). *Psychological trauma.* Washington, DC: APA.

Van der Kolk, B. A., Greenberg, M. S., Boyd, H., & Krystal, J. (1985). Inescapable shock, neurotransmitter and addiction to trauma: Towards a new psychobiology of post-traumatic stress. *Biological Psychiatry, 20,* 314-320.

Van der Kolk, B. A. (1994). The body keeps score: Memory and the evolving psychobiology of post-traumatic stress. *Harvard Review of Psychiatry, 1,* 253-265.

Vitanza, S., Vogel, L. C. M., & Marshall, L. L. (1995). Distress and symptoms of posttraumatic stress disorder in abused women. *Violence and Victims, 10* (1), 23-34.

Walker, L. E. (1983). The battered woman syndrome study. In D. Finkelhor, R. J. Gelles, G. T. Hotaling, & M. A. Straus (Ed.). *The dark side of families: Current family violence research.* Beverly Hills, CA: Sage.

Wolfe, D. A., Jaffe, P., Wilson, S. K., & Zak, L. (1985). Children of battered women: The relation of child behavior to family violence and maternal stress. *Journal of Consulting and Clinical Psychology, 53,* 657-665.

Consider the Children:
Research Informing Interventions
for Children Exposed to Domestic Violence

Debra J. Pepler
Rose Catallo
Timothy E. Moore

The research by Pepler and Moore described in this paper was funded by the Social Sciences and Humanities Research Council of Canada. The intervention and evaluation were conducted at Women's Habitat, Toronto, with support from the Laidlaw Foundation under the direction of Janet Walker, Executive Director, and Nicole Walton Allen. The authors are indebted to the women and children who participated in the research and to the women's shelters for their support. A version of this paper was presented at the University of Vermont Continuing Education Workshop on Domestic Violence, Boston, March 1996.

Women's Habitat received funding from the Laidlaw Foundation in order to carry out an evaluation of their Children's Peer Group Counselling Program. Nicole Walton Allen set up the original parameters of the project by developing the research proposal and questionnaire design. Rose Catallo input the data, analysed the results and wrote this report, in collaboration with Debra Pepler of York University.

The peer counselling groups were led by Karen Blake of L.A.M.P. or by trained counsellors from other participating community service organizations. Counsellors included Laura Bores and Clare Grebow of Catholic Family Services, Jennifer Miele of Interim Place, Vicki Lapp, Nancy Christie, Michelle Fraser, Jill Davies, Sharon Lamont, Maria Busdon and Fiona, a student placement worker.

Address correspondence to: Debra J. Pepler, Director, La Marsh Centre for Research on Violence and Conflict Resolution, York University, 4700 Keele Street, North York, Ontario, Canada M3J 1P3.

[Haworth co-indexing entry note]: "Consider the Children: Research Informing Interventions for Children Exposed to Domestic Violence." Pepler, Debra J., Rose Catallo, and Timothy E. Moore. Co-published simultaneously in *Journal of Aggression, Maltreatment & Trauma* (The Haworth Maltreatment & Trauma Press, an imprint of The Haworth Press, Inc.) Vol. 3, No. 1 (#5), 2000, pp. 37-57; and: *Children Exposed to Domestic Violence: Current Issues in Research, Intervention, Prevention, and Policy Development* (ed: Robert A. Geffner, Peter G. Jaffe, and Marlies Sudermann) The Haworth Maltreatment & Trauma Press, an imprint of The Haworth Press, Inc., 2000, pp. 37-57. Single or multiple copies of this article are available for a fee from The Haworth Document Delivery Service [1-800-342-9678, 9:00 a.m. - 5:00 p.m. (EST). E-mail address: getinfo@haworthpressinc.com].

SUMMARY. In this article, we consider interventions for children exposed to family violence in light of the research on children's problems associated with witnessing family violence. Next, we review risk and protective factors related to these children's adjustment with the view that all children are not similarly affected by exposure to family violence. Against this background, we then move to consider directions for interventions from a systemic perspective. We take into account not only the exposure to interactions between their mother and father, but also children's relationships with their mother, father, and siblings, as well as within broader systems such as the peer group, the school, and the community. We consider the critical challenges within each of these important systems for children exposed to family violence, and we propose some potential interventions to address the problems. Finally, we summarize an evaluation of an intervention that incorporates some of the elements identified by a systemic perspective. The evaluation revealed a significant improvement in children's self-reports of depression and anxiety over the course of the program. Mothers rated their children as significantly improved in emotional and hyperactive behaviour problems. There was no relation between mothers' involvement in counselling and children's improvement. Overall, the results suggest that the Peer Group Counselling Program effectively provided support to children exposed to family violence. Finally, we discuss the steps necessary to support children and families in moving toward violence-free lives. *[Article copies available for a fee from The Haworth Document Delivery Service: 1-800-342-9678. E-mail address: getinfo@haworthpressinc.com <Website: http://www.haworthpressinc.com>]*

KEYWORDS. Program evaluation, children's adjustment, siblings, peers, school, community, peer group counselling

Violent conflict is a reality for many families. In this paper, we consider the children growing up with regular exposure to violence within their own families. There are no precise estimates of how many children live with this stress, but approximately one-third of married women are estimated to have experienced violence from their current or previous partner (Statistics Canada, 1994). The majority of these women have children, which leads to estimates that 3 to 5 children in every classroom have been witnesses to woman abuse in their homes (Kincaid, 1985).

An understanding of the roots of violence is growing. A recent American Psychological Association report concluded that aggression and violence are learned behaviors (Eron, Gentry & Schlegel, 1994). Support for the conclusion that violence is learned comes from evidence that the risk of engaging in wife assault is three times as high for men who had witnessed their father abusing their mother (Statistics Canada, 1994). Once an aggressive interactional style is learned, our society provides ample reinforcement through the media to support the belief that it is appropriate to combine power and aggression. Furthermore, there are generally few consequences for abusive behavior that occurs behind closed doors.

For children growing up in violent homes, there are numerous potential lessons that result from regular exposure to family violence. First, children may learn that it is acceptable to be abusive and that violence is an effective way to get what you want. Children may learn that violence is sometimes justified–particularly when you are angry at someone. They also learn about the traditional power imbalances between men and women. The impact of exposure to family violence on children has been assessed by several research groups. In this article, we consider interventions for children exposed to family violence in light of the research on children's problems associated with witnessing family violence. Next, we review risk and protective factors related to these children's adjustment. We then consider the challenges presented for interventions from a systemic perspective and potential elements of prevention and intervention. Finally, we summarize an evaluation of an intervention that incorporates some of the elements identified by a systemic perspective.

PROBLEMS OF CHILDREN EXPOSED TO FAMILY VIOLENCE

Research on children exposed to family violence indicates that they are at risk for a wide range of both internalizing and externalizing behavior problems which vary by developmental stage (e.g., Hughes, 1988; Jaffe, Wolfe, Wilson, & Zak, 1986a; Moore & Pepler, 1998). Externalizing problems refer to behaviours that children act out, such as: temper tantrums, impulsivity, hyperactivity, aggression, conflict with siblings and with peers, cruelty to animals, and bullying. Internalizing problems are those which reflect the stresses that children endure such as: somatic complaints (e.g., headaches), sleep disturbances, anxiety, fear of separation, social withdrawal, and depression. Some research indicates that as a group, children who witness violence in their homes have levels of emotional and behavioral problems similar to children who are themselves physically abused (Wolfe & Mosk, 1983). We found that children exposed to family violence were more likely than children from non-violent homes to have an external locus of control (Moore & Pepler, 1998). In other words, they had a lower sense of predictability and control over events in their lives. Issues of control are salient in the lives of children exposed to family violence. On the one hand, there is little, if anything that they can do to stop the violence. On the other hand, children often blame themselves for the violence and occasionally take on considerable "parental" responsibility to maintain a semblance of order in their homes.

Not surprisingly, the effects of exposure to family violence extend beyond the home to children's functioning in school. Children exposed to family violence experience difficulties in paying attention and staying on task. They often fall behind in their school work because of poor attendance, which may be attributable to fear for their mothers' safety when they leave and/or illness due to the internalizing problems listed previously (Kates & Pepler, 1989).

The adjustment difficulties of children exposed to family violence clearly indicate the need for supportive interventions in several domains. In recent years, research has moved beyond describing general patterns of adjustment to considering the variation in adjustment in the face of significant stress. For example, research indicates that there is a wide range in the adjustment patterns of children exposed to family violence (Hughes & Luke, 1998; Moore & Pepler, 1998). Some children exposed to family violence show extreme adjustment difficulties, while others score well within the normal range. To understand this important variation in the behavioral profiles of children exposed to family environment, we now move to a consideration of current conceptual models that inform both research and intervention.

DEVELOPMENTAL MODEL OF RISK

Current theories related to children's adjustment difficulties focus on the interaction of risk and protective factors in relation to development. Risk factors are those which lead directly to disorder (e.g., marital conflict, parental psychopathology) (Rutter, 1990), whereas protective factors operate to buffer the effects of the risk variable (e.g., a significant adult available to support children). Risk and protective factors may reside within individuals and/or within their environments. Drawing from this theoretical perspective, Davies and Cummings (1994) have identified multiple risks experienced by children exposed to family violence. First, children witness escalating forms of aggression from their father to their mother that can often be very traumatic for the children. For example, almost half of a sample of children of battered women reported that their fathers had choked their mothers (McCloskey et al., 1995). Secondly, witnessing persistent marital conflict undermines children's emotional security and their capacity to meet the demands of everyday life (Davies & Cummings, 1994). Thirdly, children exposed to family violence may suffer from chronic levels of arousal and dysregulation. Consequently, they show high levels of emotional and behavioral reactivity when conflict arises. In our research, children's exposure to verbal aggression was the strongest predictor of adjustment difficulties (Moore & Pepler, 1998). We postulated that children may have been sensitized to verbal aggression as a potential precursor to more extreme forms of aggression in conflict situations. Children's difficulties may also have been related to a tendency to focus on and remember the conflicts within their family situations (Davies & Cummings, 1994). Finally, children exposed to family violence experience daily lessons in the use of aggression and learn to mirror the aggressive strategies used by their parents in several ways. They may model and imitate the aggressive behavior that they observe. They may learn to use disruptive behavior to distract argumentative parents and stop the conflict. Children's cognitions about the use of aggression in problem solving may develop in line with the aggressive strategies they observe. Consequently, they may use these negative strategies in interactions with their parents, siblings, and friends. These other relationships within children's lives are critical and must be considered both in terms of children's adjustment, as well as for effective interventions.

A SYSTEMIC VIEW OF THE PROBLEMS AND INTERVENTIONS

In our efforts to understand and address the problems of children exposed to family violence, we must consider all the realms of influence on their lives. Although the primary concern of this volume is exposure to violence between parents, other systems are also important in the lives of children exposed to family violence. These include their relationships with their mother, father, and siblings, as well as broader systems such as the peer group, the school, and the community. Drawing from a systemic framework, we now turn to considering the critical challenges within each of these important systems for children exposed to family violence, and we propose some potential interventions to address the problems.

Mother-Father System

The first domain of influence for the child exposed to family violence is the marital relationship (or a similar relationship between the mother and her male partner). Although conflict within the family may be confined to this relationship, it has a significant spillover effect for the children who witness it. The impact of chronic marital conflict on children is very detrimental due to the mechanisms described above. Research has identified marital discord as the strongest predictor of children's behavior problems (Emery, 1989). Family violence is the most extreme form of marital discord; therefore, children exposed to this extreme conflict may be at significantly high risk of developmental disruptions and adjustment problems.

Intervention. Multiple interventions are required to address problems within the marital relationship. First, treatment must be provided for the violent men. Interventions for batterers have been developed and evaluated with variable success (e.g., Bryant, 1994; Hanson & Whitman, 1995; Pirog-Good & Stets-Kealey, 1985). Simultaneously, there must be legal consequences for violence. The recent developments in which police can lay charges of assault without relying on the battered woman increase the likelihood that violent men will experience the legal consequences of their behavior (Statistics Canada, 1994). Another logical approach for addressing dysfunction within the marital relationship is couple counselling. Many concerns have been raised regarding this element of intervention. It is clear that the man's violent behavior must be ameliorated prior to any attempt to reconstruct the marital partnership. If the violent behaviour and attitudes that accompany it are not eradicated, the mother and children are safer and potentially healthier separated from the father.

Mother-Child System

The second system to be considered is the mother-child relationship. In spite of significant societal changes related to the family, mothers remain the primary caretakers for children. Mothers' central role is reflected in their impact on their children's well-being. Given their closeness to the children and their nurturant role, mothers can have a protective influence, buffering the effects of witnessing family violence. Their protective influence was revealed in our research: The strongest predictor of children's adjustment was low verbal aggression from mother to her children (Moore & Pepler, 1998). Conversely, the most troubled children were those whose mothers were both depressed and aggressive towards them (Pepler & Moore, 1995).

The problem facing both the mothers and children in families at risk is that women who are abused have few resources to bring to the extremely demanding task of parenting. Thus, in addition to the abuse they have to deal with, these women often experience a myriad of additional stressors (Jouriles et al., 1998). It is not surprising, therefore, if these mothers fall short in providing the nurturance and support necessary for the optimal development of their children.

Intervention. Mothers who have been abused may require diverse support in recovering from the battering and starting a new life for themselves and their children. Therefore, a range of services should be available to these women including: individual counselling, sheltered living arrangements, respite care for their children, counselling for the children, housing, legal aid, and financial aid. A challenge to providing these interventions is to reach the women who endure violent relationships and are reticent to seek support. To reach these women, governments need to be active in promoting public service programs that provide general education about family violence and that increase awareness of the problems and potential solutions. Helping women to identify the problems that they may be facing in a violent relationship must be accompanied by developing a full set of community resources to support their efforts to move out of the abusive environment.

Father-Child System

Children's relationships with their fathers comprise the third system to be considered. Often these relationships are severed when the mother and children escape an abusive home situation. When supportive services are provided within the context of a sheltered residence, the fathers are necessarily excluded from any treatment plans. On the other hand, when families are referred for services prior to a separation, there may be the possibility of considering interventions to repair the father-child relationship. There are many aspects of this relationship to take into account.

A critical question to be asked in considering intervention in the father-child relationship is whether the father has abused his children in addition to his wife. Often abusive men have an aggressive approach to multiple relationships. The patriarchal attitudes of entitlement and power underlie the use of aggression in both wife abuse and child abuse. The concern for sexual abuse of daughters should also be explored within these families.

Intervention. After careful consideration of the nature and extent of abuse within the family, treatment strategies can be considered for the abusive men. The treatment should focus on the aggressive behavior directed at both the wife and the children. Very careful deliberations are required to determine whether the abusive father should be allowed supervised access (for detailed discussion, see Jaffe & Holden, 1998).

Sibling System

In violent families, attention is generally focussed on the relationship between the mother and father, with little regard for the children and their relationships. The sibling relationship, however, is very salient in children's lives in both a positive and potentially negative sense. On the one hand, siblings can be a source of comfort and support. The close relationship between siblings may act as a buffer to the impact of marital discord (Jenkins & Smith, 1991). On the other hand, the sibling relationship has the potential to exacerbate children's aggressive behavior problems (Patterson, 1986).

In considering interventions with children exposed to family violence, it is essential to consider the impact on the sibling relationship. The intimacy and stability of this relationship may provide a milieu where children express their anger and aggression. Given the different ages of siblings, there is a built-in power differential between older and younger children within a family. Often older siblings bear heavy responsibilities for younger children, particularly when their mothers have been abused. Even though siblings can be supportive, some sibling relationships may mirror the use of power and aggression which occurs in the marital relationship.

Intervention. In developing an intervention strategy for families at risk, it is essential to assess the levels of conflict within the sibling relationship. For sibling dyads with high levels of aggressive interactions, treatment efforts should be directed at providing support for positive problem solving and mechanisms to mediate the inevitable conflict between siblings. The sibling relationship may reflect the power imbalances in the family. In this case, family therapy might be recommended to examine the dynamics and roles within the family system that maintain high levels of sibling conflict.

School System

Recently, efforts have been made to identify and support children exposed to family violence in the school context (Kates & Pepler, 1989; LaMarsh kit). There are many ways in which the academic progress of these children can be compromised. Children exposed to family violence often act out their anger, fear, and hurt within the school context. Their behaviour problems interfere not only with their own progress, but also with the learning of their class-mates (Patterson, DeBaryshe, & Ramsey, 1989). Alternatively, if the children respond by being withdrawn and quiet, they often remain unidentified. In our classroom for children of battered women, we found that many children lacked the basic elements for academic achievement. This may arise because they are absent from school a great deal and/or because when they are sitting in class, they are psychologically unavailable to learn. It is, therefore, essential to provide support to children exposed to family violence to protect them from drifting toward academic failure and low motivation.

Intervention. As the universal delivery system, schools are an ideal milieu in which to reach out to children exposed to family violence. When children are identified within the school system, extra emotional and educational support will bolster their academic accomplishments and buffer the impact of family violence. For many children exposed to family violence, schools represent the only safe and secure context in their lives. Therefore, schools can operate in two ways to address problems of family violence. First, by identifying those children exposed to family violence, they can buffer some of the deleterious effects of living in a high-risk environment. Secondly, schools can introduce violence prevention programs that begin to address some of the root causes of abuse (e.g., Response by Schools to Violence Prevention–R.S.V.P. The Community Child Abuse Council of Hamilton-Wentworth, 1994).

Peers

With age, peer relations become increasingly important influences in children's lives and are closely tied to psychosocial adjustment in the middle years of childhood (Hartup, 1996; Parker & Asher, 1987). Children living in violent homes may have limited opportunities for developing successful peer relations for several reasons. First, they may be reluctant to bring friends home to a family context in which fights explode unpredictably. Secondly, these children may avoid close friendships for fear of revealing the abuse and differences within their families. As indicated above, children may react socially by withdrawing or aggressing. Thirdly, many wife abusers are very controlling and may forbid extracurricular socializing on the part of their children. Consequently, children exposed to family violence may experience increasing isolation from the community along with their mother. They are cut off, therefore, from the normal channels for developing positive relationships with peers, such as sports, recreation activities, and community groups.

Intervention. As mothers and children begin to rebuild their lives, it is important to provide support and opportunities for successful peer interactions. If children are experiencing significant psychosocial difficulties, either withdrawal and anxiety or aggression, they may require specific skills training and counselling. Once they are able to manage comfortably in a peer context, it is important to integrate these children into community programs of interest to them. Given that children are with peers all day in the school context, significant care and effort should be made to support peer relations as part of a school strategy.

Community System

The final context in which we consider the challenges and strategies for intervention with children exposed to family violence is the community. Children grow up in the community where they are influenced by individuals, neighbourhoods, and broader societal influences such as the media. From a risk and protective factor framework, children's integration into the community is important in buffering the effects of family violence. Research has shown that a positive relationship with one significant adult may protect children from adverse risks (Rutter, 1990). The challenge, however, is that children of battered women are often isolated and unable to benefit from community connections. Therefore, the children most in need of support available within the community may be those who are hardest to reach.

Intervention. There are many ways in which children at risk can be integrated into community programs. The basic requirement is that there are appropriate and accessible community programs for all ages of children. Community programs are often considered as frills, which are quick to lose financial support in hard economic times. Compared to formal treatment, community programs cost very little and have been shown to be effective not only in engaging children, but also in reducing their behaviour problems (Jones & Offord, 1989). In addition to general recreational and sports groups in the community, those programs in which children are connected to a caring adult have considerable potential to buffer the negative effects of exposure to family violence (e.g., Big Brother/Sister, Youth Assisting Youth). All of these efforts will fall short, however, if society does not make a concerted and broad-based effort to reduce violence in the community.

A PEER COUNSELLING PROGRAM FOR CHILDREN EXPOSED TO FAMILY VIOLENCE

Some elements of the preceding interventions were contained in a Peer Group Counselling Program offered by Women's Habitat, a shelter for abused women in Toronto, Canada. The present study evaluated the impact of this program on the behavioural, social and emotional adjustment of child witnesses of family violence. There are a few related studies which have evaluated the effects of interventions for children from violent families (Hughes, 1982; Jaffe et al., 1986b; Wagar & Rodway, 1995). In her study, Hughes (1982) evaluated a model shelter-based program which included interventions with children, mothers, schools, and shelter staff. Mothers were given training on child development and parenting skills. Children were offered individual counselling, and meetings with peer, sibling, and family groups. Based on observations of the parent-child interaction after the intervention, Hughes assessed the gap between the children's needs and the mother's capabilities. Jaffe and his colleagues (1986b) conducted an evaluation of a ten-week counselling program for children who had witnessed violence in their homes. They concluded that the children had benefitted from this intervention because they could identify more positive strategies to deal with parental violence. More recently a study by Wagar and Rodway (1995) examined the effectiveness of the treatment program developed by Jaffe and his colleagues. They conducted a pre-treatment/post-treatment analysis on three variables: (1) attitudes and responses to anger, (2) knowledge of support and safety skills, and (3) children's self-blame for family violence. They found significant improvements in children's attitudes and responses to anger and in their sense of responsibility.

The original objectives of the present study were to determine: (1) the *specific* effect of peer group counselling on a number of psychological factors (attitudes, depression and anxiety) and on the behavioural adjustment of child witnesses to family violence; (2) whether concurrent maternal counselling is related to positive changes in the child's adjustment; and (3) whether there are differential effects of group counselling on boys and girls.

The two central hypotheses used to evaluate the program's effectiveness were:

1. Following the participation in the Peer Group Counselling Program, children will show significant improvements in attitudes toward violence, depression, anxiety and behavioural adjustment as compared to before the program.
2. Children whose mothers were also participating in a mother's support group will show significantly more signs of positive adjustment than children whose mothers were not concurrently participating in a counselling program.

We were also interested in examining gender differences in response to the program.

Peer Group Counselling Program Activities

The Peer Group Counselling Program was designed by Karen Blake at the Lakeshore Area Multi-Service Project Inc. (known as L.A.M.P.). The program provided support, through education, to children living in violent homes and to children who may be in a stable environment now, but who once were witnesses of family violence. Through discussion, role playing and games, the group sessions covered the following topics:

- labeling feelings such as anger, fear, guilt and humiliation;
- dealing with anger and rage, appropriate means of behaving;
- self-esteem and self-worth;
- feelings of responsibility about being part of a violent family;
- coping with family wishes and uncertain future;
- personal safety skills to prevent or escape from abuse;
- identifying and using social supports;
- sexual stereotypes and myths about the roles of men and women;
- dealing with the issues of divorce and separation; and
- coping with new parental relationships.

METHOD

The present evaluation is based on data from participants in 12 ten-week programs run between 1990 and 1994, with a maximum of seven children in each group.

Participants

Participants for this study were recruited in one of three ways: from the rolls of previous shelter residents; through the Assaulted Women's Helpline; and from outreach efforts at L.A.M.P. Through the outreach program, other organizations, such as Interim Place and the North York General Hospital, assisted in recruiting participants for the program. Approximately 84 children were involved in the program over the four years. Although maternal consent was obtained for all children attending the program, not all qualified to be included in the study. To be included in the evaluation analyses, children were required to have attended the group sessions and have completed, at the very least, a pre-treatment and a post-treatment questionnaire. Based on these criteria, forty-six (46) children from the twelve support groups were included in the analyses. The participants varied in age from 6 to 13 years, with an average age of 9 years. Data on the number of boys and girls who actually attended the program were not available; however, more questionnaires were collected from boys (27) than from girls (19).

Design

A pre-post comparison group design was used to test the central hypotheses. Each "case," a mother and child respectively, filled out the same questionnaires at four points in time: when waiting to enter the counselling group (baseline or Time1–T1); during the first week of the group (Time2–T2); after completion of the ten-week program (Time3–T3); and at a follow-up assessment six months after the group: Time4 (T4). The number of children for whom complete data were available is provided in Table 1.

Measures

Both children and their mothers completed the following questionnaires to assess attitudes, anxiety, and behavioural adjustment of children following participation in the Peer Group Counselling.

Children's Questionnaires. Children were asked to complete the following three self-report questionnaires to assess attitudes toward family violence,

TABLE 1. Number of Questionnaires Completed at Each Time Period

	Time 1	Time 2	Time 3	Time 4
Child Questionnaire	46	36	44	22
Mother's Questionnaire	41	19	37	27

depression, and anxiety. The questionnaires were administered by the group counsellor or by a Child and Youth staff member of Women's Habitat. The counsellor either read the questionnaire or allowed the child to complete it independently, depending on reading ability.

Attitudes Toward Family Violence Questionnaire (Jaffe et al., 1986b). This questionnaire comprises 41 items assessing children's attitudes about the appropriateness of using violence in a variety of contexts. The questionnaire assesses children's responses to anger, safety skills, and their sense of responsibility for the family violence. Children respond "Yes" or "No" to indicate which actions would be appropriate in a number of situations.

Child Depression Inventory (CDI) (Kovacs, 1981). The Child Depression Inventory is a self-report measure of depressive symptoms in children. Children respond to 27 questions on a 1-3 point scale from most positive to most negative statements.

Children's Manifest Anxiety Scale: What I Think and Feel (Reynolds & Richmond, 1985). This questionnaire assesses children's self-perception of anxiety. The 37 questions on a Yes/No scale are designed to measure trait anxiety. The summary score indicates the degree of anxiety symptoms.

Mother's Questionnaire. Mothers of children participating in the Peer Group Counselling Program completed the Child Behaviour Checklist (CBC) (Boyle et al., 1987). This questionnaire assesses the mother's perception of her child's behaviour problems and social competence. Parents rate their children's behaviour problems on a 136-item checklist, using a 3-point scale ranging between Never/Not True, Sometimes/Somewhat True and Often/Very True. Four disorders can be identified: conduct, hyperactivity, emotional, and somatization. The first three scales were appropriate for the children in the present study.

RESULTS

To ensure a constant and maximum number of respondents in the comparisons, the T1 data were used as the baseline measure and T3 data as the post-group measure. The measures gathered at T2 and T4 were not incorporated as it was difficult to gather follow-up information on the families who were in transition following the counselling group. Given the small number of participants, the initial analyses were conducted with the sample as a whole. Gender differences in response to the counselling program were examined separately.

Participant Profiles

Three-quarters of the children in the study were in single mother families and were quite mobile (average of three residential moves and at least two school changes at baseline). In almost every case, the child's father was identified as the mother's main violent partner. Well over half of the mothers (61%) were either separated or divorced from their partners. Approximately half of the children had weekly contact with their fathers, while the other half had no contact at all. The family income of participants ranged between $10,000 and $100,000 per year. Almost half the mothers in the sample had attended either college or university, while the other half left school before graduating from high school.

Peer Group Counselling Program Evaluation

These hypotheses were tested using Multivariate Analysis of Variance for repeated measures on the baseline (T1) and the post intervention (T3) data for both the children's and mothers' questionnaires.

The first hypothesis was that children would show significant improvements in attitudes toward violence, depression, anxiety, and behavioural adjustment.

Attitudes Toward Violence. The children's attitudes toward violence were measured on the following variables: responses to anger; reactions to provocations; rejection of people hitting each other; and feeling of responsibility for the violence. We expected that children would endorse more positive strategies and fewer negative strategies, such as fighting or hitting, after the group as compared to the baseline. There was, however, no significant difference in the reporting of positive strategies before and after the group: $F(1,42) = 0.03$, ns.

The percentages of children who indicated that they would use avoidance, communication or aggressive strategies to deal with their anger in a peer provocation situation are presented in Table 2. In general, children were most likely to endorse using communication and least likely to indicate that they would be aggressive. Although a minority of children chose aggressive strategies, there were slight increases in the proportion of children who chose threats and hitting as a strategy when provoked. These increases suggest that more specific work may be required to steer a subset of children away from considering aggression as a suitable problem solving strategy. There was likely a ceiling effect with the communication strategy: a majority of children were already choosing this strategy for problem solving.

Another aspect on the Attitudes Toward Family Violence questionnaire is how acceptable children feel it is for people to hit each other, especially from a gender perspective. We found that children understood that hitting is a violation of individual rights. Almost all of the children at baseline and after the group said it was *not* acceptable for a man to hit a woman (98% at both times). The group may have had some impact on the children's attitude about women hitting men. When asked whether it was acceptable for a woman to

TABLE 2. Percentage of Children Who Use Avoidance, Communication or Aggressive Strategies in Response to Provocation

Strategy Used	Tease		Take		Hit	
	T1	T3	T1	T3	T1	T3
Avoidance						
Ignore Them	78	78	35	33	48	39
Communication						
Ask Them to Stop	76	76	78	80	76	78
Tell Someone	61	63	74	78	76	72
Aggression						
Threaten Them	20	20	15	33	15	20
Hit Them	20	33	20	22	39	46

Note: Proportions do not add to 100% because children could say yes to more than one strategy.

hit a man, we found a significant difference, with an increase in responses indicating that hitting was *not* acceptable (from 81% to 93%).

One of the program sessions focused on the important fact that family violence is not the child's responsibility. Therefore, we expected to find a decrease in the number of children who felt they were responsible for the violence toward them and between their parents. Two questions in the Attitudes Towards Family Violence questionnaire assessed the children's feeling of responsibility for the family violence: "Do you feel mom and dad fight about you?" and "Could you have done anything to prevent your parents from arguing?" Again, we found no significant difference in the number of children who responded affirmatively to these questions before and after the group.

Children's Depression. We expected to find that the children would be better adjusted after the program than at baseline. There was a significant difference in the pre-group and post-group depression scores: $F (1,45) = 12.84$ ($p < 0.001$). Significantly more children reported a more positive response after the program than at baseline.

Children's Anxiety. We expected that the post treatment anxiety scores would be lower (better adjusted) than the baseline scores. There was a significant difference between the children's scores at T1 versus T3, $F (1,45) = 20.06$ ($p < 0.001$), with lower anxiety scores following peer group counselling.

Behavioural Adjustment. As expected, the children's behavioural adjustment, as reported by their mothers, was significantly better following the counselling, F (51) = 9.54 (p < 0.001). The univariate analyses indicated significant improvements in emotional problems, F (1,24) = 7.57 (p < .01), and for hyperactivity, F (1,23) = 6.86 (p < 0.014). To further assess the level of behavioural adjustment associated with the program, we examined the number of children above and below the Checklist's clinical threshold levels before and after the program as presented in Table 3. In general, mothers perceived their children as having few emotional and behavioural problems.

Mothers' Participation in Counselling

From a systemic perspective, interventions to support children living in violent families will be enhanced if they extend beyond the child. Therefore, we expected that children whose mothers were also participating in a mothers' support group would show significantly more signs of positive adjustment than children whose mothers were not concurrently participating in a counselling program.

The mothers' ratings on the Child Behaviour Checklist (CBC) were used to measure the children's positive adjustment. Approximately 19 mothers received ongoing counselling while their children were in the group; 11 mothers had received some counselling either just before or during the time their children were in the program; 16 mothers did not receive any counselling at all. We expected greater improvements in conduct, hyperactivity and

TABLE 3. Distribution of Children Above and Below Clinical Threshold Levels

Scale	T1	T3
Conduct		
Above Threshold (8+)	4	4
Below Threshold (0-7)	31	31
Hyperactivity		
Above Threshold (7+)	3	1
Below Threshold (0-6)	32	34
Emotional		
Above Threshold (8+)	11	8
Below Threshold (0-7)	24	27

emotional problems for children whose mothers were in counselling versus those whose mothers were not receiving support.

This hypothesis was analysed by comparing the post intervention CBC scores for the children of mothers who received the three levels of counselling, using baseline CBC scores as a covariate. A summary CBC score was used, collapsing across the categories of conduct, hyperactivity and emotional problems. There was no main effect on the children's behaviour based on the mother's participation in counselling, Multivariate F (6,42) = 1.35 (p < 0.254). In other words, there was no general effect on the mothers' perception of the children's behaviour as a function of the mother having received counselling.

The data relating mother's participation in counselling to her perceptions of her child's behaviour problems are limited in several respects. First, we do not know whether those mothers who were receiving the most counselling were the ones who needed it the most. Secondly, data on the amount, length and type of counselling the mothers received was inconsistent and incomplete; therefore, it was not possible to examine with precision any associations between the mothers' counselling and children's behaviour ratings.

Gender Differences

There were complete data for 14 girls and 17 boys available for the analysis of gender differences in responsiveness to the program. There was no significant gender by time interaction for the conduct, hyperactivity, or emotional scales. Therefore, the significant improvements in behavioural adjustment indicated above were evident in mothers' perceptions of both boys and girls enrolled in the Peer Group Counselling Program.

Limitations

Due to a number of limitations, the results of the program evaluation should be interpreted with caution. The main limitations of this project lie in the data collection procedures and subsequent analyses. First, the variability of the questionnaire administration may have had an impact on the quality of the data. It was difficult to have the same person administer the questionnaires to all participants since its completion required considerable time. Secondly, the study lacked a control group. Having a complete set of questionnaires from a group of children who did not participate in any form of intervention is essential for a robust evaluation of program effectiveness. Finally, as stated earlier, this study lacks follow-up information on the families. It was difficult to administer follow-up questionnaires since many families were in transition. In addition, since several families were in transition during the group, a number of children dropped out of the program. As a result we had a very small sample, which compromises the power of the statistical tests employed.

EVALUATION

The central objective of this study was to assess whether a Peer Group Counselling Program had a positive effect on children's behavioral and psychological adjustment. There was a significant improvement in children's self-reports of depression and anxiety over the course of the program. Mothers rated their children as significantly improved in emotional and hyperactive behaviour problems. At the onset of the program, children were generally well-adjusted in their problem solving strategies and attitudes regarding violence. These did not improve to even higher levels. There was no relation between mothers' involvement in counselling and children's improvement. Overall, the results suggest that the Peer Group Counselling Program effectively provided support to children exposed to family violence.

DEALING WITH VIOLENCE: FROM AWARENESS TO ACTION

In this article, we have considered interventions for children exposed to family violence against the background of research on children's problems associated with witnessing family violence and the potential risk and protective factors related to these children's adjustment. The challenges of intervening with these children and families have been presented from a systemic perspective. Finally, we have presented data on a preliminary evaluation of an intervention program for children which reflected some improvements in domains of concern. We conclude by considering the steps that must be taken to address issues of violence in our society.

Developing an understanding of family violence is the first step toward reducing the problem. With a sound, prospective research base, we can identify the prevalence of the problem, the causes of the problem, and the many ways in which the problem of family violence affects children and families. The second step in reducing violence is to raise the problem of family violence for open dialogue. By looking at and discussing the problem, we can move toward a broader base of understanding. When adults, such as parents, teachers, and counsellors, are committed to raising these issues and feel comfortable discussing them, children will be more open in disclosing issues related to family violence in their own lives. Finally, the efforts must move beyond individuals to encompass the many systems in which children live.

To provide an adequate safety net for children and their families, there must be a coordinated effort within the community as a whole. In this way, agencies can work together to ensure that children exposed to family violence are identified and provided with the protective supports that will enable them to weather the stresses associated with their family context. To help these children and families move toward violence-free lives, we must allocate resources for multi-dimensional programs that address problems in the lives of children exposed to family violence.

REFERENCES

Achenbach, T. M., & Edelbrock, C. S. (1983). *Manual for the Child Behavior Checklist and Revised Child Behavior Profile.* Burlington, VT: Thomas N. Achenbach, Department of Psychiatry, University of Vermont.

Boyle, M.H., Offord, D.R., Hoffman, H.G., Catlin, G.P., Byles, J.A., Cadman, D.T., Crawford, J.W., Links, P.S., Rae-Grant, N.I., & Szatmari, P. (1987). Ontario child health study. I. Methodology. *Archives of General Psychiatry, 44,* 826-831.

Bryant, N. (1994). Domestic violence and group treatment for male batterers. Special Issue: Men and groups. *Group, 18,* 235-242.

Cadsky, O., Hanson, R.K., Crawford, M., & Lalonde, C. (1996). Attrition from a male batterer treatment program: Client-treatment congruence and lifestyle instability. *Violence and Victims, 11,* 51-64.

Davies, P. & Cummings, E.M. (1994). Marital conflict and child adjustment: An emotional security hypothesis. *Psychological Bulletin, 116,* 387-411.

Emery, R. E. (1989). Family violence. *American Psychologist, 44,* 321-328.

Eron, L.D., Gentry, J.H., & Schlegel, P. (1994). Reason to hope: A psychosocial perspective on violence and youth. Washington, DC: American Psychological Association Press.

Garmezy, N. (1983). *Stress, coping and development in children.* New York, NY: McGraw-Hill.

Hanson, R.K. & Whitman, R. (1995). A rural, community action model for the treatment of abusive men. *Canadian Journal of Community Mental Health, 14,* 49-59.

Hartup, W.W. (1996). The company they keep: Friendships and their developmental significance. *Child Development, 67,* 1-13.

Hughes, H.M. (1982). Brief interventions with children in a battered women's shelter: A model preventive program. *Family Relations, 31,* 495-502.

Hughes, H.M. (1988). Psychological and behavioral correlates of family violence in child witnesses and victims. *American Journal of Orthopsychiatry, 58,* 77-90.

Hughes, H.M. & Luke, D.A. (1998). Heterogeneity in adjustment among children of battered women. In G.W. Holden, R.A. Geffner, & E.N. Jouriles (Eds.) *Children exposed to marital violence: Theory, research, and applied issues* (pp. 185-221). Washington, DC: American Psychological Association.

Jaffe, P., Wolfe, D., Wilson, S., & Zak, I. (1986a). Similarities in behavioural and social maladjustment among child victims and witnesses to family violence. *American Journal of Orthopsychiatry, 56,* 142-146.

Jaffe, P., Wilson, S., & Wolfe, D. (1986b). Promoting changes in attitudes and understanding of conflict resolution among child witnesses of family violence. *Canadian Journal of Behavioural Science, 18,* 356-366.

Jenkins, J.M., & Smith, M.A. (1990). Factors protecting children living in disharmonious homes: Maternal reports. *Journal of the American Academy of Child and Adolescent Psychiatry, 29,* 60-69.

Jones, M.B., & Offord, D.R. (1989). Reduction of antisocial behavior in poor children by nonschool skill development. *Journal of Child Psychology and Psychiatry and Allied Disciplines, 30,* 737-750.

Jouriles, E.N., McDonald, R., Stephens, N., Norwood, W., Spiller, L.C., & Ware, H.S. Breaking the cycle of violence: Helping families departing from battered women's shelters. In G.W. Holden, R.A. Geffner, & E.N. Jouriles (Eds.) *Children exposed to marital violence: Theory, research, and applied issues* (pp. 337-369). Washington, DC: American Psychological Association.

Kates, M., & Pepler, D. (1989). Programming in a reception class for children of battered women. *Canada's Mental Health.*

Kincaid, P. (1985). *The omitted reality: Husband-wife violence in Ontario and policy implications for education.* Concord, Ont.: Belsten Pub.

Kovacs, M. (1981). Rating scales to assess depression in school-aged children. *Acta Paedopsychiatrica, 46,* 305-315.

McCloskey, L.A., Figueredo, A.J., & Koss, M.P. (1995). The effects of systemic family violence on children's mental health. *Child Development, 66,* 1239-1261.

Moore, T.E., & Pepler, D.J. (In press). Correlates of adjustment in children at risk. In G. Holden & R. Geffner (Eds.) *Children exposed to marital violence: Theory, research, and intervention.* Washington, DC: American Psychological Association.

Parker, J.G., & Asher, S.R. (1987). Peer relations and later personal adjustment: Are low-accepted children at risk? *Psychological Bulletin, 102,* 357-389.

Patterson, G.R. (1986). The contribution of siblings to training for fighting: A microsocial analysis. In Olweus, D., Block, J., & Radke-Yarrow (Eds.) *Development of antisocial and prosocial behavior: Research, theories, and issues* (pp. 235-261). Orlando, FL: Academic Press.

Patterson, G.R., DeBaryshe, B.D., & Ramsey, E. (1989). A developmental perspective on antisocial behavior. *American Psychologist, 44,* 329-335.

Pepler, D., & Moore, T. (1995). Mothers' depression and aggression and the behavior problems of children in families at risk. Paper presented at the Biennial Meeting of the Society for Research in Child Development, Indianapolis, April.

Pirog-Good, M., & Stets-Kealey, J. (1985). Male batterers and battering prevention programs: A national survey. *Response to the Victimization of Women and Children, 8,* 8-12.

Reynolds, C.R., & Richmond, B.O. (1985). *Revised Children's Manifest Anxiety Scale: Manual.* Los Angeles: Western Psychological Services.

Statistics Canada. (1994). *Family violence in Canada*. Ottawa: Minister of Industry, Science, and Technology.

The Community Child Abuse Council of Hamilton-Wentworth (1994). Response by Schools to Violence Prevention (RSVP). Hamilton, Ontario: Family Violence Prevention Project.

Wagar, J., & Rodway, M. (1995). An evaluation of a group treatment approach for children who have witnessed wife abuse. *Journal of Family Violence, 10*(3), 295-306.

Wolfe, D., & Mosk, M.D. (1983). Behavioral comparisons of children from abused and distressed families. *Journal of Consulting and Clinical Psychology, 51*(5), 702-708.

Wolfe, D., Zak, L., Wilson, S., & Jaffe, P. (1986). Child witnesses to violence between parents: Critical issues in behavioral and social adjustment. *Journal of Abnormal Child Psychology, 14*, 94-104.

Witnessing Parental Violence as a Traumatic Experience Shaping the Abusive Personality

Donald G. Dutton

SUMMARY. Previous work by Dutton and his colleagues has established a clinical profile on intimately abusive adult men that is quite similar to profiles of trauma victims in many essential clinical respects. Dutton (in press) showed that arousal modulation problems, affective monitoring, cognitive problem solving deficits, externalizing attributional styles, aggression and dissociative states are common to both groups. Furthermore, intimately abusive men demonstrate similar profiles as men diagnosed independently with PTSD on the MCMI-II. Dutton (1995a, 1995b) attributed the trauma to early assaults on the self through parental shaming, accompanied by insecure attachment and physical abuse victimization. Bowlby (1973) considered insecure attachment itself both a source and consequence of trauma. Since the infant turns to the attachment-object during periods of distress seeking soothing, a failure to obtain soothing maintains high arousal and endocrine secretion. Van der Kolk (1987) considered child abuse as an "overwhelming life experience" and reviewed the defenses that children use to deal with parental abuse: hypervigilance, projection, splitting, and denial. Terr (1979) also described driven, compulsive repetitions, and reenactments that permeate dreams, play, fantasies and object relations of traumatized children. Shaming, conceptualized as verbal or behavioral attacks on the global self, has been found to generate life-

---

Address correspondence to: Donald G. Dutton, PhD, Department of Psychology, University of British Columbia, 2136 West Mall, Vancouver, BC, V6T 1Z4, Canada (e-mail: dutton@interchange.ubc.ca).

[Haworth co-indexing entry note]: "Witnessing Parental Violence as a Traumatic Experience Shaping the Abusive Personality." Dutton, Donald G. Co-published simultaneously in *Journal of Aggression, Maltreatment & Trauma* (The Haworth Maltreatment & Trauma Press, an imprint of The Haworth Press, Inc.) Vol. 3, No. 1 (#5), 2000, pp. 59-67; and: *Children Exposed to Domestic Violence: Current Issues in Research, Intervention, Prevention, and Policy Development* (ed: Robert A. Geffner, Peter G. Jaffe, and Marlies Sudermann) The Haworth Maltreatment & Trauma Press, an imprint of The Haworth Press, Inc., 2000, pp. 59-67. Single or multiple copies of this article are available for a fee from The Haworth Document Delivery Service [1-800-342-9678, 9:00 a.m. - 5:00 p.m. (EST). E-mail address: getinfo@haworthpressinc.com].

long shame-proneness or defenses involving rage. A combination of all three early experiences is traumatizing (Dutton, 1995a, 1995b; Dutton, in press). However, some evidence exists that suggests observation of interparental attacks can be substituted for physical abuse victimization as the third prong in this triad of traumatogenic experiences. *[Article copies available for a fee from The Haworth Document Delivery Service: 1-800-342-9678. E-mail address: getinfo@haworthpressinc.com <Website: http://www.haworthpressinc.com>]*

KEYWORDS. Personality disorder, attachment, spousal abuse, parenting, family violence, emotional abuse

CLINICAL DESCRIPTIONS OF SPOUSE ASSAULTERS

The general clinical profile that emerged from initial clinical sources (e.g., Ganley, 1989; Sonkin, 1987; Walker, 1979) was of a man who experienced disproportionate arousal and anger (Walker, 1979), went through cyclical tension accumulations followed by abusive outbursts and contrition (Walker, 1979), externalized blame for their actions (Ganley, 1989), experienced a restricted range of affect (Gondolf, 1985) with the exception of dysphoric states (depression), and exhibited high levels of masked dependency and emotional isolation (Sonkin, 1987) leading to extreme jealousy sometimes referred to as "conjugal paranoia." A number of theories have been put forward to explain spouse assault and these have been reviewed and criticized elsewhere (Dutton, 1995c, 1995d); broad spectrum theories such as sociobiology and feminist sociology cannot account for individual differences between serially abusive, situationally abusive and non-abusive males. Also, although social learning theory (O'Leary, 1988; Dutton, 1988) serves well in establishing the imitative and self-reinforcing functions of the acquisition of aggressive habits, and the sustaining function of rationalization or "neutralization of self-punishment," it does less well at accounting for the acquisition of private or internal events that are prominent in sustaining abusiveness. These include dysphoric states (depression, chronic anger), attributional styles (blaming of victim), defensive strategies such as externalizing and projection, insecure attachment styles, tendencies to ruminate and accumulations of internal tension. Since these phenomena are internal and unobservable, they are not "imitated" in the way that abusive behaviors are imitated. I argue that the behavioral imitation exists on a psychological substratum created by early trauma. This early trauma, which produced the psychological abuse-generating reactions described above, is itself caused by an interactive combination of events: exposure to physical abuse, shaming by a parent and insecure attachment. These events are particularly destructive to an immature ego, in the process of self-formation. While much research on trauma victims has focused on victims of childhood sexual or physical abuse, I suggest that a combination of insecure attachment, exposure to physical abuse (witnessing or being victimized) and being shamed by a parent constitutes a potent trauma source.

WITNESSING/EXPERIENCING VIOLENCE AS A SOURCE OF TRAUMA

Much has been written about the long-term effects of physical abuse of children as a risk marker for long-term abusiveness. In a national survey conducted in 1975, Straus, Gelles, and Steinmetz (1980) found that boys who grew up in abusive homes were more likely to be physically abusive toward their own wives. Children who were themselves physically abused were more likely to be abusive. Boys, in particular, were likely to "externalize," "being disruptive, acting aggressively towards objects and people, and throwing severe temper tantrums" (Jaffe, Wolfe, & Wilson, 1990, p. 41). Carmen, Reiker, and Mills (1984) suggested that boys were more likely to identify with the aggressor in the abusive home. Lisak, Hopper, and Song (1996) found that most (70%) perpetrators of physical abuse had experienced victimization (physical or sexual abuse); however, most abused men did not become perpetrators.

However, abuse directed toward the child may constitute a narrow definition of trauma. The possibility exists that witnessing a parent being struck by another parent is traumatizing. It may destroy the belief in the victim's parent's ability to protect and make life secure for the child and may force a localizing of loyalty at a premature developmental stage. Caesar (1988) found that abusive men were more likely to have witnessed interparental abuse, but her sample was small and she did not desegregate witnessing from experiencing abuse. Hughes, Parkinson, and Vargo (1989) did separate child witnesses to interparental violence who were abused or not. In terms of emotional distress and behavioral acting out, the abused/witness group was the worst, followed by the witnessed only and then a non-abused-non-witnessed control. Witnessing abuse between parents tripled the rate of use of physical abuse by men in the Straus et al. national survey (Straus et al., 1980). Both Straus et al. (1980) and Kalmuss (1984) estimated that observation of interparental aggression was a greater risk factor for use of severe violence than was being hit as a teenager. Kalmuss estimated a doubling of the odds of hitting as a function of witnessing. The odds increase for being hit was 1.5 (op. cit., p. 15).

Carlson (1984) estimated that about 3.3 million children in the US annually witnessed parental violence. Jaffe, Wolfe, and Wilson (1990) reviewed studies which put the observation rate even higher (68%-80%). Landis (1989), Rossman (1994) and Lehmann (1997) found high levels of trauma symptoms in children who had witnessed their father assault their mother. Landis (1989) and Lehmann (1997) found that over half of the children in their samples exhibited PTSD. Factors such as the duration and frequency of the witnessed violence, and multiple separations (between parents) all enhanced the probability of development of PTSD. This finding is consistent with clinical descriptive studies of children who witnessed a parent's murder, rape or suicide and which also found high rates of PTSD (Burman & Allan-Meares, 1994; Black, Hendricks, & Kaplan, 1992; Black & Kaplan, 1988; Eth & Pynoos, 1994; Malmquist, 1986; Osofsky, Wewers, Hann, & Finn, 1995; Pynoos & Eth, 1985; Pynoos & Nader, 1993). Singer, Anglin, Song, and Lunghofer (1995) conducted a large sample (n = 3735) study of adolescents that specified a variety of sources for exposure to violence, both within and outside the home. Violence exposure variables accounted for a significant amount of current trauma symptoms, including depression (R^2 = .31), anxiety (R^2 = .30), dissociation (R^2 = .23), posttraumatic stress (R^2 = .31) and total trauma (R^2 = .37). Hence, in the largest sample study conducted to date, a strong and consistent relationship was found between exposure to violence and consequent trauma experiences. In this study witnessing violence at home was the second most prevalent of eight potential sources.

INSECURE ATTACHMENT AS A SOURCE OF TRAUMA

One mechanism, apart from sheer modeling, that can occur when interparental hitting is observed, is a weakening of attachment. The notion of the victim parent as capable of proffering security and protection is destroyed by the witnessed violence. Bowlby (1969; 1973; 1977) described secure attachment as a necessary buffer against trauma. The distressed person engages in proximity seeking behaviors to the "attachment other" in order to reduce the impact of the trauma. Furthermore, expectations about relationship outcomes and the ability to self-soothe to reduce trauma effects are both consequences of attachment. Securely attached persons have more positive expectations, more optimism, even a more benign theology (Kirkpatrick & Shaver, 1992). Conversely, individuals with poor attachments, indicated by parental abuse or neglect, have poor trauma resolution skills (Cicchetti & Toth, 1995; van der Kolk & Fisler, 1995). The relationship of secure attachment to psychological functioning was sufficiently recognized that by 1996, the *Journal of Consulting & Clinical Psychology* published a special issue on attachment and psychopathology. In that issue Lyons-Ruth (1996) reviewed attachment related studies of risk factors for early aggression, finding that attachment patterns, family adversity, parental hostility "were already evident in infancy and predictive of later aggression before the onset of coercive child behavior" (p. 64). An early risk factor included elevated cortisol levels at separation. Cortisol release from the adrenal glands is stimulated by stress. Klein (1980) noted that both panic attacks and depression in humans responded to treatment with tricyclic antidepressants and MAO inhibitors and postulated that both conditions are rooted in "neurobiological sensitivity to abandonment precipitated by early life experiences" (van der Kolk, 1987, p. 46). I raise here the question of whether observation of interparental violence can *ipso facto* have effects on the attachment system through destroying the sense of a secure attachment object.

As van der Kolk (1987, p. 31) puts it, "*the essence of trauma is the loss of faith that there is order and continuity in life.*" Van der Kolk (1987) also demonstrated that secure attachment is essential for the development of core neurobiological functions in the primate brain. The development of the connection between attachment and neural development has been most fully explicated in Schore's (1994) work *Affect Regulation and the Origin of the Self*. In this work, Schore develops a psychobiological model linking maternal behaviors (such as attunement) to specific neural development, specifically to those neural mechanisms that regulate emotion (such as the limbic system).

In a group of batterers, Dutton, Saunders, Starzomski, and Bartholomew (1994) found that those with a "fearful" (insecure) attachment style self-reported the highest chronic levels of stress symptoms (r = +.51, p = .00001). Men who were in treatment for wife assault had high chronic trauma levels scores of 26 (sd = 9.8) (on the TSC-33), compared to 16 (sd = 7.9) for demographically matched controls. Dutton (1995b) found that all men's self-report subscales of the TSC-33 (anxiety, depression, sleep disturbance, dissociative states and post sexual abuse trauma-hypothesized) correlated with wives' reports of men's abusiveness. One of the mechanisms through which secure attachment may function to buffer trauma is through affect regulation. Both insecure attachment and trauma generate affect dysregulation; the effect of both in concert (as, for example, in children abused by their parents) is to produce extreme dysregulation (van der Kolk, McFarlane, & Weiseath, 1996).

COMBINED TRAUMA SOURCES

Although witnessing parental violence, being shamed and being insecurely attached are each sources of trauma in and of themselves, the combination of the three over prolonged and vulnerable developmental phases constitutes a dramatic and powerful trauma source. The child cannot turn to a secure attachment source for soothing, as none exists, yet the need created by the shaming and exposure to violence triggers enormous emotional and physiological reactions requiring soothing. Furthermore, as Pynoos (1994) points out, traumatic exposure in childhood can occur during critical periods of personality formation *"when there are ongoing revisions of the inner model of the world, self and other . . . these internal models, once organized, operate outside conscious awareness . . . they may result in isolated areas of decision making or behavior that are inconsistent with other personality attributes"* (op. cit., p. 88). It is for this latter reason that the personalities of wife assaulters are often described as incongruent with their everyday persona.

TRAUMA AND AGGRESSION

Controlling aggression is a focal issue for many trauma victims (van der Kolk, 1988). Traumatized children have trouble modulating aggression, tending to act destructively towards themselves (Ross, 1980) or others (Green, 1980). Many traumatized children have temper tantrums and fights with siblings and schoolmates (Green, 1980; Ross, 1980; Lewis et al., 1979; Lewis & Balla, 1976). Kalmuss (1984) found that witnessing violence was not sex specific; children who witnessed either parent hitting the other became more violent regardless of their gender. As From (1973) put it, sadism is "the transformation of impotence into omnipotence" (op. cit., p. 323). Dutton (1995b) found significant correlations between batterers, self-reports of trauma symptoms on the TSC-33 and wives' reports of the man's use of physical aggression. Furthermore, batterers had chronic trauma symptom levels that were significantly higher than matched controls.

Witnessing parental violence is typically part of a confounded set of traumatogenic influences on early development. Dysfunctional-violent families where interparental abuse occurs, also tend to present failures of opportunity for secure attachment, and increased risk of direct physical and emotional abuse of the child. However, in those studies that partialled out physical abuse from observation of interparental abuse, the latter seemed more likely to generate intergenerational abuse cycles.

REFERENCES

Black, D., Hendricks, J. H., & Kaplan, T. (1992). Father kills mother: Post Traumatic Stress Disorder in the children. *Psychother. Psychosomat.*, *57*, 152-157.
Black, D., & Kaplan, T. (1988). Father kills mother. *British Journal of Psychiatry*, *153*, 624-630.
Bowlby, J. (1969). Attachment and loss. Vol. 1, *Attachment*. New York: Basic
Bowlby, J. (1973). Attachment and loss. Vol. 2, *Separation*. New York: Basic.

Bowlby, J. (1977). The making and breaking of affectional bonds. *British Journal of Psychiatry, 130,* 201-210.

Burman, S., & Allan-Meares, P. (1994). Neglected victims of murder: Children's witness to parental homicide. *Social Work, 48,* 28-34.

Caesar, P. L. (1986). *Men who batter: A heterogeneous group.* Paper presented at American Psychological Association, Washington, DC.

Carlson, B. E. (1984). Children's observations on interparental violence. In A. R. Roberts (Ed.), *Battered women and their families* (pp. 37-56). New York: Springer.

Carmen, E. H., Reiker, P. P., & Mills, T. (1984). Victims of violence and psychiatric illness. *American Journal of Psychiatry, 141,* 378-379.

Cicchetti, D., Cummings, M., & Greenburg, M. (1990). An organizational perspective on attachment beyond infancy: Implications for theory, measurement and research. In M. Greenberg, D. Cicchetti, & M. Cummings (Eds.), *Attachment during the preschool years: Theory, research and intervention* (pp. 3-49). Chicago: University of Chicago Press.

Dutton, D. G. (1988). Profiling wife assaulters: Some evidence for a trimodal analysis. *Violence and Victims, 3,* 5-30.

Dutton, D. G. (1995a). *The batterer: A psychological perspective.* New York: Basic Books.

Dutton, D. G. (1995b). Trauma symptoms and PTSD-like profiles in perpetrators of intimate abuse. *Journal of Traumatic Stress, 8,* 299-316.

Dutton, D. G. (1995c). *The domestic assault of women: Psychological and criminal justice perspectives.* Vancouver, BC: UBC Press.

Dutton, D. G. (1995d). Intimate abusiveness. *Clinical Psychology: Science and Practice, 2,* 207-224.

Dutton, D.G. (in press). The traumatic origins of intimate rage. *Aggression and Violent Behavior.*

Dutton, D. G., Saunders, K., Starzomski, A., & Bartholomew, K. (1994). Intimacy-anger and insecure attachment as precursors of abuse in intimate relationships. *Journal of Applied Social Psychology, 24,* 1367-1386.

Eth, S., & Pynoos, R. S. (1994). Children who witness the homicide of a parent. *Psychiatry, 57,* 287-306.

Fromm, E. (1973). *The anatomy of human destructiveness.* New York: Fawcett.

Ganley, A. L. (1989). Integrating feminist and social learning theories of aggression. In L. Caesar & K. Hamberger (Eds.), *Treating men who batter: Theory, practice and programs.* New York: Springer.

Gondolf, E. W. (1985). *Men who batter: An integrated approach for stopping wife abuse.* Holmes Beach, CA: Learning Publications.

Jaffe, P., Wolfe, D., & Wilson, S. K. (1990). *Children of battered women.* Newbury Park, CA: Sage.

Jones, E. E. (1996). Introduction to the Special Section of Attachment and Psychopathology: Part 1. *Journal of Clinical and Consulting Psychology, 64*(1), 5-7.

Kalmuss, D. S. (1984, February). The intergenerational transmission of marital aggression. *Journal of Marriage and the Family, 46,* 11-19.

Kirkpatrick, L. A., & Shaver, P. (1992). An attachment-theoretical approach to romantic love and religious belief. *Personality and Social Psychology Bulletin, 18*(3), 266-275.

Klein, D. F. (1980). Anxiety reconceptualized. *Comprehensive Psychiatry, 6,* 411-427.

Landis, T. (1989). *Children in shelters: An exploration of dissociative processes and traumatization in some children.* Boulder: University of Colorado.

Lehmann, P. (1997). The development of PTSD in a sample of child witnesses to mother assault. *Journal of Family Violence, 12*(3), 241-257.

Lewis, D. O., & Balla, D. A. (1976). *Delinquency and psychopathology.* New York: Grune and Stratton.

Lisak, D., Hopper, J., & Song, P. (1996). Factors in the cycle of violence: Gender rigidity and emotional constriction. *Journal of Traumatic Stress, 9*(4), 721-744.

Lyons-Ruth, K. (1996). Attachment relationships among children with aggressive behavior problems: The role of disorganized early attachment patterns. *Journal of Consulting and Clinical Psychology, 64*(1), 64-73.

Maiuro, R. D., Cahn, T. S., Vitaliano, P. P., Wagner, B. C., & Zegree, J. B. (1988). Anger, hostility and depression in domestically violent versus generally assaultive men and nonviolent control subjects. *Journal of Consulting & Clinical Psychology, 56,* 17-23.

Malmquist, C. P. (1986). Children who witness parental murder: Post-traumatic aspects. *Journal of American Academy of Child Psychiatry, 25,* 320-325.

O'Leary, K. D. (1988). Physical aggression between spouses: A social learning theory perspective. In V. van Hasselt, R. Morrinson, A. S. Bellack, & M. Hersen (Eds.), *Handbook of Family Violence.* New York: Plenum Publishing.

Osofsky, J. D., Wewers, S., Hann, D. M., & Fick, A. C. (1993). Chronic community violence: What's happening to our children? *Psychiatry: Interpersonal and Biological Processes, 56*(1), 36-45.

Pynoos, R. S., & Eth, S. (1985). Children traumatized by witnessing acts of personal violence: Homicide, rape, or suicide behavior. In S. Eth & R. S. Pynoos (Eds.), *Post Traumatic Stress Disorder in children* (pp. 17-44). Washington: American Psychiatric Press.

Pynoos, R. S., & Nader, K. (1993). Issues in the treatment of Post Traumatic Stress Disorder in children and adolescents. In J. P. Wilson & B. Raphael (Eds.), *International handbook of traumatic stress syndromes.* New York: Plenum.

Rossman, B. B. (1994). Children in violent families: Diagnosis and treatment considerations. *Family Violence and Sexual Assault Bulletin, 10,* 29-34.

Schore, A. N. (1994). *Affect regulation and the origin of the self.* Hillsdale, NJ: Lawrence Erlbaum & Assoc.

Singer, M. I., Anglin, T. M., Song, L. Y., & Lunghofer, L. (1995). Adolescent's exposure to violence and associated symptoms of psychological trauma. *Journal of the American Medical Association, 273*(6), 477-482.

Sonkin, D. J. (1987). The assessment of court-mandated male batterers. In D. J. Sonkin (Ed.), *Domestic violence on trial: Psychological and legal dimensions of family violence* (pp. 174-196).

Straus, M. A., & Gelles, R. J. (1990). Societal change and change in family violence from 1975 to 1985 as revealed by two national surveys. In M. A. Straus & R. J.

Gelles (Eds.), *Physical violence in American families: Risk factors and adaptations to violence in 8,145 families* (pp. 113-132). New Brunswick: Transaction Publishers.

Terr, L. (1979). Children of Chowchilla: A study of psychic trauma. *Psychoanalytic Study of the Child, 34,* 547-623.

van der Kolk, B. (1987). *Psychological trauma.* Washington, DC: American Psychiatric Press.

van der Kolk, B. (1988). The trauma spectrum: The interaction of biological and social events in genesis of the trauma response. *Journal of Traumatic Stress, 1*(3), 273-290.

van der Kolk, B., & Fisler, R. (1995). Dissociation and fragmentary nature of traumatic memories: Overview and exploratory study. *Journal of Traumatic Stress, 8*(4), 505-525.

van der Kolk, B., McFarlane, A. C. & Weisaeth, L. (1996). *Traumatic stress.* New York: Guilford.

Walker, L. (1979). *The battered woman.* New York: Harper & Row.

The Neglected Variable of Physiology in Domestic Violence

Wanda K. Mohr
John W. Fantuzzo

SUMMARY. In the early stages of research concerning domestic violence and its effects on children, scholars have focused almost exclusively on isolated psychological variables. Little attention has been paid to events that might inform the research community about the effects of physiological factors surrounding such exposure on children's subsequent development. In order to go beyond a narrow disciplinary perspective that would exclude such important variables, a broader research agenda that includes multiple partners must be forged. The understanding of multiple etiologies and sequelae of domestic violence requires the use of comprehensive conceptual models that can bring together multiple theoretical perspectives under a broad umbrella. This article presents a developmental ecological perspective that allows for a more thorough and accurate examination of the influences of domestic violence on child development by simultaneously addressing child and environmental characteristics. *[Article copies available for a fee from The Haworth Document Delivery Service: 1-800-342-9678. E-mail address: getinfo@haworthpressinc.com <Website: http://www.haworthpressinc.com>]*

KEYWORDS. Child trauma, domestic violence, neurobiology, neurophysiology

---

Address correspondence to: Wanda K. Mohr, PhD, RN, FAAN, School of Nursing, University of Pennsylvania, 420 Guardian Drive, Philadelphia, PA 19104 (e-mail: wkmohr@pobox.upenn.edu).

[Haworth co-indexing entry note]: "The Neglected Variable of Physiology in Domestic Violence." Mohr, Wanda K., and John W. Fantuzzo. Co-published simultaneously in *Journal of Aggression, Maltreatment & Trauma* (The Haworth Maltreatment & Trauma Press, an imprint of The Haworth Press, Inc.) Vol. 3, No. 1 (#5), 2000, pp. 69-84; and: *Children Exposed to Domestic Violence: Current Issues in Research, Intervention, Prevention, and Policy Development* (ed: Robert A. Geffner, Peter G. Jaffe, and Marlies Sudermann) The Haworth Maltreatment & Trauma Press, an imprint of The Haworth Press, Inc., 2000, pp. 69-84. Single or multiple copies of this article are available for a fee from The Haworth Document Delivery Service [1-800-342-9678, 9:00 a.m. - 5:00 p.m. (EST). E-mail address: getinfo@haworthpressinc.com].

Understanding the multiple etiologies and sequelae of domestic violence requires the use of comprehensive conceptual models that can bring together multiple theoretical perspectives under a broad umbrella. A developmental ecological perspective allows for a more thorough and accurate examination of the influences of domestic violence on child development by simultaneously addressing child and environmental characteristics. In these early stages of research on domestic violence and its effects on children, an examination of the literature reveals an almost exclusive focus on isolated psychological variables. Volavka (1995) posits that sociologists, developmental specialists, child psychiatrists, psychophysiologists, and others "do not join forces to study the same subjects" (p. 171). Each studies their own set of constructs and publishes in their own journals. There is little attention to events that might inform the research community about the effects of physiological factors surrounding such exposure on children's subsequent development. With few exceptions (Rosenbaum & Hoge, 1989; Warnken, Rosenbaum, Fletcher, & Hoge, 1994) little attention is paid within the domestic violence community to the role of biology and its role in the genesis and maintenance of the events in relationships characterized by violence and interpersonal chaos.

This article is designed to review the neurobiology of violence and to examine the physiologic research concerning what takes place in the nervous system during intense environmental and emotional upheaval. It also proposes a way in which research can be broadened and expanded to include multiple variables and multiple perspectives by using a conceptual framework that captures the complexities of human beings as players in the complex transactions that constitute multilevel contexts of their environments.

A FRAMEWORK FOR STUDY

Two explanatory models have been put forth that seek to explain the role of traumatic experiences in the development of psychopathology. Reductionistic models seek to understand causation by tracing back to simpler and earlier stages. An example of this reductionistic type is the medical model that is exemplified by the notion of pathogen leading to disease (i.e., trauma being the pathogen and the ensuing psychopathology being the disease). Non-reductionistic models try to relate problems to wider rather than narrower issues. The explanatory models used in sociology are generally of this kind where the pathogens are numerous and are embedded in specific social structures. Neither of these models leave professionals with a clear or satisfactory understanding of the etiologic factors in the development and maintenance of psychopathology or maladaptive behavior.

Recognizing the need to go beyond accounts that limit themselves to either of the above models, scholars in the field of developmental psychology

(Cicchetti, 1989) have focused on an integrated approach that would bring together multiple perspectives to inform the etiology of psychopathology. According to this developmental ecological perspective, children's competencies develop across multiple domains and progress along a trajectory of critical stages in a web of complex transactions among environmental and ontogenic characteristics. Developmental psychologists (Cicchetti, 1989) posit that children must successfully negotiate the challenges of each stage in order for growth and adaptation to occur. A developmental ecological model would predict that intense environmental upheaval will disrupt the resolution of these critical developmental tasks. The effects of such upheaval on children will be determined by their developmental stage and by the specific tasks that they are attempting to negotiate (Cicchetti & Lynch, 1993). This model also stresses the important effects of ontogenic factors, such as neurophysiological variables, as well as contextal variables on children's development. It proposes that multiple transactions among many variables may enhance or hinder a mastery of stage-salient competencies (Aber & Cicchetti, 1984). Therefore, in research involving the effects of traumatic events on children, it is critical to examine both the ontogenic variables that are unique to the child, as well as understand how the interplay of proximal and distal aspects of the environment affect the resolution of critical developmental tasks (National Research Council, 1993).

THE PHYSIOLOGY OF TRAUMA

Within the past decades the work of van der Kolk, Boyd, and Krystal (1984), van der Kolk and Greenberg (1987), Pynoos, Frederick and Nader (1987), Terr (1991), Perry, Pollard, Blakley, Baker, and Vigilante (1995), and their colleagues has made it apparent that severe and repeated trauma that is left unresolved can result in a number of sequelae. Without prompt corrective measures designed to defuse and discharge the tensions set up by the intense traumatic experiences, newly activated, reverberating neural circuits can fixate, become permanent, and result in affectively charged flashbacks as well as motor behavior that is affectively driven. A full understanding of the literature on the neurobiology of the trauma response requires a basic understanding of the research that has been done on aggression and the brain, as well as an overview of the exciting new knowledge that has surfaced about neurotransmitters and their postulated effects on brain function. A brief discussion of both subjects precedes a more in-depth treatment of the hypothesized physiology underlying trauma and its effect on children.

Aggression and the Brain

All structures within the nervous system function in a similar way on the molecular level. They obey similar molecular rules mediating development, changes in response to chemical signals, and storage of information. The largest of these structures is the brain. The human brain exists in its mature form as a byproduct of genetic potential and environmental history. The brain is composed of nervous tissue and all nervous tissue is designed to change in response to external signals. This capacity allows the brain to be responsive to the environment (internal and external). The brain develops in a sequential and hierarchical fashion (i.e., from less complex brainstem to most complex limbic, cortical areas). Postnatal ontogenic experiences affect this development in ways that are only beginning to be understood (Edleman, 1989).

Neurological activity during aggressive behavior is thought to be centered on three specific brain areas: the limbic system, frontal lobe and temporal lobe. Structures in the limbic system include the hippocampus, amygdala, cingulate gyrus, and the hypothalamus (Goldberg, 1990). Alterations in functioning of the structures in the limbic system influence individuals' emotional experience and behavior and may increase or decrease the potential for aggressive behavior.

The frontal lobes mediate purposeful behavior, are involved in executive control, and exert an initiatory influence over the limbic system. The frontal lobe is the site where reason and emotion interact (Goldberg, 1990). The frontal lobes include the motor cortex, premotor area, and prefrontal area in each hemisphere. Portions of the prefrontal area are thought to act as staging areas for information received from the limbic system. Reciprocity between the staging areas of the prefrontal area and the limbic system permits regulation of hypothalamic processes by the cortex and activation of the cortex by basic drives thought to originate in the limbic system. This two-way communication link makes it possible for the areas involved to influence each other (Young, 1997). Damage to the frontal cortex impairs judgment and this may be manifested by behavioral changes that include irritability, hostility, inappropriate conduct, and *occasional* aggressive outbursts (Silver, 1987).

The temporal lobes are connected with the limbic system and they share some of the same structures, such as the hippocampus. The temporal lobes play a role in the interpretation of auditory stimuli, and they play a major role in memory. Naturally occurring lesions of the temporal lobe may elicit aggressive behavior. Temporal lobe seizures have been frequently linked with aggressive behavior, but the relationship is subject to debate and the research is fraught with problems of definition as well as methodology.

Neurotransmission

An important caveat to remember in our nascent stages of knowledge concerning the role of neurotransmission, violence, and aggression is that a surplus or deficit *of any one* neurotransmitter can only be interpreted in the context of differing effects of many neurotransmitters at differing synapses and the neural circuits involved in any behavior. A second caveat is that neurotransmission must be understood to take place as a response to a host of internal and external signals.

In recent years, research on neurotransmitters has shown that systems of neurotransmission develop and unfold throughout a person's lifetime. The neurotransmitter dopamine develops gradually and mature levels of dopamine are not present in the body until the end of the second decade of life (Coyle & Harris, 1987). On the other hand, serotonergic systems develop quite early. Alterations in neurotransmitters clearly play a role in the etiology of mental disorders (Fischback, 1992). For example, functional decreases in serotonin are central to the etiology of depression, while excessive levels are implicated in the development of mania.

The neurotransmitter frequently implicated as affecting behavior is serotonin (5-HT), a monoamine that is normally found in high concentrations in the limbic system. Serotonin plays a role in affect modulation, the capacity to tolerate pain, and the ability to feel pleasure. Other neurotransmitters that are discussed in aggression studies include dopamine, norepinephrine, and the amino acid GABA. *In animal studies* serotonin is the neurotransmitter most clearly implicated in the inhibitory control of aggression (Royalty, 1990). Animal studies also show that potentiation of GABA activity inhibits aggression (Simler, Puglisi-Allegra, & Mandel, 1983) and that dopamine and norepinephrine generally enhance aggression (Hahn, Hynes, & Fuller, 1982; Hegstrand & Eichelman, 1983; Lammers & Van Rossum, 1968).

In humans, dysfunction involving the serotonergic system has been implicated in disinhibition and aggression. Since the 1970s, research on humans has been conducted using various approaches that include: studies of the cerebrospinal fluid (Van Woerkoem, Tellken, & Minderhoud, 1977); tryptophan content in plasma and serotonin uptake in platelets (Branchey, Branchey, Shaw, & Lieber, 1984); and neuroendocrine challenges of central serotonin receptors (Coccaro, Siever, & Klar, 1989). Although the etiology and nature of the dysfunction that is involved remain unclear, the evidence strongly suggests that central serotonergic dysfunction is linked to violent behavior and impulsivity.

Physiology, Trauma, and the Interaction with Environmental Events

All of human experience is filtered by the senses. Sensory signals begin a surge of processes in the brain on a cellular and molecular level and these processes alter neuronal neurochemistry, cellular structure, and ultimately brain structure and function. The process whereby an internal representation of information comes in from the external world is dependent upon the nature of the neuronal activity that is activated by the sensing, processing and storing of signals. Variance in what is activated depends on pattern, intensity, and frequency of neuronal activity. The more intense and the more frequent a certain pattern of neural activation, the more permanent is the internal representation resulting from that activation (Schwartz & Perry, 1994). Perry and his colleagues (1995) conceptualized this representation as the processing template which resulted from these experiences and through which all new input is subsequently filtered. The more frequently a network of neurons is activated, the greater will be the internalization of information (LeDoux, Cicchetti, Xagoraris, & Romanski, 1989). Learning and the formation of memories take place through this process of internalization.

Various patterns of repeated neural activation or experience also result in sensitization. Sensitization is thought to take place when experiences activate the neurons and result in an alteration in the quality and quantity of neurotransmitter release throughout the neuronal systems that are responsible for the processing of that specific experience. Thus, sensitization takes place when a pattern of activation results in an altered, more sensitive system. When a system becomes sensitized, the same activation can result from less intense stimulation (Edleman, 1989).

Perry et al. (1995) hypothesize that traumatic experiences result in this kind of sensitization and that traumatized children exhibit response patterns commensurate with their traumatic experiences. Thus, seemingly minor stressors or cues can result in a full blown stress response. The psychophysiologic response to exposure to violence (or other traumata) includes the release of adrenergic substances and cortisone derivatives that bathe specific neurosynaptic junctions and fix the memory of the traumatic event to keep the person alert and responsive to a repetition of the trauma.

With respect to development, we have known for many years that there are different times during which different areas of the nervous system are organizing and are more sensitive to organizing experiences. Because children's brains are still in development, they are more plastic and therefore are "malleable" (Schwartz & Perry, 1994), making them more vulnerable to variances of experience. Disruption of critical environmental cues during development can lead to major abnormalities or deficits in neurodevelopment. Given certain deprivations or extremes of experiences, some of these experiences may not be reversible. Brain mediated functions such as humor, empathy, attachment, and affect regulation may be compromised. Deprivation may result in inactivation of neurochemical cues and responses, and may explain why neglected children are extremely insensitive to any replacement or remediation experiences in the form of interventions such as therapy when they become adults. In contrast, children experiencing extremes by way of developmental insults, such as abusive or otherwise violent experiences, may exhibit patterns of overactivation of neurochemical cues and responses.

The Sensitized Hyperarousal Response

Viewing a traumatic or a violent event can cause profound changes in the child's sense of the safety and security of future intimate human relationships. The helplessness of the child who is exposed to violence is influenced by the passivity that is imposed by having to watch or listen to the sights and sounds surrounding the violence and the physical mutilation it creates. The perceived danger to this child does not depend on fear of self-harm, but on the personal meaning he or she ascribes to the event, that is, the template through which he or she views the threat. The greater and more frequent the personal impact on the child the greater the likelihood a traumatic state will occur, and given enough of these states, the child responds the same way repeatedly and thus may acquire a trait.

Perry and his colleagues (1995) posit that children under severe stress respond adaptively in one of two ways. They term these the hyperarousal response and the dissociative response. The hyperarousal response involves the catecholamines that originate in the brainstem and results in increases in circulating epinephrine and associated stress steroids. By contrast the dissociative response involves dopaminergic systems and is mediated by endogenous opiod systems. Differences in adaptive responses occur as a function of both age and gender. Perry and his colleagues posit that female children are more apt to elicit a dissociative response and male children are more apt to elicit a hyperarousal response. We can take this a step further and add the contextual influence of gender roles in our society that reinforce female compliance and male dominance. In considering this as interplay, both physiological response and social learning reinforced by context thus inform us as to internalizing behaviors of females and the externalizing behaviors of males that emerge as a result of maltreatment or other trauma (Jouriles, Murphy, & O'Leary, 1989).

Due to page limitations, for the purpose of this article we will focus our discussion *only on male children*. If a male child faced with threat responds with a hyperarousal response, he will experience a dramatic increase in locus coeruleus and ventral tegmental nucleus activity. These are the brain regions that are involved in the hyperarousal response induced by the threat, and they play a critical role in regulating the stress response, arousal, vigilance, affect, attention, sleep, and the startle response. In addition, a corresponding increase in the release of norepinephrine regulates the total body response to the threat. Table 1 illustrates the sensitized hyperarousal response to a perceived threat, the continuum on which it proceeds, brain regions affected, and outcomes in terms of cognitive states.

After the initial exposure to trauma, these same systems in the brain will be reactivated when the child is exposed to reminders of the traumatic event. They may also be reactivated in response to a child's thoughts or dreams

TABLE 1. The Acute Response to Threat

adaptive response	rest (adult male)	vigilance	freeze	flight	fight
hyperarousal continuum	rest (male child)	vigilance (crying)	resistance (freezing)	defiance (posturing)	aggression
Primary Secondary (brain areas)	Neocortex subcortex	Subcortex limbic	Limbic midbrain	Midbrain brainstem	Brainstem autonomic
Cognition	abstract	concrete	"emotional"	reactive	reflexive
Mental state	CALM	AROUSAL	ALARM	FEAR	TERROR

Adapted with permission from Perry et al., 1995 (Perry, B.D., personal communication, July 8, 1997)

about the traumatic event. Such stimulus reminders may generalize leading to the repeated activation of the stress-response apparatus despite being temporally and geographically distanced from any apparent threat.

Activation of the locus coeruleus and ventral tegmental nucleus areas leads to sensitization of catecholamine systems leading to a flood of associated functional changes in brain-related functions. Given enough time a traumatized child may begin to exhibit motor hyperactivity, anxiety, behavioral impulsivity, affective lability, sleep problems, and so forth. Further, elements of the fear response become sensitized and previously neutral stressors begin to elicit exaggerated reactions. The children begin to exhibit hyperreactivity and extreme sensitivity and over time, this persistent state of fear, arousal and hyperreactivity becomes part of the child's behavioral repertoire. When exposed to reminders of the trauma event, he may respond rapidly along the continuum from mild anxiety to absolute panic. The result that is often seen in male children is a constellation of maladaptive emotional, behavioral, and cognitive problems, that have their origins in the original adaptive response to a traumatic event. These problems manifest themselves by way of "externalizing behaviors."

The helpless and frightened child begins to view the world through the lens (or template) of the original trauma and will respond accordingly. This lens is created by high levels of adrenergic and cortisone derivative substances that remain after the original trauma and which are responsible for permanently altering the neurosynaptic junctions in a way that fixates memories and impulse response. Because of these impulsive responses, these males, when they are young boys, are at a significant disadvantage in situations of high stress where demands are put on them to make "appropriate" decisions and remain rational. They already invariably feel powerless, angry, and slow to trust any adult, despite their status of dependent child. These damaged children view the world through a "template" that is highly inflexible because their experience with adults has too often been characterized by disappointment, chaos, or even violation. Anger is their galvanizing emotion and it can be manifested in aggression and hostile assaults on the environment, or turned inward in immobilizing depression, withdrawal or assaults upon the self (Perry & Pate, 1994). When this lens is one through which the male child has seen repeated beatings of his mother, it well may be that he is compelled to act in the same manner (Perry, 1997). Given what has happened physiologically, and what is mediated by proximal and distal variables consistent with meta-messages of male dominance and other cultural phenomena, the boy has a greater risk of becoming a potential batterer.

The Role of Endogenous Opiods

Exercise studies (Colt, Wardlaw, & Frantz, 1981) and studies on patients who self-mutilate (Coid, Alloilio, & Rees, 1983) report elevation of plasma beta endorphins following stress. Beta endorphins are opiods that are naturally occurring, hence endogenous. Opiods have properties that are calming. They reduce rage and aggression and they decrease feelings of paranoia and inadequacy. Van der Kolk and Greenberg (1987) suggest that exposure to severe and prolonged environmental stress and reexposure to traumatic situations evoke an endogenous opiod response and produce the same effect as ingestion of exogenous opiods. Endogenous opiods can be hypothesized in playing a role in the maintenance of the battering response, particularly in the context of reports by batterers who report a period of building tension, followed by the attack on the spouse, and then followed by the "honeymoon period" (Pagelow, 1982). The "honeymoon period" is described in the literature as one in which the batterer is extra-loving, affectionate, and contrite. It may be that the role of the violence itself is to serve to precipitate the release of these endogenous opiods which have a calm, soothing, or mildly euphoric effect that results in this "honeymoon" behavior.

PUTTING IT TOGETHER

Studies of adult victims of torture who exhibit post-traumatic stress syndrome suggested that the repeated traumatic experiences caused irreversible changes at the neurosynaptic junction (Eitinger, 1982). This happened even when the traumata were largely "psychological." Current neuroimaging and PET scan studies have confirmed this hypothesis and have traced the alterations in the direct and indirect pathways and systems involved. Severe and repeated trauma that is unresolved can set up flashbacks of affectively charged memory and of affecto-motor behavior by virtue of the systems responsible for the down regulation of the fight/flight reactions. The consequent loss of impulse control can lead to identification with the aggressor type of response to every subsequent threat or projected threat, and to a corresponding suspension of rational judgment and ability to reason or negotiate.

Research conducted on traumatized children has found that their traumatic experiences determine their apperception of stimuli (Fish-Murray, Koby, & van der Kolk, 1987), in part confirming Perry's hypothesis of the child's viewing the world through the "template" of their experiences. These same children were found to react in an intensely catastrophic manner and exhibited an impaired ability to self-correct when exposed to projective stimuli. In addition, they were found to possess highly inflexible organizing schematas across domains of functioning at a time when their preoperational thought should have been fairly loose. Conceivably, such inflexibility of thought coupled with male-sex role conditioning can play out years later in behaviors such as physical abuse of intimates and stalking during periods of separation when rigid organizing schemata are threatened, and control falters.

Dutton (1995) posits that the complex of behaviors in which the abusive male engages originates in early traumata, resulting in attachment insecurity which can result in pathological reactions to separations and estrangement. He further suggests that men who batter are more hostile and angry than nonviolent controls. Dutton and Browning (1988) found that batterers self-reported more anger in viewing videotaped situational vignettes designed to represent female closeness and abandonment. They hypothesized that batterers experienced arousal anxieties as a result of viewing the scenes, but because of male-sex role socialization, they experience this arousal as anger rather than as anxiety. Differential reinforcement, modeling, and other forms of learning increase the likelihood that anger will be expressed as aggression. Margolin, John and Gleberman (1988) found that men who are batterers report more anger and anxiety and felt more attacked by their partners following 10-minute problem solving sessions.

Research that has been guided by the developmental ecological conceptual framework suggests that abusive or neglectful experiences during childhood can lead to distorted representational models of relationships (Crittenden, 1988; Carlson, Cicchetti, Barnett, & Brunwald, 1989). Such distorted models can lead to maladaptive interpersonal relationships and these become the medium by which abusive patterns of behavior are transmitted intergenerationally. However, such representational models are not discussed within the developmental ecological perspective as mere abstractions. Rather, they are understood as having physiological correlates, in the same way in which we understand neural circuitry as foundational to the development of memory and habit. Thus, the developmental ecological perspective is extremely useful in offering a way to understand the adaptive or maladaptive development of children who grow up in an environment characterized by relationship violence.

Men who abuse have often been found to have been abused as children (Gelles, 1980; Fitch & Papantonio, 1983; Guszinski & Carrillo, 1988). Research concerning the association between aggression in the family of origin and husband to wife aggression is fairly consistent across studies (Rosenbaum & O'Leary, 1980; Capell & Heiner, 1990; Doumas, Margolin, & John, 1994). They consistently show that exposure to marital aggression in the family of origin is one predictor of being the perpetrator of marital aggression in the next generation of males and being the recipient of marital aggression for females. This supports the intergenerational "cycle of violence" hypothesis, based on social learning theory. Children learn to aggress by observing aggression, particularly that of their parents who are familiar and powerful models (Bandura, 1973). In such families the prototypic violent relationships are learned in the home early in life and then generalize to relationships with others outside the family unit. But again, this learning must be seen to have a biological component and not simply taken as psychological ephemera.

IMPLICATIONS FOR FUTURE RESEARCH AND PRACTICE

As we have suggested in this article, domestic violence and its effects on children involve a complex interplay of changing variables. These variables occur over time at different levels of the child's ecology. Distally these levels include the beliefs and values of the culture, and aspects of the community in which the child's family lives. Proximally these include family variables and ontogenic factors which exert the most direct influences on child development. The bio-physiological aspect is but one part of an exceedingly complex multi-system, multi-level puzzle. No single perspective can capture this kind of complexity. In order to avoid the blind spots inherent in a single-perspective approach, researchers must be able to study human beings from multiple perspectives.

A developmental ecological framework presents a useful perspective within which to conceptualize and address this multi-system, multi-level puzzle comprehensively. Although theoretically the community of scholars involved in violence research speak to a system approach being the standard in the field, and research in child maltreatment has used this model, studies using this comprehensive approach have been slow to appear in the area of child exposure to domestic violence. This suggests that researchers from different disciplines must begin to join in collaborative investigations that would recognize that each discipline has a fund of knowledge that can cross-pollinate others. Such collaborative efforts should be fostered, nurtured, and grounded in an exchange of information that recognizes the unique strengths that each partner brings to the partnership and a commitment to cultivate these strengths.

Single investigator research of the past must be replaced by more sophisticated study designs that go beyond analyses of the past that can generate misleading conclusions when they are used to sort out multiple interacting risk factors and reciprocal influences on outcomes. These influences include biological and psychological constructs, as well as transactional and contextual factors which necessitate more complex measurement and data analytic strategies. As none of us can presume to be expert in everything, the challenge to elegant studies means that we must place ourselves as researchers and practitioners across disciplines in a position of true collaboration and partnership with multiple players with multiple perspectives.

How would such a partnership begin? A *starting point* to effective research partnership might be to re-think the way in which we socialize our graduate students. Rather than drawing invidious distinctions and artificial boundaries between disciplines, graduate students must be socialized to considering their disciplinary approach as only one interpretive framework within the field of social sciences. Joint classes and seminars between different departments can help students to avoid a narrow parochial view and realize that each discipline's interpretive framework is one that is subjectively imposed on the process of collecting and analyzing data.

Other ways might include collaborative ventures between those who practice in the field and academics. An assumption that underlies much of what we do in the research community is that the products of our research–new knowledge–can inform policy and practice. In an ideal world theory should inform practice which should inform research which should then support or modify theoretical assumptions. This relationship makes both intuitive and intellectual sense. But often the links between research and practice are difficult to achieve.

A recent report by the National Academy of Sciences panel on "Understanding Violence Against Women" (Crowell & Burgess, 1996) called for greater understanding by the research community of the contexts of practice. The panel members posited that practitioners and researchers should come together in creative partnerships so as to better target limited resources to specific individuals who could benefit from particular types of interventions that can be demonstrated are effective in given situations.

What would such partnerships look like? One way in which such a partnership can come about is for researchers to design more methodologically complex studies than we have seen in the past. A study that is guided by a developmental ecological framework, for example, would necessitate incorporating a number of specialists from a number of different disciplines who possess expertise in their fields. Thus, a study of childhood trauma might involve the disciplines of psychology, psychiatry, social work, sociology, nursing, and any number of others, each of which would bring the strengths of their particular perspectives to the research partnership. These disciplines would consult with practitioners in ways that would involve collaborating on real life questions, and identify gaps concerning what is not yet known in order to stimulate a dialogue on questions that need to be addressed to advance both knowledge and practice. Better dialogue between "the town" and "the gown" has the potential to result in better and more relevant studies and the wider dissemination of the fruits of those studies so that interventions can be based on solid science as well as practical realities.

To be sure, such a huge venture would be difficult to fund, but one way in which this could be actuated is by establishing centers in which many scholars working in the same field can pursue the same basic questions from different perspectives. Individual projects can be funded under the umbrella of a center devoted to the pursuit of basic research, intervention research, and demonstration projects.

CONCLUSIONS

In the past there were good reasons for relying on a single perspective. Some may believe that there still are. A specialized, single perspective helps to establish a coherent intellectual reputation. Individual perspectives offer a politically motivated pattern of interpretation of the manifestations included (and excluded) in a particular research agenda in that each perspective takes a stand toward established authority.

In addition, partnerships are time consuming and they are fraught with the same drawbacks inherent in working in any team situation. These include agreements and disagreements among the various actors, the time intensive nature of working with multiple partners, logistics of communication that might be difficult among different agencies and personnel, and the necessity of keeping the vision of collective effort on the project above any one individual's personal agenda. But as Cicchetti (1993) posits: "By now, it should be apparent that extreme positions (i.e., biological or psychological; cognitive or emotional) provide overly simplistic and incorrect accounts of the developmental process. I do not think that we can afford to tolerate such lapses in logic and experimental rigor if true and lasting advances are to occur" (p. 484).

REFERENCES

Aber, J.L., & Cicchetti, D. (1984). The social-emotional development of maltreated children: An empirical and theoretical analysis. In H. Fitzgerald, B. Lester, & M. Yogman (Eds.), *Theory and research in behavioral pediatrics* (pp. 147-205). New York: Plenum.

Bandura, A. (1973). *Aggression: A social learning analysis.* Englewood Cliffs, NJ: Prentice Hall.

Branchey, L, Branchey, M., Shaw, S., & Lieber, C.S. (1984). Depression, suicide, and aggression in alcoholics and their relationship to plasma amino acids. *Psychiatry Research, 12,* 219-226.

Cappell, C., & Heiner, R.B. (1990). The intergenerational transmission of family aggression. *Journal of Family Violence, 52,* 135-152.

Cicchetti, D. (1993). Developmental psychopathology: Reactions, reflections, projections. *Developmental Review, 13*(4), 471-502.

Cicchetti, D. (1989). How research on child maltreatment has informed the study of child development: Perspectives from developmental psychopathology. In D. Cicchetti & V. Carlson (Eds.), *Child maltreatment: Theory and research on the causes and consequences of child abuse and neglect* (pp. 377-431). New York: Cambridge University Press.

Cicchetti, D., & Lynch, M. (1993). Toward an ecological/transactional model of community violence and child maltreatment: Consequences for children's development. *Psychiatry: Interpersonal and Biological Processes, 56* (1), 96-118.

Coccaro, E.F., Siever, L.J., & Klar, H.M. (1989). Serotonergic studies in patients with affective and personality disorders. *Archives of General Psychiatry, 46,* 587-599.

Coid, J., Allolio, B., & Rees, L.H. (1983). Raised plasma beta metaenkephalins in patients who habitually mutilate themselves. *Lancet, 2* (8349), 545-546.

Colt, E.W., Wardlaw, S.L., & Frantz, A.C. (1981). The effect of running on plasma beta-endorphins. *Life Sciences, 28*(14), 1637-1640.

Coyle, J.T., & Harris, J.C. (1987). The development of neurotransmitters and neuropeptides. In J.D. Noshpitz (Ed.), *Basic handbook of child psychiatry* (pp. 14-25). New York: Basic Books.

Crittenden, P.M. (1988). Distorted patterns of relationship in maltreating families: The role of internal representation models. *Journal of Reproductive and Infant Psychology, 6*(3), 183-199.

Crowell, N.A., & Burgess, A.W. (1996). *Understanding violence against women.* Washington, DC: National Academy Press.

Doumas, D., Margolin, G., & John, R.S. (1994). The intergenerational transmission of aggression across three generations. *Journal of Family Violence, 9* (2), 157-175.

Dutton, D.G. (1995). *The batterer: A psychological profile.* New York: Basic Books.

Dutton, D.G., & Browning, J.J. (1988). Concern for power, fear of intimacy, and aversive stimuli for wife abuse. In G.T. Hotaling, D. Finkelhor, J.T. Kilpatric, & M. Strauss (Eds.), *New directions in family violence research* (pp. 163-175). Newbury Park, CA: Sage.

Edleman, G. (1989). *The remembered present: A biological theory of consciousness.* New York: Basic Books.

Eitinger, L. (1982). The effects of captivity. In F.M. Ochberg & D.A. Soskis (Eds.), *Victims of terrorism* (pp. 73-93). Boulder, CO: Westview Press.

Fischback, G. (1992, Sept.). Mind and brain. *Scientific American, 267*, 48-57.

Fish-Murray, C.C., Koby, E.V., & van der Kolk, B.A. (1994). Evolving ideas: The effect of abuse on children's thought. In B.A. van der Kolk (Ed.), *Psychological trauma* (pp. 89-110). Washington, DC: American Psychiatric Association Press.

Fitch, F.J., & Papantonio, A. (1983). Men who batter: Some pertinent characteristics. *The Journal of Nervous and Mental Disease, 171*(3), 190-192.

Gelles, R.J. (1980). Violence in the family: A review of research in the seventies. *Journal of Marriage and the Family, 42* (4), 873-885.

Goldberg, S. (1990). *Clinical neuroanatomy made ridiculously simple*. Miami, FL: Medmaster.

Grusznski, R.J., & Carrillo, T.P. (1988). Who completes batterer's treatment groups? An empirical investigation. *Journal of Family Violence, 3* (2), 141-150.

Hahn, R.A., Hynes, M.D., & Fuller, R.W. (1982). Apomorphine-induced aggression in rats chronically treated with oral Clonidine: Modulation by central serotonergic mechanisms. *Journal of Pharmacological Experimental Therapeutics, 220* (2), 389-393.

Hegstrand, L.R., & Eichelman, B. (1983). Increased shock-induced fighting with supersensitive beta-adrenergic receptors. *Pharmacology, Biochemistry, & Behavior, 19*, 313-320.

Jouriles, E.N., Murphy, C.M., & O'Leary, K.D. (1989). Interspousal aggression, marital discord, and child problems. *Journal of Consulting and Clinical Psychology, 57*, 453-455.

Lammers, A. & Van Rossum, J. (1968). Bizarre social behavior in rats induced by a combination of a peripheral decarboxylase inhibitor and DOPA. *European Journal of Pharmacology, 5* (1), 103-106.

LeDoux, J.E., Cicchetti, P.O., Xagoraris, A., & Romanski, L.M. (1989). Indelibillity of subcortical emotional memories. *Journal of Cognitive Neuroscience, 1*(7), 238-243.

Margolin, G., John, R., & Gleberman, L. (1988). Affective responses to conflictual discussions in violent and nonviolent couples. *Journal of Consulting and Clinical Psychology, 56* (1), 24-33.

National Research Council. (1993). *Understanding child abuse and neglect*. Washington, DC: National Academy.

Pagelow, M.D. (1982). *Woman batterings: Victims and their experiences*. Beverly Hills, CA: Sage.

Perry, B.D. (1997). Incubated in terror: Neurodevelopmental factors in the "cycle of violence." In J. Osofsky (Ed.), *Children in a violent society* (pp. 124-149). New York: The Guilford Press.

Perry, B.D., Pollard, R.A., Blakley, T.L., Baker, W.L, & Vigilante, D. (1995). Childhood trauma, the neurobiology of adaptation, and "use-dependent" development of the brain: How "states" become "traits." *Infant Mental Health Journal, 16* (4), 271-289.

Perry, B.D., & Pate, J.E. (1994). Neurodevelopment and the psychobiological roots of post-traumatic stress disorder. In L.F. Koziol & C.E. Stout (Eds.), *The neuropsychology of mental disorders: A practical guide* (pp. 129-146). Springfield, IL: Charles Thomas Publishers.

Pynoos, R., Frederick, C., & Nader, K. (1987). Life threat and post-traumatic stress in school age children. *Archives of General Psychiatry, 44*, 1057-1063.

Rosenbaum, A., & O'Leary, K.D. (1981). Children: The unintended victims of marital violence. *American Journal of Orthopsychiatry, 51*, 692-699.

Rosenbaum, A., & Hoge, S.K. (1989). Head injury and marital aggression. *American Journal of Psychiatry, 146* (8), 1048-1051.

Royalty, J. (1990). The effects of prenatal ethanol exposure on juvenile play-fighting and postpubertal aggression in rats. *Psychology Report, 66*, 551-560.

Schwartz, E.D., & Perry, B.D. (1994). The post-traumatic response in children and adolescents. *Psychiatric Clinics of North America, 17* (2), 311-326.

Silver, J. (1987). Aggressive behavior in patients with neuropsychiatric disorders. *Neurotrauma Medical Report, 3*(2), 1-3.

Simler, S., Puglisi-Allegra, S., & Mandel, P. (1983). Effects of n-di-propylacetate on aggressive behavior and brain GABA level in isolated mice. *Pharmacology, Biochemistry, & Behavior, 18* (5), 717-720.

Terr, L.C. (1991). Childhood trauma: An outline and overview. *American Journal of Psychiatry, 148* (1), 10-20.

van der Kolk, B.A., Boyd, H., & Krystal, J. (1984). Post traumatic stress disorder as a biologically based disorder: Implications of the animal model of inescapable shock. In B.A. van der Kolk (Ed.), *Post traumatic stress disorder: Psychological and biological sequelae* (pp. 127-153). Washington, DC: American Psychiatric Press.

van der Kolk, B.A., & Greenberg, M.S. (1987). The psychobiology of the trauma response: Hyperarousal, constriction, and addiction to traumatic re-exposure. In B.A. van der Kolk (Ed.), *Psychological trauma* (pp. 63-87). Washington, DC: American Psychiatric Press Inc.

Van Woerkom, T., Tellken, A., & Minderhoud, J. (1977). Difference in neurotransmitter metabolism in frontotemporal-lobe contusion and diffuse cerebral contusion. *Lancet, 1*, 812-813.

Volavka, J. (1995). *Neurobiology of violence*. Washington, DC: American Psychiatric Press Inc.

Warnken, W.J., Rosenbaum, A., Fletcher, K.E., & Hoge, S.K. (1994). Head injured males: A population at risk for relationship aggression? *Violence and Victims, 9* (2), 153-166.

Young, P.A. (1997). *Basic clinical neuroanatomy*. Baltimore: Williams & Wilkins.

Posttraumatic Response
and Children Exposed to Parental Violence

B. B. Robbie Rossman
Joyce Ho

SUMMARY. In this article some of the literature on children's responses to natural and person-created trauma are discussed. In addition, data relevant to children's posttraumatic response as a result of exposure to interparental violence are presented. Using a factor analytic procedure, the study attempted to examine how the DSM-IV symptom clusters for Posttraumatic Stress Disorder come together for this sample of children. General suggestions are made regarding possible intervention with exposed children experiencing posttraumatic symptoms. *[Article copies available for a fee from The Haworth Document Delivery Service: 1-800-342-9678. E-mail address: getinfo@haworthpressinc.com <Website: http:// www.haworthpressinc.com>]*

KEYWORDS. PTSD, children, interparental violence, trauma, adjustment

Children growing up in spouse abusive families live in a type of war zone. Sometimes they feel they can predict the "attacks" and sometimes the aggression is unexpected. This leaves them with a sense of danger and uncertainty. Clinically we see them as showing posttraumatic distress, but we tend

---

Address correspondence to the authors at: Department of Psychology, 2155 S. Race Street, Denver, CO 80208.

[Haworth co-indexing entry note]: "Posttraumatic Response and Children Exposed to Parental Violence." Rossman, B. B. Robbie, and Joyce Ho. Co-published simultaneously in *Journal of Aggression, Maltreatment & Trauma* (The Haworth Maltreatment & Trauma Press, an imprint of The Haworth Press, Inc.) Vol. 3, No. 1 (#5), 2000, pp. 85-106; and: *Children Exposed to Domestic Violence: Current Issues in Research, Intervention, Prevention, and Policy Development* (ed: Robert A. Geffner, Peter G. Jaffe, and Marlies Sudermann) The Haworth Maltreatment & Trauma Press, an imprint of The Haworth Press, Inc., 2000, pp. 85-106. Single or multiple copies of this article are available for a fee from The Haworth Document Delivery Service [1-800-342-9678, 9:00 a.m. - 5:00 p.m. (EST). E-mail address: getinfo@haworthpressinc.com].

to see more of the extreme cases in mental health clinics, such as multiply disadvantaged families who have been referred for treatment, and the violence has been ongoing over many years. What about the children who have not come to the attention of clinical agencies? Are they as likely to show this type of distress? Would these children show more distress than children experiencing many of the same types of adversity but not exposed to parental violence? Also, would these children show posttraumatic distress of the same form as described in the Diagnostic Statistical Manual of the American Psychiatric Association (DSM-IV, American Psychiatric Association, 1994)? What are the treatment and policy implications of identifying these children as experiencing Posttraumatic Stress and Disorder (PTSD)? These are some of the questions that guide the following discussion.

POSTTRAUMATIC STRESS RESPONSE

The progression of posttraumatic response as a result of physical and psychological threat is in many ways similar to the body's response to disease stressors (the "General Adaptation Syndrome" as discussed by Selye, 1956). Comparing the two might aid in our understanding of the phenomenology of posttraumatic stress response. First, both are natural processes of the body-brain system that are intended to protect the individual. Second, both require the mobilization of resources. Here, in looking at the diagnostic features of PTSD from DSM-IV in Table 1, this mobilization can be noted in the increased arousal cluster of symptoms. These would help the individual attend to certain environmental features that might constitute a threat and respond to them with fight or flight or perhaps freeze. The avoidance and numbing symptoms could be functional to help the individual stay away from the danger both physically and emotionally, perhaps allowing the body-brain system some needed rest time. The re-experiencing symptoms might initially be functional in initiating a re-working process with regard to the threat which Horowitz and Reidbord (1992) discuss as part of a healing process following traumatic loss. Thirdly, both stress response processes involve a dysregulation of the brain-body system in order to deal with the threat. For example, in response to a virus the body elevates temperature, which is a dysregulation, in order to combat the threat. Similarly, the hyper-arousal and other aspects of posttraumatic symptoms constitute temporary dysregulation of the brain-body system to help the individual survive (see article by Mohr & Fantuzzo in this volume). Finally, the body's progressive move into a more serious disease process when all resources have been depleted is not unlike the move from posttraumatic distress symptoms and Acute Stress Disorder (DSM-IV, 1994) to formal PTSD. Thus, like the body's response to a disease stressor, posttraumatic responses may represent a normal but dysregulating reac-

TABLE 1. DSM-IV PTSD Diagnostic Criteria

A. Person exposed to traumatic event

- Threat to physical integrity of self or others
- Response of intense fear, helplessness or horror

B. Traumatic event is re-experienced (1 or more)

- Intrusive recollections of the event
- Dreams of the event
- Acting or feeling event is recurring
- Intense psychological distress to exposure to trauma cues
- Physiological reaction to exposure to trauma cues

C. Avoidance of trauma cues and numbing of responsiveness (3 or more)

- Avoid thoughts, feelings, conversations of trauma
- Avoid activities, places, people linked to trauma
- Can't recall important aspect of trauma
- Less interest or participation in important activities
- Feeling of detachment/estrangement from others
- Restricted range of feelings
- Sense of foreshortened future

D. Persistent increased arousal (2 or more)

- Difficulty sleeping
- Irritability or outbursts of anger
- Difficulty concentrating
- Hypervigilance
- Exaggerated startle response

E. Disturbance lasts longer than one month

F. Disturbance causes significant distress or impairment

tion to threatening circumstances which may re-regulate unless the threat is intense or prolonged.

Evidence suggests that some natural re-regulation of posttraumatic responses is possible. There are traumatized individuals whose symptoms abate or who do not experience diagnosable levels of PTSD in the first place. For example, Gomes-Schwartz, Horowitz, Cardarelli, and Sauzier (1990) found that one year later following disclosure, symptoms had decreased for some of the sexually abused children they interviewed, particularly if they had a supportive adult in their lives during that year. In addition, Foa and Riggs (1995) assessed the diagnosability of posttraumatic symptoms of sexually and nonsexually assaulted adults over time. At the initial assessment at two weeks post-assault, most of the sexually assaulted victims (94%) met diagnostic criteria for PTSD whereas about a quarter of the non-sexual assault victims did not (24%). Nine weeks later about half (47%) of the sexual assault victims and a quarter (22%) of the non-sexual assault victims met criteria. They noted that predictors of longer-lasting symptomatology were a high initial level of symptoms and greater use of numbing behaviors which they saw as perhaps indicative of dissociative responding. They felt that dissociative coping might keep trauma material unavailable for natural working through processes and thus retard improvement. Thus, posttraumatic responding may be a natural reaction to overwhelming fear and threat, and individuals vary in the intensity with which they experience a traumatic event and in the duration of their posttraumatic symptoms.

POSTTRAUMATIC RESPONSES AS DYSREGULATING

A striking feature of individuals exposed to intense and repetitive trauma is the extent to which their behavior and emotional responses may change and become dysregulated relative to pre-trauma status. The areas of posttraumatic dysregulation are noted most clearly in the symptoms used to diagnose PTSD. However, research is emerging that suggests that other areas of functioning may also be dysregulated in response to prolonged traumatic exposure. Two of these are neurotransmitter function and cognitive processing.

Neurotransmitter Dysregulation. Research generated by van der Kolk (1994; 1996), and Charney and his colleagues (e.g., Charney, Deutch, Krystal, Southwick, & Davies, 1993) have shed light on the brain's response to prolonged traumatic stress. Much of the work has been done with Viet Nam veterans with chronic PTSD, though other types of adult trauma victims and animal research have also been involved. Little is known about how applicable this work is for children, but it is suggestive. For a discussion of the neurotransmitter systems that have been noted as dysregulated with chronic PTSD, see Mohr and Fantuzzo in this volume. What this research has suggested is that powerful dysregulation in neurotransmitter function appears to accompany chronic posttraumatic response. Moreover, these alterations can be linked to the behavioral and emotional PTSD symptoms as well as to potential additional difficulties in cognitive processing.

Cognitive Processing Dysregulation. Several areas of theory development suggest that trauma may be associated with changes in how information is accessed and/or used.

Social Information Processing Theory (Crick & Dodge, 1994) suggests that when children are strongly aroused emotionally their information processing may become "preemptive." By preemptive processing Crick and Dodge refer to the fact that less new incoming information may be used in responding, and more of a child's response will be determined by old understandings or scripts. Unfortunately this means that the child will be less sensitive to many new features of a situation. Preemptive processing may have a counterpart in the brain system. LeDoux (1994) has speculated, based on his and others' research, that there are at least two pathways through which information is conveyed from external stimuli to the emotional response systems in the brain. One is a thalamic-amygdala pathway which is very fast and appears to respond to fragmentary aspects of the stimulus. This may be a fast track through which survival information is conveyed quickly to response centers. However, this system is more likely to be wrong. The other is the cortical-amygdala pathway which is slower, involves cortical mediation, and requires more complete stimulus information. Thus it may be that the thalamic-amygdala pathway is the one that supports the survival fast-track proposed as preemptive processing.

Cognitive Control Theory (Santostefano, 1985) suggests that we unconsciously use perceptual and cognitive processes to help us modulate arousal. One of these processes or cognitive styles is the *Leveling-Sharpening* mechanism (Santostefano, 1985). A person who is leveling information is taking it in more slowly and/or less accurately. This could serve to minimize the impact of the information and maintain normative arousal levels. At the other end of this dimension, a person who is sharpening is taking information quicker and/or more accurately. This could also help moderate arousal in creating a sense of preparedness. Santostefano found that adults preparing for their first parachute jump were leveling this type of information several days ahead of the jump, but were sharpening this information shortly before the jump. The leveling could reduce arousal about the jump farther ahead of the jump when they could do little to change the situation, whereas the sharpening ahead of the jump would be useful in noting and rehearsing all they needed to do and remember to have a successful jump. Most adults operate in a midrange on this dimension, moving back and forth as the situation demands. Young children operate more at the leveling end and then move with development into this midrange.

Rieder and Cicchetti (1989) discovered that abused preschoolers were leveling more information relative to non-abused preschoolers. Santostefano and Rieder (1984) found that school-age boys hospitalized for aggressive problems were sharpening on aggressive information relative to non-aggressive information or to boys who were hospitalized for other types of problems. Past experiences of aggressive boys may have led them to be more vigilant regarding certain types of information at the expense of other types in order to be prepared to deal with threats.

Finally, taking a Piagetian approach, Fish-Murray, Koby and van der Kolk (1987) studied the accommodation skills of abused school-age children. Accommodation skills were those that involved taking in information and changing one's schema or understandings to incorporate new aspects of the information. Assimilation processes, on the other hand, were those where new information was taken in and the information modified to fit existing schema. Piaget (1952) felt both types of skills were needed for the growth of intelligence. Fish-Murray et al. found that abused children had weaker accommodation skills in most areas, with mathematics being the best preserved, than similar non-abused children.

Thus, it appears that there may be changes or dysregulation in traumatized children's information usage. There may be differences in how they take in the information, how quickly trauma-relevant information is processed relative to other information, and in how flexible they are in dealing with new information.

CHILDREN TRAUMATIZED BY BEING EXPOSED TO PARENTAL VIOLENCE

Research has established the negative effect of living in a violent home for children and adolescents. It has been reported in multiple studies that children exposed to interparental violence have lower social competence (Wolfe, Zak, Wilson, & Jaffe, 1986; Dawud et al., 1991; Peplar & Moore, 1989; Rossman, Bingham, & Emde, 1997), and lower performance in school (Rossman et al., 1997; Wolfe & Mosk, 1983) and school-related achievement tests (Peplar & Moore, 1989). They may also have problems with aggression (Doumas, Margolin, & John, 1994; Emery, 1989; Holden & Ritchie, 1991), and adopt more rigid and aggressive approaches to problem solving (Rosenberg, 1984). Cognitive development, behavioral functioning, and social information processes may also be negatively affected (e.g., Jaffe, Wolfe, & Wilson, 1990; Rossman & Rosenberg, 1992; Sternberg et al., 1993).

While the above research is gradually shaping our knowledge regarding behavioral effects of children's exposure to interparental violence, there has been increasing research on this population that focused on traumatic responses (Devoe & Graham-Bermann, 1997; Graham-Bermann & Levendosky, 1998; Lehman, 1997; Rossman et al., 1997; Silvern & Kaersvang, 1989). Rossman et al. (1997) reported that exposed children were reported by their mothers to be experiencing more PTS symptoms than children undergoing mild life stresses. In two recent studies of child witnesses (Lehman, 1997; Devoe & Graham-Bermann, 1997), it was reported that 56% and 51% of the children met the criteria for a PTSD diagnosis, respectively. In Graham-Bermann et al.'s study (1997), the three different DSM-IV PTSD symptom groupings were examined for a sample of 64 children exposed to family violence. Thirteen percent of their sample met the DSM-IV criteria for PTSD. When examining the individual symptom groupings, 52% of the children were reported by their mothers to have at least one reexperiencing type of symptom, 42% had at least two or more arousal symptoms, and 19% showed three or more avoidance symptoms. From the above research, it is clear that traumatic stress is one of the responses of children exposed to spousal violence, and the incidence rates are similar to those for other forms of trauma that are more traditionally linked to PTSD (Fletcher, 1996; La Greca et al., 1996; McLeer, Callaghan, Henry, & Wallen, 1994).

Examining PTSD symptom groupings provides a useful addition to looking at a cumulative index of trauma stress, such as a summed symptom score, for several reasons. While a continuous summed score has been used in much research (e.g., Pynoos et al., 1987) and is a more straightforward method by which the total severity of symptoms can be assessed, looking at symptom groupings can generate a conceptual description of the pattern of trauma reactions. This could aid in future attempts to integrate what we know about trauma responses as a result of different types of exposure. Knowing the pattern of symptom groupings for exposed children, and especially identifying changes in these groupings over time, can aid in the development of targeted intervention and treatment (Koverola, 1995). In addition, examination of symptom groupings is useful because they are incorporated in current diagnostic practices. It would be important to know if existing diagnostic groupings do not work as well for describing patterns of children's PTSD responses.

Over several past projects in our lab, information has been collected as to the levels of PTSD symptomatology experienced by children aged 4-13 years who were exposed to interparental violence. These children have been recruited from four groups of largely disadvantaged families (see Table 2). Three major questions were addressed. First, would children exposed to interparental violence show higher levels of PTSD symptoms than non-exposed children? Second, although DSM-IV sets out symptom clusters of hyper-arousal, intrusions and re-experiencing, and avoidance and numbing that are used in making diagnoses (see Table 1), would these same clusters of symptoms come together for children's symptom responses? Most of the work for DSM-IV has reflected adults' responses to trauma. Finally, what aspects of children's functioning would be related to their PTSD symptom scores?

METHODS

Subjects

Participants in this study consisted of families from the community and those residing at battered women's shelters where a range of parental conflict and violence had occurred. Two hundred and eighty-five children (49% fe-

TABLE 2. Sample Description

		GROUPS			
Variable	*Non-Exposed Comm.*	*Exposed Comm.*	*Exposed Shelter*	*Exposed/ Abused Shelter*	*F Sig.*
Age/gender					
4-7yr M	34	4	31	8	
F	26	4	27	14	
8-13yr M	20	5	24	19	
F	33	1	23	12	
	113	14	105	53 (Total = 285)	
SES code	2.34^a	3.81^b	3.69^b	3.81^b	.00
% Minority	15^a	42^b	65^c	60^c	.00
CTSverb.agg.	$.95^a$	4.05^b	4.47^b	4.35^b	.00
CTSphys.agg.	$.00^a$	1.61^b	2.64^c	2.56^c	.00
Fam.Stressors	$.08^a$	$.27^b$	$.29^b$	$.28^b$	.00

Note. Means followed by different letters are significantly different ($p < .05$) using Newman-Keuls post hoc pairwise comparisons; CTS scores are scale averages across each partner; higher SES codes indicate lower SES status.

male) between the ages of 4 and 13 years (M = 7.99, SD = 2.52) and their mothers were interviewed.

All children were screened during the initial phone contact and interview for the presence or absence of child abuse reports filed with the Child Protective Services. This was done using maternal report and counselor report for shelter children. There were four exposure groups in the study as defined by family status at the initial interview:

1. Exposed/Abused Shelter group–This group consisted of children exposed to parental verbal and physical aggression who are living at battered women's shelters, and who have had a filed record of sexual or physical abuse with the Child Protective Services.
2. Exposed Shelter group–This group consisted of children exposed to parental aggression and violence who were living at a battered women's shelter at the time of recruitment. There was no filed record of abuse or neglect with the Child Protective Services.'

3. Exposed Community group–Children from this group were residing at home in the community at the time of recruitment. They have also been exposed to parental aggression and violence.
4. Non-Exposed Community group–Children from this group were residing at home in the community and had been exposed to typical parental verbal conflict. Through a brief phone interview, families in this group were screened for the absence of any parental aggression or violence as well as filed child abuse reports.

As can be noted in Table 2, the sample was ethnically diverse, mostly middle to lower socioeconomic status (SES), and particularly the exposed groups had experienced higher levels of physical and verbal aggression as well as more family stressful events.

Procedures

Recruitment for shelter families was conducted through referrals from nine battered women's shelters in the greater Denver and Front Range area. After a family was referred by a shelter Children's Program Coordinator, they were contacted by phone for an initial interview. Recruitment for community families was conducted through multiple channels, using referrals, letters and flyers. Agencies utilized included: outpatient agencies serving women in battering situations, public school systems, social service agencies, churches, clinics, and the developmental subject pool of the Department of Psychology at the University of Denver. Shelter families were interviewed at the shelter for their safety, while community families were interviewed at our laboratory at the University of Denver.

The interview required approximately two hours to complete. Mothers and children were interviewed separately, and were informed of the confidentiality of the information they provided. The mothers, and children who were over 9 years old, were then asked to sign an informed consent letter. Special care was given in explaining the study to the children to ensure their understanding. Families received monetary compensation and a small prize for the child.

Measures

Mothers in the study were asked to provide information regarding their family background, their relationship with their partner, and their perceptions of their child's behavior and emotional status. Children in the study were interviewed regarding their emotional status and were given measures that tapped their verbal ability and information usage.

Mothers completed the following instruments:

Some of the measures used and types of information gathered are listed in Table 3 and include:

1. *Family Information Demographics Questionnaire* (FIDQ). This form included information regarding the age, gender, SES (Miller, 1977) and ethnicity of each child, the child's school performance, whether they had been referred for emotional evaluation/treatment or special school problems, level of violence in the family's neighborhood, and the length of time that the child had been exposed to interparental violence.

2. *Life Events Questionnaire* (LEQ; Garmezy, Masten, & Tellegen, 1984). This measure recorded the number of stressful events that occurred in the child's family in the previous year (e.g., death, divorce). A sum score of non-child related stressful events was calculated, with higher scores indicating a higher number of events experienced. The 12-month test-retest reliability for stress scores has been shown to be between 0.53 and 0.60.

3. *Conflict Tactics Scale* (CTS; Straus, 1979).This standardized 23-item scale measures the level of spousal conflict and aggression. Mothers rated the frequency with which she and her partner engaged in three areas of spousal conflict behaviors which formed subscales: verbal reasoning, verbal aggression, and physical aggression and violence. This widely-used scale has shown to be valid and reliable in measuring adult-to-adult verbal and physical aggression (Straus, 1979). Internal consistency for mother's own verbal and physical conflict tactics were .77 and .80, respectively. For their partners, the internal consistency was .89 for verbal and .95 for physical conflict.

4. *Child Behavior Checklist* (CBCL; Achenbach & Edelbrock, 1983). This well-validated checklist asks mothers to assess their child's internalizing, externalizing, and aggressive problems, as well as their school and social functioning. Raw score scale means from the 113 items will be used rather than T scores since the sample includes a non-clinical group; however, the percentage of children in the clinical range will be determined. Total externalizing problem scores, aggressive behavior scores, and social competence scores will be calculated. Items that constitute the PTSD scale (Wolfe, Gentile, & Wolfe, 1989) will also be calculated (CBCL-PTSD).

5. *PTS-Reaction Index–Parent Form* (RI-Parent; as adapted for parent report by Rossman et al., 1997, from Pynoos et al., 1987). This scale assessed symptoms associated with PTS, according to diagnostic criteria from the DSM-III-R. Mothers were asked to rate their perception of the child's symptoms. The RI has been shown to reliably assess stress symptoms following exposure to a broad range of traumatic events.

The correlation between children diagnosed with PTSD and RI scores has been shown to be 0.91 and interrater adult agreement has averaged 94%. Internal consistency in this sample was .95.

Instruments for children were administered in an interview format as follows:

1. *Peabody Picture Vocabulary Test-Revised* (PPVT-R; Robertson & Eisenberg, 1981).The PPVT-R is a measure of verbal IQ and a valid measure of receptive vocabulary. The child is asked to choose from a set of four drawings the best match to a word presented by the examiner. There is a maximum of 150 items, with IQ norms for children ranging in age from 3 to 17 years. This test will be used to ensure group equivalence on general cognitive ability, and to ensure that verbal comprehension is adequate for the experimental tasks.

2. *Leveling/Sharpening Shootout Test* (Santostefano, 1985). This task assesses children's ability to take in information. Here, the child views 63 presentations of a picture of two cartoon-like cowboys. With every third presentation, a detail is omitted. These changes are evenly balanced between central versus peripheral and aggressive versus non-aggressive changes. Children view each picture for 5 seconds and are trained to indicate when they detect a change and what has changed. Before administering the task, children are trained using a benign picture of a chair in which details are omitted. Training is repeated until children correctly report the omitted details. A leveling/sharpening ratio score for the actual test is calculated based on the number of details correctly detected as omitted and how long it took to detect them (e.g., how many presentations after it was originally omitted). Higher scores indicate greater leveling of information, meaning that children detect fewer changes and/or take longer to detect those changes. Separate leveling/sharpening scores are calculated for aggressive and non-aggressive detail (e.g., a gun versus a rain barrel) changes. In addition, two error scores are calculated when children detect incorrect changes. Type A errors involve changes perceived in test stimuli actually present (e.g., the cloud moved or got darker). Type B errors involve imagined details that were never part of the scene (e.g., the fence is gone, when there was never a fence in the picture).

3. *PTS-Reaction Index–Child Form* (RI-Child; as adapted to include pictures by Rossman et al., 1997, from Pynoos et al., 1987). The RI-Child is a 24-item self-report measure that assesses the frequency of PTS symptoms experienced by the child. Pictures are used with each item to enable the child to fully understand the questions. Internal consistency in this sample was .89.

TABLE 3. Measures Used

TYPE OF MEASURE	
DEMOGRAPHIC:	SES, ethnicity, Life Events Questionnaire, maternal ratings of maternal availability and child taking and rejecting maternal help, neighborhood violence, time spent in a violent home, child abuse status via a filed report with Child Protective Services
PARENTAL CONFLICT:	Conflict Tactics Scales (verbal and physical aggression)
PTSD:	PTSD scale of the Child Behavior Checklist, PTSD Reaction Index (parent and child forms)
COGNITIVE:	Leveling/Sharpening Shoot Out Test (L/S ratio for aggressive and non-aggressive cues separately), PPVT Verbal IQ
CHILD ADJUSTMENT:	Child Behavior Checklist (total, internalizing and externalizing problem scores and social competence scores), maternal rating of (pre)school performance (scale of 1-9)

Analyses and Results

To address the first question of whether children exposed to interparental violence would show higher levels of PTSD symptoms than non-exposed children, Analyses of Covariance (i.e., SES and minority status were controlled since groups varied initially) were conducted for total symptom scores for children's and mothers' judgments about children's PTSD symptoms on the RI, and on the PTSD subscale of the CBCL. As noted in Table 5, there were significant group differences on these measures suggesting that exposed children had significantly higher total symptom scores than non-exposed children on all measures ($p < .00$). The Pearson correlation of these two mother-report PTSD indices were $r = .63$, $p < .00$, $n = 376$. The correlation between mothers' and children's judgments about children's PTSD symptoms for the RI was .39, $p < .000$, $n = 357$.

Following these analyses of total symptom scores, the presence versus absence symptom scores were calculated. Items from the RI were independently selected to reflect each grouping based on La Greca et al. (1996) (see Table 4). Only 16 of the 24 items of the RI were used due to the difficulty in clearly determining the grouping classification of eight of the items. Taking a conservative approach to the responses obtained from the RI, a symptom was considered to be present or "high frequency" if the participant endorsed "3–lot of the time" when being asked to rate on a 3-point scale how often a particular symptom was experienced. The meeting of PTSD diagnostic criteria B, C and D was then checked by determining how many children had "high frequency" symptoms for the appropriate number of items in each

TABLE 4. PTS-RI Items that Associate with Criteria B, C & D on the DSM-IV*

DSM-IV criteria:	PTS-RI Items:	
Criterion B: Intrusive / Re-experiencing	2.	Feeling upset and scared when you think about your parents fighting.
	3.	Picture or sounds popping into your head.
	4.	Thoughts about your parents fighting coming back into your head when you don't want them to.
	5.	Having bad dreams.
	6.	Thinking your parents might start fighting again.
	23.	Making up a story in your head (or playing a pretend game) about your parents fighting.
Criterion C: Avoidance	7.	How often feel good about things you do with friends, at school, in sports. (reverse scored)
	8.	Feeling more alone now.
	9.	Feeling so upset/sad/scared/mad that you don't want to know how you feel.
	10.	Feeling so upset/sad/scared/mad that you can't talk or cry about It.
	16.	Trying to stay away from things that make you think about your parents fighting.
Criterion D: Hyperarousal	11.	Feeling more jumpy or nervous now than you used to.
	12.	Having a hard time sleeping.
	14.	Thoughts and feelings about parents fighting get in the way of remembering things in class.
	15.	Hard time paying attention.
	24.	Feeling grumpy and mad.

* Items not included in this classification:
1. How much parents fights would upset kids.
13. Feeling bad or guilty.
17. Doing things you haven't done for a long time
    (like wetting your bed, wanting to be near someone).
18. Feeling sick. (Somatization)
19. Doing reckless things.
20. Play old games instead of new games.
21. Having new fears.
22. Not wanting to talk about parents fighting.

DSM-IV PTSD symptom grouping. It is important to note that this procedure cannot be used for formal diagnosis since the study did not assess the duration of these symptoms (Criterion E of DSM-IV), and whether these symptoms were causing clinically significant distress or impairment in functioning (Criterion F of DSM-IV).

In terms of the children's self-report of symptoms on the RI, a higher percentage of Exposed/Abused Shelter children met diagnostic criteria for PTSD than the Community children, exposed or non-exposed ($p = .03$). A substantial percentage of Exposed Shelter children also met the diagnostic criteria (24%), but they were not significantly lower than the Exposed/ Abused Shelter group, nor was the percentage significantly higher than that from the Community groups according to a Newman-Keuls post hoc test. In addition, exposed children showed the same pattern of higher behavior problems (p < .00) and poorer school (p < .00) and social (p < .00) functioning found in previous research (Jaffe, Wolfe, & Wilson, 1990; Sternberg et al., 1993) (See Table 5).

To address the second question of whether these same clusters of symptoms come together for children's symptom responses, children's reports of their symptoms on DSM-IV marker items of the RI-PTSD were factor analyzed using a Principal Components Analysis and then the resulting number of factors were rotated using an Oblimin rotation to achieve a simple struc-

TABLE 5. Analyses of Group Differences

Adjusted Group Means

Measure	Non-Exposed Comm.	Exposed Comm.	Exposed Shelter	Exposed/ Abused Shelter	Sig.
CBCL-PTSD	.22[a]	.51[b]	.50[b]	.53[b]	.00
RI-PTSD(m)	1.53[a]	2.47[b]	2.80[b]	2.69[b]	.00
RI-PTSD(c) (Y > O)	1.72[a]	1.98[b]	1.95[b]	2.04[b]	.00
%PTSDDiag.	15%[a]	5%[a]	24%	36%[b]	.03
arousal/avoid (Y > O) (G > B)	1.66[a]	2.13[b]	1.93[b]	2.07[b]	.00
dysphoric (Y > O)	1.82	1.57	1.86	2.03	ns
intrusions (Y > O)	1.79[a]	2.09[b]	2.11[b]	2.19[b]	.01
CBCL-Internal.	.17[a]	.42[b]	.35[b]	.37[b]	.00
CBCL-External.	.21[a]	.52[b]	.45[b]	.46[b]	.00
CBCL-SocialComp.	5.98	5.97	4.64	3.77	.00
SchoolPerform.	7.10	6.15	5.83	5.46	.00

Note. SES and minority status covaried. Means with different letters are significantly different (p < .05) using Newman-Keuls post hoc tests. CBCL scores are raw score scale means used as recommended for non-clinical samples (Achenbach & Edelbrock, 1983). These scores corrected by omitting PTSD items. Y and O refer to younger (4-7 years) and older (8-13 years) children and G and B refer to boys and girls.

ture where factors were allowed to relate to each other, since that seemed likely. Using skree, root one, and meaningfulness criteria, three factors were retained and rotated. The items marking each factor and their factor loadings are presented in Table 6. These factors accounted for 51.6% of the variance in children's symptom responses.

The response to the question of whether children's symptom reports would cluster in ways similar to the three DSM-IV symptom clusters would have to be "yes and no." The first factor extracted appears to be a pretty good representation of the DSM-IV re-experiencing and intrusion cluster of symptoms. However, the second factor brings together items from both the DSM-IV hyper-arousal and avoidance clusters of symptoms. In addition, the third factor combines a feeling of being disengaged with activities, school and so on, with irritable affect and traumatic play. Factoring was conducted in different age breakdowns and for exposed children only to check that they would be present in different subgroups of children. All three factors were recogniz-

TABLE 6. Groupings of PTSD Symptoms from Children's Responses

(51.6% of variance in responses explained by these factors)

LOADINGS		RE-EXPERIENCING/INTRUSION Items (6.8%)
.82	3.	Sounds about parent fighting come into your head
.77	4.	Thoughts about parent fighting pop into your head
.71	2.	You feel really upset when you think of parents fighting
.59	6.	You feel that parent fighting might happen again
.50	5.	You have bad dreams about parents fighting
		AROUSAL/AVOIDANCE Items (35.4%)
.81	18.	Feel sick more than before
.75	12.	Have a hard time sleeping
.60	8.	Feel more alone now
.52	11.	Feel more jumpy or nervous
.50	15.	Find it hard to pay attention
.49	10.	Feel so upset that you can't cry about it (parent fights)
.44	9.	Feel so upset about it you don't want to know how you feel
.36	16.	Try to stay away from things that remind you of it
		DYSPHORIA Items (9.4%)
.90	7.	Don't feel as good about things as you used to (e.g., school, friends)
.74	24.	Feel more grumpy or mad now
.52	23.	Make up pretend stories or plays about parents fighting

CORRELATIONS AMONG FACTORS:	Intrusions	Arousal/Avoid
Arousal/Avoid	.49	
Dysphoria	.11	.17

able in all of these subgroup analyses, but clearly need to be replicated in other data sets prior to taking them too seriously. Particularly the dysphoria factor is suspect since it includes so few items even though it consistently appeared in all subgroup analyses.

The coming together of arousal and avoidance symptoms in a factor seems in some ways not only different from DSM-IV groupings but also counterintuitive. However, it seems more sensible in remembering that even depression with children often involves some level of agitation rather than the more slowed down depressive state usually diagnosed in adults. It is instructive, in addition, to recall what the brain-body system may be preparing for in response to trauma, namely fight or flight. When one considers that children in parentally violent families are usually at a power disadvantage, their most effective coping strategy may be flight. When interviewing the exposed children for our study, it is not uncommon to hear them saying that when their parents fight, they would hide in their own rooms and pretend to be asleep. In certain instances, some of the children may say to us that they never really see or hear their parents fighting, when their mother's report points to the contrary due to the severe nature of the spousal aggression. It is even more interesting when siblings differed drastically in their report of how much violence they witnessed, when in fact they all lived under the same roof. One could not help but wonder in these situations, whether some of these children opted to escape from the violent situation physically and/or psychologically in order to deal with the trauma.

On the other hand, Jenkins, Smith, and Graham (1989) found in a community sample that 71% of children aged 9-12 years said they would intervene in some way in parent quarrels. This would seem directly opposed to the flight hypothesis. However, while these couples were disharmonious (i.e., reported at least one quarrel in the past year), it is not clear how many of them were physically aggressive in their interactions, which may influence their children's response. A measure of children's symptoms, interestingly, was significantly related only to two of the coping strategies children reported: self-blame and offering comfort to parents following a quarrel. Thus, children with symptom linkages to their behavior were not necessarily the ones who were most actively intervening during the quarrels. Rossman and Rosenberg (1992) found that children who reported direct action coping during parent fights were not doing as well as those who reported trying to cope so as to reduce emotional arousal.

The dysphoria factor is somewhat interesting. One gets the picture of a child who is isolated and unhappy and trying to re-work the trauma. Some of these relationships become clearer as we turn to correlations of factor scores for the three empirical children's symptom clusters with other aspects of children's functioning (see Table 7). This will enable us to examine what aspects of children's functioning are related to their PTSD symptom scores.

It can be noted in Table 7 that the arousal/avoidance and intrusion factors relate similarly to various child and family factors, which is not surprising since they correlate substantially with each other (r = .49). Higher scores on both factors are significantly associated with poorer non-aggressive intake, behavior problems, poorer school performance and social competence, being abused, living in a minority household, lower SES, greater family adversity, higher verbal and physical marital aggression and neighborhood violence, and lower maternal availability. Thus, a whole host of adversity or risk factors are associated with arousal/avoidance and intrusion symptoms. The

TABLE 7. Relation of PTSD Symptoms to Child and Family Factors

	AROUSAL/ AVOIDANCE	DYSPHORIA	INTRUSIONS
CHILD FACTORS:			
Poor Nonagg. Info. Intake	.24**	.25**	.26***
Poor Agg. Info. Intake	.09	.27**	.05
Externalizing Behav. Prob.	.26***	.01	.22***
Internalizing Behav. Prob.	.19**	−.04	.16**
School Performance	−.22***	−.09	−.16**
Social Competence	−.17**	−.60***	−.19**
Time in a Violent Home	.09	−.39***	.15*
Child Abuse	.16**	.02	.18**
FAMILY FACTORS:			
Minority Status	.35***	.08	.32***
Low SES	.29***	−.06	.35***
Family Stressors	.28***	−.15**	.33***
Spousal Verbal Agg.	.30***	−.02	.32**
Spousal Physical Agg.	.35***	−.03	.34***
Neighborhood Viol.	.27***	.11	.27***
Mom's Availability	−.16*	−.07	−.14*
Child Rejects Mom's Help	.11	.47***	.11

Note: *** p <.001, **p < .01, * p < .05, two-tail significance for each n.

intrusion factor is also related to more time in a violent family. On the other hand, higher dysphoria factor scores are significantly linked with poor non-aggressive and aggressive information intake, poorer social competence, less time in a violent home, fewer family stressors, and a child rejecting help from mother. High scores on this factor paint a picture of a child who is somewhat shut down and pulling away, but in less adverse circumstances that are not associated with parental violence. Perhaps dysphoria is an earlier reaction or a reaction to lesser exposure to neighborhood violence (a marginal relation-ship) or to adversity that is not tapped by our adversity measures. Or perhaps it simply identifies resistant, socially rejected and informationally shut down children. It is interesting that the dysphoria factor did not relate significantly to internalizing scores from the CBCL. Two possibilities exist: internalizing is a relatively broad-band scale which taps more than social withdrawal, and these other dimensions, such as depression, may not be related to dysphoria; and, methodologically, the CBCL involves adult rather than child report and it may be more difficult for adults to notice internalizing symptoms. More research is needed to determine the replicability and usefulness of this small grouping of symptoms.

CONCLUSION AND IMPLICATIONS

In sum, it appears that children's self-reported PTSD symptoms did not form neat factor groupings in this sample, except for re-experiencing-type symptoms, which came together in a manner that was similar to the DSM-IV PTSD diagnostic criteria. It would be extremely valuable to attempt to repli-cate these empirical symptom groupings in additional samples. However, they do highlight the complexity of diagnosing PTSD for children. Additional-al diagnostic complexity occurs because many symptoms that form a part of PTSD diagnosis for children also occur as key symptoms for other diagnoses often used for children and child witnesses such as Depression or ADHD (Rossman, 1994). For example, ADHD symptoms of restlessness, not listen-ing, being easily distracted, behaving without considering risk, and having a hard time sustaining attention, are all PTSD symptoms on the RI. Similarly, Depression symptoms of irritable mood, recurrent thoughts of death, psycho-motor agitation, sleep difficulties, feelings of guilt and diminished interest in activities are also all RI symptom items. This points to the potential risk of wrongly diagnosing children with PTSD as having ADHD and thus the administration of Ritalin, which may increase intrusions for some trauma-tized children.

A child's history can sometimes be used to discriminate between trauma and ADHD. For ADHD there is usually a family history of hyperactivity and attention problems as well as the child having a history of being over-active, risk-taking and impulsive from an early age. On the other hand, for PTSD diagnosis, a history of traumatic exposure is required. However, some children will have both types of history, making the diagnostic issue even more complicated. Sleep difficulties and nightmares are more common with traumatized children, but can occur with ADHD children as they adjust to medication. In sum, if there are diagnostic uncertainties with traumatized children it may be useful to wait six months to make a formal diagnosis for children exposed to parental violence to see what symptoms still seem prominent after a child has been away from a violent home for some time.

The above review of research, theory and current findings leads to several suggestions for work with children exposed to parental violence. First, it appears that some of the children may be having difficulty with information intake and/or processing. That means that information we want these children to have in treatment or about shelter rules may need to be repeated several times so that they have a better chance of incorporating it into their schema. In addition to using auditory and verbal cues in presenting information, it may be more effective to also make use of visual (in the form of pictures) and kinesthetic cues, since it is essentially repeating the information for different modes of processing. The informational difficulties may also mean that the information we receive from these children may be poorly integrated. This is because they may not have a clear picture of their negative experiences, or these experiences may not have been consolidated in memory sufficiently to be easily available. As a result, some evaluation for adequate intake and usage of new information could be helpful. If children appear to have difficulties, visual and auditory games that require information search and application (played in a setting where the children feel safe) can be used to enhance information processing.

Another implication is that exposed children will need to be evaluated for posttraumatic symptoms and distress. Indeed, similar to the traumatic effect of physical and sexual abuse, it is becoming clear that children can be as traumatized by being exposed to violence towards loved ones. Many forms of intervention from different theoretical orientations (as reviewed by Kerig et al. in this volume) are available to help children cope with posttraumatic distress and reduce symptoms. A medication evaluation may also be useful for some children.

Finally, the levels of traumatic distress experienced by some of the children suggest that longer recovery time may be needed. One policy implication of this treatment need is that communities need to work to provide more longer-term programs for battered mothers and their children. One example would be the transitional living programs provided by some crisis shelters. These may be particularly useful, not only because they provide prolonged treatment opportunities but also because children are in a safe place for a longer period of time. Safety and structure are two aspects of successful trauma intervention. Another policy implication is that it may be necessary to make longer-term treatment available in the home, particularly to battered mothers with very young children, in order to ensure that the home stays safe and that intervention services are delivered. As we learn more about the symptoms and distress experienced by children exposed to interparental violence and personal abuse, more tools will become available to relieve their distress and allow them to re-enter the pathways of normal development.

REFERENCES

Achenbach, T. M., & Edelbrock, C. S. (1983). *Manual for the Child Behavior Checklist and Revised Child Behavioral Profile.* Burlington, VT: University of Vermont.

American Psychiatric Association. (1994). Diagnostic and statistical manual of mental disorders (DSM-IV). Washington, DC: APA.

Charney, D. S., Deutch, A. Y., Krystal, J. H., Southwick, S. M., & Davis, M. (1993). Psychobiological mechanisms of posttraumatic stress disorder. *Archives of General Psychiatry, 50,* 294-305.

Cox, T. (1978). *Stress.* Baltimore, MD: University Park Press.

Crick, N. R., & Dodge, K. A. (1994). A review and reformulation of social information-processing mechanisms in children's social adjustment. *Psychological Bulletin, 115,* 74-101.

Dawud, S., Cortes, R. M., Lowensohn, O., Hart, J., Posner, S., Sternberg, K. J., & Lamb, M. E. (1991). Effects of domestic violence on children's adjustment in school. Paper presented at the meeting of the Society for Research in Child Development, Seattle, WA.

Devoe, E., & Graham-Bermann, S. (1997). Predictors of post-traumatic stress symptoms in battered women and their children. Poster presented at the Second International Conference on Children Exposed to Family Violence, London, Ontario, Canada.

Doumas, D., Margolin, G., & John, R. S. (1994). The intergenerational transmission of aggression across three generations. *Journal of Family Violence, 9,* 157-175.

Dunn, L. M. (1965). *Expanded manual for the Peabody Picture Vocabulary Test.* Circle Pines, MN: American Guidance Service, Inc.

Emery, R. E. (1989). Family violence. *American Psychologist, 44,* 321-328.

Fish-Murray, C. C., Koby, E. V., & van der Kolk, B. A. (1987). Evolving ideas: The effect of abuse on children's thought. In B. A. van der Kolk, *Psychological trauma* (pp. 89-100). Washington, DC: American Psychiatric Association.

Fletcher, K. E. (1996). Childhood posttraumatic stress disorder. In E. J. Mash & R. A. Barkley (Eds.), *Child psychopathology* (pp. 242-276). New York: Guilford.

Foa, E. B., & Riggs, D. S. (1995). Posttraumatic stress disorder following assault: Theoretical considerations and empirical findings. *Current Directions in Psychological Science, 4,* 61-65.

Frankenhaeuser, M. (1975a). Experimental approaches to the study of catecholamines and emotion. In L. Levi (Ed.), *Emotions: Their parameters and measurement* (pp. 75-97). New York: Raven Press.

Frankenhaeuser, M. (1975b). Sympathetic-adrenomedullary activity, behaviour and the psychological environment. In P. H. Venables & M. J. Christie (Eds.), *Research on psychophysiology* (pp. 135-156). New York: Wiley.

Garmezy, N., Masten, A. S., & Tellegen, A. (1984). The study of stress and competence in children: A building block for developmental psychopathology. *Child Development*, *55*, 97-111.

Gomes-Schwartz, B., Horowitz, J. M., Cardarelli, A. P., & Sauzier, M. (1990). The aftermath of child sexual abuse: 18 months later. In B. Gomes-Schwartz, J. M. Horowitz, & A. P. Cardarelli (Eds.), *Child sexual abuse: The initial effects* (pp. 132-152). Newbury Park, CA: Sage.

Graham-Bermann, S. A., & Levendosky, A. A. (1998). Traumatic stress symptoms in children of battered women. *J. Interpersonal Violence*, *13*, 111-128.

Holden, G. W., & Ritchie, K. L. (1991). Linking extreme marital discord, child rearing, and child behavior problems: Evidence from battered women. *Child Development*, *62*, 311-327.

Horowitz, M. J., & Reidbord, S. P. (1992). Memory, emotion, and response to stress. In S. Christianson (Ed.), *The handbook of emotion and memory: Research and theory* (pp. 343-358). Hillsdale, NJ: Lawrence Erlbaum Associates.

Jaffe, P. G., Wolfe, D. A., & Wilson, S. K. (1990). *Children of battered women*. Newbury Park, CA: Sage.

Jenkins, J. M., Smith, M. A., & Graham, P. J. (1989). Coping with parental quarrels. *Journal of the American Academy of Child and Adolescent Psychiatry*, *28*, 182-189.

Koverola, C. (1995). Posttraumatic stress disorder. In R.T. Ammerman & M. Hersen (Eds.), *Handbook of child behavior therapy in the psychiatric setting* (pp. 389-408). New York: Wiley-Interscience.

La Greca, A., Silverman, W. K., Vernberg, E. M., & Prinstein, M. J. (1996). Symptoms of posttraumatic stress in children after Hurricane Andrew: A prospective study. *Journal of Consulting and Clinical Psychology*, *64* (4), 712-713.

LeDeux, J. E. (1994). Emotion, memory, and the brain. *Scientific American*, June, 50-57.

Lehman, P. (1997). The development of posttraumatic stress disorder (PTSD) in a sample of child witnesses to mother assault. *Journal of Family Violence*, *12*, 241-256.

McLeer, S.V., Callaghan, M., Henry, D., & Wallen, J. (1994). Psychiatric disorders in sexually abused children. *Journal of the American Academy of Child & Adolescent Psychiatry*, *33*, 313-319.

Miller, D. (1977). *Handbook of research design and social measurement*. New York: Davis McKay Co., Inc.

Peplar, D. J., & Moore, T. E. (1989). Children exposed to family violence: Home environments and cognitive functioning. Paper presented at the meeting of the Society for Research in Child Development, Kansas City, MO.

Piaget, J. (1952). *The origins of intelligence in children*. New York: International Universities Press.

Pynoos, R. S., Frederick, C., Nader, K., Arroyo, W., Steinberg, A., Eth, S., Nunez, F., & Fairbanks, L. (1987). Life threat and posttraumatic stress in school age children. *Archives of General Psychiatry*, *44*, 1057-1063.

Rieder, C., & Cicchetti, D. (1989). Organizational perspective on cognitive control functioning and cognitive-affective balance in maltreated children. *Developmental Psychology, 25,* 382-393.

Robertson, G., & Eisenberg, J. (1981). *Peabody Picture Vocabulary Test-Revised technical supplement.* Circle Pines, MN: American Guidance Service.

Rosenberg, M. S. (1984). *The impact of witnessing interparental violence on children's behavior, perceived competence and social problem solving abilities.* Unpublished doctoral dissertation, University of Virginia, VA.

Rossman, B. B. R. (1994). Children in violent families: Current diagnostic and treatment considerations. *Family Violence and Sexual Assault Bulletin, 10,* 29-34.

Rossman, B. B. R., Bingham, R. D., & Emde, R. N. (1997). Symptomatology and adaptive functioning for children exposed to normative stressors, dog attack, and parental violence. *Journal of the American Academy of Child and Adolescent Psychiatry, 36,* 1-9.

Rossman, B. B. R., & Rosenberg, M. S. (1992). Family stress and functioning in children: The moderating effects of children's beliefs about their control over parental conflict. *Journal of Child Psychology and Psychiatry, 33,* 699-715.

Santostefano, S. (1985). *Cognitive control therapy with children and adolescents.* New York: Pergamon Press.

Santostefano, S., & Rieder, C. (1984). Cognitive controls and aggression in children: The concept of cognitive-affective balance. *Journal of Consulting and Clinical Psychology, 52,* 46-56.

Selye, H. (1956). *The stress of life.* New York: McGraw-Hill.

Silvern, L., & Kaersvang, L. (1989). The traumatized children of violent marriages. *Child Welfare, 68,* 421-436.

Sternberg, K. J., Lamb, M. E., Greenbaum, C., Cicchetti, D., Dawud, S., Cortex, R. M., Krispin, O., & Lorey, F. (1993). Effects of domestic violence on children's behavior problems and depression. *Developmental Psychology, 29,* 44-52.

Straus, M. A. (1979). Measuring intrafamily conflict and violence: The conflict tactics (CT) scales. *Journal of Marriage and the Family,* February, 75-88.

van der Kolk, B. A. (1996). The body keeps score: Approaches to the psychobiology of posttraumatic stress disorder. In B. A. van der Kolk, A. C. McFarlane, & L. Weisaeth (Eds.), *Traumatic stress: The effects of overwhelming experience on mind, body, and society* (pp. 214-241). New York: Guilford.

van der Kolk, B. A. (1994). The body keeps score: Memory and the evolving psychobiology of posttraumatic stress. *Harvard Review of Psychiatry, 1,* 253-265.

Van Meyel, R. (1997). Play based family therapy: A treatment model for preschoolers who have witnessed woman abuse. Paper presented at the Second International Conference on Children Exposed to Family Violence, London, Ontario, Canada.

Wolfe, D. A., & Mosk, M. (1983). Behavioral comparisons of children from abusive and distressed families. *Journal of Consulting and Clinical Psychology, 51,* 702-708.

Wolfe, D. A, Zak, L., Wilson, S., & Jaffe, P. (1986). Child witnesses to violence between parents: Critical issues in behavioral and social adjustment. *J. Abnorm. Child Psychol., 14,* 95-104.

Wolfe, V. V., Gentile, C., & Wolfe, D. A. (1989). The impact of sexual abuse on children: A PTSD formulation. *Behavior Therapy, 20,* 215-228.

The Relevance of Narrative Research with Children Who Witness War and Children Who Witness Woman Abuse

Helene Berman

SUMMARY. Children throughout the world have many opportunities to witness violence, in the home and on the battlefield. While the experiences of children of war and children of battered women vary considerably, their stories are, in some senses, remarkably similar. Both groups witnessed a multitude of atrocities, and almost all endured at least some degree of loss, uprooting, and separation. Despite the similarities, however, there are significant differences. Most notably, the children of war experienced their pain and suffering collectively, with family and friends who loved them and who they loved in return. In contrast, the children of battered women suffered alone, often going to elaborate lengths to ensure that others not learn about the horror in their homes. In this article, findings from a recent critical narrative study with these two groups are presented. The sample consisted of 16 children of war and 16 children of battered women, ages 10-17. The relevance of narrative research with this population is discussed and implications for researchers and clinicians are presented. *[Article copies available for a fee from The Haworth Document Delivery Service: 1-800-342-9678. E-mail address: getinfo@haworthpressinc.com <Website: http://www.haworthpressinc.com>]*

This article is funded in part by a fellowship from the Ontario Ministry of Health, The Canadian Nurses' Foundation, and the Helen Glass Award for Health Promotion Research, Sigma Theta Tau, Iota Omicron Chapter.

Address correspondence to: Helene Berman, PhD, RN, University of Western Ontario, School of Nursing, London, Ontario N6A 5C1, Canada.

[Haworth co-indexing entry note]: "The Relevance of Narrative Research with Children Who Witness War and Children Who Witness Woman Abuse." Berman, Helene. Co-published simultaneously in *Journal of Aggression, Maltreatment & Trauma* (The Haworth Maltreatment & Trauma Press, an imprint of The Haworth Press, Inc.) Vol. 3, No. 1 (#5), 2000, pp. 107-125; and: *Children Exposed to Domestic Violence: Current Issues in Research, Intervention, Prevention, and Policy Development* (ed: Robert A. Geffner, Peter G. Jaffe, and Marlies Sudermann) The Haworth Maltreatment & Trauma Press, an imprint of The Haworth Press, Inc., 2000, pp. 107-125. Single or multiple copies of this article are available for a fee from The Haworth Document Delivery Service [1-800-342-9678, 9:00 a.m. - 5:00 p.m. (EST). E-mail address: getinfo@haworthpressinc.com].

KEYWORDS. Refugee youth, health, violence, critical theory, qualitative research, children of battered women, post-traumatic stress

Your Choice

Friendship, a feeling, a thought.
A sort of caring, a sort of concern.
It is invisible, but can be seen,
It is in you, it is in me.

Hatred, a cruelty, a wall
A sort of loathing, a sort of aversion.
It is mean, it is vicious,
It is in you, it is in me.
Your Choice.

–Seth, 14 years

Children throughout the world have many opportunities to witness violence. Elsewhere in this book, statistics have been presented documenting the extent to which children witness violence directed toward their mothers in their homes. With respect to war-related violence, it is difficult to state with certainty the number of children who are witnesses. However, the U.S. National Defence Council Foundation (1996) has counted as many as 70 wars in the world today. One consequence of this scenario is that many people have been forced to escape from their homes and countries. According to the United Nations High Commissioner for Refugees (1995), there are currently 44 million refugees or displaced persons. About three-quarters of these are women and children. Given these figures, it is reasonable to assert that many children, on virtually every continent, are growing up amid some form of violence.

The experiences of children who spend their early developmental years in countries which are actively engaged in warfare vary considerably. Many have personally experienced trauma before and during escape from their homeland. Others have witnessed a multitude of atrocities, including the killing or torture of family and friends. Like children of battered women, almost all have endured at least some degree of loss, uprooting, and separation (Athey & Ahearn, 1991; Berman, 1996). In addition, children of war typically experience "cultural bereavement" and subsequent identity problems as they strive to reconcile conflicting cultural values and beliefs (Eisenbruck, 1988). As is the case with children who grow up in families where interactions between parents are characterized by violence, children who grow up in war zones may be direct recipients of violence, or they may experience it more vicariously, as witnesses to violence. It is also possible that children do not actually witness the violence, but are keenly aware that it has occurred, and profoundly affected by that knowledge.

Whether violence is expressed overtly, or in subtle and more insidious ways, in the home or on the battlefield, its effects on the health of individuals, families, and communities are becoming increasingly clear. While the body of knowledge related to children of battered women has grown substantially during the last decade, as is documented throughout this book, research with children of war is still relatively sparse. In this chapter, the relevance of narrative research with children who witness violence is examined; literature pertaining to children of war is reviewed; and the results of a recent study which included both children of war and children of battered women, including common themes and areas of divergence, are described. Although research and action have traditionally been considered to be separate and distinct activities, the use of narrative approaches to combine scholarship and advocacy is explored.

A CRITICAL NARRATIVE STUDY

The stories of children whose lives have been touched by violence are as diverse as their experiences. Yet, when we listen, we hear similarities, common themes and patterns which reflect a shared social and historical context. Traditionally, children have not been encouraged to talk openly about their experiences (Coles, 1986; Garbarino, Kostelny, & Dubrow, 1991). In her phenomenological study of children in day care, Polakow (1992) noted the tendency among researchers to examine the experiences of children through the eyes of the adults in their lives. As a result of this "adultcentric bias," the voices of children have remained relatively silent.

Narrative inquiry has been called a theoretical framework, a methodology for research and practice, and a paradigmatic perspective (Coles, 1989; Polkinghorne, 1988; Sandelowski, 1991). Although many viewpoints are recognized, one shared assumption is a consensus as to the pervasive nature of stories and storytelling (Maines & Ulmer, 1993). Individually and collectively, stories offer a way to "make sense" of our experiences. By telling stories, we do more than simply relate a sequence of events, but convey information about the context in which those events occur and meanings they hold for the storytellers, offering insight into larger cultural ideas and values.

Van Maanen (1988), in *Tales of the Field*, described a form of narrative approaches called "critical tales." The interest in such tales is to shed light on larger social, political, or economic issues. Within a critical framework, researchers go beyond the familiar aims of explanation and understanding. They seek not only to describe the world; they wish to change it. Critical narrative analysis best describes the process of knowing upon which this research was based. An assumption underlying this approach is that the contextual dimensions of children's experiences are valued and are inseparable from the ways in which children strive to bring a sense of coherence into their lives.

REVIEW OF LITERATURE

The research with children who have grown up amid war bears some similarity to the literature on children of battered women. While some children experience a multitude of physical and emotional health problems, others demonstrate remarkable resilience and strength. As Beiser and his colleagues (1995) have noted with regard to refugee children, while pre- and postmigration stressors have the potential to result in adverse sequelae, a range of mediating variables likely interact to mitigate harmful effects.

Premigration Stress

Some of the earliest insights into the responses of children to war come from studies with children and adolescents who were evacuated from their homes during World War II (Freud & Burlingham, 1943; Henshaw & Howarth, 1941). A consistent finding was that separation from families was more troublesome than the bombings. Wicks (1988) has recently noted, however, that many of these children endured abuse and neglect in the homes where they were placed, confounding the widely accepted observation that separation was more stressful than the war.

The results of more recent studies substantiate the idea that support systems and family ties are important to children during and after war (Berman, 1996; Fox, Muennich, Cowell, & Montgomery, 1994; Rumbaut, 1991). Laor, Wolmer, Mayes, Gershon, Wiezman, and Cohen (1996) observed that the capacity of mothers to act as a buffer to their children was crucial in minimizing long-term harm among Israeli pre-school children during the Gulf War. While acknowledging the significant "buffering" role of the family network, Macksoud, Aber, and Cohn (1996) observed an "optimal level of family security." Based on their work with children in Kuwait, these investigators reported that children from stable and loving families were less familiar with, and therefore less capable of, coping with the conflict around them.

Whether there is a single construct of war exposure which is harmful to children, or whether their responses depend upon the nature, type, and duration of exposure has received some attention in recent years (Athey & Ahearn, 1991; Chimienti et al., 1991; Jensen & Shaw, 1993; Kuterovac, Kyregrov, & Stuvland, 1994). Macksoud and Aber (1996) reported that the type of traumatic exposures was more important than the number of exposures in their sample of Lebanese children, 10-16 years old. Children exposed to multiple traumas, who were bereaved, separated from their parents, or had witnessed violent acts showed symptoms of PTSD. Interestingly, participation in combat was not related to increased symptomatology.

Postmigration Stress

The experience of migration is typically accompanied by many stressors. Often, there is little time to prepare for escape, making it difficult or impossible to attend to practical issues which might facilitate the resettlement process. Multiple losses, including loss of homes, friends, possessions, and in some cases, parents or siblings, are common. Poverty and racism are well-documented (Beiser et al., 1988).

Separation from family. Separation from family members after migrating to a new country has consistently been identified as a threat to the well-being of refugee youth (Fox et al., 1994; Garbarino et al., 1991). Based on their research with Cambodian refugees, Kinzie et al. (1986, 1991) found that those who, upon arrival in North America, were able to renew ties with at least one family member experienced fewer postmigration difficulties than those who lacked any family contact. These authors concluded family presence was a more important determinant of positive outcomes than either the amount or type of trauma witnessed, or the child's age or gender.

Acculturation. Acculturation is the process of mutual cultural exchange resulting from contact between cultures (Williams & Berry, 1991). Interest in the effects of acculturation on refugee populations is reflected in a variety of studies (Gil, Vega, & Dimas, 1994; Rumbaut, 1991). A positive relationship between an integration acculturation style, whereby the group's cultural identity is maintained in conjunction with efforts to become part of the larger society, and self-esteem was reported by Phinney et al. (1992). Because refugee youth are exposed to the dominant culture's values at school, they often adopt behaviors from the host country sooner than their parents, resulting in inter-generational conflict (Phinney et al., 1990; Rick & Forward, 1992).

Age and gender. The importance of age has received some attention, but results have been inconsistent. Some researchers have suggested that younger children are better able to handle their experiences; others have reached opposite conclusions (Berman, 1996; Elbedour, Bensel, & Bastien, 1993; Garbarino & Kostelny, 1996). It may be postulated that younger children lack the repertoire of coping skills and cognitive abilities available to older children and adolescents. As well, older children may have the benefit of having spent a longer period of time amid peaceful conditions. Eth and Pynoos (1985) have maintained that children's efforts to cope with traumatic stress are a function of maturity, and have described a variety of responses which correspond to children's cognitive and developmental abilities at different stages.

Like the research related to age, conclusions regarding gender are somewhat inconsistent. Several researchers have reported greater frequency of stress responses among females than among their male counterparts (Berman, 1996; Klingman, Sagi, & Raviv, 1993; Kuterovac et al., 1994). Yet others have concluded that boys exposed to violence experience higher stress levels than girls (Elbedour et al., 1993; Garbarino & Kostelny, 1996). In an examination of the effects of state terrorism and exile on indigenous Guatemalan refugee children, Miller (1996) reported no gender or age differences on the Child Behaviour Checklist. Rather than viewing either age or gender as isolated determinants of children's responses, it is possible that age and gender interact to influence responses. Dawes and Tredoux (1989) found that adolescent females were at greater risk for PTSD than adolescent males in South Africa. These investigators suggested that because it is more socially acceptable for boys to participate in warfare, they are less vulnerable than girls. Such options are not available to younger, preschool children, placing them at greater risk.

Post-Traumatic Stress Disorder (PTSD)

During the past 15 years, many investigators have documented the occurrence of PTSD in refugee youth from El Salvador and Nicaragua (Arroyo & Eth, 1985); Cambodia (Kinzie et al., 1989; Sack et al., 1985, 1995); Afghanistan (Mghir et al., 1995); South Africa (Magwaza et al., 1995); Bosnia (Weine et al., 1995); and Croatia (Ajdukovic & Ajdukovic, 1993). These studies have shown that PTSD symptoms may persist for many years (Kinzie & Sack, 1991) and that children can be traumatized in direct and indirect ways (Saigh, 1991).

Each of these studies contributes to a general understanding of the stressful nature of early exposure to violence. However, the use of PTSD as an organizing framework for understanding children's responses has some important limitations. Garbarino and his colleagues (1991) wrote about children living in war zones around the world and in the "war zones of Chicago." As these authors observed, for many of these young people, trauma is not an isolated event, but is more chronic in nature, pervading every aspect of daily life. For them, there is no "post" trauma period. The challenge they face is to find ways of making sense of events which seem quite senseless, not to get over a single bad experience.

Conceptually, concerns about ethnocentric biases underlying PTSD have been raised (Bracken, Giller, & Summerfield, 1995; DiNicola, 1996; Zur, 1996). As Bracken et al. have noted, PTSD is derived from a western philosophical orientation whereby the individual is accorded a central place, a perspective which is not shared by many cultural groups. Further, Bracken and colleagues suggest that there is a flawed assumption that responses to trauma are universally experienced, an assumption which has resulted in a tendency to overstate the similarities and minimize the differences in responses. Given these issues, it would seem incumbent upon those interested in understanding children's responses to difficult life events to acknowledge the varied political and cultural realities in which those events occur.

RESEARCH FINDINGS

A convenience sample of 16 children of war and 16 children of battered women, ages 10-17, was selected from a variety of community sources in a mid-sized city in Southwestern Ontario and a large mid-western city in the United States. The children who had witnessed war-related violence included eleven females and five males from 14 families. Of these, seven came from Bosnia, five from Somalia, two from Burundi, and two from Liberia. The children from Bosnia were Muslim. Those from Burundi were members of the Tutsi ethnic minority. All except two of these families were dependent upon public assistance. While many of the parents of the refugee children had professional positions in their native countries, they typically have been unable to find jobs in North America. The group of children who had witnessed woman abuse included nine females and seven males from twelve families. All of these families except three were receiving public assistance. None of the children were still living amid violence at the time of their participation in this study. The children of war had left the war-torn countries; the children of battered women were no longer living with their mothers' abusive partners. Although the underlying conflicts in each of these countries had been present for many years, the onset of war was preceded by years of relative peace. In this sense, the children in this research differed from children growing up in such places as Beirut, Northern Ireland, Mozambique, or South Africa who spent their childhoods never knowing what it was like to live under peaceful conditions.

The children were interviewed either individually or in small groups. The primary instrument was an interview guide which consisted of open-ended questions designed to elicit the children's stories about their lives amid violence, their lives since coming to North America or since their mothers moved away from the abusive partners, and their hopes and dreams for the future. Stories were analysed using techniques for the analysis of narrative data (Mishler, 1995; Riessman, 1992). Two weeks later, I met with the children a second time. During this session, emerging themes were shared and modified through the processes of dialogue, reflection, and critique. All of the names used are pseudonyms.

The Early Years: "It Was Just Normal"

Both groups of children perceived their early years as "normal," but what they described was vastly different. The children of war told stories about their lives before the outbreak of war, sharing rich descriptions of their homes, their schools, and their friends. Repeatedly, they spoke of cherished memories, smiling and laughing as they recalled happier times.

Maja, a 13-year-old female who came to Canada from Bosnia when she was 10 years, described a world in which her emotional and material needs were met more than adequately. She was completely unaware that something so terrible could happen to bring it all to such an abrupt end. "I was born in the city of Derventa. I was just living my normal life, I didn't think anything would happen. I had the same life I have here. There is no difference."

Medina, a 14-year-old female from Bosnia, recalled her past similarly. She had friends and family who loved her, and her view of the world was characterized by racial and ethnic tolerance.

> Just last night we were watching a tape that my mom brought from our country. There was a party, that was 1990. There were Muslims, Serbs, Croatians. There was no difference. They were all happy. They were having a good time. I asked my parents, "Did you ever think that what happened to you could happen after that party?" They started laughing because they never thought that what happened to us could be reality. We were all living really nice. We had everything. . . . If somebody told me that in 1990 a war will start in your country, I wouldn't believe it because it seemed impossible to me, I was just a kid, I didn't really think about it. But when everything started then I realized it could happen.

Claudine came to Canada from Burundi when she was 13 years old, shortly after the 1993 coup which resulted in the death of President Ndadaye and the subsequent massacre of about 50,000 Tutsis by the Hutu majority. Although Burundi is ranked the eighth poorest country in the world, and the conflict which erupted in 1993 had been simmering for many years, Claudine told about a life which was comfortable and seemingly carefree. Her family are Tutsis. Her father was an economist. Her stepmother did not work outside of the home.

> I lived in Bujumbura, the capital city. We had our own house. It was big. In Burundi, you live with a person who is taking care of your kids. Another person cooked. I lived with my family, mom, dad, my two brothers, an aunt, my grandmother, and the two people who worked for us. We had fun, you could go everywhere and now [after the war broke out] you can't because you [could] be killed and today the children can't go to school because there is violence.

Over and again, the childhood memories of the children of war were joyful. When asked to describe happy occasions, they had no difficulty doing so. Many laughed and cried as they told of treasured moments. They described lives surrounded by physical beauty and emotional contentment. They felt secure in their place in the world, believed that their worlds would remain that way forever, and as they repeatedly stated, there was no reason to believe otherwise.

The children of battered women also spoke about their "normal" lives, but the stories they told were different from the stories heard by the children of war. This group portrayed their homes as places marked by constant fighting, audible silences, and little joy. Like the children of war, many were tearful as they shared their stories, but unlike that group, their tears were not tears of joy, but a manifestation of their profound pain, sadness, and shame.

Donna, a 15-year-old female, described a litany of abuse inflicted by her stepfather, not only toward her mother, but also toward herself and her 14-year-old sister, Lucy. She described a home of constant fear, where outbursts by her stepfather were frequent, unprovoked, and unpredictable. Still, she never believed that her family life was extraordinary in any respect. "I didn't realize it was abuse until later. Then I thought it goes on like this in every family. Mom didn't say it was wrong so I just thought 'Oh, it's all right'. " Lucy portrayed life in their home in much the same way as her older sister. The atmosphere of fear which pervaded the entire home was evident in her words:

> You would only go in your bedroom to sleep, you don't go to play or nothing. You stay in the basement until it's time for bed, on the weekends you would stay down there. We had toys down there, but you couldn't play with the toys because that would make a mess. I would have to clean the basement and make sure the toilets were clean. He would swear at us and poke us a lot. It would leave bruises. Or he'd slap us across the head and say, "You're stupid." We never showed mom the bruises because we were scared. We weren't allowed around our mom because he was possessive.

Lucy seemed to have some intuitive sense that her family life was not the way other families interacted. Yet, she reluctantly accepted her stepfather's insistence that fighting is the norm in most families. "He just told me everybody's house is like this. I always asked him, 'Then how come on TV they don't show that?' And he always just said, 'It's not true on TV. All parents fight all the time. It's just something that happens.' After a while, I began to believe it."

Asked to recall happy moments, these children typically described occasions which were intended to be joyous or fun, but which "ended in disaster." Birthday parties often ended in fighting, family outings deteriorated, and were in some cases abruptly terminated, over seemingly trivial disputes. For many, the happier times occurred when they were in the shelter with their mothers. It was there that they first began to learn that what was going on in their homes was perhaps not the way it ought to be. And it was there that people seemed to care about them. Noting this irony, one perceptive female stated, "It's like the happy times and the sad times were all mixed up."

The perception that their lives were "normal" was heard again and again. Yet, the "normal" everyday world inhabited by children of war was one which bore little resemblance to the "normal" everyday world of children of battered women. For the children of war, this "normal" world was characterized by peace, love for family and friends, and safety. The "normal" world which the children of battered women spoke of was a place where violence and intimidation pervaded many facets of daily life, where interactions were characterized by conflict and tension, and where disappointments were expected. In retrospect, these children repeatedly stated that they now recognize that their experiences were not "normal," but at the time, many believed that what went on in their homes was no different from what occurred in most people's homes.

When the Skiing Fields Became Cannon Fields

The eruption of war marked a sudden end to everything the children of war knew and loved. Peace was replaced by killings, torture, and other violent acts, which became commonplace and random. Taken-for-granted assumptions about the world were shattered; the predictable became unpredictable; neighbors turned against neighbors. Their sense of safety and security was destroyed, leaving them frightened and confused. As twelve-year-old Sonja stated:

> Sarajevo is an Olympic city. It is surrounded by beautiful mountains on which we used to ski and enjoy the sunshine, until one day when the skiing fields became cannon fields. I couldn't understand what was happening. I could see people were worried, and I could hear the scary sounds of gunshots and bombs. We stopped going to school and stopped playing outside. Very bad people were bombing our city and killing our children, mothers, and fathers. A bomb fell in front of my house. Everybody said that we are lucky. Lucky because we were all inside but nobody got hurt.

The sudden end to a world that Sonja loved was clear in her words, "We had a perfect life and all of a sudden this happened." Similar stories were repeated over and again. Most described their recollections of the outbreak of war with vivid detail. Stjepan and Gabrijela were eight and nine years old, respectively, when the war in Bosnia began. Their father was arrested and tortured at a concentration camp for about eight months. Although the children never actually saw their father being beaten, they later saw the scars. Gabrijela recalled that time.

> I saw lots of people die. They used to put people in the school and then blow the schools up. We were in the school and they were preparing to

blow it up but some guy came, he was Muslim but was working for Serbs just to stay alive, and he told them not to blow up the school so they didn't. Women and children were together and the men were in different ones. They used to beat men up and we used to hear them yelling. They would surround your town with tanks. If you didn't come out of your house then they blow it up.

Stjepan, when asked if he remembered when the war started, initially stated that he forgot most of it. After a few thoughtful moments, he spoke.

I was playing outside. I heard bullets and my mom called me to come home. I was like "No, no, I want to play." I didn't know what was going on. Two hours later the army came and took my dad. I cried. After 15 days they brought him back. He was all in blood. They just brought him so we could see him. Then they took him back. They used to bring people and just throw them out, dead people that they beat up so they would die. The men were beaten up so bad that they were all black from the blood that dried.

Stories such as these were told repeatedly. The children recalled soldiers bursting into their homes and bedrooms in the middle of the night, arresting their fathers, and leaving them feeling confused, betrayed, fearful, and sad. There was no preparation for the horror that ensued.

He Wasn't Mean to Me, He Just Never Talked to Me

The children of battered women did not know a life of peace prior to the onset of violence. Violence had been an integral part of family life for as long as they could remember. Sometimes it was subtle and insidious; other times, it was explicit and explosive. In either case, it was always there.

Mardelle, 15 years old, witnessed the abuse of her mother by two men, first by her biological father, and several years later, by her mother's boyfriend. The interlude between relationships was recalled by Mardelle as the "good years," adding that she and her mother would often share special times together. This phase was interrupted when her mother entered into a new relationship, one which quickly became violent.

He was abusive to my mom, not really to me. Emotionally to me, seeing my mom. I think that was abuse, to see my mom go through it. He wasn't really mean to me, he just never talked to me . . . He acted like he loved her a lot. But his problem was alcohol or something. If he drank he would get really possessive and take his anger out on her. Like one time he sliced my mom's stomach with a knife when she was pregnant. Just like a little slice, not real big or nothing. He took an anger control class and was doing good until he got angry at the teacher. Mom usually forgave him and took him back.

Mardelle has never seen any man play a positive role in her family's life and recalled the happiest times as those when she was alone with her mother. She calmly described the incident in which her mother was stabbed, adding that this was not as frightening to her as a later occasion when he threatened to kill her baby sister. One remarkable insight was Mardelle's recognition that witnessing violence against her mother constitutes a form of abuse.

The chronic and incessant nature of the fighting was noted by Erica. "When we woke up in the morning they'd fight and when we came home from school they'd be fighting still. When they weren't fighting, there was just silence. The only time he said anything was to complain about the food, or us, or to put us down."

From these stories, it is apparent that the children of war experienced something quite unlike the children of battered women. For the former, violence represented a sudden, but temporary, interruption to previously peaceful lives, whereas the latter group experienced violence as a defining feature of family life for as long as they could remember. For both groups, however, the effects of violence continued to be felt long after the violence ended.

The Public and Private Face of Violence

Children who live amid violence, regardless of its particular manifestations, share some aspects of the experience. What they see, what they hear, and in some senses, what they feel, is similar. Yet, as this research demonstrates, the way in which violence in the home is experienced is qualitatively different from the way in which the violence of war is experienced.

In part, these differences stem from social and political constructions of war and domestic violence. Wars are fought in the public realm. There are official declarations of war; there are rules of "fair play"; and there are international bodies established to ensure that the war-makers abide by the rules. The purpose of such efforts are, presumably, to ensure that war in the modern world is less heinous than war in earlier times. Despite any admirable intentions, the disturbing reality is that the weapons which are available today can wreak far more devastation and destruction, not only on soldiers, but also on civilians and the environment, than ever before.

The "private wars" in the home unfold in a different manner. Like war, domestic violence has also been going on for centuries. But unlike war, woman abuse is not publicly declared, nor is it publicly fought. There are no rules of "fair play," there are no bodies set up to monitor the conduct of men who abuse their intimate female partners, particularly if the woman is successful at keeping it hidden.

In this research, both groups heard and saw the sounds and sights of violence, of people getting hurt. The children recounted long nights when they lay awake, too immobilized by their fear to do anything. The children of war told of hiding out in the basements of their friends and neighbours, listening to the anguished cries as bombs and grenades fell around them. They felt profound anger, sadness, and confusion. Schools closed, they were not allowed to play outside, and all efforts were directed to the common struggle to stay alive. Any semblance of normalcy came to an abrupt and total end. While it is difficult to imagine anything more terrifying, these children were among family, friends, and neighbors who shared the same bewildering and frightening emotions. For them, violence was experienced communally and collectively with people they loved, and who loved them in return.

The children of battered women also spent many sleepless nights listening to the sounds of violence. But the sounds which they heard came from within their homes, from violence inflicted upon their mothers. Occasionally siblings supported one another, but more often, they lay in their beds feigning sleep. They described many of the same feelings as the children of war. But they also spoke of shame and embarrassment. For these children, violence did not interrupt the routines of daily life. Each morning they were expected to proceed with their usual activities, to go to school and maintain the facade of normalcy, that nothing untoward was happening in their homes. The need for such pretense was also a significant distinguishing feature in the experiences of the two groups of children. For children of war, there was no shame, embarrassment, or need to hide the realities of the violence which had come to dominate their everyday lives.

For the children of battered women, there was no formal acknowledgment of war. Instead, they bore silent and unacknowledged witness to their own suffering. While much of what they heard and saw was remarkably similar to what the children of war heard and saw, these children were forced to endure their pain and sorrow in secrecy and silence, isolated and alone.

The Aftermath of Violence

Violence holds different meanings for children. In this research, war represented an erosion of basic assumptions about the expected and taken-for-granted order of things. In contrast, the children of battered women had not known lives without violence, and no such assumptions about the orderly nature of events had ever been embraced.

In her novel, *The Bean Tree*, Barbara Kingsolver wrote about a woman and her daughter named Turtle, as they travel through life, facing obstacles at every turn. Ultimately, they discover that their capacity to overcome challenges far exceeds what they'd ever anticipated. This ability to discover inner strengths, to grow and learn in previously unforeseen ways, was clear in the words of the children who shared their stories. Many were able to construe benefit from their experiences. The children of war often described themselves as "the lucky ones." Although all experienced separation from one or both parents for varying lengths of time during the war, and many of their fathers were imprisoned and tortured, they were able to get out of the country, and all were eventually reunited with both parents. As Monique explained:

> I think a lot about my family and friends, what happened to me, and my future. Some of my friends were killed, they were burned, it was at a boarding school, where they killed all the Tutsis, about 150 people. So I guess I am lucky.

Mirza, a 15-year-old boy from Bosnia stated, "I am lucky because we came out of the war. We're alive and nothing the worst happened." Similar thoughts were echoed by many, but they also expressed concern for friends and family less fortunate than themselves, even for those they did not know, but who were imprisoned, tortured, or killed.

Some children expressed a sense of hope for the future. In Medina's words, "It's important that you don't forget what you survived, but try to go on with your life. Try to have something in your future, to be something and somebody. And never forget your country. Now I have everything that I want. I have my parents and my friends. That's the most important thing."

Many of the children of battered women were also able to identify positive outcomes of their painful early years. One female spoke about her determination to help make the world a more peaceful place. Seth, a perceptive 14-year-old male stated, "Well, everything that I've gone through makes me who I am today. It's made me stronger . . . like I lost some self-esteem but I've regained a lot of it and I've even got more."

It would be misleading, however, to suggest that their problems are over, or that they no longer suffer. Such a conclusion would be far from the truth. While many demonstrate impressive strengths and resources, their earlier experiences continue to haunt them. Learning to cope with trauma ought not be confused with healing from trauma. Both groups of children told of persistent feelings of loneliness, eating and sleeping difficulties, recurrent headaches, and intrusive thoughts and fears. Some recounted feeling immobilized and depressed. Medina, awakened in the middle of the night by two armed soldiers who had come to arrest her father, poignantly explained the terror she continues to experience whenever someone knocks too loudly at the door.

The children of war described an array of difficulties they faced adjusting to life in North America. Many, unfamiliar with the language or the culture, the subtle and not-so-subtle rules and expectations, encountered teasing and bullying in their new schools. The children from African countries experienced racism, often for the first time in their lives. As one female from Somalia stated, "I am happy to be away from the war, but now I must learn about racism. It, too, is like a war." Despite the challenges these children continue to face, almost all asserted that today they are doing well in school and have many friends.

DISCUSSION

In her research with children in the West Bank, Punamaki (1989, 1996) reported that, despite the constant threat of danger these children faced, they were able to derive strength from their ideological commitment to, and identification with, their country's struggle. Seemingly protective factors such as age, gender, or family supports were less compelling determinants of children's responses. The important role of ideology has been described with respect to children in Mozambique (Boothby, 1994), South Africa (Dawes, 1990), and elsewhere (Coles, 1986; Garbarino et al., 1991). According to these authors, ideology can serve both positive and negative purposes. On the one hand, it can provide a context that enables children to understand the chaotic circumstances of their lives, thereby enhancing their capacity to cope. Alternatively, ideological commitment might serve as the justification for continued violence, ultimately exposing children to more danger.

The role of ideology is somewhat ambiguous in this research and the challenge to find sense out of the seemingly senseless was complex. The children of war did not typically articulate an explicit commitment to the political struggle, and their understandings of the conflicts were simplistic and abstract: fighting is bad, violence is bad. Still, they expressed fierce loyalty to their families, and to "their people." As Mirza, a 14-year-old boy from Bosnia stated, "I don't hate the Serbs, but I can never forgive them for what they did to my people." Similar sentiments were expressed by the Tutsi children from Burundi toward the Hutu majority. There was no ambivalence as to which side they were on; as to who the enemy was. Despite naive explanations for the war, they believed that there was a right side and a wrong side. And there was no doubt that they were on the right side. Although they stated that they could not forgive or forget, none of the children expressed a desire for revenge.

The children of battered women felt shame and embarrassment about the violence which permeated their family interactions. These children never knew what it means to live in a home where needs are met, where positive emotions are openly expressed and encouraged, or where there is order and predictability. Unlike the children of war, these children had tremendous ambivalence as to who the enemy was.

Seven had participated in a group program for children who witness woman abuse. This program helped them understand that violence directed toward women is an expression of male domination; that it is a means of control which is manifested in many ways; and that it is a phenomenon which has historical, cultural, and social roots. Such understandings enabled the children to see that they were not to blame and that violence in their lives was not simply the result of bad, nasty, or misguided individuals, or peculiar to their family. They recognized that violence was socially produced and experienced in situations which have been handed down for countless generations. While such knowledge did not, in their eyes, absolve their fathers from accountability for their actions, nor lessen the pain, it did provide a means to understand.

In this research, children were given an opportunity to examine the violence in their own lives, as well as violence in general. Through a mutual process of dialogue and reflection, new insights were gleaned. My interactions with the children, the way the interviews unfolded, were always different. Common to all, however, was the desire among the children to tell their stories. Many had never done so before. Too often, it is assumed that children are unable to discuss sensitive issues. The reality is that they are quite capable of talking about their experiences, welcome the opportunity to do so, and can teach us a great deal about the dynamics of violence, about coping and survival.

In their paper about survivors of the holocaust, Gallant and Cross (1992) wrote, "Suffering and survivorship are intrinsic to life and the self journey, not external to it. Survivors show us that to endure trauma, we must learn to confront the paradoxical, that life may be conflictual as well as harmonious, meaning is discursive as much as received, and wholeness for the self must be salvaged out of fragmentation" (p. 240). Though commonsense notions of tragedy distance it from everyday life with terms like "sad tales," it should not be removed from our conception of normal life and social order. Research on children growing up amid violence requires the development of discursive techniques which allow the researcher to understand the subjective experience in which meaning develops out of trauma, and the development of strategies that enable and empower children to bring about change.

Because this article is about giving voice to a group of children whom we have not heard from a great deal, I would like to close as I began, with the voice of one child. This passage is from a speech which was written by Sonja shortly after she arrived in Canada.

Human greatness is the ability to forgive. The world would be very strange if people only gained desire for revenge. I read what happened in World War II. It was the same: occupation, killing, destroying. War stopped and people have started to live a normal life. They could live it because they were capable of forgiving. I cannot forget people's faces and eyes looking toward the Heavens. I cannot forget children's tears, people's hands waving goodbye, and my father's words, 'See you soon' on the day when my mom, my brother, and I between bombs and gunshots left Sarajevo. After that I pray to God every night. Never again will there be a war anywhere on earth. Please, now is the time for happiness, understanding, and forgiveness.

REFERENCES

Ajdukovic, M., & Ajdukovic, D. (1993). Psychological well-being of refugee children. *Child Abuse & Neglect, 17*, 843-854.

Arroyo, W., & Eth, S. (1985). Children traumatized by Central American warfare. In S. Eth & R. S. Pynoos (Eds.), *Post-traumatic stress disorder in children* (pp. 103-120). Washington, DC: American Psychiatric Press.

Athey, J. L., & Ahearn, F. (1991). The mental health of refugee children: An overview. In F. Ahearn & J. Athey (Eds.), *Refugee children: Theory, research, and services* (pp. 3-19). Baltimore, MD: Johns Hopkins University Press.

Beiser, M., Barwick, C., Berry, J., da Costa, G., Fantino, A., Ganesan, S., Lee, C., Milne, W., Naidoo, J., Prince, R., Tousignant, M., & Vela, E. (1988). *After the door has been opened: Mental health issues affecting immigrants and refugees*. Ottawa, ON: Ministries of Multiculturalism and Citizenship, and Health and Welfare.

Beiser, M., Dion, R., Gotowiec, M., Hyman, I., & Vu, N. (1995). Immigrant and refugee children in Canada. *Canadian Journal of Psychiatry, 40* (2), 67-72.

Berman, H. (1996). Growing up amid violence: A critical narrative analysis of children of war and children of battered women (Doctoral dissertation, Wayne State University, Detroit, 1996). *Dissertation Abstracts International, 57*(12B), 9715809.

Bodman, F. (1941). War conditions and the mental health of the child. *British Medical Journal, 2*, 486-488.

Boothby, N. (1994). Trauma and violence among refugee children. In A. J. Marsella, T. Bornemann, S. Ekblad, & J. Orley (Eds.), *Amidst peril and pain: The mental health and well-being of the world's refugees* (pp. 239-259). Washington, DC: American Psychological Association.

Bracken, P. J., Giller, J. E., & Summerfield, D. (1995). Psychological responses to war and atrocity: The limitations of current concepts. *Social Science Medicine, 40*, 1073-1082.

Chimienti, G., Nasr, J., & Khalifeh, I. (1991). Children's reactions to war-related stress: Affective symptoms and behavior problems. *Social Psychology and Psychiatric Epidemiology, 24*, 282-287.

Coles, R. (1986). *The political life of children*. Boston: Atlantic Monthly.

Dawes, A., & Tredoux, C. (1989). Emotional status of children exposed to political violence in the Crossroads squatter area during 1986-1987. *Psychology in Society, 12*, 33-47.

Dawes, A. (1990). The effects of political violence on children: A consideration of South African and related studies. *International Journal of Psychology, 25*, 13-31.

DiNicola, V. (1996). Ethnocultural aspects of PTSD and related disorders among children and adolescents. In A. Marsella, M. Friedman, E. Gerrity, & R. Scurfield (Eds.), *Ethnocultural aspects of post-traumatic stress disorder: Issues, research, and clinical applications* (pp. 389-414), Washington, DC: APA.

Eisenbruck, M. (1988). The mental health of refugee children and their cultural development. *International Migration Review, 22*, 282-300.

Elbedour, S., Bensel, R. T., & Bastien, D. (1993). Ecological integrated model of children of war: Individual and social psychology. *Child Abuse & Neglect, 17*, 805-819.

Eth, S., & Pynoos, R. (1985). Developmental perspective on psychic trauma in childhood. In C. Figley (Ed.), *Trauma and its wake: The study and treatment of post-traumatic stress disorder* (pp. 36-52). New York: Brunner/Mazel.

Fox, P., Muennich, P., Cowell, J., & Montgomery, A. (1994). The effects of violence on health and adjustment of Southeast Asian refugee children: An integrative review. *Public Health Nursing, 11*, 195-201.

Freud, A., & Burlingham, D. (1943). *War and children.* New York: Medical War Books, Ernst Willard.

Gallant, M. J., & Cross, J. E. (1992). Surviving destruction of the self: Challenged identity in the holocaust. *Studies in Symbolic Interaction, 13*, 221-246.

Garbarino, J., Kostelny, K., & Dubrow, N. (1991). *No place to be a child: Growing up in a war zone.* Lexington, MA: D. C. Heath & Co.

Gil, A. G., Vega, W., & Dimas, J. (1994). Acculturative stress and personal adjustment among hispanic adolescent boys. *Journal of Community Psychology, 22*, 43-54.

Henshaw, E. M., & Howarth, H. E. (1941). Observed effects of wartime conditions on children. *Mental Health, 2*, 93-101.

Jensen, P., & Shaw, J. (1993). Children as victims of war: Current knowledge and future research needs. *Journal of the American Academy of Child and Adolescent Psychiatry, 32*, 697-708.

Kinzie, J. D., Sack, W., Angell, R., Clarke, G., & Rath, B. (1989). A three-year follow-up of Cambodian young people traumatized as children. *Journal of the American Academy of Child Psychiatry, 28*, 501-504.

Kinzie, J. D., & Sack, W. H. (1991). Severely traumatized Cambodian children: Research findings and clinical implications. In F. Ahearn & J. Athey (Eds.), *Refugee children: Theory, research, and services.* Baltimore, MD: Johns Hopkins University Press.

Klingman, A., Sagi, A., & Raviv, A. (1993). The effect of war on Israeli children. In L. A. Leavitt & N. A. Fox (Eds.), *The psychological effects of war and violence on children* (pp. 75-92). Hillsdale, NJ: Lawrence Erlbaum Associates.

Kuterovac, G., Dyregrov, A., & Stuvland, R. (1994). Children in war: A silent majority under stress. *British Journal of Medical Psychology, 67*, 363-375.

Laor, N., Wolmer, L., Mayes, L., Gershon, A., Wiezman, R., & Cohen, D. J. (1996). Israeli preschool children under Scuds: A 30-month follow-up. *Journal of the American Academy of Child and Adolescent Psychiatry, 36*, 349-356.

Macksoud, M., & Aber, J. (1996). The war experiences and psychosocial development of children in Lebanon. *Child Development, 67*, 70-88.

Macksoud, M., Aber, J., & Cohn, I. (1996). Assessing the impact of war on children. In R. Apfel & B. Simon (Eds.), *Minefields in their hearts: The mental health of children in war and communal violence* (218-230). New Haven, CO: Yale University Press.

Magwaza, A., Killian, B., Petersen, I., & Pillay, Y. (1995). The effects of chronic violence on preschool children living in South African townships. *Child Abuse & Neglect, 17*, 795-803.

Maines, D., & Ulmer, J. (1993). The relevance of narrative for interactionist thought. *Studies in Symbolic Interaction, 14*, 109-124.

Mghir, R., Freed, W., Raskin, A., & Katon, W. (1995). Depression and posttraumatic stress disorder among a community sample of adolescent and young adult Afghan refugees. *Journal of Nervous and Mental Disease, 183*(1), 24-30.

Mishler, E. (1995). Models of narrative analysis: A typology. *Journal of Narrative and Life History, 5*, 87-123.

National Defense Council Foundation (1996, Jan. 3). *The London Free Press*, p. A5.

Phinney, B., Lochner, B., & Murphy, R. (1990). Ethnic identity and psychological adjustment. In A. Stiffman & L. Davis (Eds.), *Ethnic issues in adolescent mental health* (pp. 53-72), Newbury Park, CA: Sage.

Phinney, J., Chavira, V., & Williamson, L. (1992). Acculturation attitudes and self-esteem among high school and college students. *Youth & Society, 23*, 299-312.

Polakow, V. (1992). *The erosion of childhood*. Chicago: University of Chicago Press.

Polkinghorne, D. E. (1988). *Narrative knowing and the human sciences*. Albany, NY: State University of New York Press.

Punamaki, R. (1989). Factors affecting the mental health of Palestinian children exposed to political violence. *International Journal of Mental Health, 18*, 63-79.

Punamaki, R. (1996). Can ideological commitment protect children's psychosocial well-being in situations of political violence? *Child Development, 67*, 55-69.

Rick, K., & Forward, J. (1992). Acculturation and perceived intergenerational differences among Hmong youth. *Journal of Cross-Cultural Psychology, 23*, 85-94.

Riessman, C. K. (1993). *Narrative analysis*. Newbury Park, CA: Sage Publications.

Rumbaut, R. G. (1991). The agony of exile: A study of the migration and adaptation of Indochinese refugeee adults and children. In F. Ahearn & J. Athey (Eds.), *Refugee children: Theory, research, and services* (pp. 53-92). Baltimore, MD: Johns Hopkins University Press.

Sack, W., Angell, R., Kinzie, J. D., & Rath, B. (1985). The psychiatric effects of massive trauma on Cambodian children II: The family, the home, and the school. *Journal of the American Academy of Child Psychiatry, 25*, 377-383.

Sack, W., Clarke, G., & Seeley, J. (1995). Posttraumatic stress disorder across two generations. *Journal of American Academy of Child and Adolescent Pscyhiatry, 34*, 1160-1166.

Saigh, P. A. (1991). The development of posttraumatic stress disorder following four different types of traumatization. *Behavioral Research Therapy, 29*, 213-216.

Sandelowski, M. (1991). Telling stories: Narrative approaches in qualitative research. *IMAGE: Journal of Nursing Scholarship, 23*, 161-165.

United Nations High Commissioner for Refugees (1995). *The state of the world's refugees: In search of solutions*. New York: Oxford University Press.

Van Maanen, J. (1988). *Tales of the field*. Chicago: University of Chicago Press.

Weine, S., Becker, D., McGlashan, T., Vojvoda, D., Hartman, S., & Roblins, J. (1995). Adolescent survivors of "ethnic cleansing": Observations on the first year in America. *Journal of the American Academy of Child and Adolescent Psychiatry, 34*, 1153-1159.

Wicks, B. (1988). *No time to wave goodbye*. London: Bloomsbury Press.

Williams, C., & Berry, J. (1991). Primary prevention of acculturative stress among refugees. *American Psychologist, 46*, 632-641.

Zur, J. (1996). From PTSD to voices in context: From an "experience-far" to an "experience-near" understanding of responses to war and atrocity across cultures. *International Journal of Social Psychiatry, 42*, 305-317.

Evaluation of the London (Ontario) Community Group Treatment Programme for Children Who Have Witnessed Woman Abuse

Marlies Sudermann
Larry Marshall
Susan Loosely

SUMMARY. Group intervention for children exposed to woman abuse is increasingly used to respond to the psychological needs of children exposed to woman abuse. This article describes a community group model of intervention for children exposed to woman abuse, and an evaluation approach used to assess the impact of such groups. The collaborative development of questionnaire/interview evaluation instruments for this purpose is described, and the set of instruments is pre-

Address correspondence to: Dr. Marlies Sudermann, Thames Valley District School Board, 1250 Dundas Street E., P.O. Box 5888, London, ON N5W 5P2, Canada.

[Haworth co-indexing entry note]: "Evaluation of the London (Ontario) Community Group Treatment Programme for Children Who Have Witnessed Woman Abuse." Sudermann, Marlies, Larry Marshall, and Susan Loosely. Co-published simultaneously in *Journal of Aggression, Maltreatment & Trauma* (The Haworth Maltreatment & Trauma Press, an imprint of The Haworth Press, Inc.) Vol. 3, No. 1 (#5), 2000, pp. 127-146; and: *Children Exposed to Domestic Violence: Current Issues in Research, Intervention, Prevention, and Policy Development* (ed: Robert A. Geffner, Peter G. Jaffe, and Marlies Sudermann) The Haworth Maltreatment & Trauma Press, an imprint of The Haworth Press, Inc., 2000, pp. 127-146. Single or multiple copies of this article are available for a fee from The Haworth Document Delivery Service [1-800-342-9678, 9:00 a.m. - 5:00 p.m. (EST). E-mail address: getinfo@haworthpressinc.com].

sented in its entirety. The main instrument, entitled *Child/Teen Witness to Woman Abuse Questionnaire,* was tailored to the content of the groups and covers topics such as definitions and understanding of abuse, safety skills, beliefs and attitudes about abuse, perceived responsibility for abuse, alternatives to violence, non-violent conflict resolution strategies, and help seeking skills. Both closed-ended and open-ended questions are employed. Separate questionnaires assess consumer (mother/caregiver and child) satisfaction and feedback. The results of a study evaluating the groups are described, which showed good changes from pre to post intervention, as well as a high degree of satisfaction among children and mothers with regard to the groups. Feedback from children and mothers as to suggested improvements in the group is also described. *[Article copies available for a fee from The Haworth Document Delivery Service: 1-800-342-9678. E-mail address: getinfo@haworthpressinc.com <Website: http://www.haworthpressinc.com>]*

KEYWORDS. Questionnaire, assessment instrument, peer support, family violence, trauma, survivors, adolescents, secondary prevention

INTRODUCTION

Intervention for children exposed to woman abuse is a pressing need in many communities, because of the severe emotional and behavioural consequences of witnessing violence between the adults in the home. The other articles in this book, as well as other publications (e.g., Sudermann & Jaffe, in press; Peled, Jaffe, & Edleson, 1995; Sternberg, Lamb, Greenbaum, Cicchetti, Dawud, Cortes, Krispin, & Lorey, 1993; Fantuzzo, dePaola, Lambert, Martino, Anderson, & Sutton, 1991), amply document the deleterious effects on children who live in family war zones. Also, for both males and females, childhood exposure to family violence is a predictor of poor emotional and behavioural adjustment in adulthood (Straus, 1992). Since exposure to woman abuse as a child is the leading risk factor and predictor for males abusing women (Jaffe, Wolfe, & Wilson, 1990), interventions designed to ameliorate this risk and prevent violence in this group of children while they are still young would appear to be a high priority in order to prevent future woman abuse (and other violent assaults). However, interventions for children exposed to woman abuse have only recently been developed, and implementation and evaluation of such interventions are only at a beginning stage. The present article will describe the London (Ontario) Community Group Treatment Programme for Children Exposed to Woman Abuse; will discuss the development of an instrument to evaluate this group intervention, the Child/Teen Witness to Woman Abuse Questionnaire; and finally will report on the results of a small evaluation study with this instrument which found very encouraging results. At the end of the article, the Child/Teen Witness to Woman Abuse Questionnaire is reproduced.

Group intervention is the most frequently described therapeutic modality offered to children who have been exposed to woman abuse (Peled & Davis, 1995). A number of authors, including Alessi and Hearn, 1984; Layzer, Goodson, and DeLange, 1986; Wilson, Cameron, Jaffe, and Wolfe (1989); Peled and Davis (1995); and Bentley, Lehmann, Loosely, Marshall, Rabenstein, and Sudermann (1997) have described interventions involving a series of semi-structured group sessions. These programmes are intended to assist children and adolescents to process their experiences of witnessing woman abuse in a supportive environment. Common themes or goals in these approaches include offering children and adolescents opportunities to talk about their experiences of witnessing woman abuse and violence between the adults in their home (breaking the secret or breaking the silence); dispelling myths about woman abuse and family violence; imparting improved safety skills; teaching non-violent values; and practising respectful ways of relating with others. Improving self-esteem, learning about sources of help available in the community, and preventing sexual abuse and dating violence are additional goals which are often included in these group interventions. Art and play activities are employed along with group exercises and discussion. Longer-term goals of group interventions include decreasing emotional and behavioural problems in children and adolescents who have witnessed woman abuse, and breaking the intergenerational cycle of violence.

While there are other approaches to therapy and intervention with children who have witnessed woman abuse, such as individual therapy (Silvern, Karyl, & Landis, 1995) and art therapy (Malchiodi, 1990), semi-structured group therapy may have become the most frequently employed intervention modality because it allows children to process their experiences with their peer group, which assists in learning and breaking the silence; because a group format is often enjoyable and familiar to children in that it is similar to community children's activities; and because it offers a cost-effective intervention. Also, the structured format encourages consistent coverage of topics and treatment activities.

Evaluation of interventions for children exposed to woman abuse have to date been rather scarce, which is not unusual for new areas of endeavour. One early pilot evaluation of groups for child witnesses of woman abuse completed by Jaffe, Wilson, and Wolfe (1986) found some positive changes in children's attitudes about responsibility for violence, their self-esteem, and their skills for keeping themselves safe in woman abuse situations.

Peled and Edleson (1992) conducted a qualitative evaluation of groups at the Minneapolis Domestic Abuse Project Children's Program and found some interesting results. The Minnesota program consists of ten structured sessions designed to assist children with breaking the secret around domestic violence, sharing experiences, learning to protect themselves, and learning assertive conflict resolution, among the main goals. The evaluation found some positive results, and some unintended negative results as well. The positive results were that children learned to define abuse, to resolve conflicts with siblings and peers more positively, to better protect themselves if the abuse recurred, and to understand that they were not alone with the problem of domestic violence. Some of the unintended consequences were that some children were more reluctant to discuss the domestic violence with their mother because they had misinterpreted the directive to keep group discussions confidential, some children were uncomfortable with the sexual abuse prevention discussion, and some children found it difficult to think about the abuse they had witnessed. However, overall, the outcomes of the group were considered positive and affirming for the children.

It is notable that Peled and Edleson chose an exclusively qualitative approach to their evaluation effort for a number of reasons, including: the goals of their programme were very general; the agency context required a non-intrusive evaluation approach which enhanced staff participation; concerns about the use of standardized measures with young children; the need to address unintended effects of the programme; a need to evaluate programme processes as well as results; and a scarcity of information needed to construct valid and reliable standardized instruments (Peled & Davis, 1995).

It is clear that the development of therapeutic approaches for children who witness woman abuse is still in a relatively early stage, and that further evaluation efforts are needed. Evaluation is a crucial function if interventions are to be developed and refined. Evaluation is also important for purposes of funding agencies, which increasingly require indications of effectiveness in order to continue to support programmes.

Issues which remain to be addressed include quantitative and qualitative assessment of the effectiveness of group intervention in the short, medium and long-term in respect to reducing children's emotional and behaviour problems, improving the children's adjustment in relationships, at home, at school and in the community, and preventing subsequent violence by children exposed to woman abuse. The satisfaction and comfort level of children and their mothers with the group processes is clearly an important issue. Other areas in need of investigation include the effectiveness of various forms of group intervention, and the effectiveness (or lack thereof) of specific components and processes within the group intervention; characteristics and training of effective group leaders; the importance of group composition; and needs for follow-up or booster sessions. Which children will benefit from group intervention, and which require alternative or extended therapy for these issues is another major area requiring investigation. It may be that children who have experienced different severity, duration, and age of onset of exposure to woman abuse require different therapeutic approaches. Children with different severities of post-traumatic stress symptoms, and different personality characteristics, strengths and coping styles may require different therapeutic modalities and approaches.

Given all of the potential evaluation needs and challenges which have been identified with respect to group intervention for children who have witnessed woman abuse, it is not surprising that evaluation efforts must be developed over time, as it would be impossible to meet all the evaluation needs in one study, with one method, or using only one source of information.

DESCRIPTION OF LONDON COMMUNITY GROUP TREATMENT PROGRAMME FOR CHILD WITNESSES OF WOMAN ABUSE

The London Community Group Treatment Programme for Child Witnesses of Woman Abuse originated in the mid 1980s, and a description and evaluation of earlier groups are to be found in Jaffe, Wilson, and Wolfe (1986). Currently, the model of service delivery for the group's treatment is an inter-agency collaborative model, which uses single point access referral, through one group programme coordinator, with the assistance of group co-facilitators from diverse member agencies. The co-facilitators each facilitate a few groups together with the programme coordinator. Groups are offered at different sites in the community at member agencies, including a child protective service (Children's Aid Society of London and Middlesex); a children's mental health centre (Madame Vanier Children's Services); a centre for preventative services for young children and their families (Merrymount Children's Centre); a women's shelter (Women's Community House); a second-stage housing for women and children who have survived and left abusive relationships (Second Stage Housing) and a youth detention facility (Craigwood Youth Services), among others. Approximately 25 groups are held per year, with an average of 7 to 8 participants per group.

Age and Gender Groupings. Children aged 4 to 16 are accepted, and are grouped together with other children of similar developmental level. Common age groupings include: 4 and 5 year-olds; 6-8 years; 7-9 years, and 10-12 years and teen groups. In the younger age groups, it has been found that gender composition of the group is less important, but in the older age groups, including pre-teens and teens, having a gender-balanced group is considered more important in order to enable the participants to address issues related to gender.

Preparation for Group. Pre-group interviews are completed in order to assess the appropriateness of the child's group participation, and to familiarize the child and mother with the group leader and the group programme. The pre-group interview with the mother present gives the child permission to talk about the violence. This is considered to be the first step in breaking the silence around the violence which the child has witnessed. The nature of violence which the child has witnessed and experienced is discussed, in order for the group leader to understand the issues the child will need to address in group. Also, the issues of whether the violence has now stopped, and whether the child will feel safe participating in the group are addressed. If the violence is still ongoing, or the child is denying the violence occurred in the past, the participation in group may be deferred until these issues can be addressed. Also, children who are in extreme turmoil, with regard to their behaviour and family situation, may be deferred for group participation until these issues have become more resolved, and the child is more ready to take advantage of a therapeutic group intervention. The pre-group interview is also an opportunity for the child to learn to talk about the violence which has occurred in a more open manner, and to learn language to describe his or her experience more accurately.

Group Processes and Content. A manual has recently been published describing the procedures and exercises employed in the groups (Bentley, Lehmann, Loosely, Marshall, Rabenstein, & Sudermann, 1997), and the reader is referred to this manual, entitled *Group Treatment for Children Who Witness Woman Abuse: A Manual for Practitioners,* for details of group exercises and techniques. Variations in the sessions are described in the manual for young children (pre-school-kindergarten age), for adolescents, and for adolescents in young offender facilities.

The groups usually meet for ten sessions (up to 12) and focus on (a) increasing the participants' adaptive functioning and remediating the social-behavioural problems associated with witnessing violence; (b) creating sufficient change to prevent violence in the child's future relationships, and (c) ensuring the child learns safety skills to keep herself or himself safe during any recurrence of violent episodes in the family environment.

The topics addressed during the sessions include: definitions of and language to describe violence, including emotional, physical and sexual violence, with terminology adapted to different developmental levels; recognizing, understanding, and communicating feelings; talking about violence in families; anger and conflict resolution; responsibility for violence and myths about family violence and woman abuse; power and control as they relate to different forms of abuse; safety planning; dating violence or sexual abuse prevention (depending on the child's age) and self-esteem.

Creating and maintaining an emotionally supportive, safe group atmosphere is an important part of the treatment process. Group rules are defined and developed to prevent any verbal abuse or disrespect occurring in the groups, and to promote support and respect among group members. Creating a group environment where children have fun and experience nurturance is another important goal for group facilitators, and to this end, snacks and fun activities are provided. Each child is given opportunities to be heard and listened to within the group, and group leaders report that this is a very powerful experience for many children. At the final session of the group, there is a celebration, and group completion certificates are given to the children.

Maternal/Caregiver Involvement. In the community group treatment model, there have been different levels of maternal involvement. Examples include child only groups, where there is less mother involvement; mother-child groups, which are described in the article of this book by Stephanie Rabenstein and Peter Lehmann, and which have a high level of maternal involvement; and parallel integrated groups, in which mothers have their own group sessions at times, and at other times participate in the children's groups. Where mothers are involved, the program emphasizes understanding the effects on children of witnessing wife abuse so that they can meet the trauma needs of their children more effectively.

Guiding Principles. Because of the multiple group facilitators who bring their creativity and individual styles to the Community Group Treatment Programme, a set of Guiding Principles have been created, to direct group facilitators in their preparation for weekly sessions, and to assist the facilitators in holding each other accountable for the content and process of each group through monthly meetings. These guiding principles were developed by Stephanie Rabenstein (1997) and are as follows:

1. Is the group providing ample opportunities for children to tell their stories and be heard, believed and validated?
2. Does the group ensure that the children know how to protect themselves emotionally and physically by developing and practicing safety plans?
3. Does the group convey the message that all types of violence and abuse are unacceptable?
4. Does the group convey that abusive behaviour is a choice and that responsibility lies with the person perpetrating the violence and abuse?
5. Does the group explore the expression of anger and other emotions and provide non-abusive alternatives?
6. Does this group explore alternative means of conflict resolutions?
7. Does the group provide a positive environment where all the activities are learner centred and esteem building?

The community group treatment model is well accepted in the community, as reflected by a high rate of referrals from a broad range of referral sources. Mothers of children who have been exposed to woman abuse often advocate for the need for intervention for their children, as they know their children have been deeply affected by the abusive situation in the home, and feel the need for children to have the opportunity to talk about their experience and receive intervention for the trauma they have experienced.

COLLABORATIVE DEVELOPMENT OF CHILD/TEEN WITNESS TO WOMAN ABUSE QUESTIONNAIRES

The impetus to conduct an evaluation of the Community Group Treatment Programme for Children Who Have Witnessed Woman Abuse came from a need to provide accountability to funders of the service, as well as out of a need to learn more about how effectively the programme was meeting its goals, how it was perceived by participants and their mothers, and how the programme could be improved.

Existing tests and questionnaires were not considered suitable for this evaluation of children's groups for a number of reasons. Most broad-ranging questionnaires about children's emotions and behaviours have been designed to assess such a well-established set of behaviours and characteristics that they would not necessarily be sensitive to the specific nature of a group intervention. Also, most such questionnaires do not address issues specific to witnessing woman abuse, and would not capture knowledge such as is taught in such groups. Questionnaires which specifically addressed trauma and witnessing family violence or woman abuse were not readily available, although some have since appeared (e.g., Lehmann, 1997; Wolfe & Lehmann, 1992). For these reasons, it was considered best to design a new questionnaire set which would reflect the goals and intended learnings in the group. In order to obtain the best quality product, a group process was instituted where input was sought from the group designers, leaders and administrators, as to content of the evaluation questionnaires. A draft was constructed, and successive drafts were refined for wording and content by the group. In this way a unique questionnaire was constructed. The resulting set of questionnaires addressed learning in the group by children and adolescents, as well as child/adolescent satisfaction with the group and satisfaction with the group by mothers/caregivers. Suggestions for improvement by child and teen participants and mothers or caregivers were also included in each of the satisfaction/feedback questionnaires.

The resulting document is reproduced at the end of this article. As can be seen from examining it, there is a combination of quantitative and qualitative questions, and a variety of response formats. The Child/Teen Witness to Woman Abuse Questionnaire can be administered in a small group, individual or interview format depending on the age and needs of the child or adolescent. The questions are focussed on several main areas, including: understanding of the definition of different forms of abuse; safety skills, knowledge, beliefs and attitudes toward woman abuse; alternatives to violence in interpersonal conflict resolution; excuses for abuse, and sources of other learning about woman abuse. The feedback questionnaires encourage the participants to express their views of the value of the groups, their comfort with the group process and format, and to make suggestions as to improvements.

The response format and scoring system allows for both quantitative responses and qualitative/opinion responses, so that a wide range of responses can be assessed, and individualized issues can be brought forward, for example, in safety skills.

THE EVALUATION STUDY

Goals and Hypotheses of the Study

The purpose of the study described here was to assess whether the children's groups were meeting their short-term goals, whether the children were learning the psycho-educational content presented, whether children felt comfortable in the groups, and to assess whether the children could suggest any changes they might like to see in the groups. Similarly, feedback was wanted from mothers (and foster mothers) of the participants. The hypotheses of the study were as follows:

1. That children would increase their knowledge of safe behaviour during violent episodes between their parental figures and their knowledge of helping persons and agencies.
2. That children would improve their stated approaches to handling conflicts with peers and learn to use non-violent conflict resolution strategies.
3. That children would improve their knowledge and attitudes with regard to responsibility for violence and excuses for woman abuse, and would stop believing myths about wife assault/woman abuse.
4. That participants' appraisal of the groups would be positive with regard to personal and psychological comfort in the group, as well as learning from the group.
5. That participants' mothers or alternate caretakers would appraise the groups positively in terms of the participants' learning as well as, possibly, improvement in behaviour.

Sample and Methodology

Child/Teen Witness to Woman Abuse Questionnaires were administered to 31 children ranging in age from 7 to 15 years. The average age was 11.6

years, and there were 17 girls and 14 boys. Group leaders and a research assistant administered the questionnaires individually prior to the start of the groups, usually during the pre-group interview, and again at the last session. Questionnaires were read to some children who had difficulty reading, particularly the younger children. Mothers and caregivers completed the questionnaires which were either mailed out to them, or brought to their homes by a research assistant. Completion of the questionnaires was voluntary, and not tied to provision of service, although very few people refused.

Results of the Study

The results of the study indicated that the children and teens were learning the intended content in the groups, and were changing their attitudes and beliefs about woman abuse, peer abuse and other forms of violence in the intended direction. Improvements in knowledge and learning were particularly evident in areas such as defining verbal abuse (name-calling, threats) as abuse; and in defining low-level physical violence, such as slapping, as abuse. Children and teens changed their views of the cause of abuse between their parents, putting less responsibility on themselves, and more on the perpetrator of the abuse. They learned that it is not their job to intervene, and that their first priority should be to keep themselves safe. For example, before the intervention, 55 percent of children and teens replied "false" to the statement that "sometimes children are the cause of parents' abusive behaviour/fights" while after intervention, 84 percent replied "false" to this assertion. Prior to the intervention, 59 percent of the children replied that they would try to stop a fight between their parents, while after the intervention, only 10 percent endorsed this statement. There were also positive changes in the children's knowledge of community resources and persons from whom to get help, and positive changes in their stated approaches to their own responses to peers in conflict situations.

In terms of the children's satisfaction with the groups, 60.7 percent of the children responded at 5 (a lot), on a five-point scale, while 32 percent rated the group at 4 (quite a lot). Children rated the groups highly in terms of what they had learned also, with 64 percent rating the groups at 5 (a lot) and 29 percent at 4 (quite a lot). In both these areas, there were no ratings below 3. The verbal comments were very positive, and there were few negative comments. A few children indicated that it had been difficult for them to talk about the abuse in their family, but most of these children felt it helped them. Some children commented that the groups helped them understand violence and their feelings. Ninety-two percent of the children said they would recommend the group to a friend who had violence problems in his or her family.

The mother's/caregiver's evaluations also were very positive about the value of the groups. In response to the question "How much do you think the group helped your child?," 56 percent of the mothers responded "a lot" (5 on a five-point scale), and 30 percent responded with "quite a lot" (4). There were no evaluations below 3 (a little) on this item.

Seventy-four percent of mothers and caregivers indicated that they had noticed changes in their child as a result of group participation, while 26 percent noticed no change. The changes reported were all positive, with one exception. Changes noticed by mothers included better behaviour, less violence against siblings, listening better, and the child not being as frustrated. Several mothers noted their children were more confident and outspoken. Some sample comments about what the mothers and caregivers liked about their child's participation in the groups included "He appears happier. He seemed really relaxed with the others." "It gave them a chance to express themselves" and "It forced us to talk about issues that are most times easier to ignore." The one negative comment in this regard was "I was concerned because of the escalation in his violent behaviour. It seemed he was left hanging after the group's end." This comment applied to a child who was in clear need of further intervention, due to severe emotional and behavioural disturbance. Children who have witnessed extreme violence, have had severe reactions to the violence, and/or have other concurrent issues, and who do not respond well to group intervention should go on to further treatment as a priority.

The one area which was identified for improvement by quite a few mothers in the feedback from mothers and caregivers was that they desired more information about what their children were learning in the groups. They felt that sometimes they were unsure what their child had learned or had been told. They felt that if they received more information they could reinforce it better at home. There were probably one or two mothers who felt uneasy about the message in the group that violence was not acceptable at all, in that they relied on some forms of physical discipline. This is an area which can be addressed in the mother-child model and not as well in the child-only model.

Mothers'/caregivers' other suggestions about what could be done to improve groups were also most interesting. Several mothers felt the need for more frequent or more intensive groups. One mother suggested that the group leaders spend some individual time with children at the end of the session, to allow shy children to talk more. One mother suggested including sessions on assertiveness and making friends in the group. Another mother suggested a group for children who are having more difficulty with the issue, and another mother suggested working on the issue of shame and embarrassing feelings. Another mother expressed gratitude that her children could take the group a second time, as she felt they needed this to process the issues more fully. Quite a few mothers noted that they could think of no improvements at that time, and had positive comments on the groups. Further information on the results of the study, and the verbatim comments can be found in Marshall, Miller, Miller-Hewitt, Sudermann and Watson (1995).

LIMITATIONS OF THE STUDY AND FUTURE DIRECTIONS

Clearly, this questionnaire and initial study, however encouraging and positive the results were, represents a starting effort and much more in the way of evaluation and instrument development needs to be done. Test-retest reliability, internal consistency reliability, factor structure and other psycho-metric properties of the Child/Teen Witness to Woman Abuse Questionnaire need to be addressed. In addition, the correlation of the questionnaire with other measures and ratings of actual behaviour would be useful.

A much larger sample is required in order to address issues of age and gender differences in response to the groups, as well as response of children who have different types and extents of experiences of witnessing family violence.

The issue of having group leaders administer the questionnaires has some methodological implications regarding demand characteristics, especially for the children, although having a familiar person is also more comfortable for the children rather than being introduced to yet another person to whom personal details and traumas are revealed. The issue of how much change would be attained with no intervention also presents itself, and a waiting list control group would address this.

Many other research ideas present themselves in the context of this study, including the impact of the group on conflict resolution of these children in real peer and relationship situations, the overall longitudinal course of the adjustment of these children, and the ideal timing of group involvement with respect to the cessation of the abuse. Nevertheless, this study and the Child/Teen Witness to Woman Abuse Questionnaire represent a first step towards evaluation of children's groups, with very encouraging results.

REFERENCES

Alessi, J.J., & Hearn, K. (1984). Group treatment of children in shelters for battered women. In A.R. Roberts (Ed.), *Battered women and their families* (pp. 49-61). New York: Springer.

Bentley, L., Lehmann, P., Loosely, S., Marshall, L., Rabenstein, S., & Sudermann, M. (1997). *Group treatment for children who witness woman abuse.* London, ON: Community Group Treatment Program.

Hughes, H.M. (1986). Research with children in shelters: Implications for clinical services. *Children Today.*

Jaffe, P., Wolfe, D.A., & Wilson, S.K. (1990). *Children of battered women*. Thousand Oaks, CA: Sage.

Jaffe, P., Wilson, S., & Wolfe, D.A. (1986). Promoting changes in attitudes and understanding of conflict among child witnesses of family violence. *Canadian Journal of Behavioural Science, 18(4)*, 356-380.

Layzer, J.I., Goodson, B.D., & DeLange, C. (1986). Children in shelters. *Response to Victimization of Women and Children, 9(2)*, pp. 2-5.

Lehmann, P. (1997). The development of posttraumatic stress disorder (PTSD) in a sample of child witnesses to mother assault. *Journal of Family Violence, Vol. 12*, No. 3, 241-257.

Malchiodi, C.A. (1990). *Breaking the silence: Art therapy with children from violent homes*. New York: Brunner/Mazel.

Marshall, L., Miller, N., Miller-Hewitt, S., Sudermann, M., & Watson, L. (1995). *Evaluation of groups for children who have witnessed violence*. London, ON: London Family Court Clinic and Centre for Research on Violence Against Women and Children at University of Western Ontario.

Peled, E., & Davis, D. (1995). *Groupwork with children of battered women: A practitioner's manual*. Thousand Oaks, CA: Sage Publications.

Peled, E., Jaffe, P.G., & Edleson, J.L. (1995). *Ending the cycle of violence: Community responses to children of battered women*. Thousand Oaks, CA: Sage Publications.

Peled, E., & Edleson, J.L. (1992). Multiple perspectives on groupwork with children of battered women. *Violence and Victims*, 7, 327-346.

Silvern, L., Karyl, J., & Landis, T.Y. (1995). Individual psychotherapy for the traumatized children of abused woman. In E. Peled, P.G. Jaffe, & J.L. Edleson (Eds.), *Ending the cycle of violence: Community responses to children of battered women* (pp. 43-76). Thousand Oaks, CA: Sage Publications.

Sternberg, K.L., Lamb, M.E., Greenbaum, C., Cicchetti, D., Dawud, S., Cortes, R.M., Krispin, O., & Lorey, F. (1993). Effects of domestic violence on children's behavior problems and depression. *Developmental Psychology, 29(1)*, 44-52.

Sudermann, M., & Jaffe, P.G. (1997). *Children and youth who witness violence: New directions in intervention and prevention*. In D.A. Wolfe, R.J., McMahon, & R. DeV. Peters (Eds.), *Child abuse: New direction in prevention and treatment across the lifespan*. Thousand Oaks, CA: Sage Publications.

Wilson, S.K., Cameron, S., Jaffe, P., & Wolfe, D. (1989). Children exposed to wife abuse: An intervention model. *Social Casework: The Journal of Contemporary Social Work, 70(3)*, 180-184.

Wolfe, V.V., & Lehmann, P.J. (1992). *The children's impact of traumatic events scale–Family violence version*. Unpublished assessment instrument. London, ON: Children's Hospital of Western Ontario.

February 22, 1995

Child/Teen Witness to
Woman Abuse Questionnaire

LONDON FAMILY COURT CLINIC INC.

Marlies Sudermann, Ph.D., C.Psych.
London Family Court Clinic

with the assistance of:

Larry Marshall
Nancy Miller
Sandra Miller-Hewitt
Lynn Watson

Pre-Post Child/Teen Questionnaire/Interview

CASE ID

YOUR LEADER WILL FILL IN THIS SECTION, OR GIVE YOU INSTRUCTIONS

Pre-test _____   Post-Test _____   Date Test Administered: _____ _____ _____
                                                                   Day   Month   Year

   Type of Group: Child Only(1) _____   Mme Vanier(2) _____   Parallel(3) _____

Gender of child: F _____   M _____   Date of Birth _____ _____ _____
                                                              Day   Month   Year

Group Start Date: _____ _____ _____   For Post Test: Number of Sessions attended _____
                  Day   Month   Year

For updates on this questionnaire, contact:

Dr. Marlies Sudermann
London Family Court Clinic
254 Pall Mall Street, Suite 200
LONDON ON CANADA N6A 5P6
e-mail: marlies@lfcc.on.ca

A. DEFINITIONS OF WOMAN ABUSE

	Yes	Not Sure	No
1. If a man does this to a woman, is it abuse?			
a) Hits with a fist	Y	NS	N
b) Slaps	Y	NS	N
c) Calls names	Y	NS	N
d) Threatens to hurt her	Y	NS	N
e) Threatens to break one of her things	Y	NS	N
f) Kisses her even if she says, "No."	Y	NS	N

B. SAFETY SKILLS

2. If the adults in your house were fighting, what could you do to keep yourself safe?

a)

b)

c)

3. a) If someone tried to hurt your Mom, what would you do?

	Yes	Not Sure	No
b) Would you try to stop the fighting?	Yes	Not Sure	No

4. What phone number(s) can you call to get help in an emergency? Give more than one answer if you can.

Phone Number	Place or Person Called
_____	_____
_____	_____
_____	_____

5. If there were fights in your family, who would you talk to? You may give more than one answer.

a.

b.

c.

C. KNOWLEDGE/ATTITUDES ABOUT WOMAN ABUSE	True	Not Sure	False
6. Some fighting and hitting (between a dad and a mom) is OK.	T	NS	F
7. Alcohol or drugs cause woman abuse.	T	NS	F
8. Woman abuse happens in a lot of families.	T	NS	F
9. A fight can clear the air and settle things.	T	NS	F
10. Sometimes, moms do things they deserve to be hit for.	T	NS	F
11. It is OK to hit another person.	T	NS	F
12. Sometimes children are the cause of parents' abusive behaviour/fights.	T	NS	F
13. Children are to blame if dad hits mom.	T	NS	F
14. Children should try to stop parents from fighting.	T	NS	F

D. ALTERNATIVES TO VIOLENCE/ANGER CONTROL

15. If you were on the school bus, and someone took your hat or backpack, what could you do?

a)

b)

c)

16. When I am mad at someone, I:	Always	Very Often	Sometimes	Almost Never	Never
a) I tell someone when I'm angry with them	5	4	3	2	1
b) Get help to settle the problem	5	4	3	2	1
c) Plan to get back at the person	5	4	3	2	1
d) Yell or scream at the person	5	4	3	2	1
e) Hit, punch, or kick	5	4	3	2	1
f) Go away to cool off	5	4	3	2	1
g) Destroy objects or throw things	5	4	3	2	1
h) Try to think of how the other person feels	5	4	3	2	1

E. EXCUSES FOR VIOLENCE/ABUSE	Yes	Sometimes	Never
17. a) Is it okay for you to swear at another kid your own age?	Y	S	N
b) What if the other kid is really bugging you?	Y	S	N
c) What if the other kid has sworn at you?	Y	S	N
d) What if the other kid has stolen from you?	Y	S	N
e) What if the other kid hit you?	Y	S	N
18. a) Is it okay for you to make fun of another kid your own age?	Y	S	N
b) What if the other kid is really bugging you?	Y	S	N
c) What if the other kid has sworn at you?	Y	S	N
d) What if the other kid has stolen from you?	Y	S	N
e) What if the other kid hit you?	Y	S	N
19. a) Is it okay for you to hit another kid your own age?	Y	S	N
b) What if the other kid is really bugging you?	Y	S	N
c) What if the other kid has sworn at you?	Y	S	N
d) What if the other kid has stolen from you?	Y	S	N
e) What if the other kid hit you?	Y	S	N
20. a) Is it okay for a man to hit his wife or girlfriend?	Y	S	N
b) What if she has stayed out late?	Y	S	N
c) What if she has been drinking?	Y	S	N
d) What if she has hit the kids?	Y	S	N
21. a) Is it okay for a woman to hit her husband or boyfriend?	Y	S	N
b) What if he has stayed out late?	Y	S	N
c) What if he has been drinking?	Y	S	N
d) What if he has hit the kids?	Y	S	N

22. Anna and John can hear their Dad and Mom arguing downstairs. Dad is angry that the house is a mess. Anna and John are upstairs in their rooms. They can hear the fight getting worse. They hear a smashing sound. Then they hear their Mom scream, "Why did you break that?" Then they hear their Dad hitting their Mom.

a) What should Anna and John do?

	Yes	Maybe	No
i) Go downstairs and break up the fight.	Y	M	N
ii) Telephone police or emergency services.	Y	M	N
iii) Telephone a neighbour or relative for help.	Y	M	N
iv) Stay in a safe place and stay out of the fight.	Y	M	N

b) Whose fault is it that Mom is getting hit?

c) Where and how can Anna and John get help for themselves, after the fight stops?

F. OTHER LEARNING ABOUT VIOLENCE AND WOMAN ABUSE

23. Have you learned about violence, violence prevention or woman abuse at school?

YES _____   NO _____

If yes, describe what you learned.

24. Have you seen any t.v. programs about family violence or woman abuse?

YES _____   NO _____

If yes, describe the shows you have seen.

<table>
<tr><td>

┌─────────────────────┐
│   — — — — │
│   **CASE ID** │
└─────────────────────┘

</td></tr>
</table>

Person's Relationship to the child:
Mother: _____
Foster Mother: _____
Other: _____

Post-Group
Mother's/Caretaker's Evaluation

1. What did you like about your child's participation in the group?

2. How much do you think the group helped your child?

A Lot		A Little		Not at All
5	4	3	2	1

3. Have you noticed any change in your child as a result of participation in the group?

   Yes   No

   If you answered yes, what changes did you notice?

4. How much information did you receive about what your child was learning and doing in the group?

A Lot		A Little		Not at All
5	4	3	2	1

5. What would you suggest that should be done differently in future groups?

┌─────────────────────┐
│   — — — — │
│   **CASE ID** │
└─────────────────────┘

Post-Group
Children's Evaluation

1. How much did you like the group?   **A Lot**   **A Little**   **Not at All**

                                                5   4   3   2   1

2. What did you like about the group?

3. What did you dislike about the group?

4. How much did you learn in the group?   **A Lot**   **A Little**   **Not at All**

                                                5   4   3   2   1

5. Would you tell a friend who has problems in her or his family to come to this kind of group?

                                                                Yes   No

Helping Children Who Reside
at Shelters for Battered Women:
Lessons Learned

Nanette Stephens
Renee McDonald
Ernest N. Jouriles

SUMMARY. The need for mental health/psychoeducational services for children in battered women's shelters is discussed. In addition to questions of types, targets, and timing of services, the need for a careful evaluation of all shelter-based services for children is emphasized. Suggestions and guidelines are provided for designing, implementing, and evaluating services for children in battered women's shelters. *[Article copies available for a fee from The Haworth Document Delivery Service: 1-800-342-9678. E-mail address: getinfo@haworthpressinc.com <Website: http://www.haworthpressinc.com>]*

KEYWORDS. Services, programs, youth, domestic violence, evaluation, spousal aggression

Are mental health/psychoeducational services really needed for children who are residing in battered women's shelters? If so, what specific kinds of services should be offered, to whom should services be offered, and when should these services be delivered? These are key questions to consider when

Address correspondence to: Nanette Stephens, PhD, Department of Psychology, University of Houston, 4800 Calhoun, Houston, TX 77204-5341.

[Haworth co-indexing entry note]: "Helping Children Who Reside at Shelters for Battered Women: Lessons Learned." Stephens, Nanette, Renee McDonald, and Ernest N. Jouriles. Co-published simultaneously in *Journal of Aggression, Maltreatment & Trauma* (The Haworth Maltreatment & Trauma Press, an imprint of The Haworth Press, Inc.) Vol. 3, No. 1 (#5), 2000, pp. 147-160; and: *Children Exposed to Domestic Violence: Current Issues in Research, Intervention, Prevention, and Policy Development* (ed: Robert A. Geffner, Peter G. Jaffe, and Marlies Sudermann) The Haworth Maltreatment & Trauma Press, an imprint of The Haworth Press, Inc., 2000, pp. 147-160. Single or multiple copies of this article are available for a fee from The Haworth Document Delivery Service [1-800-342-9678, 9:00 a.m. - 5:00 p.m. (EST). E-mail address: getinfo@haworthpressinc.com].

planning services for children who reside in shelters for battered women. In this article, we address these questions and provide some guidelines derived from our experience in designing shelter-based children's services. Finally, we close with some specific suggestions for planning, implementing, and evaluating services for children living in shelters for battered women.

IS THERE A NEED FOR CHILDREN'S SERVICES IN BATTERED WOMEN'S SHELTERS?

The answer to this question may seem obvious to many. However, individuals who are not working directly with families in shelters for battered women often lack accurate information about the circumstances and needs of many of these women and children. First, it is important to note that shelters for battered women typically house more children than women. For example, in Texas more than 10,000 women and 15,000 of their children sought refuge in shelters for battered women in 1996 (Texas Council on Family Violence, 1997). One might argue on the basis of these figures alone that some type of service should be available for children at battered women's shelters.

Second, most, if not all, children in shelters for battered women have been directly or indirectly exposed to domestic violence. Research indicates that this experience in and of itself is likely to engender at least short-term distress in children (see prior articles in this volume; also Cummings & Davies, 1994), with greater frequency of exposure to domestic violence increasing the likelihood of child problems (e.g., Jouriles, Norwood, McDonald, Vincent, & Mahoney, 1996). In addition to the extreme distress and disruption posed by exposure to domestic violence, other stressors and hardships are all too common for many of these families. Table 1 summarizes demographic information we gathered from families seeking residential services from five Houston, Texas area battered women's shelters.

As can be seen in Table 1, many of the families are dealing with consequences of poverty in addition to domestic violence. Often, families have no means of transportation and lack basic material resources such as furniture, clothing, and essential household goods (Jouriles et al., 1998). Others have experienced frequent moves, social isolation, drug and/or alcohol problems, and other types of mental health problems (e.g., mood disorders, anxiety: Jouriles et al., 1998). Tragically, many of the women and children served by women's shelters have experienced child abuse and/or neglect, as well (Jouriles & Norwood, 1995).

Given the host of difficulties that many of these families face, it comes as no surprise that reviews of the research on children of battered women have concluded that these children, particularly those who are residing with their mothers at battered women's shelters, are at great risk for a variety of adjust-

TABLE 1

	Mode	Mean (SD)	Range
# Children per Family	2	2.5 (1.3)	1-9
Age of Mother	30	30.9 (5.9)	20-50
Yrs. Ed/Mother	12	11.3 (2.3)	3-17
Yrs. Ed/Partner	12	11.6 (2.5)	3-18
Family's Yearly Pre-shelter Income (mother and partner)	0	$3,706 (11,785)	$0-156,000

Note: data for each demographic variable were collected from over 400 families with children ages 3 and older, from 1989-1996 (the number of families providing data for each category, however, was different).

ment problems in comparison to children who have not been exposed to domestic violence (see Jaffe, Wolfe, & Wilson, 1990; Kolbo, Blakely, & Engleman, 1996; McDonald & Jouriles, 1991, for reviews of the empirical literature). Although it appears that some of these children are functioning well despite the hardships they have experienced (Hughes & Luke, 1998), many others are experiencing severe adjustment problems. Examples of such problems include externalizing behavior problems (e.g., aggressive, antisocial, oppositional behaviors), internalizing behavior problems (e.g., anxiety, depression, withdrawal, somatic complaints), academic problems, problems relating to peers, and low self-esteem (Christopoulos et al., 1987; Davidson, 1978; Hilberman & Munson, 1977-78; Jaffe et al., 1990; Kolbo et al., 1996; Levine, 1975; McDonald & Jouriles, 1991). Furthermore, there is some evidence that these problems are stable, that is, they do not necessarily disappear or improve when the family separates from the batterer (e.g., Jouriles et al., 1998). In fact, some children continue to have difficulties into their adult years. For example, data indicate that a male child's exposure to his mother's physical abuse increases the risk that he will be a batterer as an adult (Hotaling & Sugarman, 1986), and a female child's exposure to her mother's physical abuse increases the likelihood that she will experience depression as an adult (Henning, Leitenberg, Coffey, Turner, & Bennett, 1996).

Thus, the answer to the question of whether there is a need for children's services in battered women's shelters is a resounding "Yes!" Recognizing this need, many shelters have recently begun to develop programs and services for children (Alessi & Hearn, 1984; Grusznski, Brink, & Edleson, 1988; Hughes, 1997; Peled & Edleson, 1995). Those involved in the development and implementation of such programs can readily attest to a number of difficult and complex questions that confront program developers: Which services should be offered? Which children should be targeted to receive services? When should services be initiated and terminated? We turn to these questions in the following section.

TYPES, TARGETS, AND TIMING OF SERVICES

In the paragraphs above, we touched on the broad range of problems and needs of children residing in battered women's shelters. Unfortunately, there is no "one size fits all" service or program that can meet all of the complicated and diverse needs of many of these children. Thus, it is essential that program developers carefully consider and stipulate the purpose or intended function of the services they are designing. For example, shelter workers might wish to design services that increase children's safety, improve children's self-esteem, or reduce children's aggression. Obviously, choices about the purposes or functions of services will depend greatly upon the needs, resources, and philosophy of a particular shelter.

Once the purposes or functions of the services are determined, the following questions arise: What types of services (e.g., play groups for children, individual counseling) best achieve these purposes? How do we select or identify which children will receive and/or benefit from the services? When should we initiate services? In our work in several battered women's shelters in the Houston, Texas area over the last 10 years, we have seen many types of shelter-sponsored children's programs and services, including play groups, shelter-based day care, out-of-shelter day care, child advocacy groups, anger management groups, homework groups, tutorial services, arts/crafts programs, field trips, and reading rooms/groups. Individual counseling, play therapy, art therapy, and group therapy for children are also often provided in shelters. In addition to the services offered to children, many shelters offer services to mothers that are intended to directly benefit their children (e.g., parent education classes). Many services are typically made available to all residents of the shelter (with the exception of infants), and it is not unusual for participation in these services to be *required* as a condition of shelter stay. This impressive array of services and activities may suggest to some that sheltered children's needs are being adequately and effectively addressed. We believe, however, that it is impossible to tell if this is the case because of the absence of outcome data systematically evaluating these services. In fact, we suspect that, in the majority of cases, children's needs are *not* being sufficiently addressed by shelter-based services. Why do many well-intended shelter services and programs fall short of meeting the needs of children of battered women? We believe that a number of issues makes the planning and implementation of services for sheltered children a difficult undertaking.

First, as discussed earlier, sheltered children often have needs that are diverse, complex, and difficult to address. Importantly, most of these children do not have the same needs. Some children have school-related problems, and others do not. Some children are in crisis and/or are very fearful and depressed, while others are very aggressive and defiant. Some children have many of these problems, while others appear to be functioning very well in spite of the difficulties they have experienced. This variability in children's adjustment problems (coupled with the lack of a "one size fits all" service) makes it difficult to plan and implement services that will meet the specific needs of all children.

Second, assumptions about the causes or sources of a child's problem(s) may affect how issues pertaining to the type, target, and timing of services are addressed. It is easy to assume that many sheltered children's problems are a direct and primary result of domestic violence and therefore ought to be addressed by services focused on ameliorating the effects of domestic violence. In reality, however, there are often multiple causes for these children's problems. In addition, it is often difficult and sometimes impossible to precisely determine the cause(s) or source(s) of the problem. Exposure to domestic violence is not likely to be good for any child, but this experience is not *necessarily* the most pressing or deleterious concern for *all* sheltered children. In other words, domestic violence is not always the sole cause or even the most serious cause of the problems that these children are having. For example, we noted previously that many children living in battered women's shelters have been physically abused or neglected. Many sheltered families are living well below the poverty line, and as a result have often had inadequate medical care and have lived in unsafe neighborhoods and/or in crowded living conditions. In many shelters, residents often have histories of drug and alcohol problems as well. Because all of these conditions are associated with the development of adjustment problems in children, it is very difficult to sort out which of these influences, in addition to domestic violence, is responsible for a particular child's behavioral and emotional difficulties. Services derived from a tacit assumption that the problems of all children of battered women are primarily caused by domestic violence may result in treating the wrong causal agent or ignoring other factors that may be contributing to the child's problems. That is, services that primarily involve issues related to domestic violence may focus on events that are not always directly and/or immediately related to a child's adjustment and may overlook or ignore other critical, immediate concerns (e.g., physical or sexual abuse, child neglect).

Third, most shelters have restricted resources, including limited staff, limited funds for training materials, and limited space suitable for children's services. Often, because of these constraints, children receive no shelter-based services at all or else such services are provided to children in groups (e.g., anger management, coping skills groups). When group services embody a counseling or other mental-health component, other concerns emerge. For example, the ages of children residing in a shelter at any given time may vary widely, and children of very different ages and developmental levels are sometimes included in the same groups. This variability in child developmental status suggests that in some groups, less mature children may be exposed to concepts that they cannot comprehend or use. In other cases, children's needs may be so varied and complex that a group approach is benign at best, and confusing and distressing at worst. Taken together, these differences are likely to make the use of group counseling services potentially problematic.

Fourth, the duration of most shelter stays is quite limited. Most of the shelters we work with have a 30-day limit, although a few families are granted extensions for 1-3 months. Many families only remain in shelter a day or two, and some depart with little or no warning. Children generally have no control over how long their family remains at the shelter, and consequently have no control (and often no knowledge) of how long they will be able to receive services. Uncertainties regarding the duration of shelter stay raise very important ethical and clinical concerns about initiating services with children and then being unable to follow through with the services. This issue is especially critical because many of the problems that some of these children are experiencing are very complex and are likely to take longer than a few days or weeks to address. In some cases, it is even possible that more harm than good may be caused when these types of difficult problems are only partially addressed with very short-term and/or incomplete interventions.

Fifth, although shelter entry may seem to be a logical time for a family to begin to receive mental health services, it must be remembered that the vast majority of families come to shelters first and foremost for refuge from violence, not for counseling or therapy. The concept of "readiness for change" (see Prochaska & DiClemente, 1984) or receptiveness/readiness for services suggests that it is a mistake to assume that every child who comes to a shelter wants a particular type of service or is ready to benefit from that service. In our work, we have observed that when children arrive at a shelter, they often have a very different understanding of their family's situation than their mothers or shelter staff. For example, some children have no idea of why they have come to a shelter. Other children are angry and resentful because they blame their mothers for taking them away from their fathers, their homes, their schools, and/or their neighborhood friends. In addition, approximately 10% of children ages 8 years or older whom we have interviewed have told us that they have never seen their fathers physically abuse (e.g., hit, push, kick) their mothers. In contrast, other children frankly acknowledged that they witnessed their mother's abuse, and many admitted to witnessing domestic violence that involved a knife or gun. Thus, children often come to shelters at very different levels of awareness and readiness to talk about or address the violence and the other problems in their lives, as well.

It is clear thus far that issues regarding delivery of sheltered children's services are complex and demand serious deliberation given the potential consequences of such services. Added to the concerns described above is a sixth issue that involves the difficulty of attempting to address a child's problems without consideration of "the bigger picture" (e.g., the child's and family's context). That is, where do all of the above considerations fit in terms of a particular child's family and circumstances, and what role will a mother have in her child's treatment? Many times, mothers are relatively unaware of the nature and content of the services provided to their children. More importantly, it is possible that some skills that appear appropriate and adaptive for children who have been exposed to domestic violence may actually be inappropriate and even detrimental for some children. For example, many mothers return to their abusive partners after exiting a shelter (Okun, 1988). In such families, children who have recently learned that it is acceptable to express their feelings about family violence or who have learned self-advocacy skills in a shelter may be at increased risk of harm or maltreatment should they apply these skills at home, particularly if their actions may be perceived as "talking back" or noncompliance (e.g., a child phones 911 instead of following a parent's order to go to the bedroom during a violent marital interaction). Similarly, formulating safety plans for children without access to important information about family dynamics and circumstances, which may unexpectedly change following shelter departure, may put children at greater risk in certain situations. Hence, at times, providing treatment or counseling services for a child without including or consulting the child's mother, without full knowledge of the child's history, and without knowing the circumstances the child will face after he or she exits the shelter may create iatronegic treatment effects. Simply put, well-intended intervention efforts that are not fully integrated with significant influences and factors in the child's life may exacerbate the child's difficulties.

To summarize, questions of types, targets, and timing of services for children in shelters are complicated by a number of factors:

1. the diversity and complexity of many sheltered children's behavior and adjustment problems,
2. the difficulty of identifying precise causes and sources of the children's problems,
3. limited shelter resources,
4. the limited and uncertain duration of shelter stays,

5. the variation in children's readiness/ability to profit from services,
6. the difficulty in obtaining critical contextual information and consulting with and including mothers in their children's services.

Given this daunting list of concerns, answers to questions about types, targets, and timing of shelter-based services will undoubtedly vary from shelter-to-shelter, and will depend greatly on the resources available. Our multi-disciplinary, clinical-research team, which includes social workers, shelter staff, college student volunteers, community therapists, and researchers, continues to conduct research, which focuses on identifying specific needs of children living in Houston, Texas-area battered women's shelters. We are also developing and implementing services to meet some of those needs. Recommendations for shelter-based programs and activities for children, gleaned from our work with children of battered women over the past decade, are presented in the following section.

RECOMMENDATIONS FOR CHILDREN'S SERVICES

First, we recommend that shelters have well-trained staff who are familiar with available community resources (e.g., community mental health agencies, child protective services, health-care agencies). Within a family's first 24-48 hours of their shelter stay, a staff member should implement a screening interview for the purpose of identifying family and child problems that require immediate attention. Examples of such problems, which unfortunately are not uncommon in battered women's shelters, are suicidal feelings, unmet medical needs, and child maltreatment. For some families with such critical needs, referrals to community-based resources and agencies may be sufficient. For others, additional assistance may be necessary, such as help in setting up appointments with referral agencies, providing transportation to such agencies, helping families understand the need for such referrals, and alerting families to the availability of services to address their problems. Although many sheltered families are familiar with some social service agencies (e.g., AFDC, WIC), others are less aware of resources that provide legal, mental health, or child protective services. After initial referrals are made, shelter staff may then help families by encouraging compliance with referral agencies' recommendations, and continuing to monitor the family's status with respect to the problems that necessitated referral. This latter issue is especially important when concerns about child abuse or neglect arise.

Related to the above issue, a shelter's ability to provide appropriate and timely referrals will depend on the staff's level of training and experience in recognizing the presence of a problem (i.e., the extent to which a problem is directly observable or has consequences for staff or other shelter residents).

That is, such referrals are often made when either a shelter worker or shelter resident "notices" that a problem exists (e.g., child abuse, severe maternal depression, child illness), or when a family member asks for help. Many other families who have problems that are not overtly observable (e.g., suicidal feelings, covert child abuse) may thus "fall through the cracks," and/or may remain unaware that help exists for the kinds of problems they are experiencing. To address this concern, we recommend that shelters implement a systematic method for identifying problems that demand immediate attention. We recommend that each family who enters a shelter be screened for the presence of specific critical problems that occur with some frequency in shelter populations. The most obvious such problems are mother or child suicidality or severe depression, physical and sexual abuse and/or neglect of children, and unaddressed medical problems (e.g., illness requiring medical treatment). Although it has been postulated that many children who are exposed to marital violence develop Post-Traumatic Stress Disorder (e.g., see Rossman & Ho, 2000, this volume; Kerig, Fedorowicz, Brown, & Warren, 2000, this volume; also Rossman, 1998; Silvern, Landis, & Karyl, 1990), this remains an area of considerable controversy that we believe warrants additional, careful study before such symptomatology is routinely assumed to be present among sheltered children of battered women. A number of interviews, questionnaires and checklists have been developed that could be readily adapted by shelter staff in consultation with mental health professionals to meet the needs of specific shelters, to ensure that screening interviews are systematic and standardized, and to reduce the likelihood that serious problems will be overlooked.

Our second recommendation is that shelters offer a variety of activities for the sole purpose of making a family's shelter stay more pleasant and positive for everyone (i.e., children, mothers, and shelter staff). Because shelters are often highly structured environments, it is difficult for most families to feel "at home." In many shelters, women must complete assigned chores at specific times, must sign in and out (for safety) when leaving and returning, must eat meals at set times, and must attend certain shelter meetings. In addition, privacy is often compromised, and families are typically required to comply with shelter rules that govern children's behavior and stipulate how mothers may respond to child misbehaviors. In addition, most families who have to seek refuge at shelters are highly distressed and are attempting to cope with many difficult and often long-standing problems. Many mothers are trying to deal with their children's adjustment problems; others are concerned about the anticipated effects on their children of divorce and dissolution of the family. Some mothers are pressured by their children to leave the shelter because the children are bored or just "want to go home." The extreme stress that is associated with feelings of being in danger, and at times even pursued by a batterer, can further elevate the level of tension and strain within a shelter, as can the high levels of behavioral and emotional problems of many sheltered children. When such families come together with other similarly stressed families in an unfamiliar shelter environment, the potential for conflict, strain, and premature shelter departure is increased. Thus, activities that provide opportunities for mothers and children to "take a break" from this stress and tension are highly recommended.

During the initial years of our team's work, we were contacted by a shelter to assist in the development of a children's program with the goal of reducing the level of chaos within the shelter. While this goal may not have been very ambitious, it was reasonable, appropriate, and practical. Because there were no shelter-based children's activities at that time, mothers and children were left to their own devices to find ways for the children to spend their time. One of the very negative side-effects of this was that families were leaving the shelter prematurely, and in some cases returning to their batterers, because of the chaotic shelter environment or the fact that many children were bored and restless. One of our first steps, then, was to organize structured activities for the children. Our team recruited volunteers so that we would be able to provide a relatively small child-to-adult volunteer ratio. We trained the volunteers in basic child-management and nurturing skills, and we supplied ideas and materials for enjoyable activities that children of different ages could do for several hours a day such as arts and crafts, sporting activities and games, field trips, etc. While participating in these activities, the children were also receiving a great deal of positive adult attention and were interacting with positive adult role models. The children looked forward to this program and to being with the volunteers who came to play with them, and the level of chaos in the shelter dropped drastically. The children's program also allowed mothers to have some time to just relax or accomplish necessary tasks, such as doing laundry, meeting with shelter caseworkers, apartment/job-hunting, etc. One unanticipated side-effect of this program was that having the children organized and engaged in activities also gave shelter staff a break, as they had been accustomed to having the children "underfoot" throughout the shelter all day. The success of this program is evidenced by the fact that it continues today, virtually unchanged from when it began, and we have been asked to implement the same type of children's program in other shelters. This type of program makes very few demands on shelter staff (e.g., they have to notify mothers of the existence of the program and tell the children's program volunteers which children will attend the program each day), and provides benefits to children, mothers, and shelter staff. Given the low demands, the range of benefits, and the continued success of this early effort, we recommend this type of service, at a minimum, for all shelters.

Third, we offer a two-part recommendation with respect to shelter-based services geared toward addressing children's adjustment problems: *Proceed with Caution* and *Evaluate the Services Offered.* Although we certainly do not want to discourage providing mental health/psychoeducational services for children, we maintain that there is a significant potential for inadvertently doing harm to some children if a broad-brushed approach is used in implementing such interventions. Thus, we recommend that all mental health/psychoeducational interventions be carefully evaluated to determine whether the services are having the desired effects. An example illustrates this point:

At one shelter where we were working, the shelter staff devised what we thought was a very clever short-term intervention using a videotape for children to watch with a counselor. This videotape, which depicted children hearing their parents yell at each other, utilized a talking teddy bear as a narrator who emphasized to the children that (1) they were not alone; that is, there were other children who had parents who argued and fought, and (2) they were not to blame for their parents' fights. The children were then provided with coloring books with pictures of the teddy bear and drawings with captions reiterating the two points covered in the videotape.

At first, we were very pleased with the creativity and apparent utility of this intervention, and the shelter director and shelter counselor indicated that they felt that the children were enjoying and benefiting from the program. Our initial enthusiasm was further bolstered by our analysis of data we had collected from a small sample of children who had been exposed to severe domestic violence. The results of our analysis had indeed indicated that many children actually did blame themselves for their parents' violence, and the more the children blamed themselves, the more likely they were to report that they felt depressed, were anxious, and had low self-esteem. The intervention thus appeared to offer an effective, short-term solution for an apparently common problem. In order to document how effective the intervention was, we decided to conduct a small evaluation study. Much to our dismay, we found that the children who watched the videotape and used the coloring book with their counselor actually blamed themselves *MORE* for their parents' violence *after* the intervention than before the intervention. In other words, this intervention had the opposite of its desired effect. Moreover, it had this opposite effect on each child who received the service during the evaluation study! We still do not know why this occurred, but we speculate that the intervention sensitized children to the idea of self-blame. It is also worth pointing out that this intervention was a "child-only" service. That is, mothers were not involved in the intervention except to give their children permission to participate. We later found out that some mothers actually felt that their children *were* to blame for the domestic violence and directly told them so. Regardless of the reasons for the ineffectiveness of the intervention, it illustrates the point that a thoughtful, well-intended effort to help children can have unintended negative consequences.

Again, we do not make this point to discourage people from developing and implementing interventions to help children and their families, but to highlight the need to *evaluate the effects of interventions.* Not all interventions or therapies have the desired effects, not all interventions or services are helpful to all children, and not all shelters are able to provide a full range of programs and interventions for children. Thus, given the limited resources of most shelters, the careful evaluation of services that are intended to address children's mental health needs is not only ethical and responsible behavior, but it can also be a means of demonstrating the cost-effectiveness of such services and interventions.

The diverse circumstances of sheltered families, the wide range of variability of children's needs, the limited funds and resources that are typical in many shelters, and the short and often unpredictable amount of time that most families spend in a shelter make the development, implementation, and evaluation of services for children a complicated and challenging endeavor. A necessary and critical first step, however, in the development of any type of service is a thorough assessment of needs, followed by a thoughtful and careful specification of which needs will be addressed by which services (i.e., clear statements about the types, targets/recipients, and timing of services to meet specific needs). After these specifications are made, it is often helpful to review and evaluate how other shelters and service agencies have addressed the same types of needs and goals, making adaptations, as appropriate, for specific shelter situations and needs. Following the initial implementation of services, the critical, but often neglected, next step is to evaluate whether the services accomplished the specified goals. Information from this step then can lead to decisions about whether to continue and/or modify the services. Thus, the fundamental steps in planning, implementing, and evaluating services for sheltered children are:

1. assessment of needs,
2. specification of types, targets, and timing of services to meet certain needs and goals,
3. design and selection of services to meet specific goals,
4. implementation of services,
5. evaluation of services, and
6. decisions to continue, discontinue, or modify services.
7. Decisions to modify services should, of course, be followed by an evaluation of the effects of those modified services.

REFERENCES

Alessi, J. J., & Hearn, K. (1984). Group treatment of children in shelters for battered women. In A. R. Roberts (Ed.), *Battered women and their families* (pp. 49-61). New York: Springer.

Christopoulos, C., Cohn, D. A., Shaw, D. S., Joyce, S., Sullivan-Hanson, J., Kraft, S. P., & Emery, R. E. (1987). Children of abused women: Adjustment at time of shelter residence. *Journal of Marriage and the Family, 49*, 611-619.

Cummings, E. M., & Davies, P. (1994). *Children and marital conflict: The impact of family dispute and resolution.* New York: Guilford.

Davidson, T. (1978). *Conjugal crime: Understanding and changing the wifebeating pattern.* New York: Hawthorn.

Grusznski, R. J., Brink, J. C., & Edleson, J. L. (1988). Support and education groups for children of battered women. *Child Welfare, 68*, 431-444.

Henning, K., Leitenberg, H., Coffey, P., Turner, T., & Bennett, R. T. (1996). Long-term psychological and social impact of witnessing physical conflict between parents. *Journal of Interpersonal Violence, 11*(1), 35-51.

Hilberman, E., & Munson, K. (1977-78). Sixty battered women. *Victimology: An International Journal, 2*, 460-470.

Hotaling, G., & Sugarman, D. (1986). An analysis of risk markers in husband to wife violence: The current state of knowledge. *Violence and Victims, 1*(2), 101-124.

Hughes, H. M. (1997). Research concerning children of battered women: Clinical implications. In R. Geffner, S. Sorenson, & P. Lundberg-Love (Eds.), *Violence and sexual abuse at home: Current issues in spousal battering and child maltreatment* (pp. 225-244). New York: The Haworth Press, Inc.

Hughes, H. M., & Luke, D. A. (1998). Heterogeneity in adjustment among children of battered women. In G. Holden, R. Geffner, & E. N. Jouriles (Eds.), *Children exposed to marital violence: Theory, research, and applied issues* (pp. 185-221). Washington, DC: American Psychological Association.

Jaffe, P. G., Wolfe, D. A., & Wilson, S. K. (1990). *Children of battered women.* Newbury Park: Sage Publications.

Jouriles, E. N., McDonald, R., Stephens, N., Norwood, W. D., Spiller, L. C., & Ware, H. S. (1998). Breaking the cycle of violence: Helping families departing from battered women's shelters. In G. Holden, R. Geffner, & E. N. Jouriles (Eds.), *Children exposed to family violence: Theory, research, and applied issues* (pp. 337-369). Washington, DC: American Psychological Association.

Jouriles, E. N., & Norwood, W. D. (1995). Physical aggression toward boys and girls in families characterized by the battering of women. *Journal of Family Psychology, 9*, 69-78.

Jouriles, E. N., Norwood, W. D., McDonald, R., Vincent, J. P., & Mahoney, A. (1996). Physical violence and other forms of marital aggression: Links with children's behavior problems. *Journal of Family Psychology, 2*(10), 223-234.

Kerig, P., Fedorowicz, A., Brown, C., & Warren, S. (2000). Assessment and intervention for PTSD in children exposed to violence. In R. Geffner, P. G. Jaffe, & M. Sudermann (Eds.), *Children exposed to domestic violence: Current issues in research, intervention, prevention and policy development.* New York: The Haworth Press, Inc.

Kolbo, J. R., Blakely, E. H., & Engleman, D. (1996). Children who witness domestic violence: A review of empirical literature. *Journal of Interpersonal Violence, 11*, 281-293.

Levine, M. (1975). Interparental violence and its effects on the children: A study of 50 families in general practice. *Medical Science Law, 15*, 172-176.

McDonald, R., & Jouriles, E. N. (1991). Marital aggression and child behavior problems: Research findings, mechanisms, and intervention strategies. *The Behavior Therapist, 14*, 189-192.

Okun, L. (1988). Termination or resumption of cohabitation in woman battering relationships: A statistical study. In G. T. Hotaling, D. Finkelhor, J. T. Kirkpatrick, & M. A. Straus (Eds.), *Coping with family violence: Research and policy perspectives* (pp. 107-119). New York: Sage.

Peled, E., & Edleson, J. L. (1995). Process and outcome in small groups for children of battered women. In E. Peled, P. G. Jaffe, & J. L. Edleson (Eds.), *Ending the cycle of violence: Community responses to children of battered women* (pp. 77-96). Newbury Park, CA: Sage.

Prochaska, J. O., & DiClemente, C. C. (1984). *The transtheoretical approach: Crossing traditional boundaries of therapy.* Homewood, IL: Dow Jones, Irwin.

Rossman, B. B. R. (2000). Descartes's error and posttraumatic stress disorder: Cognition and emotion in children who are exposed to parental violence. In G. W. Holden, R. Geffner, & E. N. Jouriles (Eds.), *Children exposed to marital violence: Theory, research, and applied issues* (pp. 223-256). Washington, DC: American Psychological Association.

Rossman, B. B. R., & Ho, J. (2000). Posttraumatic responses and children exposed to family violence. In R. Geffner, P. G. Jaffe, & M. Sudermann (Eds.), *Children exposed to domestic violence: Current issues in research, intervention, prevention, and policy development.* New York: The Haworth Press, Inc.

Silvern, L., Landis, T., & Karyl, J. (1990). *Identifying trauma in children of violent marriages.* Paper presented at the 1990 National Symposium on Child Victimization, Atlanta, GA.

Texas Council on Family Violence. (1997). Family violence statistics in Texas. Available from Texas Council on Family Violence, 8701 N. MoPac Expressway, Ste. 450, Austin, TX.

Assessment and Intervention for PTSD in Children Exposed to Violence

Patricia K. Kerig
Anne E. Fedorowicz
Corina A. Brown
Michelle Warren

SUMMARY. Recent research has established that exposure to domestic violence is a major risk factor for posttraumatic stress disorder (PTSD) in children. However, one issue that has been relatively neglected in research conducted to date concerns developmental differences: both in the expression of PTSD symptoms across childhood and adolescence, and in the techniques appropriate for assessing and intervening with PTSD in children at different ages. The available literature is reviewed concerning the conceptualization, measurement, and treatment of PTSD in children, with special attention to the case of children of battered women. Guidelines are provided for developmentally sensitive approaches to assessment and treatment. *[Article copies available for a fee from The Haworth Document Delivery Service: 1-800-342-9678. E-mail address: getinfo@haworthpressinc.com <Website: http://www.haworthpressinc.com>]*

KEYWORDS. Domestic violence, children, posttraumatic stress disorder, psychotherapy, assessment

Portions of this paper are based on: Kerig, P.K., Fedorowicz, A. E., Warren, M., and Brown, C. A. (1997, June), *Clinical issues in assessment and intervention with PTSD in children exposed to violence*. Paper presented in J. Fantuzzo (Chair), *Exposure to violence and PTSD in children*, Second International Conference on Children Exposed to Violence, London, Ontario.

Address correspondence to: Patricia K. Kerig, PhD, School of Psychology, James Madison University, Harrisonburg, VA 22807-7401 (e-mail: kerigpk@jmu.edu).

[Haworth co-indexing entry note]: "Assessment and Intervention for PTSD in Children Exposed to Violence." Kerig, Patricia K. et al. Co-published simultaneously in *Journal of Aggression, Maltreatment & Trauma* (The Haworth Maltreatment & Trauma Press, an imprint The Haworth Press, Inc.) Vol. 3, No. 1 (#5), 2000, pp. 161-184; and: *Children Exposed to Domestic Violence: Current Issues in Research, Intervention, Prevention, and Policy Development* (ed: Robert A. Geffner, Peter G. Jaffe, and Marlies Sudermann) The Haworth Maltreatment & Trauma Press, an imprint of The Haworth Press, Inc., 2000, pp. 161-184. Single or multiple copies of this article are available for a fee from The Haworth Document Delivery Service [1-800-342-9678, 9:00 a.m. - 5:00 p.m. (EST). E-mail address: getinfo@haworthpressinc.com].

Research has clearly established that posttraumatic stress disorder (PTSD) is a potential consequence of exposure to family violence (Arroyo & Eth, 1995; Jaffe, Sudermann, & Reitzel, 1992; Peled, Jaffe, & Edelson, 1995), including woman abuse (Graham-Bermann & Levendosky, 1998; Pynoos & Eth, 1985; Rossman & Ho, this volume). However, before we can help children to overcome exposure to domestic violence, there are a number of issues that need to be considered. In particular, there are important developmental differences in how the symptoms of PTSD are expressed, how they should be assessed, and which interventions are most effective for children of various ages.

ASSESSMENT OF PTSD SYMPTOMS IN CHILDREN EXPOSED TO VIOLENCE

Conceptual Models of the Effects of Trauma on Children

A number of theorists have recently presented comprehensive models for understanding the effects of trauma, including Foy, Madvig, Pynoos, and Camilleri (1996), Koverola (1995), Pynoos, Steinberg, and Goenjian (1996), and Vernberg, La Greca, Silverman, and Prinstein (1996). Although each model offers unique insights, they also converge on a number of similar themes. For example, these models are *integrative* and consider the child as a whole person, taking into account multiple domains of functioning. In addition, they are *contextual,* considering the child in the context of the family, peer group, and the larger society. Thirdly, these models are *developmental,* and consider the ways in which children interpret and respond to traumatic experiences at different ages. In particular, Pynoos (1993; Pynoos, Steinberg, & Wriath, 1995) emphasizes the utility of using developmental psychopathology as a framework for understanding individual differences in the effects of trauma across the life span. Developmental psychopathology focuses attention on the mechanisms of development underlying psychopathology, such as emotion regulation, self-efficacy, and the successful navigation of stage-salient issues, in order to understand the factors that predict the child's reactions to traumatic experiences.

There are a number of dimensions that should be considered in assessing the impact of trauma on children, including characteristics of the child, the social environment, and the traumatic experience itself (Koverola, 1995). All these factors interact with one another to shape specific outcomes for individual children, and each can provide either a source of protection, or increased risk, for the development of psychopathology in children exposed to violence (Foy et al., 1996).

Areas for Assessment

Assessment of children's functioning. In order to conduct a comprehensive assessment of the impact of traumatic stress, Koverola (1995) suggests that we look at the child's functioning in many domains, including the cognitive, affective, moral, interpersonal, sexual, and physical. It is important to consider how each of these domains might have been affected by the trauma, and how they might be hindering the child from going forward in development. In addition, Vernberg et al. (1996) and Pynoos et al. (1995) suggest that we should also assess vulnerabilities of the child, such as temperament and prior history of traumatization, which might "potentiate" the risk of PTSD (Foy et al., 1996). In addition, they point to the need to assess sources of resiliency and competence, such as the child's coping strategies and self-esteem, which might moderate the risk.

Assessment of the social environment. Traumatic experiences have a direct impact on children's functioning, as well as an indirect impact through their effects on the family, the community, and society (Koverola, 1995). Therefore, the child's social context also needs to be assessed. For example, are family members supportive of the child, or are the parents themselves traumatized, thus adding to the child's distress (Keppel-Benson & Ollendick, 1993; Foy et al., 1996)? Are there resources available in the community for the child and the family (Koverola, 1995)? Are there larger societal influences at play; for example, do social norms and values regarding shame and secrecy inhibit a family from talking about the experience openly?

Assessment of the traumatic experience. A number of characteristics of the traumatic experience can differentially affect children's adjustment. These include the frequency and duration of the stressor, and the relationship of the victim and perpetrator (see Table 1). In addition, certain trauma characteristics have been specifically related to increased risk of PTSD. Significantly, PTSD is more likely to develop when children are exposed to acts of human aggression, as in the case of domestic violence. However, while it is helpful to consider all of the characteristics listed in Table 1, it is also necessary to tailor each assessment to the specific events the child has experienced (Koverola, 1995). Each traumatic event may have its own particular characteristics that make it threatening to the child.

Type I vs. Type II trauma. Another important characteristic to assess, as Terr argues (1991), is whether the trauma can be characterized as Type I or Type II. Type I traumas are responses to a single, sudden, unexpected stressor (e.g., an automobile accident) while Type II traumas follow from long-standing, repeated stressors (e.g., chronic family violence). While Type I symptoms fit the DSM-IV criteria for PTSD, some Type II symptoms are not well-captured by DSM, such as dissociation. It is important to be aware of the markers of Type II traumatization, because many of them are subtle, and may

TABLE 1. Characteristics of Traumatic Events Related to PTSD

Characteristics of the traumatic experience to be assessed:
- Type of traumatic experience
  - ◆ **Type I Trauma**
    - ◇ Single, sudden stressor (e.g., witnessing death of a parent)
    - ◇ Distinct and full memories
    - ◇ Symptoms fit the DSM-IV criteria:
      - * Repetition, avoidance, and hyper-arousal
  - ◆ **Type II Trauma**
    - ◇ Long-standing, repeated trauma (e. g., chronic sexual abuse)
    - ◇ Blurred memories of the traumatic events
    - ◇ Symptoms may be inconsistent with DSM-IV criteria
      - * Denial, self-hypnosis, dissociation, withdrawal, absence of feeling
      - * Sense of rage or unremitting sadness, self-destructive behavior
- Timing, frequency, and duration of the traumatic experience
- Force and degree of exposure to the traumatic experience
- Resolution of the traumatic experience
- Age at onset
- Number of perpetrators and their relationship to the victim
- Frequency of traumatic reminders

Characteristics related to increased risk for PTSD:
- Human aggression (e.g., woman abuse)
- Fright or life threat to self or significant others
- Prospect of loss or disruption
- Physical injury, great destruction of property
- Experienced first-hand

Sources: Keppel-Benson & Ollendick (1993); Koverola (1995); Pynoos et al. (1995); Schaefer (1994); Terr (1991); Vernberg et al. (1996); Vogel & Vernberg (1993).

go unnoticed. Further, Type II traumas may result from stressors which take place in secrecy and silence, such as sexual abuse and woman battering. Therefore, in contrast to dramatic and public events that are called to the attention of observers, Type II traumas may be overlooked. This is of concern, given the serious long-term-consequences of Type II traumatization.

Developmental Differences in Symptoms of PTSD

The developmental level of the child is important to consider in clinical work, as age will affect how the symptoms of PTSD manifest themselves, as well as how they can be assessed. In this next section, we review developmental differences in the ways that symptoms of PTSD are evidenced in the preschool, school-age, adolescent, and adult years. As presented in DSM-IV, the symptoms of PTSD fall into three distinct clusters: (1) Re-experiencing; (2) Avoidance and numbing; and (3) Increased arousal.

Re-experiencing. This first cluster of symptoms is the only one for which DSM-IV recognizes differences between children and adults. Table 2 presents the DSM-IV criteria in bold, with age-related considerations derived from research and clinical observations in regular font. For example, while adults may have recurrent and distressing recollections of the event, including images or thoughts, in young children intrusive recollections more often take the form of behavior, such as repetitive play about the traumatic event (Terr, 1988). Older children may have repetitive fantasies of being rescued or seeking revenge.

DSM-IV also notes that children are more likely than adults to have frightening dreams without recognizable content, or night terrors. If children's dreams do have content, Eth (1989) describes common post-traumatic dreams as concerning their own premature death. Children with PTSD may also believe that their dreams are prophetic. In addition, while adults may experience dissociative flashbacks in which they feel as if the traumatic event was recurring, children are more likely to experience only sounds or visual images of the event, which are likely to emerge when they are in a state of relaxation (Pynoos & Nader, 1990). Elementary school-age children, in particular, are prone to reenacting traumatic events or inventing trauma games such as "murder" (Armsworth & Holaday, 1993). Children are also likely to

TABLE 2. DSM-IV Cluster A Symptoms: Re-Experiencing

Adult	Adolescent	School-age	Preschool
1. recurrent recollections	recurrent revenge/rescue fantasies	recurrent revenge/rescue fantasies	**repetitive play**
2. distressing dreams	**nightmares**	**nightmares** night terrors	**nightmares** night terrors
3. feeling that event is recurring	**feeling that event is recurring**	intrusive sounds, images trauma re-enactment	intrusive sounds, images trauma re-enactment
4. distress when exposed to traumatic cues	trauma-specific and mundane fears	trauma-specific and mundane fears	separation anxiety stranger anxiety regressive fears
5. physiological reactivity upon exposure	reactivity and somatic complaints	reactivity and somatic complaints	eating problems, sensitivity to loud noise

Note: Bold represents DSM-IV criteria.
Sources: Eth (1989); Eth & Pynoos (1994); Ribbe, Lipovsky, & Freedy (1995); and Terr (1985; 1991).

develop specific fears of stimuli associated with the traumatic event, as well as more general fears that have a regressive quality, such as fear of the dark, of strangers, or of sleeping alone.

Avoidance and numbing. The second cluster includes a number of specific symptoms that differ in children and adults (see Table 3). For example, while adults may make efforts to avoid thoughts or feelings associated with the trauma, in children this takes the form not of active avoidance, but rather of "spacing out." Further, although adults may be unable to recall important aspects of the trauma, children rarely demonstrate total amnesia for traumatic events (Bruck, Ceci, & Hembroke, 1998). Instead, children tend to show cognitive-perceptual difficulties (Eth, 1989). Preschoolers are likely to experience confusion about significant details of an event. Children of all ages may misperceive the timing and sequencing of events, a phenomenon referred to as time skew, or misjudge events as having been predictors of the trauma, termed omen formation (Terr, 1985).

TABLE 3. DSM-IV Cluster B Symptoms: Avoidance/Numbing

Adult	Adolescent	School-age	Preschool
1. avoidance of thoughts or feelings about event	"spacing out"	"spacing out"	"spacing out"
2. avoidance of people, places, or activities	phobic behavior	phobic behavior	phobic behavior
3. inability to recall event	time skew omen formation	time skew omen formation	cognitive confusion
4. diminished interest in activities	truancy	school refusal	regressive behaviors
5. detachment from others	isolation acting out against others	withdrawal from peers lack of interest in play	anxious attachment
6. restricted range of affect	sadness, guilt	sadness, guilt sense of aloneness	sadness, helplessness
7. sense of foreshortened future	**sense of foreshortened future**	**sense of foreshortened future**	**sense of foreshortened future**

Note: Bold represents DSM-IV criteria.
Sources: Eth (1989); Eth & Pynoos (1994); Ribbe, Lipovsky, & Freedy (1995); and Terr (1985; 1991).

Diminished interest in activities is likely to take the form of insecure behavior in preschoolers, who may be no longer willing to leave the home independently. They may become immobilized or regressed, wanting to be fed or dressed, losing bowel or bladder control, or clinging to caregivers. In contrast, diminished interest may manifest as school refusal in older children, or as truancy in adolescents. Similarly, while estrangement from others may result in symptoms of anxious attachment in preschoolers, school-aged children are more likely to withdraw from peer and play groups, and adolescents may act out against others, such as by stealing and fighting. The restricted range of affect associated with PTSD is most likely to emerge as depression or sadness in children. Munson (1995) argues that much of children's repetitive play is a way to communicate their distress to others, in order to overcome feelings of "aloneness." Children also struggle against feelings of helplessness, sometimes attempting to achieve a sense of control by implicating themselves in the negative event; for example, Pynoos and Eth (1986) describe a child who regretted that she had not unloaded her father's gun.

While a sense of a foreshortened future is listed in DSM-IV as a general symptom, in fact this is a symptom that was first observed in children, and may apply to them more than to adults. Many traumatized children do not expect to marry, have children, or have a normal life span (Saigh, 1992). Some children do not expect to live longer than a few days or months, and have a sense of "futurelessness." Some of the symptoms of avoidance, such as "spacing out," "withdrawal," and "confusion," require particular attention, because they suggest the possible use of dissociation, a defensive strategy indicative of serious adjustment problems in individuals exposed to severe and chronic traumas (Putnam, Helmers, & Trickett, 1993).

Dissociative symptoms in children. It is important to be aware of developmental differences in the symptoms of dissociation, because the ways in which these symptoms are evident in children and adolescents are not identical to dissociative states in adults. While adults often report dissociative flashback experiences of reliving the trauma, the symptoms of dissociation in children generally include inattention, or appearing to be in a daze or trance. During this state, children lose track of time, are unresponsive to external stimuli, and lack awareness of what is going on around them (Putnam et al., 1993).

As outlined in Table 4, there are physiological, cognitive, behavioral, and personality changes during dissociative states, some of which may be overlooked in children. Symptoms such as being "tuned out" or in a daze may be misattributed to a child's quiet nature, or even interpreted as evidence that the child is functioning well, since the child is not misbehaving or in obvious distress. Further, children themselves may report that all is well, and defend against acknowledging their disturbing experiences. Splitting of internal and external experiences has been noted as a common defense in traumatized chil-

TABLE 4. Dissociative Symptoms in Children

Cognitive symptoms
- Spacing out, appearing to be in a daze or trance
- Losing track of time
- Loss of memory about self, periods of time, recent actions
- Loss of memory about the traumatic event
- Forgetfulness or confusion about everyday things

Motor symptoms
- Rapid or extreme changes in behavior
- Diminished responsiveness to environmental stimuli

Physiological symptoms
- Rapidly changing somatic complaints

Personality changes
- Extreme changes in personality or behavior
- Regression (e.g., thumb-sucking, baby-talk, imaginary playmates)

Other symptoms
- Lack of responsivity to external stimuli
- Lack of awareness of what is going on around self
- Unexplained injuries, talking of dying, self-mutilation
- Answering to another name or referring to self by another name
- Sleepwalking

dren (Fischer & Ayoub, 1994; Lipovsky, 1991). Other subtle symptoms, such as confusion and forgetting about everyday things, may simply go unnoticed. Further, some symptoms of dissociation may be confused with those of other disorders. For example, a child who is often unresponsive to others, forgetful, or careless may be misdiagnosed with attention deficit hyperactivity disorder. However, these symptoms take on a new meaning when they follow exposure to a trauma, particularly a severe and chronic stressor such as family violence.

Increased arousal. Few significant developmental differences have been reported in regard to this third cluster of symptoms (see Table 5). However, it is worth noting that adolescents may demonstrate the opposite of insomnia, and withdraw into heavy sleep. Traumatized children are particularly noted to be unable to inhibit startle responses after even brief exposure to stimulation (Ornitz & Pynoos, 1989).

TABLE 5. DSM-IV Cluster C Symptoms: Increased Arousal

Adult	Adolescent	School-age	Preschool
1. difficulty sleeping	insomnia or withdrawal into heavy sleep	difficulty falling asleep	difficulty falling asleep
2. irritability/ anger	angry or aggressive behavior	oppositionaly acting out	tantrums acting out
3. difficulty concentrating	academic difficulties	academic difficulties	inattention to instructions
4. hypervigilence	hypervigilence	obsession with trauma details	sensitivity to auditory stimuli
5. exaggerated startle response	**exaggerated startle response**	**exaggerated startle response**	**exaggerated startle response**

Note: Bold represents DSM-IV criteria.
Sources: Eth (1989); Eth & Pynoos (1994); Ribbe, Lipovsky, & Freedy (1995); and Terr (1985; 1991).

Techniques for Assessing PTSD Symptoms in Children

The material presented above focuses on *what* information the clinician needs to gather in order to assess PTSD in children exposed to domestic violence. This next section concerns how we can obtain that information.

Interviews. The first question to be considered when obtaining interview data is, Who do you talk to? If possible, it is helpful to include in the assessment both children and adults (such as parents, police, and teachers). Children and adults can contribute different, but equally important, kinds of information. For example, children are good reporters of their own level of stress and subjective symptoms, such as anxiety, which are often underestimated by adults (McNally, 1991). Adults, on the other hand, may be better sources of information about children's behavior, such as aggression or avoidance (Nader & Pynoos, 1992).

Further, adults may be able to provide more accurate information about what actually took place during traumatic events; unless, of course, they themselves are also suffering from trauma. The child's own perceptions may be distorted due to shock, time skew, or omen formation, as noted above. This is particularly the case for younger children, who are more likely to be confused, or to have significant misunderstandings about the experience (Pynoos & Nader, 1988). However, it is still important to talk to children directly, in order to obtain their subjective impressions. For example, even if circumstances were not truly life-threatening, did the child think s/he might be killed or seriously injured (Lipovsky, 1991)? Or, on the other hand, regardless of whether those around the child were attempting to help, did the child *perceive* others to be supportive during the event? Questions such as these will yield information about both risk and protective factors associated with the traumatic experience.

During an interview, the clinician should keep in mind the developmental level of the child, in regard to cognitive, language, and emotional development. For example, younger children will require the interviewer to use more concrete referents and simple sentences. In addition, younger children may require more emotional support from caregivers during an interview (Steward, Bussey, Goodman, & Saywitz, 1993).

Measures for PTSD assessment. A number of structured interviews, observer rating scales, and self-report questionnaires available to assess PTSD symptoms are listed in Table 6. McNally (1996) provides an overview of these assessment tools. Although many of these measures are promising, the majority are still in the early stages of development, and complete psychometric information is not yet available. In addition, few of these measures are appropriate for use with preschool children. A further limitation is that almost all of these measures have been designed to assess Type I single-episode traumas, such as accidents and natural disasters, rather than Type II chronic stressors, such as exposure to family violence. Consequently, for the assessment of children exposed to domestic violence, particularly young children, clinical interviews continue to be an important source of data.

INTERVENTIONS WITH CHILDREN TRAUMATIZED BY FAMILY VIOLENCE

The importance of carefully assessing PTSD becomes clear when we turn to the task of developing interventions that can counter the negative effects of trauma on children. There is as yet little empirical research on treatments for childhood PTSD; however, clinical work with traumatized children provides some guidance. Just as we described an integrative model of assessment, leading professionals in the field have emphasized the need for an integrative approach to treatment as well (Parson, 1996; Schwartz & Prout, 1991). For example, while interventions with traumatized children have been discussed extensively from psychodynamic (Terr, 1990) and cognitive-behavioral (Lipovsky, 1992) points of view, there is general agreement that neither of these treatment approaches is effective on its own (Koverola, 1995; Shalev, Bonne, & Eth, 1996; Terr, 1990). Therefore, the best approach may be an integration of different techniques on the basis of an individual child's traumatic reaction, needs, and developmental status (Silvern, Karyl, & Landis,

TABLE 6. Assessment Tools: Interviews, Questionnaires, and Rating Scales

Structured interviews

PTSD

- PTSD module for the K-SADS-E (McLeer, Callaghan, Henry, & Wallen, 1994). Ages 3 to 16.
- Childhood Post-Traumatic Stress Disorder Reaction Index (Pynoos et al., 1987). Ages 5 to adolescence.
- Diagnostic Interview for Children and Adolescents (Welner, Reich, Herjanic, Jung, & Amadao, 1987; see Earls, Smith, Reich, & Jung, 1988). Ages 7 to 19.
- Children's Impact of Traumatic Events Scale-Revised (Wolfe, Gentile, Michienzi, Sas, & Wolfe, 1991). Ages 8 to 16.
- Children's Posttraumatic Stress Disorder Inventory (Saigh, 1989). Ages 9 to 13.

Dissociation

- Child Interview for Subjective Dissociative Experiences (Liner, 1989). Ages 7 to 12.

Self-report questionnaires

PTSD

- PTSD Reaction Index Questionnaire (Schwarzwald, Weisenberg, Waysman, Solomon, & Klingman, 1993). Ages 5 to 13.
- Impact of Events Scale (Horowitz, Wilner, & Alvarez, 1979). Ages 5 to adolescence.
- School Trauma Survey (Hyman, Zelikoff, & Clarke, 1988). Young adults (retrospective reports).

Dissociation

- Children's Perceptual Alteration Scale (Evers-Szostak, & Sanders, 1992). Ages 7 to 12.
- Adolescent Dissociative Experiences Scale (Armstrong, Putnam, & Carlson, 1994). Ages 12 to 18.

Associated symptoms

- Depression: Child Depression Inventory (Kovacs, 1992). Ages 8 to 17.
- Anxiety: Revised Children's Manifest Anxiety Scale (Reynolds & Richmond, 1978). Ages 9 to 12.
- Futurelessness: About the Future (Saigh, 1992). School-aged children.

Parent and teacher rating scales

PTSD

- Child Post-Traumatic Stress Disorder Inventory: Parent Interview (Nader & Pynoos, 1989). Ages 5 to 13.
- Crisis Behavior Rating Scale (Felner, Norton, Cowen, & Farber, 1981). Early school-aged children.

Dissociation

- Child Dissociative Checklist (Putnam, Helmers, & Trickett, 1993). Ages 3 to 19.
- Child Behavior Checklist subscale (Malinosky-Rummell, 1991). Ages 4 to 18.

1995). As Schaefer (1994) has emphasized, "only by combining several therapeutic factors does this treatment become powerful enough to enable children to overcome the extraordinary emotional ordeal they experience in the wake of a trauma" (p. 315). Further, authors from various perspectives have converged on similar themes regarding the goals, and even methods of treatment. Two goals for intervention with PTSD emerge as central across theoretical perspectives: re-exposure to traumatic cues, and clearing up cognitive distortions.

Re-Exposure to Traumatic Cues

The primary goal of treatment with traumatized children is to facilitate the child's ability to gain mastery over the traumatic experience. Clinicians writing from different perspectives agree that this requires that the child be re-exposed to traumatic cues in a therapeutic way (Gillis, 1993; Parson, 1997; Ribbe, Lipovsky, & Freedy, 1995; Schaefer, 1994; Terr, 1990). Traumatic experiences evoke strong and dysregulating emotions. Subsequently these emotions, whether through the mechanism of unconscious processes as in psychodynamic theory or classical conditioning in the behaviorist perspective, come to be evoked by cues associated with the event. Therefore, the immediate goals of re-exposure are to disconnect the association children have formed between traumatic cues and anxiety, and to minimize children's tendency to avoid traumatic material. In the longer term, re-exposure allows children to comprehend the trauma, integrate it, and move past it. According to Gillis (1993), "Children learn that the event was not so overwhelming that they cannot stand the painful memories associated with it" (p. 172).

Therapeutic re-exposure needs to be differentiated from re-exposure which is *re*-traumatizing. For example, children may re-expose themselves through post-traumatic play, in which a child repetitively and compulsively reenacts traumatic themes without experiencing anxiety relief (Marvasti, 1993; Terr, 1983). Post-traumatic play has a driven quality to it, and is devoid of freedom or pleasure (Schaefer, 1994). Further, during post-traumatic play the child does not have access to the feelings aroused, or the ability to verbalize them. Thus, merely reliving the event may only serve to stimulate feelings of helplessness and terror, and prevent their resolution (Terr, 1983).

Therapeutic re-exposure differs in that it takes place in the presence of a supportive adult, the re-exposure is gradual, and the child maintains a feeling of control over the experience. The therapist fosters this by helping the child to recognize when s/he is distressed, and by respecting the child's limits as to how much of the material s/he can process at one time (Gillis, 1993). Children should be provided with some control over the pace of re-exposure, even if that pace is slow (Ribbe et al., 1995). At the same time, however, it is necessary to strike a balance so as not to encourage the avoidant strategies children have adopted for coping with traumatic events. The therapist can best achieve this by conveying an attitude of calm and confidence that gently conveys the firm belief that the child can face this material without becoming overwhelmed.

Sometimes adults fear that they may re-traumatize children further by encouraging them to talk about traumatic events. However, we can be reassured by the fact that both research and clinical work have documented that talking about traumatic experiences with a supportive adult is relieving, rather than distressing, for children (Gil, 1991; Nader & Pynoos, 1991; Pynoos & Eth, 1986; Silvern et al., 1995; Terr, 1990). This is particularly the case for children exposed to domestic violence, for whom the burden of secrecy and fear of the repercussions of disclosure are additional sources of stress (Silvern et al., 1995). Thus, "although the desire to protect children from further discomfort by shielding them from trauma-related cues is well intentioned . . . it is not always in the children's best interests" (Lyons, 1987, p. 354).

Open discussion. Re-exposure to traumatic cues is largely accomplished through open discussion of the experience (Pynoos & Eth, 1986), also referred to as "straight talk" (Silvern et al., 1995) or debriefing (Yule & Canterbury, 1994). Pynoos and Eth (1986) have developed interviews that guide open discussion of a child's reactions to a traumatic event. The interviewer uses support and empathy to encourage children to openly discuss, play out, or draw each aspect of the traumatic experience. The child's misconceptions and worries about the event can be brought out into the open, as well as feelings the child might be uncomfortable acknowledging, such as self-blame and desires for revenge. Calm discussion of the event helps children to de-mystify the experience, and to overcome their feelings of helplessness and terror. Younger children may require more structure and support in this process, and will need concrete, simple, and present-oriented language. In addition, Parson (1997) emphasizes the need to understand and respect the defenses used by traumatized children (e.g., avoidance, dissociation, and passive aggression) and to proceed carefully in order to avoid overwhelming the child. The interview ends with a summary in which the child's experiences are described as understandable, realistic, and common among children exposed to similar events. Although this technique has been developed for purposes of crisis intervention in general (Arroyo & Eth, 1995; Nader & Pynoos, 1991), it is easily adapted to situations of domestic violence.

Silvern et al.'s (1995) straight talk approach is less structured and intended for use within a therapy relationship. This technique has been tailored specifically for use with children of battered women. Silvern et al. (1995) emphasize the need to focus on children's personal understanding of the event, and their concerns about safety, helplessness, guilt, and self-blame. Further, the authors argue that while play and artwork can help children to "symbolically express" their reactions, it is essential to work toward direct verbal disclosure in order to insure that aspects of the traumatic experiences are not distorted or avoided. Therefore, the goals of straight talk are to help children to clarify, reframe, and normalize their experiences so that the event can be coherently integrated (Silvern & Kaersvang, 1989).

Behavioral techniques. Classical conditioning techniques, such as systematic desensitization and flooding, are also used to re-expose children to traumatic cues. The cues can include all aspects of the experience, such as sensory details that might arouse anxiety (sights, sounds, and smells), as well as the child's thoughts and feelings. Treatment requires the creation of a safe and non-threatening environment, through which the child is given the opportunity to disconnect the association between anxiety and cues reminiscent of the event, extinguish the traumatic reaction, and decrease avoidance. Both of these techniques require special training and a high level of clinical skill.

Systematic desensitization requires that the child be imaginally exposed to a hierarchy of anxiety-producing scenes, while in a state of deep muscle relaxation (Parson, 1997). A less formal approach can also be used, by encouraging children to discuss tolerable aspects of the violence experienced, alternating with relaxation when the discussion becomes too overwhelming (Lipovsky, 1991). With either approach, children learn that they can cope with and master the anxiety associated with the traumatic experience. Systematic desensitization can be used not only to decrease avoidance, but also to alleviate children's post-traumatic fears (Terr, 1985).

Imaginal flooding is an alternative technique in which the child is asked to repeatedly imagine the traumatic event for short periods of time (Saigh, Yule, & Inamdar, 1996). Scenes are created based on information obtained from the child, and incorporate all aspects of the experience, including visual, auditory, olfactory, and physical cues, as well as behaviors and thoughts (Lipovsky, 1991). In contrast to systematic desensitization, flooding involves extended and uninterrupted presentations of traumatic cues (Saigh et al., 1996). It is believed that this prolonged exposure facilitates long-term extinction of the conditioned anxiety.

Empirical tests of this approach have reported that flooding is associated with a reduction in PTSD symptoms in children exposed to Type I traumas (Saigh et al., 1996), while its effectiveness with Type II traumas such as domestic violence is not known. Moreover, research with adults has yielded mixed results, with flooding potentially exacerbating symptoms of PTSD (Shalev et al., 1996). Given the potential negative consequences of flooding, this is an approach that should be used only with caution. Lipovsky (1992) recommends that flooding be combined with systematic desensitization when working with traumatized children, in order to avoid overwhelming them with negative affect. In this manner, children can be re-exposed to traumatic cues gradually, from the least traumatic cue to the most traumatic, while using relaxation or distraction to prevent excessive discomfort. Further, flooding and systematic desensitization may be more effective for older than younger children. Preschoolers may find it harder to tolerate the anxiety engendered, and may lack the cognitive skills that are required to visualize the traumatic experience (Saigh et al., 1996).

Psychodynamic play therapy. Play therapy may be the most effective way of re-exposing younger children to traumatic cues. From a psychodynamic perspective, abreactive play permits a child to release the intense emotions associated with the trauma (Terr, 1985), and may be especially useful with young children, for whom playing "hard, dirty, and rough" relieves anxiety. Play is also the most natural way for children to express their feelings and work them through. This process has been described as "spontaneous mastery play" (Schaefer, 1994), or "adaptive play reenactment" (Zero to Three, 1994), in which children unconsciously recreate the traumatic experience in their play and, with each repetition, weaken the negative affect associated with the trauma. Re-exposure through play also provides the child with the opportunity to review the traumatic material in a way which places it more accurately in the past, rather than being experienced as recurring in the present (Silvern et al., 1995).

However, as mentioned previously, some spontaneous play is not helpful; that is, post-traumatic play. Because of the re-traumatizing quality of this type of play, children may need more active intervention from the therapist. For example, the therapist can interrupt the driven and repetitive nature of post-traumatic play by providing interpretations of the play themes that link them to the traumatic event, such as "I wonder if you ever felt you were going to die when your mommy was screaming, like this baby doll just did?" (Schaefer, 1994, p. 309-310). Interpretations are used to help children gain self-awareness regarding their reactions to the trauma, and thus to "accept as real what tends to be experienced as unreal" (Schaefer, 1994, p. 310).

Further, Terr (1990) cautions that children's post-traumatic play can be resistant to interpretations. She suggests a number of alternative ways in which clinicians can intervene in post-traumatic play, including: (a) focusing on the feelings the child is experiencing (terror, shame, anger, helplessness, excitement, etc.) and connecting these feelings to the past; (b) drawing connections between the traumatic event and other repetitive behaviors, dreams, or fantasies; (c) discussing the child's feelings of helplessness, and the resulting omens or rationalizations the child has developed to compensate; (d) pointing out overgeneralizations and displacements; (e) emphasizing more adaptive ways of coping with the trauma; and (f) helping the child to move past the experience by focusing on rehabilitation and rewards in his/her present life.

Gil (1991) also suggests that a child's post-traumatic play can be interrupted by encouraging the child to take on different roles within the reenactment, offering a more positive resolution, or simply redirecting the child. For example, one boy achieved relief from anxiety when he was able to play out calling the police and having his father arrested, something that, at the time, he was too frozen with fear to do. If the child is now in the safety of a shelter, the therapist may also contrast the terror and helplessness associated with the traumatic event to the child's current situation.

Ultimately, the therapist may have to intervene in the course of post-traumatic play a number of times and in a number of different ways, before the child is able to develop a sense of control or resolution. In addition, children are strongly motivated to avoid traumatic cues, which also calls for the use of more structured play techniques to facilitate re-exposure.

Cognitive-behavioral play therapy. Cognitive-behavioral approaches to play therapy require the therapist to guide and structure the play by planfully providing play objects reminiscent of the experience, and encouraging children to act it out (Lipovsky, 1992). For example, if a mother were severely injured and taken away in an ambulance, the therapist can provide the child with a doll house, ambulance, and figures of police officers and family members with which to act out the trauma. The same approach may also be taken through drawings, story-telling, or puppet play.

Family therapy. Systemic family therapies also provide ways of re-exposing children to traumatic cues. For example, Wachtel (1994) describes the use of "negative reminiscing," in which adults are encouraged to openly discuss traumatic memories with their children. This is particularly useful for children who were very young when the trauma occurred, and who therefore have only hazy and confusing memories of it, or when children believe that the violence is a secret or taboo topic that they are not allowed to discuss. An additional benefit of family work is that a therapeutic benefit is provided to all the children in the family. Siblings together can be taught safety and coping skills, and can be encouraged to provide support for one another.

A caution about this technique is that it requires that the mother be comfortable discussing the traumatic episode, and that she have worked through it sufficiently so as to be able to talk about it calmly and help her children tolerate the feelings aroused. For example, mothers traumatized by abuse may be unable to carry out this kind of work until later in their own recovery (Terr, 1989). Therefore, this approach is appropriate only after a significant amount of therapeutic work with the mother, and will require ongoing support of her. Inclusion of the perpetrating parent is highly controversial, given the potential risk for re-traumatization of the child. Thus, the father would be included only under special circumstances, such as when he has successfully completed an intervention for batterers and has committed to behaving non-violently.

Ultimately, whether re-experiencing takes place during spontaneous play or is guided by the therapist, occurs during individual sessions or in the context of family treatment, the goal is for the child to work through the experience and gain mastery over it. Schaefer (1994) states that mastery of the trauma has been achieved when a child:

1. feels in control of the outcome of his/her play
2. can play out a satisfactory ending to the scenario
3. feels free to express and release negative emotions, and
4. exhibits a realistic understanding of the traumatic event.

Clearing up Cognitive Distortions

A second goal common to all treatments is to clear up cognitive distortions and maladaptive beliefs that children might have developed. For example, as mentioned previously, omen formation may lead children to believe that they could have predicted the violence or prevented it from happening (Terr, 1985). Children may also have maladaptive beliefs such as that they caused the violence, or that their mother is to blame (Kerig, 1998). Children also may believe that some of their feelings are bad and wrong, such as their anger or violent revenge fantasies. Such beliefs may increase children's emotional distress, and interfere with their ability to work through the trauma (Ribbe et al., 1995).

Psychodynamic approaches change beliefs through the interpretation of play themes, which allows children to gain insight and develop more realistic views of their role in the traumatic experience. Children can also use fantasy play to construct more positive resolutions to the event, which will in turn allow them to gain mastery and approach the future with greater optimism. For example, Terr (1983) suggests that post-traumatic play can be interrupted by helping children to construct a realistic solution that might have helped them during the traumatic event (e.g., calling 911, going to a neighbor's house). The goals of this kind of problem-solving are to help children to realize that they were not in control of the violence, and to encourage them to see that they now have the skills to cope with similar events in the future. This can help relieve children of the guilt and fear that are often associated with exposure to domestic violence.

With older children, more formal cognitive therapy techniques can be used to challenge distorted ideas about self-blame and encourage more adaptive ways of thinking (Parson, 1997; Lipovsky, 1991). Two such techniques are self-instruction and positive cognitive restructuring. For example, children can be given messages to repeat to themselves when they engage in negative cognitions (e.g.,"When parents hit each other, it is never the kid's fault") or ruminative worrying ("My family is safe. We're OK!"). Cognitive restructuring can be facilitated by focusing children's attention on positive characteristics of their family ("My brothers and sisters look out for each other"), just as maternal blame can be countered by drawing attention to the mother's positive qualities ("My mom cares about me. She wants to make sure I'm safe") (Kerig, 1998).

However, these interventions require some cognitive sophistication, and thus they may not be effective with younger children. Simpler techniques, such as thought-stopping, can be used to help younger children interrupt their negative self-talk (e.g., children can be taught to stop, press their internal "pause button" and "rewind"). Particularly with younger children, the focus may need to be on clarifying misperceptions about the traumatic event itself. For example, one young girl believed that, because the police who took her father away were carrying guns, they were intending to shoot him.

Summary of Developmental Considerations

Although the work on child PTSD to date has been criticized for its neglect of developmental issues (Horowitz, 1996), such considerations are extremely important in choosing interventions that will be effective with children at various ages. Based on the foregoing review of the literature, a summary of developmental considerations for intervention with PTSD in children is presented in Table 7.

Other Treatment Issues for Children with PTSD

There are other important goals of treatment for PTSD in children. First, *anxiety reduction* can be a very important goal in and of itself. Excessive anxiety is disruptive to children's functioning, while, on the other hand, children gain a general sense of self-efficacy when they learn techniques with which to modulate their own distress (Klingman, 1993). Secondly, traumatized children often having difficulty accessing their feelings. *Emotional numbing* can be countered by helping children recognize and label their emotions (Gillis, 1993).

A third important goal is to provide *education* to children about their own traumatic reactions (Pynoos & Eth, 1986). Preparing children for the possibility that they might have nightmares, or that loud noises may startle them or remind them of the traumatic event, can help to normalize their experiences and alleviate their emotional distress (Lipovsky, 1992; Ribbe et al., 1995). For example, children may misinterpret the symptoms of PTSD as indications that they are "going crazy" (Gillis, 1993), and find it reassuring to learn that these are expectable reactions shared by other children.

TABLE 7. Developmental Model for Intervention with PTSD in Children

Goal	Adolescent	School-age	Preschool
Re-exposure			
• Express emotions	Open discussion	Open discussion	Abreactive play
• Reduce anxiety	Desensitization	Desensitization	Structured play
• Reduce sensitivity to traumatic cues	Family therapy	Family therapy	Family therapy
• Minimize avoidance			
Reduce cognitive distortions			
• Minimize misperceptions, self-blame, and maladaptive beliefs	Interpretation	Mastery play	Mastery play
• Gain understanding of PTSD symptoms	Cognitive restructuring	Cognitive-behavioral play therapy	Cognitive-behavioral play therapy
• Learn constructive coping strategies			
• Gain mastery		Cognitive restructuring	Thought-stopping
Integration			
• Increase capacity to trust	Long-term therapy	Long-term therapy	Long-term therapy
• Break cycle of victimization			
• Re-work and re-integrate at each stage of development			

A further treatment consideration, emphasized from all perspectives, is the importance of *early intervention*. Early intervention can prevent long-term emotional difficulties by interrupting maladaptive processes before they become entrenched, and promoting adaptive ways of coping with the trauma (Lipovsky, 1991). Battered women's shelters, for example, may provide an important opportunity to provide early intervention with children traumatized by exposure to woman abuse. At the same time, however, for many children exposed to chronic violence, short-term crisis intervention may not be sufficient. Particularly for children who have undergone repeated exposure to traumatizing events, such as those characterized by Type II traumas (Terr,

1990), *long-term psychotherapy* may be necessary. Several authors, including Friedrich (1996), Gaensbauer and Siegel (1995), Gil (1991), Gillis (1993), Lipovsky (1991, 1992), and Parson (1997), provide guides for long-term therapeutic approaches with children.

CONCLUSION

In conclusion, the development of an integrative treatment plan for children exposed to domestic violence requires that a number of considerations be made during assessment, including the nature of the traumatic reaction, the child's family context, the child's unique vulnerabilities and competencies, and the child's stage of development. While we can be informed by integrative and developmental models, the guiding force for treatment must, above all, be determined by the particular needs of the individual child.

REFERENCES

American Journal of Psychiatry, 152, 1329-1335.

Armstrong, J., Putnam, F., & Carlson, E. (1994). *Adolescent Dissociative Experiences Scale (A-DES)*. Unpublished manuscript. University of Southern California, Los Angeles, CA.

Armsworth, M. W., & Holaday, M. (1993). The effects of psychological trauma on children and adolescents. *Journal of Counseling and Development, 72*, 49-56.

Arroyo, W., & Eth, S. (1995). Assessment following violence-witnessing trauma. In E. Peled, P. G. Jaffe, & J. L. Edelson (Eds.), *Ending the cycle of violence: Community responses to children of battered women* (pp. 27-42). Thousand Oaks, CA: Sage.

Bruck, M., Ceci, S. J., & Hembroke, H. (1998). Reliability and credibility of young children's reports: From research to policy and practice. *American Psychologist, 53*, 136-151.

Earls, F., Smith, E., Reich, W., & Jung, K. G. (1988). Investigating psychopathological consequences of a disaster in children: A pilot study incorporating a structured diagnostic interview. *Journal of the American Academy of Child and Adolescent Psychiatry, 27*, 90-95.

Eth, S. (1989). Post-traumatic stress disorder in childhood. In M. Hersen & C. G. Last (Eds.), *Handbook of child and adult psychopathology: A longitudinal perspective* (pp. 263-274). New York: Pergamon.

Eth, S., & Pynoos, R. S. (1994). Children who witness the homicide of a parent. *Psychiatry, 57*, 287-306.

Evers-Szostak, M., & Sanders, S. (1992). The Children's Perceptual Alteration Scale (CPAS): A measure of children's dissociation. *Dissociation, 5*, 91-97.

Felner, R. D., Norton, P. L., Cowen, E. L., & Farber, S. (1981). A prevention program for children experiencing life crisis. *Professional Psychology, 12*, 446-452.

Fischer, K. W., & Ayoub, C. (1994). Affective splitting and dissociation in normal and maltreated children: Developmental pathways for self in relationships. In D. Cicchetti & S. L. Toth (Eds.), *Rochester symposium on developmental psychopathology: Disorders and dysfunctions of the self* (pp. 149-222). New York: Rochester.

Foy, D. W., Madvig, B. T., Pynoos, R. S., & Camilleri, A. J. (1996). Etiologic factors in the development of posttraumatic stress disorder in children and adolescents. *Journal of School Psychology, 34*, 133-145.

Friedrich, W. N. (1996). An integrated model of psychotherapy for abused children. In J. Briere, L. Berliner, J. A. Bulkley, C. Jenny, & T. Reid (Eds.), *The APSAC handbook on child maltreatment* (pp. 104-118). Thousand Oaks, CA: Sage.

Gaensbauer, T. J., & Siegel, C. H. (1995). Therapeutic approaches to posttraumatic stress disorder in infants and toddlers. *Infant Mental Health Journal, 16*, 292-305.

Gil, E. (1991). *The healing power of play: Working with abused children.* New York: Guilford.

Gillis, H. M. (1993). Individual and small-group psychotherapy for children involved in trauma and disaster. In C. F. Saylor (Ed.), *Children and disasters* (pp. 165-186). New York: Plenum.

Graham-Bermann, S. A., & Levendosky, A. A. (1998). Traumatic stress symptoms in children of battered women. *Journal of Interpersonal Violence, 13*, 111-138.

Horowitz, F. D. (1996). Developmental perspectives on child and adolescent posttraumatic stress disorder. *Journal of School Psychology, 34*, 189-191.

Horowitz, M., Wilner, N., & Alvarez, W. (1979). Impact of Events Scale: A measure of subjective stress. *Psychosomatic Medicine, 41*, 209-218.

Hyman, I. A., Zelikoff, W., & Clarke, J. (1988). Psychological and physical abuse in the schools: A paradigm for understanding post-traumatic stress disorder in children and youth. *Journal of Traumatic Stress, 1*, 243-267.

Jaffe, P. G., Sudermann, M., & Reitzel, D. (1992). Child witnesses of marital violence. In R. T. Ammerman & M. Hersen (Eds.), *Assessment of family violence: A clinical and legal sourcebook* (pp. 313-331). New York: Wiley.

Keppel-Benson, J. M., & Ollendick, T. H. (1993). Post-traumatic stress disorder in children and adolescents. In C. F. Saylor (Ed.), *Children and disasters* (pp. 29-43). New York: Plenum Press.

Kerig, P. K. (1998, October). *In search of protective factors for children exposed to interparental conflict and violence.* Paper presented at the Third International Conference on Children Exposed to Violence, San Diego.

Klingman, A. (1993). School-based intervention following a disaster. In C. F. Saylor (Ed.), *Children and disasters* (pp. 165-186). New York: Plenum.

Kovacs, M. (1992). *Children's Depression Inventory manual.* Toronto: Multi-Health Systems.

Koverola, C. (1995). Posttraumatic stress disorder. In R. T. Ammerman & M. Hersen (Eds.), *Handbook of child behavior therapy in the psychiatric setting* (pp. 389-408). New York: Wiley.

Liner, D. (1989). *Child Interview for Subjective Dissociative Experiences scoring manual.* Unpublished measure. Georgia State University, Atlanta, GA.

Lipovsky, J. A. (1991). Posttraumatic stress disorder in children. *Family & Community Health, 14*, 42-51.

Lipovsky, J. A. (1992). Assessment and treatment of post-traumatic stress disorder in child survivors of sexual assault. In D. W. Foy (Ed.), *Treating PTSD: Cognitive behavioural strategies* (pp. 127-164). New York: Guilford.

Lyons, J. A. (1987). Posttraumatic stress disorder in children and adolescents: A review of the literature. *Developmental and Behavioral Pediatrics, 8*, 349-356.

Malinosky-Rummel, R. R., & Hoier, T. A. (1991). Validating measures of dissociation in sexually abused and nonabused children. *Behavioral Assessment, 13*, 341-357.

Marvasti, J. A. (1993). "Please hurt me again": Posttraumatic play therapy with an abused child. In T. Kottman & C. Schaefer (Eds.), *Play therapy in action: A casebook for practitioners* (pp. 485-525). Northvale, NJ: Aronson.

McLeer, S. V., Callaghan, M., Henry, D., & Wallen, J. (1994). Psychiatric disorders in sexually abused children. *Journal of American Academy of Child and Adolescent Psychiatry, 27*, 650-654.

McNally, R. J. (1991). Assessment of posttraumatic stress disorder in children. *Psychological Assessment, 3*, 531-537.

McNally, R. J. (1996). Assessment of posttraumatic stress disorder in children and adolescents. *Journal of School Psychology, 34*, 147-161.

Munson, C. E. (1995). Overview of diagnosis and treatment of psychological trauma in children. *Early Child Development and Care, 106*, 149-166.

Nader, K., & Pynoos, R. S. (1992, August). *Parental report of children's responses to life threat.* Paper presented at the meetings of the American Psychiatric Association, Washington, DC.

Nader, K. O., & Pynoos, R. S. (1991). Play and drawing techniques as tools for interviewing traumatized children. In C. E. Schaefer, K. Gitlin, & A. Sandgrund (Eds.), *Play diagnosis and assessment* (pp. 375-389). New York: Wiley.

Ornitz, E., & Pynoos, R. S. (1989). Startle modulation in children with post-traumatic stress disorder. *American Journal of Psychiatry, 147*, 866-870.

Parson, E. R. (1996). Child traumatherapy and the effects of trauma, loss, and dissociation: A multisystems approach to helping children exposed to lethal urban community violence. *Journal of Contemporary Psychotherapy, 26*, 117-162.

Parson, E. R. (1997). Posttraumatic child therapy (P-TCT): Assessment and treatment factors in clinical work with inner-city children exposed to catastrophic community violence. *Journal of Interpersonal Violence, 12*, 172-194.

Peled, E., Jaffe, P. G., & Edleson, J. L. (1995). *Ending the cycle of violence.* Thousand Oaks, CA: Sage.

Putnam, F. W., Helmers, K., & Trickett, P. K. (1993). Development, reliability, and validity of a child dissociation scale. *Child Abuse & Neglect, 17*, 731-741.

Pynoos, R. S. (1993). Traumatic stress and developmental psychopathology in children and adolescents. In J. Oldham, M. Riba, & A. Tasman (Eds.), *American Psychiatric Press Review of Psychiatry* (Vol. 12, pp. 205-238). Washington, DC: American Psychiatric Press.

Pynoos, R. S., & Eth, S. (1985). Children traumatized by witnessing acts of personal violence: Homicide, rape, or suicide behavior. In S. Eth & R. S. Pynoos (Eds.),

Post-traumatic stress disorder in children (pp. 19-43). Washington, DC: American Psychiatric Press.

Pynoos, R. S., & Eth, S. (1986). Witness to violence: The child interview. *Journal of the American Academy of Child Psychiatry, 25*, 306-319.

Pynoos, R. S., Frederick, C., Nader, K., Arroyo, W., Steinberg, A., Eth, S., Nunez, F., & Fairbanks, L. (1987). Life threat and posttraumatic stress in school age children. *Archives of General Psychiatry, 44*, 1057-1063.

Pynoos, R. S., & Nader, K. (1988). Psychological first aid and treatment approach to children exposed to community violence: Research implications. *Journal of Traumatic Stress, 1*, 445-473.

Pynoos, R. S., & Nader, K. (1990). Children's exposure to violence and traumatic death. *Psychiatric Annals, 20*, 334-344.

Pynoos, R. S., Steinberg, A. M., & Goenjian, A. (1996). Traumatic stress in childhood and adolescence: Recent developments and current controversies. In B. A. van der Kolk, A. C. MacFarlane, & L. Weisarth (Eds.), *Traumatic stress: The effects of overwhelming experience on mind, body, and society* (pp. 331-358). New York: Guilford.

Pynoos, R. S., Steinberg, A. M., & Wriath, R. (1995). A developmental model of childhood traumatic stress. In D. Cicchetti & D. J. Cohen (Eds.), *Developmental psychopathology. Vol. II: Risk, disorder, and adaptation* (pp. 72-95). New York: Wiley.

Reynolds, C., & Richmond, B. (1978). What I think and feel: A revised measure of children's manifest anxiety. *Journal of Abnormal Child Psychology, 6*, 271-280.

Ribbe, D. P., Lipovsky, J. A., & Freedy, J. R. (1995). Post-traumatic stress disorder. In A. R. Eisen, C. A. Kearney, & C. E. Schaefer (Eds.), *Clinical handbook of anxiety disorder in children and adolescents* (pp. 315-356). Northvale, NJ: Jason Aronson.

Rossman, B. B. R., & Ho, J. (2000). Posttraumatic response and children exposed to parental violence. In R. Geffner, P. Jaffe, & M. Sudermann (Eds.), *Children exposed to domestic violence: Current issues in research, intervention, prevention, and policy development.* (pp. 85-106). New York: The Haworth Press, Inc.

Saigh, P. A. (1989). The development and validation of the Children's Posttraumatic Stress Disorder Inventory. *International Journal of Special Education, 4*, 75-84.

Saigh, P. A. (1992). *About the future.* Unpublished manuscript, Graduate Center of the City University of New York.

Saigh, P. A., Yule, W., & Inamdar, S. C. (1996). Imaginal flooding of traumatized children and adolescents. *Journal of School Psychology, 34*, 163-183.

Schaefer, C. E. (1994). Play therapy for psychic trauma in children. In K. O'Connor & C. E. Schaefer (Eds.), *Handbook of play therapy* (pp. 297-318). New York: Wiley.

Schwartzwald, J., Weisenberg, M., Waysman, M., Solomon, A., & Klingman, A. (1993). Stress reaction of school-age children to the bombardment of SCUD missiles. *Journal of Abnormal Psychology, 102*, 404-410.

Schwarz, R. A., & Prout, M. F. (1991). Integrative approaches in the treatment of post-traumatic stress disorder. *Psychotherapy, 28*, 364-373.

Shalev, A. Y., Bonne, O., & Eth, S. (1996). Treatment of post-traumatic stress disorder: A review. *Psychosomatic Medicine, 58*, 165-182.

Silvern, L., & Kaersvang, L. (1989). The traumatized children of violent marriages. *Child Welfare, 68*, 421-436.

Silvern, L., Karyl, J., & Landis, T. Y. (1995). Individual psychotherapy for the traumatized children of abused women. In E. Peled, P. G. Jaffe, & J. L. Edelson (Eds.), *Ending the cycle of violence: Community responses to children of battered women* (pp. 43-76). Thousand Oaks, CA: Sage.

Steward, M. S., Bussey, K., Goodman, G. S., & Saywitz, K. J. (1993). Implications of developmental research for interviewing children. *Child Abuse & Neglect, 17*, 25-37.

Terr, L. C. (1983). Play therapy and psychic trauma: A preliminary report. In C. E. Schaefer & K. J. O'Connor (Eds.), *Handbook of play therapy* (pp. 308-319). New York: Wiley.

Terr, L. C. (1985). Psychic trauma in children and adolescents. *Psychiatric Clinics of North America, 8*, 815-835.

Terr, L. C. (1988). What happens to early memories of trauma? A study of twenty children under age five at the time of documented traumatic events. *Journal of the American Academy of Child and Adolescent Psychiatry, 27*, 96-104.

Terr, L. C. (1989). Treating psychic trauma in children: A preliminary discussion. *Journal of Traumatic Stress, 2*, 3-20.

Terr, L. C. (1990). *Too scared to cry: Psychic trauma in childhood.* New York: Harper & Row.

Terr, L. C. (1991). Childhood traumas: An outline and overview. *American Journal of Psychiatry, 148*, 10-20.

Vernberg, E. M., La Greca, A. M., Silverman, W. K., & Prinstein, M. J. (1996). Prediction of posttraumatic stress symptoms in children after Hurricane Andrew. *Journal of Abnormal Psychology, 105*, 237-248.

Vogel, J., & Vernberg, E. M. (1993). Children's psychological responses to disaster. *Journal of Clinical Child Psychology, 22*, 470-484.

Wachtel, E. F. (1994). *Treating troubled children and their families.* New York: Guilford.

Welner, Z., Reich, W., Herjanic, B., Jung, K. G., & Amadao, H. (1987). Reliability, validity, and parent-child agreement studies of the Diagnostic Interview for Children and Adolescents (DICA). *Journal of the American Academy of Child and Adolescent Psychiatry, 26*, 649-653.

Wolfe, V. V., Gentile, C., Michienzi, T., Sas, L., & Wolfe, D. A. (1991). The Children's Impact of Traumatic Events Scale: A measure of post-sexual abuse PTSD symptoms. *Behavioral Assessment, 13*, 359-383.

Yule, W., & Canterbury, Y. (1994). The treatment of post traumatic stress disorder in children and adolescents. *International Review of Psychiatry, 6*, 141-151.

Zero to Three (1994). *Diagnostic classification of mental health and developmental disorders of infancy and early childhood.* Arlington, VA: Zero to Three/National Center for Clinical Infant Programs.

Mothers and Children Together:
A Family Group Treatment Approach

Stephanie Rabenstein
Peter Lehmann

SUMMARY. Treatment groups for both mothers and children together who have experienced mother assault is a unique therapeutic milieu which has been underutilized in the treatment field. This article presents a 10-week feminist-informed family systems group model as part of a treatment approach for children exposed to family violence and can be used with families of children from pre-school to adolescence. This model provides a context in which the experience of family violence can be debriefed, and issues related to trauma, safety, secrecy, and post-abuse family restructuring can be addressed by family members together. In addition, play and art therapy based interventions are presented and are tailored for the beginning, middle, and end of the group process.. *[Article copies available for a fee from The Haworth Document Delivery Service: 1-800-342-9678. E-mail address: getinfo@haworthpressinc.com <Website: http://www.haworthpressinc.com>]*

KEYWORDS. Trauma, family therapy, mother assault, art/play techniques

Group leader: Kyle, what made you decide you wanted to be the big brother to stop Dad from hurting Mom?

Kyle: Because . . . I didn't want to see it. I didn't want him to do it so I wanted to stop him.

Address correspondence to: Stephanie Rabenstein, Madame Vanier Children's Services, 871 Trafalgar Street, London, Ontario, N52 1E6, Canada.

[Haworth co-indexing entry note]: "Mothers and Children Together: A Family Group Treatment Approach." Rabenstein, Stephanie, and Peter Lehmann. Co-published simultaneously in *Journal of Aggression, Maltreatment & Trauma* (The Haworth Maltreatment & Trauma Press, an imprint of The Haworth Press, Inc.) Vol. 3, No. 1 (#5), 2000, pp. 185-205; and: *Children Exposed to Domestic Violence: Current Issues in Research, Intervention, Prevention, and Policy Development* (ed: Robert A. Geffner, Peter G. Jaffe, and Marlies Sudermann) The Haworth Maltreatment & Trauma Press, an imprint of The Haworth Press, Inc., 2000, pp. 185-205. Single or multiple copies of this article are available for a fee from The Haworth Document Delivery Service [1-800-342-9678, 9:00 a.m. - 5:00 p.m. (EST). E-mail address: getinfo@haworthpressinc.com].

185

Laurie's mother: Kyle probably . . . maybe, I don't know if he did, he wished he had an older brother, him being the only.

Kyle: Yeah, I wish I was older, then I wouldn't have just sat there.

Leader: And that's maybe why you thought at the end (of the skit) to be the cop too?

Kyle: Yeah (laughs), 'cause I was big . . .

Laurie's mother: Then he could do something . . .

Kyle: (I could be) Constable Butler . . .

Group laughter.

Kyle's mother: Maybe someday!

Leader: . . . When that was happening years ago, you were not able to do that. And that's not your fault.

Laurie's mother: Sometimes, whether the children believe it or not, and what I told mine, because they feel, too, they should have been there, too, to help me . . . is that they did help me in a lot of ways by staying out of the way so that they weren't getting hurt also and I would have had three of us to take care of. . . .

Kyle's mother: I felt even worse when Kyle was there. I thought, why couldn't he have been at my mom's. . . . I wish to God that he hadn't even been there at all.

From a mother-child group discussion of an impromptu skit the children acted out for their mothers.

(Note: All identifying personal information has been changed.)

INTRODUCTION

The purpose of this article is to examine the use of a conjoint mother and child treatment group as one of many treatment options appropriate for children in the aftermath of mother assault. Interest in intervention approaches with child and caretaker survivors of violence has come from concerns that childhood exposure to violence is epidemic and constitutes a major mental health priority (McAlister Groves, 1996; Osofsky, 1997). This point has not been lost to domestic violence researchers and for the past 20 years many studies have documented how children of all ages are negatively impacted by witnessing mother assault. Such children have repeatedly been found to exhibit any number of internalizing, externalizing, and social competency problem behaviors (for reviews see Barnett, Miller Perrin, & Perrin, 1997; Carlson, 1996; Fantuzzo & Lindquist, 1989; Jaffe, Sudermann, & Reitzel, 1992). In addition, posttraumatic stress disorder (PTSD) symptoms have been reported in anecdotal (Osofsky & Fenichel, 1994, 1996; Rossman & Rosenberg, 1997; Silvern & Kaersvang, 1989; Silvern, Karyl, & Landis, 1995; Terr, 1990) and empirical reports (Graham-Bermann & Levendosky, in press; Lehmann, 1997) of child witnesses.

Consistent with the empirical research has been the emergence of theoretical models to explain children's responses to witnessing mother assault. At least five main theories have been proposed and include a social learning model (Jaffe, Wolfe, & Wilson, 1990), the family disruption hypothesis (Jouriles, Barling, & O'Leary, 1987), PTSD (Pynoos, 1994), emotional insecurity (Davies & Cummings, 1994), and a family systems paradigm (Figley, 1989).

Clinicians, too, responding to this social problem have begun to provide a number of interventions to meet the needs of children. Although there is little empirical information to guide treatment, most providers have relied on the development of methods by way of case studies and theoretical writings (Hughes, 1997). Despite these limits, a number of approaches from many disciplines may be seen as useful for short- and long-term intervention.

A striking absence in the clinical literature is the systematic survey of children's mental health centers for child clients who have witnessed mother assault in their homes. These children can present with the same range of symptoms as those reported in shelters for battered women. However, there is no global recognition that a thorough assessment of these children must include assessing for the presence of woman abuse in the home. The role of children's mental health centers in child witness treatment is an intriguing and important question that requires exploration but is beyond the scope of the current discussion. Ironically, children's mental health centers working within a family systems paradigm can provide a setting that is ideal for engaging children and their families in treating the effects of exposure to mother assault. The main objective of this article will be to delineate one such approach for intervening with child witnesses and their mothers using a family group treatment modality. It is comprised of two sections. First, a theoretical framework for a mother-child group model is addressed within a feminist-informed family systems framework followed by an outline of group goals. Finally, a few of the central group interventions are highlighted from the beginning of the group to the end.

MOTHER-CHILD GROUP TREATMENT: THEORY AND GOALS

This literature clarifies the variety of approaches used to intervene with children exposed to mother assault and other forms of violence. While there may be differences in the goals and methodologies of these approaches, each has the advantage of addressing multiple issues relevant to child witnesses. A family group approach may be seen as an additional tool for mental health providers useful in contexts such as children's mental health and family service settings. The section below highlights our conceptual perspective for the use of a feminist-informed mother-child group followed by an outline of group goals.

Feminist-Informed Family Systems Perspective

A classical family systems paradigm views not only the individuals who comprise the family but their ways of relating to each other and the system as a whole, as a valuable source of information, resource and intervention. Therefore, a systems perspective encourages working with more than one family member whenever possible. When a feminist-informed lens is overlaid on the family systems perspective, mother assault is seen as a multi-dimensioned phenomenon where issues of family structure and power differentials between family members are played out.

Family therapy's awareness of woman abuse as a serious problem affecting families is due to the feminist critique of family therapy and the subsequent development of feminist family therapy. Four central principles form the theoretical foundation for the mother-child group.

1. We are committed to the belief that all women and men are equal and that it is wrong for women to be subordinate (Avis, 1986; Kanuha, 1996; Pressman, 1989). In practice, we reject society's normalization of violence, the stereotypical roles and political beliefs that frame women's and children's oppression. All family members have the right to develop to their full potential and be allowed to make choices that will enhance the overall effectiveness of their lives. We also recognize that societal institutions (e.g., media, courts, police) historically have reinforced male dominance and we work with families to advocate for themselves.

Violence cuts across boundaries established by economics, race, culture, and sexual orientation. The belief in equality is also firmly grounded in a focus not only on gender but also on class, race and culture, all of which interact to shape family life (Kliman, 1995). A perspective sensitive to all of these dimensions is imperative and acknowledges that the manifestation, treatment, effects, and/or prevention of violence against women and children may differ across economic, ethnic and cultural groups (Fontes, 1997).

2. Each person in the family is responsible for his or her behavior (Barrett, Trepper, & Fish, 1990; Goldner, Penn, Sheinberg, & Walker, 1990). The recognition of individual responsibility is paramount in the transition to post-violence family life. We reject the societal notion that ascribes blame and guilt to women for their partner's violence and in its place we emphasize the understanding that everyone makes personal choices for which they must be accountable. By stressing that adults have choice in determining their beliefs and behavior, we believe that family members can begin to recognize a personal sense of efficacy and empowerment that can disrupt the perpetuation of abuse.

Further, we take a non-neutral stance towards the issue of violence, arguing that all violence is wrong. We confront the abusive language, images, behaviors and cognitions of the men, women and children we work with in congruence with our promotion of non-violence between family members.

3. All family members have a right to personal safety (Domestic Abuse Intervention Project, 1997). As family therapists working from a non-neutral position, we view violence as the central issue and not a symptom of other issues such as communication or problems of family structure (Avis, 1992; Bograd, 1984). Thus, safety of all family members is our first priority. Treatment efforts keep this in mind at all times. One way of attending to safety is by recognizing that men who abuse employ various forms of power and control to force their will on women and children. Therefore, we continually assess for potential risk and educate appropriate family members about these risk factors. Because safety is the priority, we agree with Shamai (1996) that in some cases preserving an intact family structure can be dangerous and damaging and we will support a woman's decision to permanently leave her partner. As the author states, it is the responsibility of the therapist to recognize and accept that separation may become necessary when continuation of the relationship is dangerous (p. 212).

Safety also includes protecting children from harm. The feminist-informed family systems paradigm allows the therapist to hold women as well as men responsible for their directly abusive behavior towards their children *and* holds men and women accountable for insuring the child's well-being at all times. This always occurs within a context that recognizes the pervasive influence that larger social, political and cultural systems have on men, women and families. We disagree with Ash and Cahn (cited in Peled, 1996) that feminism is "limited to the degree that it fails to give some account of the aspects of women which seem ugly and undesirable" (p. 140).

When we work with families where there has been domestic violence, we punctuate our discussions with the family member perpetrating the abuse. This is most frequently men using violence against their female partners (Bograd, 1992; Jaffe, Sudermann, & Reitzel, 1992). If, as the literature indicates, children who witness this horrific behavior are indeed abused children (Echlin & Marshall, 1995), then who do we identify as the perpetrator of this abuse? First and foremost, it is the man perpetrating the violence, albeit indirectly, against the child. *At the same time*, we advocate that the mother as an adult and a parent is responsible for protecting children from harm. We expect the same of non-offending mothers in cases of incest. We do not minimize the reality that some mothers choose not to protect their children by either returning to their partner or by becoming abusive towards their own children (O'Keefe, 1995; Peled, 1996). These are delicate places to tread not only for treatment providers but also child welfare workers (Echlin & Marshall, 1995, present a thorough discussion of these issues). As family therapists, we walk slowly and carefully in our work with abusive fathers and battered mothers believing that a firm stand on the responsibilities of both parents when domestic violence occurs does not automatically preclude effective work with either. We concur with Rondeau, Lindsay, Beaudoin, and Brodeur (1997) that the aim of intervention should involve a "social ethic" (p. 285) where violence is seen as an act of domination and interest must first serve the victim. Children cannot feel free and secure if they are victims of violence within their home. A social ethic requires therapists to help both parents recognize that the victimization of children through witnessing, even if they are not direct recipients of a blow, is harmful to that child.

4. *Familiarity with the non-systemic literature is essential* (Barrett et al., 1990). Advances made in the field of violence against women and children suggest that no single conceptual model can explain the complexity of this very serious problem. In its place are developing frameworks consisting of multifactor interactional theories (Barnett et al., 1997) that illuminate the impact of violence by describing the interrelationships between individual, familial, and cultural components. We find this helpful and as a result have turned our attention to the notion that familial exposure to acts of violence constitutes traumatic events. These events leave direct victim and witness members feeling helpless, terrorized and vulnerable to developing symptoms of posttraumatic stress disorder. Interest in the field of traumatology has led us to strategies dealing with the traumatic aftereffects of violence (Lehmann, Rabenstein, Duff, & Van Meyel, 1994).

MOTHER-CHILD GROUP TREATMENT: INTERVENTIONS

The mother-child group model is one of three models that comprise the Community Group Treatment Program for Children Who Have Witnessed Woman Abuse, a community-based, multi-agency committee in London, Ontario that runs groups for child witnesses to mother assault. The mother-child group occupies a unique place in the array of treatment options available to the child and her or his family.

One of the strengths of group therapy in general is that group discussions among people who share a similar experience break through the social isolation, minimization, and denial that can characterize the victimization experience. This is certainly true for the mother-child group. This group highlights and builds upon the interaction between all participants across family and age boundaries. Children have their own parent, other children, other mothers, as well as group leaders to validate their experiences, challenge misperceptions and share ideas with.

Mothers are supported as heads of their family. Group leaders constantly reinforce that the management of a child's behavior rests with her. Mothers have the authority to make decisions in the interests of their children and our role is to collaborate and not impose. At the same time, we reserve the right to provide expectations when parenting becomes inappropriate and will gently challenge or allow a parent or support a parent through a confrontation by other parents.

The majority of children who complete the mother-child group are from single parent homes in which the mother is head of the household. Typically, the abuser is out of the home but may have some contact with the child. The model requires that mothers are at a point where they recognize the effects of violence on their children and are ready to support and assist their youngster. This means that families who are in crisis usually are not suited for this group until the crisis subsides.

The groups generally follow many of the weekly themes outlined in Bentley et al. (1997) and Sudermann, Marshall, and Loosely (this volume). Some of these themes include: identification of various abusive behaviors, exploration of emotions, identification and deconstruction of harmful myths about violence and gender, conflict resolution, safety planning and esteem building. However, while we believe it is important to provide information, the content of group discussion is tailored to the families present. Weekly agendas are flexible and adapted to the needs of the participants. We count on the ideas of the parents to direct our planning and solicit their input about what the most relevant or pressing issues are for them and their children. At other times, we simply follow the group process.

Goals of the Mother-Child Group

The mother-child group has five goals. Each goal is outlined as follows along with a rationale for its consideration.

Supporting the Restructuring of the Family

As Pressman (1987) has pointed out, mothers who are abused are often relegated by the abusive partner to a power position equal to or less than that of the children in the family. One unfortunate outcome is that mothers often speak of their use of physical discipline and other ineffective and negative parenting practices (e.g., lack of consistency, yelling or screaming) in attempts to regain control over the child's acting out. One of the primary tasks for the family is for the mother to establish or reestablish her leadership by setting limits on her children's behavior in non-abusive ways (Lehmann et al., 1994). The group provides ample opportunities for mothers to examine these executive skills. Leaders step back and encourage mothers as they deal directly with their own children in navigating transitional activities and confront disruptive behavior throughout the hour and a half. We purposely move away from the traditional patriarchal model of parenting where roles are assigned by gender to that of "role symmetry" (Bilinkoff, 1995, p. 101), an alternative parenting style incorporating elements of work and nurturing.

Providing a Place for Families to Talk About Abuse in Safe Ways

Family therapists have devoted much thought to secrecy in families. Family therapist pioneer Peggy Papp (1993) reminds us that secrets in families are not innately bad. "Parents are continuously confronted with decisions concerning how to impart information to their children about the world they live in" (p. 66). Problems occur when the natural sensitivity and judgment of parents is clouded by feelings of guilt, shame, fear, etc., or the desire to protect the child. These feelings interfere with the parents' ability to communicate about the issue, making the parent anxious and guarded. Often adults in the family underestimate the child's ability to handle the secret information (Papp, 1993). Their children, sensing that information is being withheld, become confused, anxious and internalize the feeling that something is not right. At the same time, children may withhold information from their parent to protect themselves and/or the parent. Finally, family members will also keep "shared secrets" in the family safe from the outside world (Papp). These three types of secrets converge frequently for many families where there has been mother assault.

We have observed that children look to their mothers for direction about whether or not it is safe to talk about the family's secrets. Mothers hold the missing pieces of information needed by the children to better understand his or her situation. Mothers will also set the tone for which "shared secrets" are appropriate for the family to talk about. Further, the mother is also the person best suited for helping her child determine where is it safe to talk about what with whom, since she knows the child and the circumstances under which the child may be at risk. For example, a mother and child may decide it is not safe to tell the non-custodial father who perpetrated the mother assault that the family participates in the group. With the mother's guidance, the children can decide what or what not to say to the father.

Mothers are central figures in all of these types of endeavors whether or not they are present at the time of discussion. The mother-child group brings the parent into the room with her son or daughter and provides opportunities for families to work through these issues together.

Children's revelations in group are not limited to their experiences of domestic violence. When a secure environment has been created, children will often disclose previously untold experiences of direct physical or sexual abuse. Research by Sas, Cunningham and Hurley (1995) indicates that parents play the greatest role in many aspects of a child's disclosure of sexual abuse. Parents are the adults their children will most often tell first. Parents are also directly responsible for acting in the best interest of their children and the people most empowered to do so. This underscores the importance and efficacy of having mothers present as we broach all of these topics. It also requires a preparedness on the part of group leaders who must manage the crisis a child's unexpected disclosure can precipitate for that child, his or her mother and others in the group. Leaders simultaneously support the child and the mother, contain the information and activate procedures for bringing a disclosure to the attention of the proper authorities if necessary.

Debriefing Traumatic Stories

Mothers frequently have an incomplete understanding about what the child knows about the violence. Meanwhile, her child has constructed ideas about what has taken place based on pieces of information he or she has gleaned from what she or he has seen, heard or imagined. The shame and secrecy of the abuse coupled with the developmental level of the child and the stress the child has experienced often results in inaccurate or incomplete narratives about what took place (Papp, 1993). Therapeutic space is created that allows family members to tell their individual and shared stories.

Inviting a Family-Wide Stance Against All Abusive Behavior in the Home

Having mothers present allows us to address abusive behaviors that may continue among family members in the home even after the abuser has left. It is simply not enough to mandate that "all abuse in this house stops!" Hurtful interactions between parents, children, and siblings need to be concretely identified and replaced by more appropriate means of expressing strong emotions and resolving conflict.

One way of addressing this is by inviting members to search for non-violent alternatives in the extended family and community. On the content level, the "search of exceptions" to prevailing beliefs about power and control is done through exercises that require the group to identify non-violent and nurturing extended family or community members as role models. Positive choices for non-violence, integral parts of creating a new, peaceful foundation for family life, are highlighted and supported.

Creating a Non-Violent Future

The final goal, creating a non-violent future for the family, arises from contextualizing the violence as part of, in many cases, the family's deep history–stretching back through generations. When the intergenerational transmission of abusive interactions and sexist beliefs is identified, conscious choices can be made by the family to create a non-violent future. Our focus on a non-violent future opens space for children and families to create their own "healing theory" (Figley, 1989). These are stories through which children and mothers can gain a sense of new direction and hope because they recognize the positive but perhaps unconscious decisions for a more fear-free and peaceful existence than they have been making. Opportunities are provided for the family to purposefully denounce the legacy of violence in favor of peace for the current generation and those to come.

Described below are some of the key intervention activities that form the bulwark of the mother-child group. They have been clustered according to where in the three-phased life of the group they are most often effective and appropriate.

Beginning: The Selection of Families and the Pre-Group Interview

Traditionally, families refer themselves or are referred by child welfare workers, shelter workers, women's advocacy workers or family therapists. Families are interviewed by the leaders prior to the group. Siblings are welcomed into the interview if the child and mother would like them there regardless of whether or not the brother or sister will be participating. Rather than a precursor to treatment, this first family interview provides an opportunity for assessment and treatment to begin. For some, it is the first time that family members have had a focused conversation about the violence, verbally acknowledging and labeling it. Thus, the pre-group interview can be a microcosm of the group itself. The leader's first question directed to mother is "What does your child know about why you are all here today?" From the beginning, this establishes her as the person in charge of the flow of information, a theme that will thread throughout the group.

Group leaders make conscious use of specific, simple and realistic language when referring to the abuse while at the same time respecting the language the client family uses to describe the abuse. The interview incorporates a checklist of abusive behaviors that leaders ask about specifically such as verbal battering, hitting, kicking, slapping, threats, mind games, sexual and financial abuse, etc. (Loosely et al. 1997). The form includes questions about who is in the family, who the abuser was/is and whether alcohol/drugs was/is involved. This written tool provides information leaders can access at a glance and enables them to plan specifically based on the needs and experiences of the participating families. Additional screening questions determine if the child is able to acknowledge the violence and abuse in the home, if the child is ready to talk about it and if it is safe for the child to do so in a group context. Finally, the child is asked, "How do you think your dad would feel about you being involved in a group where you would be talking about his abusive behavior?" whether or not the child sees the father. This question can provide an understanding of how the child perceives his or her safety and introduces the family to the concept of a family safety plan.

Secrets and the Privacy Box

Throughout the model's development we have grappled with ways to convey the notions of good secrets, bad secrets and privacy, a daunting enough task with families who have not been victimized by the intimate and undisclosed horror of violence in the home. We have also searched for ways to delineate secrecy from confidentiality, an essential part of positive group process. Hence, the following ideas.

Early in the first session, when we identify the purpose of the group, we say that sometimes families find it hard to talk about the hurtful things that happened at home. They think that these things only happened to them and not other kids and moms. The abuse is a "bad secret" that nobody talks about, sometimes not even with each other. We tell mothers that it is their leadership in the family and their commitment to family healing that has brought the family to the group. Then we ask mothers to give their children verbal permission to talk about the abuse "right here and now, in the group."

We give them the latitude to move apart from the rest, to whisper, to do whatever is most appropriate for them and their child in order to complete this ritual. The purpose is for mother to give a clear, direct, non-ambiguous message that, in this setting, the child can talk about what happened. As a type of enactment (Nichols, 1997), directions for this exercise must be explicit and the mechanics must be made clear.

Following this ritual, the leaders show the group a metal strong box. Attached to the key are a handful of colorful ribbons. As participants watch, the box is opened. The leader describes the box as being like the group. "One of the first things we will do in group each week is open the box," the group is told. "When the box is open and group begins, we will be talking about what has happened at your house and how you felt about it. Other people will share their stories too. What we talk about in group is private or 'confidential'. When the group is over, other people's stories go in the box for safekeeping until next week but you can take your stories home and discuss them with your family if you choose. The only stories, thoughts or feelings you can talk about outside of this room are your own or your family's. It is important that you take care of other family's stories by keeping them in group (or in the box) and not telling anyone outside of this room about a story that does not involve you."

Use of this metaphor began with families of children three to six years of age. However, the power and clarity it brings to these concepts has prompted us to use them with all ages.

Hand Portraits

The anxiety and uncertainty of coming together as strangers in a group for the first time is a common part of group process. The Hand Portrait exercise is a low-risk, creative activity that helps to ease first-session tensions.

In the first session, a Polaroid photograph of each family is taken and incorporated into a Hand Portrait (Sawicki, 1991). As a team, each family is directed to create a poster of themselves using the photo and tracings of each member's hand. Inside the hand, participants fill in words or pictures that describe themselves and then fill in the surrounding area with motifs that exemplify their family. This activity is a vehicle through which members become better acquainted, and as a family art technique, provides an early opportunity for families to express themselves non-verbally and work cooperatively. It also provides leaders with the chance to observe the interactions of family members within group. Families are asked to introduce themselves through their posters, which are then hung for the duration of the 12-week group.

Abusive Behaviors Poster

Following the Hand Portrait, group leaders ask the children to move to the front of the room where three laminated posters with pictures and headings illustrating verbal abuse/threats/racism, physical abuse and sexual abuse have been hung (Bentley et al., 1997). The leaders systematically work through each of the posters asking the children for their definitions of each type of abusive behavior and requesting examples. With young children, leaders will often call upon mothers to clarify in the child's language a concept that is unclear to the child. The responses are written out on post-it notes, which the children then stick underneath the appropriate heading. Sometimes a child's decision about where to place the example is unexpected. With an emphasis on interaction and process, we are curious about why a child may categorize an abusive act in an atypical way. We are more likely to ask the child about their choice rather than immediately correct it. This simple, yet impactful, exercise provides information about: what the children have witnessed and are willing to disclose; how they identify these behaviors; which topics provoke a non-verbal reaction (increased fidgeting or agitation, a move closer to the parent, physical withdrawal, etc.); and how the children relate to the leaders, the other children and their mothers. Again, these posters remain in the room throughout the life of the group and post-its are readily available each week so that as behaviors are identified, they can be added to the lists. These lists often prove to be illuminating for mothers who thought their children were unaware of what was taking place. We make a point of asking mothers whether there are any surprises on these lists and if so, why they thought their children were unaware of the occurrences.

Middle: The Use of Videos and Art

Videos

Videos are a tremendous resource in the mother-child group. Their impact can be so great that thought and care must precede their use. The visual and auditory images in fictional accounts of family violence, bullying or other types of abuse can trigger traumatic memories for adults and children alike. We have found that it is safest to show videos after a certain level of group familiarity and trust has been established. Adequate preparation for the parents and children is essential as is more structure imposed by leaders to manage higher levels of anxiety.

Mothers have given us clear feedback that they prefer previewing the videos instead of seeing them for the first time with the children. We routinely schedule a separate evening for mothers only to watch and then reflect on their personal feelings and thoughts about the films. It is also a chance for them to prepare for the children's potential responses.

We will often show *Facing up* (1994), a movie about bullying first. It provides an introduction to issues of power, control and anger but from a slightly safer emotional distance since it depicts the experiences of a boy in school, not at home. We then view *It's not always happy at my house* (1989), *What about us?* (1994), or *The Crown Prince* (1989), three films that show domestic violence in families of various configurations. The choice of film should depend on the age and make-up of the group.

We stress that what is being viewed is a story portrayed by actors. We say, "Sometimes when moms and kids watch this program, they remember what happened to them and have many feelings. Some of what happens in this story might be the same as what happened to you and some of it may be different." We provide tissue boxes and ample paper and markers for the children to draw as they watch. We tell them that at the end of the film we will talk about their pictures, thoughts and feelings. The session is always scheduled so that there is enough time to talk through the feelings and provide as much closure as possible prior to the end of that session.

Safe and Unsafe Places

This family art activity, "Safe and Unsafe Places," suggested by play and art therapist Betty Bedard-Bidwell (Personal communication, February, 1994), can be a valuable indicator of how a child sees his or her family in terms of physical and emotional safety. It can highlight specific beliefs that the child has about safety and the child's safety skills. All group participants are given a large piece of paper which they fold in half. On the left side (projectively representing the past) they are asked to draw a picture of an unsafe place. On the right (representing the present/future) they are asked to draw a safe place. Families discuss their pictures in family groups first and then share, if they desire, with the group at large. Leaders query parents about their impressions of the children's art. The information gleaned from this exercise shapes the safety planning activities for the subsequent week. In a conversation about his drawing of a somewhat chaotic building, it became clear that 6-year-old Joshua did not know his own street address or phone number. His mother revealed that she, Joshua, and her younger son, who was also in the group, had relocated several times within two years. A fun-filled drill using play phones and emphasizing the memorization of each child's home address was devised and implemented the following week (Jon DeActis, personal communication, January, 1998).

Rainbow of Feelings

Anger and conflict are pervasive themes for all of the families who attend group. Judy Jones, a child care worker at Madame Vanier Children's Services who specializes in work with very young children, has developed the Rainbow of Feelings (Jones, 1997). This art exercise has become one of the center-pieces of the mother-child group. It beautifully illustrates that anger is one of many necessary and important feelings that all people have. First, the children are given several red strips of paper and tape and told to use the paper to make a rainbow on the wall. As they attempt to do this, a conversation ensues about whether a rainbow can be created with only one color. The children are given more strips in a variety of hues. They are told to create a rainbow using a whole range of colors and then asked what kind of rainbow they are able to make now. The connection is made between the necessity of many colors in the making of a rainbow, and the necessity of many feelings for a person. Children and adults are asked, "If you were given a new puppy, but the only feeling you could have was anger, what would happen?" or "If you were being blamed for something you did not do but all you could feel was happy, what would happen?" Participants may be asked to act out their responses to these scenarios, which are often comical and poignant.

Fire as a Metaphor for Anger

Jones (1997) has also created activities that use fire as a metaphor for anger. Leaders initiate a discussion about the uses of fire (cooking, heating, etc.). Children are questioned about what happens when fire gets out of control (houses and people can be destroyed and hurt). Finally, the children are asked about what is needed in order for fire to be used safely (i.e., containment, monitoring). "Sometimes anger, like fire, can get out of control," the children are told. Mothers and children then brainstorm about ways they have found to use anger appropriately and keep it contained. The children go outside with a leader to collect boulders to bring into the group room. The anger management strategies are written on the rocks, which are then placed in the shape of a fire pit. Anger-provoking situations are written on red and orange tissue paper, crumbled up and placed inside the circle to symbolize the flames of the anger/fire as the group discusses ways of expressing anger appropriately in each situation.

The Ending

As with all group therapy, the ending phase of the mother-child group is characterized by activities that promote consolidation of and reflection on new learning and bring closure to the group experience. Closure is of central importance to these families whose lives are often marked by harsh, painful and incomplete endings.

Creating a Peaceful Future

In the second to the last meeting, families receive an invitation that reads: You have been working very hard to rebuild your family life on a foundation of peace and happiness that replaces the old home life built on abuse and fear. You are invited to make or bring in something that tells us about the changes in your family and your hopes for the future.

One family brought a bag of chips to share because when the abusive partner was in the home, no one was allowed to buy this treat. Other families have drawn before-the-abuse-stopped and after-the-abuse pictures. The "M." family created a colorful and abstract family rainbow using pieces of paper in various sizes glued on to a large piece of paper. The children wrote the following description:

> The Rainbow represent the moods of the family. The sparkles
> represent our family's feelings.
> Orange is for confused.

Blue is for sad feelings.
Red is for mad feelings.
Yellow is for holding our feelings in.
Purple means you are having all the feelings at once.
Pink is for happiness.

Imbedded in this activity is the message that each family has been working hard together to recover from the effects of family violence prior to and outside of the group. They will continue this important effort long after the group has ended.

Some families who live under the siege of violence do not have the room or the energy to play together. Mothers who themselves were children exposed to violence often did not have the chance to play when they were young and must learn how to be playful from their own children. Group may be the first time the mothers have the emotional space to come alongside their children and engage in playful fun. As an enactment (Nichols, 1997), this activity invites the family to take their experience back to their home by collaborating on the creation of an important symbol in an interactive and inventive manner.

The Children's Skit About Family Violence

A skit about family violence acted out by the children is developed and rehearsed for performance in the final session. It can also be an improvised psychodramatic activity; introduced, rehearsed and performed as part of the final session. Videotaping the final product for the children to view themselves can enhance the therapeutic impact of the experience (Efron & Veenendaal, 1988). Traditionally, we separate the parents and children for the rehearsal. One co-leader departs with the mothers for adult-only time used to debrief the group experience. Meanwhile, the children are asked to develop a skit about family violence. The roles that the children assume and the dramatic sequences that unfold can reflect themes of importance for each child. Depending on the ages, issues and group process, the leader may impose more structure or less structure on the activity dictated by the children's ability to work together and stay focused on the task at hand.

The mothers return to the room for the performance. When the skit concludes, the play is debriefed with the families. Illustrations of the alternative stories of peace and safety in the skit are highlighted. Since the activity is situated at the time of closure, any areas of concern are addressed with each family privately during the post-group interview.

Concluding Party

As with all of the groups for children who witness violence (Bentley et al., 1997), the final session is marked by a celebration that includes food and a graduation ceremony. We affirm for the families and ourselves that breaking secrets, talking about abuse and feelings and building peaceful lives demands courage and hard work. Their accomplishments are recognized and celebrated. The requisite snack that the leaders provide each week is supplemented with special party food like pizza. Families are invited to contribute dishes or snacks if they desire. Not only is food a central element in celebrations around the world but in the context of these treatment groups, food is a symbol of nurturance and comfort amidst an anxiety-provoking hour and a half–a consistent and anticipated element of each of the twelve sessions.

The session and group draw to a close with exercises that invite the group to reflect on what they have learned. Each participant receives a personalized certificate formally presented by the leaders. Thus, group closure is symbolized on many levels which includes the more private post-group interviews with individual families that take place within the following two weeks.

Post-Group Interviews

The post-group family interview provides a chance to meet with each family one last time to process what the group experience has been like for them, to reinforce their strengths and identify areas for future work, if necessary. A written summary of the family's participation is given to the mother. A copy of this is forwarded to any referral sources that may be involved. Often families are encouraged to re-refer the children to another group in the Community Group Treatment Program since key issues of anger, responsibility, safety, etc., change as family situations evolve and as children mature.

Certainly, leading the mother-child group is not for the faint-hearted. Working with mothers and children creates a rich and challenging interactive field that requires energy, vigilance and strong group facilitation skills not to mention ample time to prepare and debrief. Working with adults and their children brings a different level of accountability for the leadership. However, we believe that the power of the group experience for families who have survived family violence cannot be duplicated in any other treatment modality. Working together as a family within a group of other families creates a unique opportunity for validation, healing and transformation.

CONCLUSION

This article has described a group for children exposed to mother assault and their mothers. This specific model has emerged from a feminist-informed, family systems perspective and seeks to address issues for these children and their mothers within a supportive and validating environment that acknowledges alternative stories of strength and resilience.

As the body of clinical literature addressing the treatment of children exposed to domestic violence continues to broaden, groups for children and their most significant caregiver will continue to provide a unique place in the treatment spectrum. The opportunity to address issues of critical importance to the well-being of the child in the family context will continue to develop.

REFERENCES

Avis, J. M. (1986). Feminist issues in family therapy. In F. Piercy & D. Sprenkle (Eds.), *Family therapy sourcebook* (pp. 213-242). New York: Guilford.

Avis, J. M. (1992). Where are all the family therapists: Abuse and violence within families and family therapy's response. *Journal of Marital and Family Therapy, 18,* 225-232.

Barnett, O. W., Miller-Perrin, C. L., & Perrin, R. D. (1997). *Family violence across the lifespan: An introduction.* Thousand Oaks, CA: Sage.

Barrett, M. J., Trepper, T. S., & Stone Fish, L. (1990). Feminist-informed family therapy for the treatment of intrafamily child sexual abuse. *Journal of Family Psychology, 4,* 151-166.

Bentley, L., Lehmann, P., Loosley, S., Marshall, L., Rabenstein, S., & Sudermann, M. (1997). *Group treatment for children who witness woman abuse.* London, ON: Community Group Treatment Program.

Bilinkoff, J. (1995). Empowering battered women as mothers. In E. Peled, P. G. Jaffe, & J. L. Edleson, *Ending the cycle of violence: Community responses to children of battered women* (pp. 97-105). Thousand Oaks, CA: Sage.

Bograd, M. (1984). Family systems approaches to wife battering: A feminist critique. *American Journal of Orthopsychiatry 54,* 558-568.

Bograd, M. (1992). Values in conflict: Challenges to family therapists' thinking. *Journal of Marital and Family Therapy, 18,* 3, 245-256.

Carlson, B. E. (1996). Children of battered women: Research, programs, and services. In A. R. Roberts (Ed.), *Helping battered women: New perspectives and remedies* (pp. 172-187). New York: Oxford University Press.

Davies, P. T., & Cummings, E. M. (1994). Marital conflict and child adjustment: An emotional security hypothesis. *Psychological Bulletin, 116,* 387-411.

Domestic Abuse Intervention Project. (1997). *Creating a process of change for men who batter.* Unpublished manuscript.

Echlin, C. & Marshall, L. (1995). Child protection services for children of battered women: Practice and controversy. In E. Peled, P. G. Jaffe, & J. L. Edleson (Eds.), *Ending the cycle of violence: Community responses to children of battered women* (pp. 170-186). Newbury Park, CA: Sage Publications.

Efron, D., & Veenendaal, K. (1988). Videotaping in groups for children of substance abusers: A strategy for emotionally disturbed, acting out children. *Alcoholism Treatment Quarterly, 4,* 71-85.

Facing Up-Video (1992). Committee for Children. 172 20th Avenue, Seattle, WA.

Fantuzzo, J., & Lindquist, C. (1989). The effects of observing conjugal violence on children: A review and analysis of research methodology. *Journal of Family Violence, 4,* 77-94.

Figley, C. R. (1989). *Helping traumatized families.* San Francisco, CA: Jossey-Bass.

Fontes, Aronson, L. (1997). Conducting ethical cross-cultural research on family violence. In G. Kaufman Kantor & J. L. Jasinski (Eds.), *Out of the darkness: Contemporary perspectives on family violence* (pp. 296-312). Thousand Oaks: Sage.

Goldner, V., Penn, P., Sheinberg, M., & Walker, G. (1990). Love and violence: Gender paradoxes in volatile attachments. *Family Process, 29,* 343-364.

Graham-Berman, S. A., & Levendosky, A. A. (in press). Traumatic stress symptoms in children of battered women. *Journal of Interpersonal Violence.*

Hughes, H. M. (1997). Research concerning children of battered women: Clinical implications. *Journal of Aggression, Maltreatment & Trauma, 1,* 225-244.

It's not always happy at our house. (1989) L.M. Media Marketing Services, Ltd., 115 Torbay Road, Markham, Ontario.

Jaffe, P. G., Sudermann, M., & Reitzel, D. (1992). Child witnesses of marital violence. In R. T. Ammerman & M. Hersen (Eds.), *Assessment of family violence: A clinical and legal sourcebook* (pp. 313-331). New York: John Wiley & Sons.

Jaffe, P. G., Wolfe, D. A., & Wilson, S. (1990). *Children of battered women.* Newbury Park, CA: Sage.

Jones, J. (1997). *Violence prevention: A model for discussing violence with young children.* Unpublished paper.

Jouriles, E., Barling, J., & O'Leary, D. K. (1987). Predicting child behavior problems in maritally violent families. *Journal of Abnormal Child Psychology, 15,* 165-173.

Kanuha, V. (1996). Domestic violence, racism, and the battered women's movement in the United States. In J. L. Edleson & Z. C. Eisikovits (Eds.), *Future interventions with battered women and their families* (pp. 34-52). Thousand Oaks, CA: Sage.

Kliman, J. (1995). The interweaving of gender, class, and race in family therapy. In M. P. Mirkin (Ed.), *Women in context: Toward a feminist reconstruction of psychotherapy* (pp. 25-47). New York: The Guilford Press.

Lehmann, P. (1997). The development of posttraumatic stress disorder (PTSD) in a sample of child witnesses to mother assault. *Journal of Family Violence, 12,* 241-257.

Lehmann, P., Rabenstein, S., Duff, J., & Van Meyel, R. (1994). A multi-dimensional model for treating families that have survived mother assault. *Contemporary Family Therapy, 16,* 7-25.

McAlister Groves, B. (1996). Growing up in a violent world: The impact of family and community violence on young children and their families. In E. J. Erwin (Ed.), *Putting children first: Visions for a brighter future for young children and their families* (pp. 31-52). Boston: Brooks.

Murphy, L., Pynoos, R. S., & Boyd James, C. (1997). The trauma/grief-focused group psychotherapy module of an elementary school-based violence prevention/

intervention program. In J. D. Osofsky (Ed.), *Children in a violent society* (pp. 223-255). New York: Guilford.

Nichols, M. (1997). The art of the enactment: How to get real conversation going in the consulting room. *Family Therapy Networker,* November/December, 23.

O'Keefe, M. (1995). Predictors of child abuse in maritally violent families. *Journal of Interpersonal Violence, 10,* 3-25.

Osofsky, J. D. (Ed.) (1997). *Children in a violent society.* New York: Guilford.

Osofsky, J. D., & Fenichel, E. (Eds.). (1994). *Hurt, healing, hope: Caring for infants and toddlers in violent environments.* Washington, DC: Zero to Three.

Papp, P. (1993). The worm in the bud: Secrets between parents and children. In E. Imber-Black (Ed.), *Secrets in families and family therapy* (pp. 66-85). New York: W.W. Norton & Co., Inc.

Peled, E. (1996). "Secondary" victims no more: Refocusing intervention with children. In J. L. Edleson & C. Eisikovits (Eds.), *Future interventions with battered women and their families* (pp. 125-153). Thousand Oaks, CA: Sage Publications.

Pressman, B. (1987). The place of family of origin therapy in the treatment of wife abuse. In A. J. Hovestadt & M. Fine (Eds.), *Family of origin therapy: The family therapy collections* (pp. 45-56). Rockville, MD: Aspen.

Pressman, B. (1989). Treatment of wife abuse: The case for feminist therapy. In B. Pressman, G. Cameron, & M. Rothery (Eds.), *Intervening with assaulted women: Current theory, research, and practice* (pp. 21-46). Hillsdale, NJ: Lawrence Erlbaum.

Pynoos, R. S. (1994). Traumatic stress and developmental psychopathology in children and adolescents. In R. S. Pynoos (Ed.), *Posttraumatic stress disorders: A clinical review* (pp. 65-98). Lutherville, MD: Sidran.

Rondeau, G., Lindsay, L., Beaudoin, G., & Brodeur. (1997). Ethical dimensions of intervention with violent partners: Priorities in the values and beliefs of practitioners. In G. Kaufman Kantor & J. L. Jasinski (Eds.), *Out of the darkness: Contemporary perspectives on family violence* (pp. 282-295). Thousand Oaks, CA: Sage.

Rossman, B. B. R., & Rosenberg, M. S. (1997). Psychological maltreatment: A needs analysis and application for children in violent families. In R. Geffner, S. B. Sorenson, & P. K. Lundberg-Love (Eds.). *Violence and sexual abuse at home: Current issues in spousal battering and child maltreatment* (pp. 245-262). New York, NY: The Haworth Press, Inc.

Sas, L. D., Cunningham, A. H., & Hurley, P. (1995). *Tipping the balance to tell the secret: Public discovery of child sexual abuse.* London, ON: London Family Court and Health Canada.

Sawicki, W. (1991). *Juggling cultures.* London, ON: London Intercommunity Health Centre.

Shamai, M. (1996). Couple therapy with battered women and abusive men: Does it have a future? In J. L. Edleson & Z. C. Eisikovits (Eds.), *Future interventions with battered women and their families* (pp. 201-215). Thousand Oaks, CA: Sage Publications.

Silvern, L., & Kearsvang, L. (1989). The traumatized children of violent marriages. *Child Welfare, LXVIII,* 421-436. ⋅

Silvern, L., Karyl, J., & Landis, T. Y. (1995). Individual psychotherapy for the traumatized children of abused women. In E. Peled, P. G. Jaffe, & J. L. Edleson (Eds.), *Ending the cycle of violence: Community responses to children of battered women* (pp. 43-76). Newbury Park, CA: Sage.

Terr, L. (1990). *Too scared to cry: Psychic trauma in childhood*. New York: Harper & Row.

What about us?-Video (1993). Kinetic Productions, 408 Dundas Street East, Toronto, Ontario.

Child Protection Workers
and Battered Women's Advocates
Working Together to End Violence
Against Women and Children

Carole Echlin
Bina Osthoff

SUMMARY. Child protection workers and battered women's advocates are challenged to stop working against one another and to start working together to end violence against women and children. Recognizing that there are many difficulties in working collaboratively, the authors maintain that because the issues of child protection and violence against women are intertwined, the need for a collaborative response is imperative. Examples of this collaboration are described. *[Article copies available for a fee from The Haworth Document Delivery Service: 1-800-342-9678. E-mail address: getinfo@haworthpressinc.com <Website: http://www.haworthpressinc.com>]*

KEYWORDS. Child welfare, battered women's advocates, woman abuse, collaborative response

To effectively address the serious and prevalent problem of violence against women and children within our communities, coordinated and com-

Address correspondence to: Carole Echlin, 42 Kirkton Court, London, Ontario, Canada, N5X ITZ.

[Haworth co-indexing entry note]: "Child Protection Workers and Battered Women's Advocates Working Together to End Violence Against Women and Children." Echlin, Carole, and Bina Osthoff. Co-published simultaneously in *Journal of Aggression, Maltreatment & Trauma* (The Haworth Maltreatment & Trauma Press, an imprint of The Haworth Press, Inc.) Vol. 3, No. 1 (#5), 2000, pp. 207-219; and: *Children Exposed to Domestic Violence: Current Issues in Research, Intervention, Prevention, and Policy Development* (ed: Robert A. Geffner, Peter G. Jaffe, and Marlies Sudermann) The Haworth Maltreatment & Trauma Press, an imprint of The Haworth Press, Inc., 2000, pp. 207-219. Single or multiple copies of this article are available for a fee from The Haworth Document Delivery Service [1-800-342-9678, 9:00 a.m. - 5:00 p.m. (EST). E-mail address: getinfo@haworthpressinc.com].

prehensive efforts that focus on battered women's concerns for their children must be undertaken by child protection workers and battered women's advocates. Given the high rate of co-occurrence of woman abuse and child abuse (Straus & Gelles, 1990), one would expect to find a high level of cooperation and collaboration among child protection workers and battered women's advocates. While collaborative efforts between these two sectors are growing, tensions still exist. Working together requires that battered women's advocates and child protection workers address these obstacles so that they no longer interfere.

Why doesn't she just take her kids and get the heck out?

Why are child protection workers blaming the victim? Can't they see she has enough to cope with? (Cummings & Mooney, 1988)

In 1995, three reporters from the *Toronto Star* newspaper devoted eight months of full time investigation to research woman abuse. The following is taken from their report:

During the week of June 30th to July 6th in Toronto, Ontario, 133 cases of woman abuse began their journey through the court system; 127 of the victims were women and six were men. Five of the women were pregnant when beaten. Eight were sexually assaulted. A dozen women had their hair pulled out as a result of being dragged across the floor. Almost two dozen women were choked. Twelve women were assaulted with knives and sixteen were attacked with objects such as chunks of wood, telephones and even a bicycle.

Almost one-third of these attacks were witnessed by children, who were on average about eight years old. Seven of these youngsters called 911 and nine were assaulted themselves during the attacks. (Armstrong, Daly & Mallan, 1995)

For battered women's advocates and child protection workers this report is not *news*. We are quite aware that women are being beaten, raped, isolated, coerced, threatened and murdered by their partners. We also know that the children of battered women are witnessing these atrocities and that many of these children are also being directly abused by the perpetrators. In reference to the severity of woman abuse, feminist activist and writer Charlotte Bunch has commented that "if any other group were so systematically murdered, tortured and raped we would have a civil emergency" (Bunch, 1991). She states that: "woman abuse in its many forms is the most pervasive and insidious form of human rights abuse." Nevertheless, responses to these injustices are often inadequate. Some interventions for woman abuse and/or child protection are based on feminist principles and enhance the strategies to end woman abuse, while other interventions follow competing discourses and can confuse and minimize the issues. Some interventions even put women and children in danger.

Sadly, for many of the victims of woman abuse, battered women's advocates and child protection workers have found themselves working at cross purposes when trying to intervene. This needs to stop. Given that woman abuse and child victimization occur in tandem, the authors believe that effective intervention in such cases must be coordinated. This requires that battered women's advocates and child protection workers challenge the competing discourses and reduce the fragmentation in current interventions so that proactive collaborative policies and legislation can be developed and implemented.

This article is a call to action. It is a call to child protection workers and battered women's advocates specifically, to start working together to end woman abuse. Further, it is a call for proactive intervention and legislative changes that empower mothers to protect their children by integrating the child's best interests with the mother's safety needs. Finally, it is a call to hold the perpetrators of woman abuse and child abuse accountable for their actions. Implementation of such action requires a critical analysis of the systems and approaches that promote and perpetuate woman abuse. Also required is the political will to take individual as well as collaborative, collective action to ensure social justice for all women and children.

To meet this challenge, both child protection workers and battered women's advocates must identify the harm that witnessing woman abuse has on children; understand the forms and dynamics of woman abuse; understand the risks to children from abuse and neglect; develop an understanding of why women stay in abusive relationships for periods of time and offer ideas for collaborative intervention in woman abuse cases.

A FAMILY'S TRUE STORY

The following account comes from the police reports regarding charges of assault against Robert Earl Gaudry. Mr. Gaudry was thirty-two years old with a lengthy history of violent assaults, the majority of assaults against his common-law partner of eight years. In this report a child about six years old was exposed to the violent acts of his father locking up his mother in the bathroom, forcing her head under the hot water tap, breaking her nose, perforating her eardrum, and ripping her ear in half during a brutal attack. The report continues that while the mother was being abused, the sixteen-year-old brother was attempting to put the six-year-old and three-year-old daughter to bed. According to the report, as the six-year-old was going to bed, he remembers that at the end of another fight his older brother was pulled from his bed and ordered by his father to clean up his battered and bleeding mother (Fauler, 1995).

How could a child protection worker intervene in the case presented? Would a worker offer services? If services were offered would a worker remove the children? Why or why not?

Variations in attitudes, laws, knowledge and practice have led to a multitude of responses by child protection workers in cases of woman abuse. In our experience, some communities may not offer intervention in the case presented while in other communities, services may be offered while in yet other communities the children may be removed from their home. Why do practices differ so widely?

Society's beliefs about the oppression of women, the role of the mother, the best interests of children and men's accountability, all impact the policies, laws and interventions that we subsequently develop and follow. These variations in attitudes, awareness, laws and practices result in fragmented responses to women and children exposed to woman abuse.

Over the years, service providers are becoming more aware of and concerned with the impact that witnessing woman abuse has on children. While this increased awareness is a positive step for children, it has not yet reduced the existing tension between child protection services and battered women's advocates who intervene in woman abuse cases. Although battered women's advocates and child protection workers share a common goal–to end violence in families–relations between the two systems over the years have been very strained (Callahan, 1993; Gordon, 1988). In fact, there has been a long history of hostility and antagonism between the two groups. Schechter and Edleson (1994) report that the separate historical developments in child welfare and services to battered women have been compounded by different philosophies, different professional terminologies, and even the value placed on different outcomes. This has resulted in mistrust and suspicion between the two groups.

Complicating and exacerbating the situation, has been the lack of legislation in both the United States and Canada which provides a workable definition of child abuse that includes children who witness woman abuse. For example, in six of the ten provinces in Canada there is legislation which defines children's exposure to "domestic violence" as a ground to declare children to be in need of protection. However, in the other provinces there is no legislation or policies that protect child witnesses to woman abuse although provisions regarding "psychological abuse" are sometimes employed to this end. Furthermore, in the provinces where these laws do exist they are often too vague, or too broad. As well, the majority of these laws use the term "severe domestic violence" but offer no guidelines on how to define what is meant by severe. Another criticism of the legislation has been the use of gender neutral terms like "domestic violence" rather than woman abuse, which obscures the attribution of responsibility (Echlin & Marshall, 1995).

In her article, *Children Who Witness Women Battering: Concerns and Dilemmas in the Construction of a Social Problem* (1993), Einat Peled identified similar problems in the United States. She reported that there were no federal or state laws in the United States that specified that children who witness woman abuse were children in need of protection. She also reported that while virtually all states had emotional abuse as a reportable condition, conceptualizing it was a major problem. Given the imprecision of the definition and the difficulty in proving that the psychological maltreatment of the child was caused by witnessing woman abuse, she reports that child protection services were left to decide when and how to intervene (Peled, 1993).

For these reasons, confusion, frustration and fragmentation in response to child protection cases involving woman abuse is not surprising. What is clear, however, is that women and children are suffering both by the perpetrators of the abuse and as a result of inadequate societal protection.

ASSESSING FOR WOMAN ABUSE

To ensure the safety of women and children in woman abuse situations it is imperative that an assessment for woman abuse be undertaken in all child protection cases and that all interventions be grounded in a solid understanding of the complexities of meeting the needs of both the battered women and their children.

Currently, there are many differing discourses and interventions in cases of woman abuse. Critical to creating a collaborative effort between child protection workers and battered women's advocates is the articulation of *common* principles and belief statements. The ideology used to define woman abuse informs the conceptualization of the causes perpetuating factors and dynamics of woman abuse in families and, in turn, directly influences the interventions and solutions.

A feminist approach to woman abuse acknowledges that we live in a world where sexist ideas, attitudes and structures give rise to discrimination, violence and oppression of women. In a feminist analysis, ending sexism, along with other forms of oppression, requires that we challenge abuses of power in individual and family situations, as well as within political, economic and structural systems (LCCEWA, 1994).

This belief statement is supported by the United Nations definition of gender-based abuse. According to the United Nations Fourth World Conference on Women (1995), violence against women means: "any act of gender-based violence that results in, or is likely to result in, physical, sexual or psychological harm or suffering to women, including threats of such acts, coercion or arbitrary deprivations of liberty, whether occurring in public or private life." The report describes the persistence of violence against women as a manifestation of historically unequal power relations between men and women, which have led to domination over and discrimination against women by men and which have prevented women's full advancement. Violence against women is one of the crucial social mechanisms by which women are forced into a subordinate position compared to men.

This social reality of systematic gender inequality requires that responses to the needs of children who witness woman abuse be constructed within the framework of a solid understanding of the definitions and dynamics of woman abuse and according to the common belief statements articulated. Without a clear analysis, misinformation, biases and conflicting agendas can hinder strategies for intervention. For example, one primary myth that hinders intervention in woman abuse cases suggests that women allow the abuse and that women could prevent the abuse and protect their children if they choose to do so. This myth is contradictory to the definition of woman abuse which states that the abuse is systematic and intentional. Also problematic in this fallacy is the profound minimization of the impact of abuse and the obstacles in society that perpetuate and promote woman abuse. When this myth is maintained, the perpetrator is protected from responsibility in actively pursuing power and control over the woman and children. The abuser's responsibility to end the violence and keep the children safe is not addressed. Serious consequences result when this myth is applied to the case of battered women and especially battered mothers who may be under scrutiny regarding the care of their children. Victim blaming is the result, which is often voiced by the question, *"Why doesn't she just leave?"*

WHY DO WOMEN STAY?

"I always stayed in this relationship because I'd sooner have him in front of me than behind me. I don't know if you understand that or not . . . it was better for me to know where he was than not to know." ("Elizabeth," describing her fear in the video: *Make a Difference [1994]*).

Inherent in the accusation *"Why Do Women Stay?"* is the misinformed belief that leaving the abusive partner is the best and only safety plan. In contrast to this, women report the relentless retaliation from the abuser after separation and research confirms that woman abuse tends to escalate when women leave the relationship (Campbell, 1992). For the children of abused women, separation does not end the violence and uncertainty with which they had lived (Shepard, 1992).

It is ironic that in the repetition of the accusation "*Why Do Women Stay?*" that the real question "*Why do abusers continue to abuse their partners and their children?*" never gets asked and therefore never gets addressed.

In each of the Making Connections Groups offered at the LBWAC, advocates discuss with women the victim blaming inherent in the accusation "*Why Do Women Stay?*" Women are also asked about the barriers they face in seeking safety for themselves and their children. Interestingly, in group after group similar reasons recur including the following:

WOMEN'S BARRIERS TO SEEKING SAFETY

- *Retaliation by abuser.* Women report that many abusers threaten to kill themselves, the woman or other family members if they believe the woman is taking action to protect herself and the children. Barnard, Vera, Vera and Newman (1982), report that a battered woman's chance of being killed by her partner rises more than 30 fold after she leaves him.
- *Abuse towards the children.* Women report that their children's safety is often their primary concern when they are negotiating a safety plan. Some women feel that they can mitigate their children's safety more effectively by staying in the relationship. Abuse of children by a batterer is more likely when the marriage is dissolving, the couple has separated and the husband/father is highly committed to continued dominance and control of the mother and children (Bowker, Armitell, & McFerron, 1988).
- *Child abduction.* Women report that they have been terrorized by their abusive partner's threats to abduct their children. Half of all abductions occur during court-ordered visitation, and fathers abduct their children mainly to hurt mothers (Heger & Grief, 1991).
- *Child custody issues.* Custody and access orders guarantee the abuser continued contact with the victim. Friendly parent provisions, coerced mediation, access arrangements and joint custody are but a few of the dangerous barriers that women confront when attempting to take action for the safety of themselves and their children. Women's fears of losing custody are also well founded. Taylor (1993) states that custody and access workers in Vancouver believe that abusive men are over-represented in the group of men that fight for custody of their children. Saunders (1993) reports that they are also more likely to receive favourable rulings from the courts.
- *Gender bias in the legal system.* Women have learned to fear the legal system. They report that they are "*damned if they do and damned if they don't*" in regard to reporting child abuse and/or woman abuse.

Women are often accused of making false accusations of child abuse, and alienating the children from their father. Or women are accused of being simply bitter, nasty wives. Conversely, if a woman either does not know about or does not report abuse, then she is labelled "neglectful" and "uncaring" (Tapp, 1994). The Canadian Panel on Violence Against Women (1993) crystallizes the risk for women in seeking legal recourse to protect themselves and their children, as follows: "the legal system remains self-serving, perpetuating ineffective and inadequate laws, policies, practices–and indeed, practitioners–which only serve to continue the denial of violence against women."

- *Lack of resources.* Community systems have too often failed to respond effectively to protect battered women and their children. During a six-month period ending in 1996, a survey of the LBWAC clients indicated that many women were staying with or returning to an abusive partner due to cuts in income maintenance programs, second stage housing and legal aid (LBWAC, 1996).
- *Cultural conditioning.* Many women report that the abusers often give them hope that they will change. Social pressure from family/friends/ church to stay together further challenges women. Joan Bilinkoff (1995) states that "women are taught by our culture to invest their identities in their relationships or marriages. Women are taught also to take major responsibility for the success or failure of the relationships."

If you were the woman in the Gaudry case, given the very real barriers, no-win situations, dangers, victim blaming and backlash inherent in woman abuse situations, what would you do to protect yourself and your children? As a society we must take responsibility for the lack of safe choices for women. Blaming the individual woman for not leaving the situation ignores the social and cultural dynamics of oppressions and obscures society's accountability. Anne Tapp (1994) reports that "When we in the battered women's movement, or the courts or the social service system judge a woman to be a bad mom because she returns to her abuser, we are in effect supporting the same socioeconomic and political structures that afford her too few options in the first place." Further, Ganley and Schechter (1996) report that charging the non-offending woman with failure to protect children, overtly or covertly makes mothers responsible for actions of their batterers, while ignoring the domestic violence perpetrator's responsibility.

Violence against women and children must be of international concern. The impact on women and children is devastating. However, to portray women solely as victims is not sufficient. Women in the LBWAC Making Connections Group talk about the tactics of abuse that they are subjected to by their partners and the impact of this abuse. They also discuss the many strategies and survival skills they employ to protect themselves and their children. With the goal of ensuring children's safety by empowering mothers, it is important for child protection workers and battered women's advocates to acknowledge women's experience in attempting to achieve safety for themselves and their children and collaboratively build on women's survival skills when developing safety plans, referrals and case management strategies.

Like Ganley and Schechter, we are aware that not all battered women are perfect parents and that some battered women would abuse or neglect their children whether or not they were being abused themselves. Ganley and Schechter (1996) report further that some mothers deny the problem of woman abuse or refuse help, and some children are in so much danger from their fathers or mothers that they have to be placed in alternative forms of care. We, however, also believe that it is important to focus on the fact that children are often much safer when their mothers are not being abused (Ganley & Schechter, 1996).

MAKING A DIFFERENCE: STRENGTHENING COMMUNITY RESPONSES AND COLLABORATION

Identifying and documenting interventions and solutions is an important step in the goal of ending violence against women and children. The real challenge, we believe, is creating the collaboration in ideology and practise and garnering the political will to implement the recommendations. Making a difference requires full partnership of all members of society in prioritizing women's and children's safety and advocating for action that shifts the status quo. Both child protection workers and battered women's advocates have a critical role in the achievement of this goal. The child protection and battered women's advocacy organizations have mandates that address their individual clients as well as community betterment. We suggest that the community betterment component be strengthened to promote these solutions:

- Define woman abuse as a serious social problem: woman abuse has devastating consequences for women, children and society. Woman abuse will not decrease until its existence is recognized;
- Increase awareness among both child protection and other community service providers that witnessing violence is harmful to children;
- Develop policy for children's protective services that will enhance child safety in woman abuse situations by supporting the non-offending parent and holding the perpetrator responsible for the abuse;
- Advocate for changes in child custody and child welfare legislation that reflect the reality of violence in women's and children's lives;

- Ensure that victims of violence have access to services that provide options for safety and that enable women to care for and protect themselves and their children;
- Challenge the myths that undermine protection issues: once a battered woman, always a battered woman, women provoked the abuse and/or deserved it, women allow the abuse, woman abuse is really mutual abuse;
- Educate ourselves and others about the oppression and victimization of children as well as the oppression and victimization of women;
- Collaboratively develop protocols with women's advocates, child protection workers, officers of the court and medical personnel. Include cross training;
- Change/create laws that are meaningful, useful and accessible to battered women and children and that address woman abuse as the potentially lethal crime that it is.
- Advocate for a justice system that protects victims by holding perpetrators accountable for stopping woman abuse; and,
- Share all of the above information with women, men and children.

Are we prepared to meet the challenge? In recognizing the insidious nature of woman abuse and the monumental task ahead of us as a community and especially for child protection workers and battered women's advocates, it is important to remember that many battered women and children are facing these same obstacles individually, every day.

INNOVATIVE PROGRAMS FOR ABUSED WOMEN AND CHILDREN EXPOSED TO WOMAN ABUSE

In recognition of the need to develop interventions which coordinate the protection of children found to have been abused or neglected with services for their battered mothers, the Family Development Clinic Staff at the Children's Hospital in Boston, Massachusetts created an innovative project called Advocacy for Women and Kids in Emergencies (AWAKE) in 1986. This was the first program in the United States in a pediatric setting which served battered women and their children at the same time (Sheeran, 1996). AWAKE believes that by providing help to battered women in conjunction with clinical services to children, both populations are served more effectively (Schechter & Gary 1992). Ganley and Schechter (1996) report that: "[Initiatives like this] suggest several shifts in traditional child practice," including the following:

1. Identifying domestic violence is critical to the safety of children.
2. Helping battered women and providing services to them is necessary to keep children safe.

3. Holding perpetrators of domestic violence accountable for stopping the violence is essential to protecting children.

In the London, Ontario community, battered women's advocates and child welfare workers are recognizing that the issues of child protection and violence against women are intertwined. Collaborative actions that address the challenge to better respond to women and children in situations of woman abuse are growing. For example, representatives from battered women's organizations and child protection services are members of the London Coordinating Committee to End Woman Abuse; protocols have been established between some battered women's organizations and child protection services; and, representatives from the respective agencies have presented together at workshops and seminars on the topics of abused women and their children. As an outcome of the increased collaboration efforts, two agencies (the London Children's Aid Society and the London Battered Women's Advocacy Centre) are exploring the development of a group program to meet the needs of abused women involved with the Children's Aid Society, who might otherwise not access services. The focus of the proposed group is to offer an educational group to women which includes information regarding the dynamics of woman abuse, safety plans, and resources in the community. Given the non-voluntary nature of some of the work of the Children's Aid Society and the completely voluntary nature of the London Battered Women's Advocacy Centre, this proposed group requires that the two agencies explore the fragmentation in mandates so that the women's service needs are effectively addressed.

On a broader scale, within the Province of Ontario's violence against women prevention initiative, "Agenda for Action," the Ministry of Community and Social Services received funds to provide training to child protection workers on issues of domestic violence. Because the two issues–child protection and violence against women–are often intertwined, the Ministry is involving both the child protection and violence against women sectors in the creation of a mechanism for collaboration between agencies at the local level. The two goals of the project are: to improve services to vulnerable and abused children and to abused women through joint training in the two sectors, and to develop a model protocol for collaboration between child protection and violence against women service providers (Howarth et al., 1998).

Right now, we have the opportunity to make a difference. The authors are issuing a call to ensure that the direction taken in needed legislative and policy changes are constructed with the recognition that the children's best interests must be connected to the mother's safety needs. The authors also believe that it is imperative that child protection workers and battered women's advocates are involved in the development of the legislative and policy changes because without this expertise, the new provisions could be flawed. In addition, more innovative programs addressing both the needs of children exposed to woman abuse and their mothers need to be developed, evaluated and disseminated.

The need for comprehensive collaborative action is clear. May we all heed the message by Ann Jones:

> We can't make the world safe for children by making it ever more dangerous for their mothers. (*The Monitor,* 1993)

REFERENCES

Armstrong, J., Daly, R., & Mallan, C. (1996). Hitting Again. *The Sunday Star,* Ontario Edition, 16-17.

Barnard, W. W., Vera, H., Vera, M. I., & Newman, G. (1982). Till Death Do Us Part: A Study of Spouse Murder. *Bulletin of the American Academy of Psychiatry and the Law,* 10, 271-280.

Bilinkoff, J. (1995). Empowering Battered Women as Mothers. In E. Peled, P. Jaffe & J. Edleson (Eds.), *Ending the Cycle of Violence: Community Responses to Children of Battered Women* (pp. 97-105). Newbury Park, CA: Sage Publications.

Bowker, L. H., Arbitell, M., & McFerron, J. R. (1988). On the Relationship Between Wife Beating and Child Abuse. In K. Yllo & M. Bograd (Eds.), *Perspectives on Wife Abuse.* Newbury Park, CA: Sage.

Bunch, C. (1991). As stated in After the Montreal Massacre [Film]. The National Film Board of Canada, Studio D and the Canadian Broadcasting Company. Montreal, Quebec.

Callahan, M. (1993). Feminist Approaches: Women Re-create Child Welfare. In B. Wharf (Ed.), *Rethinking Child Welfare in Canada.* Toronto: McClelland & Stewart.

Campbell, J. C. (1992). If I Can't Have You, No One Can: Power and Control in Homicide of Female Partners. In J. Radford & D. Russell (Eds.), *Femicide: The Politics of Woman Killing* (pp. 99-113). New York: Twayne Publishers.

Canadian Panel on Violence Against Women. (1993) *Changing the Landscape: Ending Violence–Achieving Equality.* Ottawa: Ministry of Supply and Services Canada.

Company Communications. (1994). Make a Difference [Film]. Carol Campbell and Cora Engel Ryan. London.

Cummings, N. & Mooney, A. (1988). Child Protective Workers and Battered Women's Advocates: A Strategy for Family Violence Intervention. *Responses,* 11(2), 4-9.

Echlin, C. & Marshall, L. (1995). Child Protection Services for Children of Battered Women: Practice and Controversy. In E. Peled, P. Jaffe & J. Edleson (Eds.), *Ending the Cycle of Violence: Community Responses to Children of Battered Women* (pp. 170-185). Newbury Park, CA: Sage.

Fauler, L. (1995). *Edmonton Journal,* Edmonton, Alberta.

Ganley, L. & Schechter, S. (1996). *Domestic Violence: A National Curriculum for Child Protective Services.* Family Prevention Fund, 383 Rhode Island Street, Suite 304, San Francisco, CA.

Gordon, L. (1988). *Heroes of Their Own Lives: The Politics and History of Family Violence.* New York: Penguin.

Hegar, Rebecca, L. & Grief, Geoffrey, L. (1991). Abduction of Children by Their Parents: A Survey of the Problem. *Social Work,* 36, 421-424.

Howarth, J. B. et al. (1998). Background letter re: The CAS/VAW Protocol and Training Project. Belwood, Ontario.

Jones, Ann. (1993). Children of a Lesser Mom: Women Who Fail to Save Their Kids from Abusive Men May Be Guilty of Neglect. But the Courts Are Calling It Murder. *The Monitor,* Lear's, May (32).

London Battered Women's Advocacy Centre (1996). Statistical Review of Client Needs at the London Battered Women's Advocacy Centre. Cited in *The London Battered Women's Advocacy Centre 1995/1996 Annual Report.*

London Coordinating Committee to End Woman Abuse, *Strategic Plan.* (1994).

Peled, Einat (1993). Children Who Witness Woman Battering: Concerns and Dilemmas in the Construction of a Social Problem. *Children and Youth Services Review,* 15, 43-52.

Saunders, D. (1993). Custody Decisions in Families Experiencing Woman Abuse. *Social Work, 39,* 51-59.

Schechter, S. & Edleson, J. L. (1994). In the Best Interest of Women and Children: A Call for Collaboration Between Child Welfare and Domestic Violence Constituencies. Briefing paper presented at the conference on Domestic Violence and Child Welfare Integrating Policy and Practise for Families, Wingspread, Racine, WI, June 8-10, 1994.

Schechter, S. & Gary, L. T. (1992). Health Care Services for Battered Women and Their Abused Children. Boston: Children's Hospital. Cited in A. Ganley, & S. Schechter. Domestic Violence: A National Curriculum for Child Protective Services. Family Violence Prevention Fund, 1996.

Sheeran, Maureen. (1996). Massachusetts Department of Social Services Protects Children by Protecting Mothers. *Synergy: The Newsletter of the Resource Centre on Domestic Violence: Child Protection and Custody,* 2(1), 6-8.

Shepard, M. (1992). Child-Visiting and Domestic Abuse. *Child Welfare,* 74(4), 357-365.

Straus, M. A. & Gelles, R. J. (Eds.) (1990). *Physical Violence in American Families.* New Brunswick, NJ: Transaction Publishers.

Tapp, Anne. (1994). Mother-Accountability or Mother Blaming. *National Coalition Against Domestic Violence–Voice, Special Edition Domestic Violence and the Law, Winter,* pp. 13-14.

Taylor, G. (1993). Child Custody and Access. *Vis á Vis: National Newsletter on Family Violence, Canadian Council on Social Development,* 10(3), 4.

United Nations, *Report of the Fourth World Conference on Women: Platform for Action* (1995). p. 51-52.

The Role of Attitudes and Awareness
in Anti-Violence Education

N. Zoe Hilton

SUMMARY. Most interventions for the prevention of violence in relationships aim at attitudes and awareness. Prevailing attitudes in our society already condemn violence, however, and wife assault is viewed as
particularly serious. Some research shows that perpetrators have attitudes more supportive of violence than other people do, but the link between attitudes and behavior can be complex. Trying to persuade
people to change their attitudes in one direction can lead instead to
people taking more extreme versions of their existing attitudes. Some
interventions that raise awareness and promote availability of services
appear to teach participants to take the problem less seriously. Most students report neither undesirable attitudes nor low awareness of violence
in relationships. But their behavior appears inconsistent with their
reported attitudes and awareness. If interpersonal violence has its roots in
a problem more fundamental than the views of contemporary society, then
anti-violence education based on attitudes and awareness will have limited

Grant T. Harris, PhD, and Marnie E. Rice, PhD, were co-investigators in the
research described in this article and provided comments on the manuscript. The
author would like to thank the participating students and staff; Ross Spearn, Jacquie
Black, and the Simcoe County Board of Education; the many workshop presenters;
and Catherine Cormier, Carole Lang, Sandy Lavigne, and Tina Smith Krans for
research assistance. This work was supported by the Ontario Ministry of Health
(SD-CE-93183) and the Ontario Mental Health Foundation, but the opinions expressed are the author's.

Address correspondence to: N. Zoe Hilton, PhD, Research Psychologist, Mental
Health Centre, 500 Church Street, Penetanguishene, ON L9M 1G3 Canada (e-mail:
zhilton@ mhcp.on.ca).

[Haworth co-indexing entry note]: "The Role of Attitudes and Awareness in Anti-Violence Education."
Hilton, N. Zoe. Co-published simultaneously in *Journal of Aggression, Maltreatment & Trauma* (The Haworth
Maltreatment & Trauma Press, an imprint of The Haworth Press, Inc.) Vol. 3, No. 1 (#5), 2000, pp. 221-238;
and: *Children Exposed to Domestic Violence: Current Issues in Research, Intervention, Prevention, and
Policy Development* (ed: Robert A. Geffner, Peter G. Jaffe, and Marlies Sudermann) The Haworth Maltreatment & Trauma Press, an imprint of The Haworth Press, Inc., 2000, pp. 221-238. Single or multiple copies of
this article are available for a fee from The Haworth Document Delivery Service [1-800-342-9678, 9:00 a.m. -
5:00 p.m. (EST). E-mail address: getinfo@haworthpressinc.com].

221

benefits, and possibly some harmful effects. This article encourages a cautious rethinking of assumptions underlying current anti-violence education and alternative theories of violent behavior. It offers some suggestions for ways to reduce violent behavior, and encourages integration of violence prevention efforts into regular curricula and extra-curricular activities. *[Article copies available for a fee from The Haworth Document Delivery Service: 1-800-342-9678. E-mail address: getinfo@haworthpressinc.com <Website: http://www.haworthpressinc.com>]*

KEYWORDS. Dating, evaluation, high school, self-report, theory, violence, witness

RETHINKING THE ROLE OF ATTITUDES AND AWARENESS IN ANTI-VIOLENCE EDUCATION

In recent years much information has been gathered on the prevalence and incidence of violence in dating relationships. There are many reports of the prevalence of physical violence in high school students' relationships (e.g., Day, 1990; Fitzpatrick & Halliday, 1992; Gray & Foshee, 1997; Henton, Cate, Koval, Lloyd, & Christopher, 1983; Hilton, Harris, & Rice, 1998; Mercer, 1987; O'Keeffe, Brokapp, & Chew, 1986; Peterson & Olday, 1992; Roscoe & Callahan, 1985; Roscoe & Kelsey, 1986; Sudermann & Jaffe, 1993). Sexual coercion is also reported by teens in dating relationships (Ageton, 1983; Davis, Peck, & Storment, 1993; Hilton et al., 1998; Poitras & Lavoie, 1995; Sudermann & Jaffe, 1993). Marital violence often originates in dating violence (e.g., Avni, 1991; O'Leary, Malone, & Tyree, 1994; Roscoe & Benaske, 1985), and dating violence can be a very serious problem in itself (e.g., Levy, 1991).

Most interventions for the prevention of violence in relationships aim, among other things, at attitudes and awareness (e.g., Feltey, Ainslie, & Geib, 1991; Jaffe, Sudermann, Reitzel, & Killip, 1992; Krajewski, Rybarik, Dosch, & Gilmore, 1996; Lavoie, Vézina, Piché, & Boivin, 1995; Sudermann, 1997; Sudermann, Jaffe, & Hastings, 1995; Tulloch & Tulloch, 1992; Winkel & de Kleuver, 1997). Trying to change students' attitudes and awareness through general violence prevention education, rather than targeting interventions for "at risk" students, assumes that there are general social attitudes that need changing (e.g., Falchikov, 1996). Prevailing attitudes in our society do not condone violence, however, and wife assault is seen as particularly serious (e.g., Bethke & DeJoy, 1993; Gentemann, 1984; Harris, 1991; Tulloch & Tulloch, 1992; Wolfgang, Figlio, Tracy, & Singer, 1985). Some research shows that perpetrators have attitudes more supportive of violence than other people do (e.g., Bookwala, Frieze, Smith, & Ryan, 1992; Riggs & O'Leary,

1996; Sugarman & Hotaling, 1989), but it is questionable from attitude research whether attitudes cause behavior, and the real link between attitudes and behavior can be complex (Eagly & Chaiken, 1993). Also, studies over the past 30 years show that trying to persuade people to change their attitudes in one direction can lead instead to people taking more extreme versions of their existing attitudes (Brehm, 1966; Eagly & Chaiken, 1993; Winkel & deKleuver, 1997). Some evaluations of violence-prevention education have found this kind of "attitude backlash." Jaffe et al. (1992), while finding overall improvements in girls' attitudes and beliefs following anti-violence education, report that boys' responses were just as likely to have worsened as to have improved. In particular, boys showed an increase in endorsement of date rape. They hypothesized that students showing this backlash were those already involved in violent relationships.

Evidence that some students–perhaps those most in need of intervention–respond in an undesirable way to anti-violence education, instructs us to reflect on the goals of anti-violence education, the assumptions underlying these goals, and the alternatives available. For example, Jaffe et al. (1992) point out that perpetrators need interventions to prevent reoccurrence of violence rather than primary prevention. Perhaps we should drop large-scale anti-violence education in favor of interventions targeted to high-risk students. On the other hand, perhaps other purposes can be met by attempts to change attitudes and raise awareness. In this chapter I will consider four main questions to help us rethink the role of attitudes and awareness in anti-violence education:

- what are high school students' attitudes towards violence, and what influences attitudes?
- how aware of violence are students, and what influences their awareness?
- are there drawbacks to current anti-violence education, and how could we improve it?
- what assumptions underlie current anti-violence education, and what alternatives exist?

ATTITUDES TOWARDS VIOLENCE AMONG PEERS

Acceptance of Date Rape

Researchers evaluating anti-violence education have tested a variety of attitudes or opinions. Some attitudes are presented as statements and students are asked to indicate whether they think the statement is true, or how strongly they agree or disagree with the statement. Jaffe et al. (1992; cf Davis et al.,

1993; Day, 1990; Goodchilds, Zellman, Johnson, & Giarusso, 1988) asked students, "Is it all right if a male holds a female down and forces her to engage in sexual intercourse if . . . " followed by nine conditions. Boys were significantly more likely than girls to endorse date rape items, but overall "relatively small percentages of students endorsed any of the items" (p. 114).

We used the same questions about date rape attitudes, slightly reworded, in an evaluation of an anti-violence education session closely based on the model used by Jaffe et al. (1992). In the first phase of this research and intervention project, we provided half a day of anti-violence education for students at nine high schools in Simcoe County, Ontario. Also similar to Jaffe et al. (1992), we provided staff training, suggested courses of action for those who were being abused or were peers of those being abused, and promoted curriculum integration; however, unlike the original model, we did not plan follow-up activities or engage in school or board policy review. The high schools ranged in enrollment from under 400 to over 1700 and were located in municipalities with populations ranging from 1,600 to 70,000. The population of the county was generally representative of the province of Ontario as a whole with respect to the distribution of age, education, and unemployment (Simcoe County District Health Council, 1992). A week before the education, all students (N = 2168, 51.7% male, 48.3% female) completed a brief question sheet that included the date rape attitude questions. The question sheet was administered by teachers in the classroom. Students also completed the sheet after the education session and six weeks later as part of an evaluation (Hilton, Harris, Rice, Smith Krans, & Lavigne, in press) but for this article, responses before the intervention are of interest in themselves.

Table 1 shows the responses from our students to the date rape attitude questions. The percentage of students who said "Yes" to each situation is slightly lower than that reported by Jaffe et al. (1992). As in Jaffe et al. (1992), boys were significantly more likely to endorse date rape items than were girls, χ^2 (1, N = 2167) = 94.76, p < .001, but fewer than 10% said "Yes" to any of the items. Other, less representative samples have revealed much higher endorsement of date rape items (e.g., Goodchilds et al., 1988). Yet, when students in our sample were asked to report on their experiences of aggression and sexual coercion, they reported rates in the high range of what is reported in the literature for such behaviors, even among comparable studies using detailed questions like the Conflict Tactics Scales (CTS; Straus, 1979, 1990) and the Sexual Experiences Survey (SES; Koss & Oros, 1982). For example, about 20% of boys reported perpetrating an act of sexual aggression against a girl about their own age, and 55% of girls reported being a victim (Hilton et al., 1998)–yet attitudes in this sample were very "desirable"! This finding raises the question of the value of trying to change attitudes, if violence is still high among students with the "right" attitudes.

Perceived Seriousness of Aggression

Each student participating in our anti-violence education also took part in more extensive studies of attitudes towards aggression. In one of these studies, 411 grade 11 students (52.8% male, 47.2% female) listened to audio taped scenes of aggression played by teenage actors. Some scenes portrayed male-to-female violence, while others portrayed male-to-male, female-to-male, or female-to-female violence. There was a set of scenes of physical aggression for each victim-perpetrator combination, a set of nonphysical aggression scenes for each victim-perpetrator combination, and a set of sexual aggression scenes for each opposite sex combination. Each student heard one set of scenes, e.g., male-to-female sexual aggression, male-to-male physical aggression, etc. Students rated each scene in their set for how serious the aggression was, from 1–not to 5–extremely. The mean ratings were all above the midpoint (Table 2).

Scenes of sexual aggression were rated the most serious; and nonphysical aggression, least serious, F (2, 396) = 8.88, p < .001. Table 2 shows that sexual aggression was rated more serious when perpetrated by a male against a female, and nonphysical aggression was rated least serious when occurring between same sex peers. In general, male-to-female aggression was rated the most serious victim-perpetrator combination; male-to-male aggression, least serious; and aggression by females, in between, F (2, 396) = 22.33, p < .001.

TABLE 1. Is It Ok If a Guy Holds a Girl Down and Forces Her to Have Sex If . . .

	Percent Responding "Yes"	
	Boys	Girls
a. He spends a lot of money on her	3.3	0.3
b. He is so turned on he can't stop	2.9	0.3
c. She's had sex with other guys	3.3	0.5
d. She's stoned or drunk	4.6	0.7
e. She lets him touch her above the waist	4.8	0.8
f. She says she will have sex and then changes her mind	5.8	0.9
g. They have dated a long time	4.8	0.7
h. She gets him turned on	5.3	0.8
i. She has led him on	8.2	1.6
Any of the above items	9.9	2.6

TABLE 2. Mean Ratings (and Standard Deviations) of Seriousness of Aggression

	Type of Aggression		
	Nonphysical	Physical	Sexual
Female-to-female	3.01 (.69)	3.44 (.65)	--
Female-to-male	3.43 (.56)	3.60 (.41)	3.52 (.57)
Male-to-female	3.57 (.49)	3.75 (.57)	3.84 (.62)
Male-to-male	3.00 (.66)	3.26 (.68)	--

Note: Intra-sex sexual aggression was not studied.

We also found that girls tended to rate aggression as more serious than did boys, $F (1, 396) = 10.63, p < .01$. On the other hand, there was no interaction between students' sex and the different forms of aggression; that is, boys and girls agreed on relatively how serious the scenes of aggression were.

We also looked at the relation between attitudes and behavior among students in this study. Students self-reported on their experiences as victims or perpetrators of violence with their male and female peers in the past twelve months. Questions included items from the CTS physical violence subscale (Straus, 1979, 1990), items modified from the SES (Koss & Oros, 1982), and items based on nonphysical forms of abuse reported by battered women in a study by Follingstad, Rutledge, Berg, Hause, and Polek (1990) (see Hilton et al., 1998, for more details). For girls, self-reported experience of violence was not related to overall ratings of seriousness of violence; however, boys who reported being perpetrators of violence, and those who reported being victims (including male-to-male violence), rated violence less serious overall than did boys with no self-reported experience of violence.

In another study, a different sample of students self-reported on their experiences of peer violence and their attitudes towards date rape. We found no differences between victims and perpetrators in their responses to the date rape attitude questions before anti-violence education, nor in their attitude change after education (Hilton et al., in press).

Thus, it appears that most students do not endorse "bad" attitudes. Nor do they condone male-to-female violence more than other forms of violence. Sexual violence is considered especially serious. Perhaps perpetrators of violence accept violence more than do students with no recent experience of peer violence, yet they do not differ substantially in this respect from victims.

AWARENESS OF VIOLENCE AMONG PEERS

Awareness of Dating Violence Among Peers

One way awareness has been operationalized for evaluation is by asking, "Do you know someone who has experienced abuse (physically, sexually, or emotionally) in a dating relationship?" (Jaffe et al., 1992). Jaffe and his colleagues found that 54.0% of students, including 47.5% of boys and 60.5% of girls, replied "Yes" to this question. We asked the same question of the 2168 students described previously. Overall, nearly two-thirds of the students (62.3%) reported that they knew someone who has experienced some form of dating abuse. Significantly more girls (71.5%) than boys (54.5%) were aware of dating abuse among their acquaintances, $^2 (1, N = 2167) = 67.46, p < .001$. Thus our results, similar to those reported in previous research, indicate a high level of awareness of abuse in a dating relationship.

We also operationalized relative awareness by asking students how common they think different forms of violence are. Ninety-four students with no dating experience (55.6% male, 44.4% female) participated in this study. We described each type of aggression. For example, for physical aggression, we listed the Conflict Tactics Scale (Straus, 1979, 1990) violence items, then asked, "How common is it for a guy to do these things to a girl?" or a girl to a guy. Students rated how common it is on a scale from 1–not to 5–very. The mean ratings were around the mid-point. Male-to-female violence was seen as more common than female-to-male, $F (1, 47) = 62.30, p < .001$. Nonphysical aggression was seen as the most common type of aggression; physical aggression, the least, with sexual aggression, including nonphysical coercion, in between, $F (2, 47) = 5.75, p < .05$. Girls and boys agreed on how common male-to-female violence is, but girls rated female-to-male violence as more common than boys did, $M = 2.09$ vs. 1.68, $t (51) = 2.16, p < .05$.

Effect of Witnessing Violence

In this study, we explored several variables that might influence awareness. Because of mandatory reporting concerns, we did not ask about experience of child abuse. We did, however, ask students whether they had witnessed aggression between their parents. Nearly half (48.8%) of students reported knowing of physical aggression between their parents, and 21.3% reported seeing at least one act of violence (17.0% father-to-mother, 19.1% mother-to-father). These students might be considered "at risk" of violence themselves. The more parental violence students witnessed, the more common they rated peer aggression by girls, $r = 0.35, p < .01$, and peer aggression by boys, $r = 0.29, p < .05$. Witnessing peer violence itself was not significantly associated with awareness of peer violence.

These findings suggest that we do not need awareness education for students who witness violence in the home. Smith and Williams (1992) found that teenagers who were abused by their parents differed little from other students in their opinions about dating violence; however, abused students were more likely to stay in a violent dating relationship and to be violent themselves. Secondary interventions for such children are increasingly available (e.g., Jaffe, Wolfe, & Wilson, 1990; Peled & Edelson, 1995; and see other articles in this volume). In general, we should be as cautious about efforts to raise awareness as about education to change attitudes. In a recent longitudinal study, teenage boys who reported never having been a perpetrator of dating violence at time 1 were more likely to self-report dating violence eighteen months later (time 2) if they had perceived dating violence as normal and prevalent at time 1 (Foshee, Bangdiwala, & Mok, 1997). Furthermore, female college students attending primary and secondary interventions for eating disorders reported more disordered eating habits afterward than students who did not attend (Mann, Nolen-Hoeksema, Huang, Burgard, Wright, & Hanson, 1997). The researchers concluded that students learned that eating disorders were normal and that remedies were easily available; therefore, the intervention taught students to take the problem less seriously.

DRAWBACKS AND ALTERNATIVES

These findings raise the question of why we should try to change attitudes and awareness. Do we wish to alter perpetrators' perceptions, and consequently change their behavior? But perpetrators do not differ substantially from victims in their attitudes or perceptions of violence Also, awareness of violence is not low, especially for male-to-female violence, and especially among potentially "at-risk" students. Students tend to have socially desirable attitudes, especially towards male-to-female violence. And trying to change people's attitudes has the potential hazard of causing an attitude backlash. There is some indication in the psychological literature that attitudes might be adapted to existing behavior, to help people justify what they have done, or to "neutralize" self-punishment (Dutton, 1986; Hilton, 1993; Schauss, Chase, & Hawkins, 1997). That is, pro-violence attitudes might be less of a cause for violence than an excuse for it. Attitude-change education is unlikely to change behavior if that behavior has a more fundamental origin.

Do we wish to increase victims' likelihood of ending an abusive relationship or seeking outside help? If so, assertive behavior taught more directly using the social learning procedures of modeling, practising, and reinforcement might be more effective. These direct skills-teaching techniques are better suited to integration in classroom curricula than to single assembly-type lectures. The practical knowledge of resources for outside help can also be conveyed in the classroom.

Do we wish to increase the likelihood that students and school personnel will provide emotional support and practical services to victims of violence? If so, we might better put our efforts into facilitating the development of peer support services and specialized counseling skills for staff. Students indicate that they want schools to take a leading role in violence prevention (Jaffe & Reitzel, 1990). We asked the 94 students with no dating experience, described above, to indicate how they found out about violence in dating relationships. Although their schools had working relationships with outreach counselors from their local women's shelters, and provided some education about violence, only 16.0% of students reported that school was a source of information. School was the second least likely source of information about violence in relationships, next to discussing it at home (8.5%). Students were most likely to say they heard about it from friends (59.1%), followed by knowing a victim (for girls, 57.1%) or seeing it happen (for boys, 45.7%).

Do we wish to raise awareness of violence to a more desirable level? This question is a particularly challenging one. What is a desirable level of awareness? Perhaps we would like students to have an accurate perception of the prevalence of aggression. Yet, the available statistics on absolute rates of interpersonal violence are of questionable validity (Hilton et al., 1998; cf Langley, Martin, & Nada-Raja, 1997). Relative rates of violence might be more valid. Students in our sample believe that male-to-female violence is more common than female-to-male violence, which is supported by other aspects of our research. Perhaps we would like students to recognize aggression as normal and ubiquitous. As with attempts to change attitudes, there could be a danger in this approach, because of suggestive evidence that perceiving violence as normal predicts boys' perpetration of dating violence (Foshee et al., 1997). Problem behavior could also increase when students see remedies as easily available (Mann et al., 1997; see also Helweg-Larsen & Collins, 1997). Raising awareness of the barriers of leaving an abusive relationship, on the other hand, might have equally undesirable effects. We need to consider carefully what it is we wish to raise awareness of, and for what purpose. We should also rigorously evaluate our efforts, and not assume that the worst outcome is "no change": we can do harm (Winkel & deKleuver, 1997).

Do we wish to raise awareness and alter attitudes to the point of "zero tolerance"? If so, we should consider how realistic it is to expect all students to endorse only what we deem desirable attitudes, and the truthfulness of their responses if they do. The influence of socially desirable response sets must be taken into account in evaluations that rely entirely on self-report at the expense of knowledge tests or, more importantly, behavioral observations. A recent meta-analysis by Sugarman and Hotaling (1997) confirmed that perpetrator self-reports are more strongly correlated with social desirability scores than are victim reports. And in our own studies, perpetrator reports of male-to-female violence are less internally consistent than victim reports (Hilton et al., 1998). Socially desirable responding could explain some of the desirable changes in attitudes that have been reported in the literature on anti-violence education.

ASSUMPTIONS AND ALTERNATIVES

Attitudes and Contemporary Society

There is evidence that the stronger their desire to respond in a socially approved manner, the less likely are both males and females to report their perpetration of violence (Sugarman & Hotaling, 1997). This finding is inconsistent with the claim that society's attitudes condone violence against women (Brown, 1990; Dobash & Dobash, 1979; Ferraro & Pope, 1993; Straus, 1976). Much attention was paid to a survey reported by Stark and McEvoy in 1970, finding that 25% of men and 16% of women believed it was acceptable for a man to hit his wife on "appropriate" occasions. As has been argued, however, such minority opinions, although disturbing, do not constitute a "norm" supporting wife assault (Dutton, 1988). Stark and McEvoy (1970) found a slightly higher rate of acceptance of a woman hitting her husband (26% of men, 19% of women). Studies of different forms of violence find that a man beating his wife is rated worse than beating a stranger (Greenblat, 1985), although the intimacy of relationship interacts with the offender's history of violence (Hilton, 1993b). In another study, female college students rated wife beating the most morally wrong of 20 acts that included armed robbery and the use of poison gas on civilians (Gentemann, 1984). Some students approve of wife assault or dating violence in certain situations, but few endorse it in situations other than play or self-defense (Gentemann, 1984; Roscoe, 1985). Assaults against wives or girlfriends, however, receive lower ratings of approval, acceptance, and normalcy than assaults on husbands or boyfriends in scenarios of specific situations (Bethke & deJoy, 1993; Harris, 1991; Hilton, 1992).

This area of research suggests that attitudes towards violence against women are not generally undesirable. Most ratings of violence in these studies, moreover, indicate that it is a serious and undesirable behavior (see also Wolfgang et al., 1985). It seems, however, that people find reasons to justify or mitigate violence in certain situations. One situation in which violence against women is sometimes perceived as likely or justified is the arousal of sexual jealousy or possessiveness (e.g., Dutton, 1988; Hilton, 1992; Gentemann, 1984; Greenblat, 1985; Wilson & Daly, 1993). Interventions to counter tendencies to endorse, commit, or reinforce violence under these circumstances might be helpful. Potential victims might also benefit from education about the situational risks of violence.

Attitudes and Behavior

Some members of society are less strong in their condemnation of violence against women: e.g., males versus females (Burke, Stets, & Pirog-Good, 1989; Falchikov, 1996; Gentemann, 1984; Hilton, 1993b; Jaffe et al., 1992; Stets, 1991); police versus battered women's advocates (Foshee & Linder, 1997; Saunders & Size, 1986); and students with "traditional" versus egalitarian sex role attitudes (Gentemann, 1984; Greenblat, 1985; Walker, Rowe, & Quinsey, 1993). Self-reported perpetrators of violence also fall into this category (e.g., Burt, 1983; Cate et al., 1982; Dutton, 1988; Henton, Cate, Koval, Lloyd, & Christopher, 1983; Saunders, Lynch, Grayson, & Linz, 1987; Stith, 1990; though see Bethke & DeJoy, 1993; Walker et al., 1993). Whether such attitudes precede violence against women is an empirical question that remains unanswered in the absence of suitable longitudinal research. Our research indicates that victims also tend to endorse violence more than students reporting no violence. People who have more exposure to violence might habituate to it, perceive it as less serious, and underestimate its occurrence (cf. Harris, Rice, & Preston, 1989).

Socially desirable responding can perhaps also describe a finding in research of self-reported aggression by high school students: boys tend to report doing less male-to-female violence than females report experiencing (e.g., Hilton, Harris, & Rice, 1997; Mercer, 1987; Poitras & Lavoie, 1995). We find this discrepancy in our surveys of high school students. The sample included 930 grade 11 students (51.2% male, 48.8% female) from 13 schools including those described earlier. We asked students about either perpetration or victimization of nonphysical and physical aggression acts, described above. We also asked: "what is the worst injury you have caused to a girl" or to a guy, on a scale labeled from "no injury" to "had to stay in hospital"; and "what is the most afraid a girl has been of you" or a guy has been of you, on a scale labeled from not at all afraid to terrified most of the time. There were corresponding questions for the victim questionnaires. All questionnaires asked about experiences with girls and boys.

Table 3 shows the reported prevalence rates for physical aggression: the most common is male-to-male, and the least common is female-to-female. In general, perpetrators and victims agree on the prevalence of violence, but not for male-to-female aggression. It cannot be simply that perpetrators under-report violence, because only male perpetrators under-report only male-to-female violence. In our research, male perpetrators disagree with female victims on the rate of minor and severe male-to-female aggression, and the fear and injury resulting. Boys in our earlier study said male-to-female violence was more common, but that "awareness" contrasts with their self-reported behavior. Boys agreed that male-to-female aggression was most serious. So maybe the boys have the "right" attitude and respond to the survey questionnaires in a socially desirable way. According to this interpretation, however, we have desirable attitudes coexisting with undesirable behavior. We cannot expect to change behavior by changing attitudes, if the behavior has a more fundamental origin.

Behavior and Evolutionary Advantage

What makes male-to-female violence socially undesirable? What makes it acceptable for boys to "take responsibility" for male-to-male violence? Possible answers to these questions can be found in theories using evolutionary concepts such as parental investment theory (Daly & Wilson, 1983) and a theory of sexual proprietary violence (Wilson & Daly, 1993). Essentially, a behavior that had an advantage in terms of evolutionary success would be passed on to the offspring of the parent who exhibited that behavior. It is important to note that a behavior that had an evolutionary advantage in the distant past need not necessarily be adaptive or condoned in the contemporary social environment. Having an evolutionary basis, moreover, does not rule out effects of the environment in changing that behavior. Applying evolutionary-based theories to self-report data suggests an element of impression management that is tailored to the environment. Elsewhere, we have provided a detailed explanation of evolutionary theories, and how they can help us to understand interpersonal violence today (Hilton, Harris, & Rice, 1997). Only a brief description will be given here.

A theory based on evolutionary concepts suggests that boys' violence serves different functions depending on whether the target is male or female. It is a theory that deserves cautious consideration as it helps interpret the discrepancies in self-report data. In the distant past (and perhaps even today), there was an advantage to a male keeping a female in his control, so that he could have sex with her and ultimately reproduce. The risks of violence to the female and her offspring, though, would be undesirable to the female; therefore, the female would prefer a mate who would not use violent and controlling behavior. So males might have tried to hide this behavior, especially from other females who might be potential mates. This theory also posits that there was an advantage to

TABLE 3. Self-Reported Rates of Physical Aggression

	Percentage Reporting Experience as	
	Victim	Perpetrator
Female-to-female	35.7	31.9
Female-to-male	54.6	59.0
Male-to-female	58.2	20.0
Male-to-male	78.4	75.4

having a reputation for male-to-male aggression, because the aggressive male would gain status among other males. Debra Pepler (1997), observing bullying in the school yard, has described it as a "theatrical" behavior.

RETHINKING ANTI-VIOLENCE EDUCATION

The implication of evolutionary theories for anti-violence education is similar to that arising from the research on attitudes and behavior: we must focus on changing the problem behavior itself. Behavior will not change if it has its origin in a more fundamental problem. Having an evolutionary basis does not mean that a behavior cannot change, if the environmental contingencies change. Indeed, people working in the field of anti-violence education agree that violent behavior is constantly being modified through social controls, upbringing, education, and other efforts.

One possible way to change behavior is to teach skills for non-violent relationships. If one purpose of male-to-male aggression is to gain status, there are more socially desirable ways to achieve this goal. Perhaps social skills and leadership skills would be beneficial, as might using peer support to advantage as has been done with "prosocial gangs" (Goldstein & Glick, 1994). If male-to-female aggression is done to control a female and maintain a monogamous relationship, this effect could be achieved at least as successfully if the female enjoys the relationship. In this respect, the Alternatives to Violence approach shows promise (Wolfe, Wekerle, & Scott, 1997). These interventions might be most effective when targeted to those most likely to become perpetrators or victims of violence.

For perpetrators, victims, and all high school students, it is imperative that adults model and reinforce non-violent and non-coercive behavior. Efforts to reward prosocial behavior are being made in some elementary schools (e.g., Gamache & Snapp, 1995; Peterson, 1997) but bullies are often rewarded by popularity among peers (Pepler, 1997) and perpetrators receive what might actually be a reward (i.e., time off school or suspension) for violent behavior. For a victim of abuse, assertive behavior is punished by the abuser and extinguished by victim-blaming and gaps in the helping services. When a victim does not have the resources to escape a violent relationship, the violence is reinforced. Services should be increased, particularly for 16- to 18-year-olds who are often too old for children's services and too young for adult services. Students indicate that their peers are their top source of information about violence in relationships. Peer counseling training should include accurate information about risks of violence and sources of professional help. For the student body as a whole, we feel that one of the most valuable workshops in our anti-violence education session was "how to help a friend." Practical support to help victims succeed in leaving violent relationships could be a particularly effective strategy, as violence begins to lose its effectiveness at keeping females in relationships.

CONCLUSION

Violence prevention efforts designed to change attitudes and awareness receive overwhelmingly positive reviews from school staff and enthusiastic participation from community agencies. Students have stood up in assemblies we provided to state that the education should be available more widely, and they have been applauded by their peers. Written student feedback also suggests that we can make a big difference in some lives:

> I learned that I was in a very abusive relationship. These workshops really opened my eyes, and I broke up with him. I would like to thank the organizers of this workshop, because I am now a changed person, and enjoy life much more.

In light of our data and other research, however, the priority given to this approach to violence prevention should be reconsidered. On the whole, students do not report undesirable attitudes nor low awareness of violence in relationships. What students–especially boys–report to be their behavior, however, is inconsistent with their reported attitudes and awareness. The research reviewed here suggests that the interpersonal violence has its roots in a problem more fundamental than the attitudes of contemporary society. It further suggests that anti-violence education based on attitudes and awareness will have limited benefits, and possibly some harmful effects. Curriculum integration and regular classroom skills–teaching sessions that model, instruct, and reinforce prosocial behavior might offer greater benefit. Activities requiring students to advocate for behavior change also show promise (Kelly, McAuliffe, Sikkema, Murphy, Somlai, Mulry, Miller, Stevenson, & Fernandez, 1997; Linz, Fuson, & Donnerstein, 1990; Wolfe et al., 1997; cf. Jaffe et al., 1992, re: "action planning").

Rather than leading to undue pessimism, it is hoped that this article will encourage cautious steps forward in violence prevention for high schools. We should think carefully about the validity of assumptions underlying any anti-violence education, about alternative theories of violent behavior, and about the ways we can most effectively and efficiently reduce violent behavior while avoiding undesirable effects. In all our efforts, we should include empirically sound evaluations.

REFERENCES

Avni, N. (1991). Battered wives: Characteristics of their courtship days. *Journal of Interpersonal Violence, 6*, 232-239.

Bethke, T.M. & DeJoy, D.M. (1993). An experimental study of factors influencing the acceptability of dating violence. *Journal of Interpersonal Violence, 8*, 339-349.

Bookwala, J., Frieze, I.H., Smith, C., & Ryan, K. (1992). Predictors of dating violence: A multivariate analysis. *Violence and Victims, 7*, 297-311.

Brehm, J.W. (1966). *A theory of psychological reactance.* New York: Academic Press.

Brown, R. (1990). The challenge of family violence: An international review. In R. Roesch, D.G. Dutton, & V.F. Sacco (Eds.), *Family violence: Perspectives on treatment, research, and policy,* pp. 5-19. Burnaby, BC: British Columbia Institute on Family Violence.

Burke, P.J., Stets, J.E., & Pirog-Good, M.A. (1989). Gender identity, self-esteem, and physical and sexual abuse in dating relationships. In M.A. Pirog-Good & J.E. Stets (Eds.), *Violence in dating relationships: Emerging social issues,* pp. 72-93. New York: Praeger.

Cate, R.M., Henton, J.M., Koval, J., Christopher, F.S., & Lloyd, S. (1982). Premarital abuse: A social psychological perspective. *Journal of Family Issues, 3,* 79-90.

Daly, M. & Wilson, M. (1983). *Sex, evolution, and behaviour (Second edition).* Belmont, CA: Wadsworth.

Davis, T.C., Peck, G.Q., & Storment, J. (1993). Acquaintance rape and the high school student. *Journal of Adolescent Health, 14,* 220-224.

Dobash, R.E. & Dobash, R. (1979). *Violence against wives: A case against the patriarchy.* New York: The Free Press.

Dutton, D.G. (1986). Wife assaulters' explanations for assault: The neutralization of self-punishment. *Canadian Journal of Behavioral Science, 18,* 381-390.

Dutton, D.G. (1988). *The domestic assault of women: Psychological and criminal justice perspectives.* Boston: Allyn & Bacon.

Eagly, A.H. & Chaiken, S. (1993). *The psychology of attitudes.* New York, NY: Harcourt Brace Jovanovich College Publishers.

Falchikov, N. (1996). Adolescent attitudes to the abuse of women: Are wives and nonmarital partners viewed differently? *Journal of Interpersonal Violence, 11,* 391-409.

Feltey, K.M., Ainslie, J.J., & Geib, A. (1991). Sexual coercion attitudes among high school students: The influence of gender and rape education. *Youth and Society, 23,* 229-250.

Ferraro, K.J. & Pope, L. (1993). Irreconcilable differences: Battered women, police, and the law. In N.Z. Hilton (Ed.), *Legal responses to wife assault: Current trends and evaluation,* pp. 96-123. Newbury Park, CA: Sage.

Fitzpatrick, D. (1990). *Violence against young women in teen dating relationships.* Amherst, NS: Cumberland County Transition House Association.

Follingstad, D.R., Rutledge, L.L., Berg, B.J., Hause, E.S., & Polek, D.S. (1990). The role of emotional abuse in physically abusive relationships. *Journal of Family Violence, 5,* 107-120.

Foshee, V., Bangdiwala, S., & Mok, M.C. (1997, July). Longitudinal predictors of adolescent dating violence. Paper presented at the 5th International Family Violence Research Conference, Durham, NH.

Foshee, V. & Linder, G.F. (1997). Factors influencing service provider motivation to help adolescent victims of partner violence. *Journal of Interpersonal Violence, 12,* 648-664.

Gamache, D. & Snapps, S. (1995). Teach your children well: Elementary schools and violence prevention. In E. Peled, P.G. Jaffe, & J.L. Edleson (Eds.), *Ending the cycle of violence: Community responses to children of battered women*, pp. 209-231. Thousand Oaks, CA: Sage.

Gentemann, K.M. (1984). Wife beating: Attitudes of a nonclinical population. *Victimology, 9*, 109-119.

Goldstein, A.P. & Glick, B. (1994). *The prosocial gang: Implementing aggression replacement training.* Thousand Oaks, CA: Sage.

Goodchilds, J.D., Zellman, G.L., Johnson, P.B., & Giarrusso, R. (1988). Adolescents and their perceptions of sexual interactions. In A.W. Burgess, *Rape and sexual assault II*, pp. 245-270. New York: Garland Publishing Inc.

Gray, H.M. & Foshee, V. (1997). Adolescent dating violence. *Journal of Interpersonal Violence, 12*, 126-141.

Greenblat, C.S. (1985). Don't hit your wife . . . unless . . . : Preliminary findings on normative support for the use of physical force by husbands. *Victimology, 10*, 221-241.

Harris, M.B. (1991). Effects of sex of aggressor, sex of target, and relationship on evaluations of physical aggression. *Journal of Interpersonal Violence, 6*, 174-186.

Harris, G.T., Rice, M.E., & Preston, D.L. (1989). Staff and patient perceptions of the least restrictive alternatives for the short term control of disturbed behavior. *Journal of Psychiatry and Law, 17*, 239-263.

Henton, J., Cate, R., Koval, J., Lloyd, S., & Christopher, S. (1983). Romance and violence in dating relationships. *Journal of Family Issues, 4*, 467-482.

Hewleg-Larsen, M. & Collins, B.E. (1997). A social psychological perspective on the role of knowledge about AIDS in AIDS prevention. *Current Directions in Psychological Science, 6*, 23-26.

Hilton, N.Z. (1992). Reactance and frustration in wife assault. *Dissertation Abstracts International, 54*, 09B.

Hilton, N.Z. (1993). Childhood victimization and lack of empathy in child molesters: Explanation or excuse? *International Journal of Offender Therapy and Comparative Criminology, 37*, 287-296.

Hilton, N.Z. (1993b). Police intervention and public opinion. In N.Z. Hilton (Ed.), *Legal responses to wife assault: Current trends and evaluation.* Newbury Park: Sage.

Hilton, N.Z., Harris, G.T., & Rice, M.E. (1998). On the validity of self-reported rates of interpersonal violence. *Journal of Interpersonal Violence, 13*, 58-72.

Hilton, N.Z., Harris, G.T., & Rice, M.E. (1997). Aggression by adolescent males. Manuscript in preparation.

Hilton, N.Z., Harris, G.T., & Rice, M.E., Smith Krans, T., & Lavigne, S. (in press). Anti-violence education evaluation in high schools. *Journal of Interpersonal Violence.*

Jaffe, P.G., Sudermann, M., Reitzel, D., & Killip, S.M. (1992). An evaluation of a secondary school primary prevention program on violence in intimate relationships. *Violence and Victims, 7*, 129-146.

Jaffe, P.G., Wolfe, D.A., & Wilson, S.K. (1990). *Children of battered women.* Newbury Park, CA: Sage.

Kelly, J.A., McAuliffe, T.L., Sikkema, K.J., Murphy, D.A., Somlai, A.M., Mulry, G., Miller, J.G., Stevenson, L.Y., & Fernandez, M.I. (1997). Reduction in risk behavior among adults with severe mental illness who learned to advocate for HIV prevention. *Psychiatric Services, 48,* 1283-1288.

Koss, M.P. & Oros, C. (1982). The sexual experiences survey: Reliability and validity. *Journal of Consulting and Clinical Psychology, 50,* 455-457.

Krajewski, S.S., Rybarik, M.F., Dosch, M.F., & Gilmore, G.D. (1996). Results of a curriculum intervention with seventh graders regarding violence in relationships. *Journal of Family Violence, 11,* 93-112.

Langley, J., Martin, J., & Nada-Raja, S. (1997). Physical assault among 21-year-olds by partners. *Journal of Interpersonal Violence, 12,* 675-684.

Lavoie, F., Vézina, L., Piché, C., & Boivin, M. (1995). Evaluation of a prevention program for violence in teen dating relationships. *Journal of Interpersonal Violence, 10,* 516-524.

Linz, D., Fuson, I.A., & Donnerstein, E. (1990). Mitigating the negative effects of sexually violent mass communications through preexposure briefings. *Communication Research, 17,* 641-674.

Mann, T., Nolen-Hoeksama, S., Huang, K., Burgard, D., Wright, A., & Hanson, K. (1997). Are two interventions worse than none? Joint primary and secondary prevention of eating disorders in college females. *Health Psychology, 16,* 215-225.

Mercer, S.L. (1987). *Not a pretty picture: An exploratory study of violence against women in high school dating relationships.* Toronto: Education Wife Assault.

O'Keeffe, N.K., Brockapp, K., & Chew, E. (1986). Teen dating violence. *Social Work,* 465-468.

Peled, E. & Edleson, J.L. (1995). Process and outcome in small groups for children of battered women. In E. Peled, P.G. Jaffe, & J.L. Edleson (Eds.), *Ending the cycle of violence: Community responses to children of battered women,* pp. 72-96. Thousand Oaks, CA: Sage.

Pepler, D. (1997, June). Paper presented at the Second International Conference on Children Exposed to Family Violence: Assessment, Intervention, Prevention, and Research Strategies, London, ON, Canada.

Peterson, K. (1997, June). Paper presented at the Second International Conference on Children Exposed to Family Violence: Assessment, Intervention, Prevention, and Research Strategies, London, ON, Canada.

Peterson, S. & Olday, D.E. (1992). How was your date last night? Intimate relationship violence among high school students. *Human Services in the Rural Environment, 16,* 24-29.

Poitras, M. & Lavoie, F. (1995). A preliminary study of the prevalence of sexual violence in adolescent heterosexual dating relationships in a Quebec sample. *Violence and Victims, 10,* 299-313.

Riggs, D.S. & O'Leary, K.D. (1996). Aggression between heterosexual dating partners. *Journal of Interpersonal Violence, 11,* 519-540.

Roscoe, B. (1985). Courtship violence: Acceptable forms and situations. *College Student Journal, 19,* 389-393.

Roscoe, B. & Benaske, N. (1985). Courtship violence experienced by abused wives: Similarities in patterns of abuse. *Family Relations, 34,* 419-424.

Roscoe, B. & Callahan, J.E. (1985). Adolescents' self-report of violence in families and dating relationships. *Adolescence, 20,* 545-566.

Roscoe, B. & Kelsey, T. (1986). *Dating violence among high school students. Psychology, A Quarterly Journal of Human Behavior, 23*, 53-59.

Schauss, S.L., Chase, P.N., & Hawkins, R.P. (1997). Environment-behavior relations, behavior therapy and the process of persuasion and attitude change. *Journal of Behavior Therapy and Experimental Psychiatry, 28*, 31-40.

Stark, R. & McEvoy, J. (1970). Middle-class violence. *Psychology Today* (November), 52-54 & 110-112.

Straus, M.A. (1976). Sexual inequality, cultural norms, and wife-beating. *Victimology, 1*, 54-70.

Straus, M.A. (1979). Measuring intrafamily conflict and violence: The Conflict Tactics (CT) Scales. *Journal of Marriage and the Family, 41*, 75-88.

Straus, M.A. (1990). The Conflict Tactics Scales and its critics: An evaluation and new data on validity and reliability. In M.A. Straus & R.J. Gelles (Eds.), *Physical violence in American families: Risk factors and adaptations to violence in 8,145 families*. New Brunswick: Transaction Publishers.

Sudermann, M. (1997, June). Innovative school-based violence prevention. Paper presented at the Second International Conference on Children Exposed to Family Violence: Assessment, Intervention, Prevention, and Research Strategies, London, ON, Canada.

Sudermann, M. & Jaffe, P.G. (1993, August). Violence in teen dating relationships: Evaluation of a large scale primary prevention programme. Paper presented at the American Psychological Association Annual Meeting, Toronto.

Sudermann, M., Jaffe, P.G., & Hastings, E. (1995). Violence prevention programs in secondary (high) schools. In E. Peled, P.G. Jaffe, & J.L. Edleson (Eds.), *Ending the cycle of violence: Community responses to children of battered women*, pp. 232-254. Thousand Oaks, CA: Sage.

Sugarman, D.B. & Hotaling, G.T. (1989). Dating violence: Prevalence, context, and risk markers. In M.A. Pirog-Good & J.E. Stets (Eds.), *Violence in dating relationships: Emerging social issues*, pp. 3-32. New York: Praeger.

Sugarman, D.B. & Hotaling, G.T. (1997). Intimate violence and social desirability: A meta-analytic review. *Journal of Interpersonal Violence, 12*, 275-290.

Tulloch, M.L. & Tulloch, J.C. (1992). Attitudes to domestic violence: School students' responses to a television drama. *Australian Journal of Marriage and Family, 13*, 62-69.

Walker, W.D., Rowe, R.C., & Quinsey, V.L. (1993). Authoritarianism and sexual aggression. *Journal of Personality and Social Psychology, 65*, 1036-1045.

Wilson, M. & Daly, M. (1993). An evolutionary psychological perspective on male sexual proprietariness and violence against wives. *Violence and Victims, 8*, 271-294.

Winkel, F.W. & de Kleuver, E. (1997). Communication aimed at changing cognitions about sexual intimidation. *Journal of Interpersonal Violence, 12*, 513-529.

Wolfe, D.A., Wekerle, C., & Scott, K. (1997). *Alternatives to violence: Empowering youth to develop healthy relationships*. Thousand Oaks, CA: Sage.

Wolfgang, M.E., Figlio, R.M., Tracy, P.E., & Singer, S.I. (1985). *The national survey of crime severity*. Washington, DC: US Government.

POLICY DEVELOPMENT
AND INTERNATIONAL ISSUES

Controversies
in Family Preservation Programs

Richard J. Gelles

SUMMARY. This paper examines the controversies over the use of family preservation policies to prevent and treat child abuse and neglect. Policies that aim to preserve families in which child maltreatment has occurred are at least a century old. However, there is renewed interest in such policies, given the dramatic rise in child abuse and neglect reports and a large number of children who spend time in out-of-home placements. New intensive family preservation services were advanced as able to assure the safety of children while working toward a lasting preservation of the family unit. The paper summarizes the research on intensive family preservation services and reports that such programs do not reduce placements nor do they appear to enhance child safety.

Parts of this article were presented at the Conference on *Children Exposed to Family Violence,* June, 1997, London, Ontario, Canada.

Address correspondence to: Richard J. Gelles, School of Social Work, Caster Building, 3701 Locust Walk, University of Pennsylvania, Philadelphia, PA 19104.

[Haworth co-indexing entry note]: "Controversies in Family Preservation Programs." Gelles, Richard J. Co-published simultaneously in *Journal of Aggression, Maltreatment & Trauma* (The Haworth Maltreatment & Trauma Press, an imprint of The Haworth Press, Inc.) Vol. 3, No. 1 (#5), 2000, pp. 239-252; and: *Children Exposed to Domestic Violence: Current Issues in Research, Intervention, Prevention, and Policy Development* (ed: Robert A. Geffner, Peter G. Jaffe, and Marlies Sudermann) The Haworth Maltreatment & Trauma Press, an imprint of The Haworth Press, Inc., 2000, pp. 239-252. Single or multiple copies of this article are available for a fee from The Haworth Document Delivery Service [1-800-342-9678, 9:00 a.m. - 5:00 p.m. (EST). E-mail address: getinfo@haworthpressinc.com].

239

The paper concludes by proposing that risk assessments and assessments of readiness to change could improve decision-making regarding which families might be aided by family preservation and which children should be protected by terminating their parents' rights. *[Article copies available for a fee from The Haworth Document Delivery Service: 1-800-342-9678. E-mail address: getinfo@haworthpressinc.com <Website: http:// www.haworthpressinc.com>]*

KEYWORDS. Abuse, neglect, intensive family preservation, reasonable efforts, placement, change, risk assessment

The scene is a courtroom. A wife seeks a restraining order to protect her from the battering and abuse of her new husband. In the short fifteen months of their marriage, her new husband has physically and emotionally abused her, including one attack that left her with a fractured elbow. As part of her evidence, the woman presents police records that her husband not only beat her, but beat his former wife, fracturing her skull and breaking her legs and ribs.

The judge considers the evidence. Clearly the woman before him has been battered and abused. Clearly, the man from whom she seeks protection has a history of abusive and dangerous behavior. The judge, however, decides not to issue the requested restraining order.

"I believe in the institution of marriage," the judge states. "I believe that it is healthier for people to be married than to go through the trauma of separation and divorce," he continues. "Thus," he states, "This is what I am going to do. Instead of issuing a restraining order at this time, I am going to ask you to return home to your husband. We have a new program in our city called 'Intensive Marriage Preservation'. I am going to require you and your husband to be part of this program. The program will assign a 'Marriage Preservation Worker' to your family. This worker has a very small number of families with whom she works. She will be available to you whenever you need her, every hour of every day. She will work to identify the strengths in your relationship and will visit your home at least three times each week for the next 20 weeks. She can work with you and help your husband with anger management. I know your husband attacked you and almost killed his first wife, but I have read that this 'Marriage Preservation Program' is quite effective and has a very good safety record. I will ask you to check back with me in six months. Now, go home with your husband and work to preserve your marriage."

How would domestic violence advocates react to such a scenario? Would they, or could they, trust that the woman would be safe? Would they assume that such a program is effective and safe? Would they agree that intensive efforts should be made to save this marriage? Or, would advocates be so outraged that they would seek the removal of the judge?

What if the program the judge advocated was identified by the federal government as the intervention-of-choice for dealing with domestic violence? What if such a program received $250,000,000 in federal support, even if there was actually no scientific evidence that it was actually effective? How would domestic violence advocates react?

What if the federal government not only funded such a program, but required judges to use such a program before issuing restraining orders? How would domestic violence advocates respond to such legislation?

The scenario described above seems almost absurd when considered within the framework of domestic violence. No advocate, researcher, or even a layperson with a shred of common sense would, in my opinion, agree that the judge's actions and the federal government's policy makes sense in light of what researchers and clinicians know about domestic violence. Common sense alone would argue that if a man beats a woman nearly to death, it would be wholly inappropriate to require another woman to remain in a marriage with him, especially if he has already been violent towards her.

And yet, such a scenario occurs every day, in courtrooms in every state and county. The only difference is that one small thing about this case was changed. The case was one of child abuse, not wife abuse. The child, a fifteen-month-old boy, had been the subject of a number of child abuse and neglect reports. His sister had been beaten badly enough to fracture her skull, ribs, and legs when she was six months old. While children do not seek restraining orders, child welfare agencies can remove children and place them in out-of-home placements. Juvenile and family courts have the option of terminating parental rights. In this case, the six-month-old girl was removed from her parents and after 18 months the parents voluntarily terminated their parental rights. The fifteen-month-old boy remained with his parents. While a judge did not order "intensive family preservation," the family did receive the normal complement of child welfare/family preservation services. Unfortunately, the normal complement of services did not assure the safety of the boy, and he was smothered by his mother when he was fifteen months of age (Gelles, 1996).

THE POLICY OF FAMILY PRESERVATION

Family preservation programs are not new. They go back at least to the turn of the century with the settlement house movement, Hull House and Jane Addams. The settlement house movement aimed to help families cope with stress and poverty and keep the families together. Family preservation programs are designed to help children and families, including extended and adoptive families, which are at risk of abuse or delinquency, or are in crisis.

Family preservation programs have been a key component of the child welfare system for nearly a century: The rediscovery of child abuse and neglect in the early 1960s and the conceptualization of the problem as one arising out of the psychopathology of the parents or caretakers, changed child welfare emphasis from one of preserving families to one of protecting children (Kempe et al., 1962; Steele & Pollock, 1968). Intensive family preservation programs re-emerged in the mid-1970s in response to an exponential increase in child abuse and neglect reporting and a similar exponential increase in foster care placements and the cost to public child welfare agencies of such placements. The conceptual model that explained child maltreatment also shifted in the 1970s away from a medical, psychopathological model, to a more social model that emphasized stress, poverty, social isolation, and a lack of understanding of proper parenting behaviors and skills (Gelles, 1973; Gil, 1970). It was assumed that family preservation programs, both traditional child welfare efforts at family reunification and the newer "intensive" family preservation services, would be effective–based on assumptions about the causes of child abuse and neglect, the cost-effectiveness of the programs, and based on the assumption that children fared better with their birth parents.

This article examines the policy and practice of family preservation. There are a number of important problems with both the traditional and newer "intensive" family preservation services. First, the policy and the programs are based on an inadequate understanding of the causes of abuse and neglect and the process and amenability to change of caregivers that maltreat their children. Second, although intensive family preservation services have been touted as effective, cost-effective, and able to balance child safety with the goal of family preservation, rigorous empirical research has not yet supported any of these claims of effectiveness (National Research Council, 1998).

The current debate between preservation and safety resembles the swing of a pendulum. The forces behind the pushes of the pendulum from one side (preservation) to the other (safety) tend to be high profile cases of child abuse fatalities or inappropriate intrusions of state child welfare agencies into families who have not placed their children at risk. A more constructive discussion is to examine under what conditions family preservation might be effective if such services were better targeted to the families where there is a low risk of abuse and a high likelihood of change.

FAMILY PRESERVATION AND THE DOCTRINE OF REASONABLE EFFORTS

Child abuse and neglect have, for more than a century, been conceptualized as a child welfare problem that is best responded to by the social service or child welfare system. Child maltreatment has been viewed as a child welfare matter. The basic assumption that guides intervention is that social and clinical interventions are more effective in protecting children and preventing the reoccurrence of abuse and neglect than arrest, prosecution, or other legal interventions. At the core of family preservation is the belief that children do best when cared for and raised by their biological caretakers. The theoretical and empirical work on attachment (Bowlby, 1958, 1969; Harlow, 1958, 1961; Lindsey, 1994) has been used to support this assumption, but even professionals and policy makers who are unfamiliar with research on attachment endorse the assumption that the preferred method of intervening in cases of child maltreatment is to preserve the family, so long as the safety of the child can be assured.

Mandatory reporting laws enacted in the 1960s combined with public awareness campaigns and technological developments, such as toll-free lines (800 numbers) resulted in extraordinary increases in reports of child abuse and neglect. By 1978, there were a little less than one million reports of child maltreatment in the United States each year as well as approximately 500,000 children in foster care placements in the United States (Pelton, 1989; Tatara, 1993). The combination of increased reports, increased numbers of children in out-of-home placements, and the cost of such placements, raised concerns across the child welfare system.

The Adoption Assistance and Child Welfare Act of 1980

The emphasis on family preservation policy was crystallized by the federal Adoption Assistance and Child Welfare Act of 1980 (Public Law 96-272), which experts and advocates generally consider the most significant legislation in the history of child welfare. The two major child welfare provisions of the act were on permanency planning and "reasonable efforts." Permanency planning was a response to concerns over what child welfare experts had labeled "foster care drift." Although data on foster care were scarce and often incomplete at that time, researchers and practitioners generally believed that too many children were going into foster care each year and staying too long, without any concern for permanence (Lindsey, 1994). Permanency planning mandated that states develop permanency plans for children–either that they be returned to their birth parents or placed for adoption, within eighteen months of entrance into the child welfare system. The second child welfare provision of the legislation was embodied in the two words, "reasonable efforts." Again, aimed at reducing foster care drift and inappropriate out-of-home placement, the policy of "reasonable efforts" was stated in a brief, but important section of the legislation:

> . . . in each case, reasonable efforts will be made
> (A) prior to the placement of a child in foster care, to
> prevent or eliminate the need for removal of a child
> from his home, and (B) to make it possible for the child
> to return to his home. (471 a 15, p. 503)

States had to demonstrate that they made reasonable efforts and that they were in compliance with the permanency planning provision of the law in order to qualify for federal funding for adoption and foster care.

The Adoption Assistance and Child Welfare Act of 1980 appeared to have the desired effect. Data on foster care placements indicated that out-of-home placements declined to under 300,000 per year by the mid-1980s (Pelton, 1989; Tatara, 1993). The reduction, however, did not continue, and by the mid-1990s foster care placements approached 600,000 per year (Tatara, 1993).

Despite the good intentions behind the law and apparent initial success in reducing foster care placements, the Adoption Assistance and Child Welfare Act of 1980 had some unintended consequences. One problem was the ambiguity around the very concept of "reasonable efforts." Nowhere in the federal legislation or ensuing legal decisions in state courts, was the concept "reasonable efforts" ever clearly defined. As a result, child protection workers, administrators, legal staff, and judges had no guidelines for how much or how long they had to make efforts at reunification before moving to permanent out-of-home placement for abused and neglected children. A second problem was the actual implementation of the law. Because there were no specific definitions or guidelines for what constituted "reasonable" and because family preservation was a long-held value of the child welfare system, child welfare workers and administrators often interpreted "reasonable efforts" to mean that they should make "every possible effort" to keep children with, or reunite them, with the birth parents.

Intensive Family Preservation Services

There are now many variations of family preservation services in use across the country, including "Homebuilders," an approach developed in Tacoma, Washington in 1974. The core goal of such programs is to maintain child safety in the home, or to facilitate a safe and lasting reunification. Intensive family preservation services are another variation of family preservation services. These types of programs are designed for families that have a serious crisis threatening the stability of the family and the safety of the family members.

There are many variations of intensive family preservation services programs; the essential feature is that such programs are short-term, crisis intervention. Services are meant to be provided in the client's home. The length of the sessions can be variable. Unlike traditional family preservation services, intensive family preservation services are available seven days a week, twenty-four hours a day. Perhaps the most important feature of intensive family preservation services is that caseloads are small; caseworkers may have only two or three cases. In addition, the length of time is brief and fixed at a specific number of weeks. Both hard and soft services are provided. Hard services include food stamps, housing, homemaker services; soft services include parent education classes and individual and/or family counseling.

ARE INTENSIVE FAMILY PRESERVATION SERVICES EFFECTIVE?

The initial evaluations of intensive family preservation services were uniformly enthusiastic. The programs were claimed to have reduced the placement of children, reduced the cost of out-of-home placement, and, at the same time, assured the safety of children. Foundation program officers and program administrators claimed that families involved in intensive family preservation services had low rates of placement and "100 percent safety records" (Barthel, 1991; Forsythe, 1992). Susan Kelley, Director of the Division of Family Preservation Services, Office of Children and Youth Services for the state of Michigan, testified before Congress that of 2,505 families who participated in Michigan's Families First program in the first year, one incident of abuse was reported (Barthel, 1991).

There were, however, major methodological and design limitations of the early evaluations of intensive family preservation services. The vast majority of the evaluations of intensive family preservation services either employed no control group or used a comparison group that was not an appropriate match for the group receiving treatment. Moreover, there were questions raised about whether "placement avoidance" was the appropriate outcome measure for the evaluations. Rossi (1992) cautioned that "placement avoidance" was not a proper outcome variable since placement avoidance was itself the treatment. Rossi (1992) concluded that the evaluation studies did not convincingly demonstrate that intensive family preservation services reduced placement or reduced child welfare costs. The claim that children were safe was not actually evaluated in these early studies.

There have been at least 46 evaluations of intensive family preservation services, of one form or another (Heneghan, Horwitz, & Leventhal, 1996; Lindsey, 1994; National Research Council, 1998). Of these 46 evaluations and of nearly 850 published articles on intensive family preservation, only 10 studies actually evaluated intensive family preservation services, included outcome data in the report, and used a control group of some kind. The National Academy of Sciences (National Research Council, 1998) review of prevention and treatment evaluations identified 13 evaluations of intensive family preservation services that employed experimental or quasi-experimental designs. In California, New Jersey, and Illinois, the evaluations used randomly assigned control groups, included outcome data, and had large enough samples to allow for rigorous evaluation. In all three studies, there were either small or insignificant differences between the group receiving intensive family preservation services and the control group receiving traditional casework services. Even in terms of placement avoidance, there was no difference between the two groups. These results suggest that earlier claims that intensive family preservation services were successful in reducing placement were obtained because of the low overall rate of placement in child welfare agencies. These results also point to how difficult it is for child welfare caseworkers to accurately classify a family as "high risk" for being placed, since 80 to 90 percent of the children in the control group were not placed, even though these children were theoretically selected for the study because they were at high risk of being placed.

As noted above, the outcome measures of most evaluations do not include data specifically designed to measure child outcome. Thus, it is also impossible to verify the claim of the safety record of intensive family preservation services. Critics of intensive family preservation services programs argue that children are injured or even killed when they are inappropriately returned to their abusive caretakers (Gelles, 1996). Indeed, there is considerable anecdotal evidence that such children are injured and killed when left with or returned to abusive parents. However, as yet, no data exist on whether children involved in intensive family preservation services have higher rates of re-injury or fatalities compared to children served by traditional child welfare services.

Thus, the empirical case for intensive family preservation has yet to be made. Amid the claims and counter claims on intensive family preservation and following the funding of the Family Preservation and Support Act of 1993, the Department of Health and Human Services funded a national evaluation of family preservation and support services. This evaluation, conducted by Westat, The Chapin Hall Center for Children, and James Bell Associates is examining a full range of family preservation and support programs at a number of sites across the country. The study is using a randomized trial design with a variety of outcome measures, including placement, cost, and family functioning.

The claims for the effectiveness of intensive family preservation have not been supported to date by scientific evidence; therefore, there is concern for the widespread adoption of intensive family preservation services. Peter Rossi, for one, criticized the states and the federal government for running ". . . pell mell into family preservation without considering the evidence for it" (MacDonald, 1994).

WHY FAMILY PRESERVATION POLICIES ARE INEFFECTIVE

There are a number of reasons why intensive family preservation services, specifically, and the broader policy of family reunification are not effective.

First, it is possible that intensive family preservation services, in and of themselves, are simply not effective. The theory behind the program may be faulty and the programs themselves, therefore, may not be addressing the key causal mechanisms that cause child abuse. Second, the programs may be effective, but they may not be implemented properly by the agencies and workers that are using the programs. When the evaluation data for the Illinois Family First program were made public (Schuerman, Rzepnicki, & Littell, 1994), an initial reaction was that there was considerable variation in how intensive family preservation was being implemented at the different sites in Illinois. The overall implementation was also not true to the "Homebuilders" model of intensive family preservation. Thus, the lack of support for the effectiveness was blamed on the programs not being properly implemented. Third, the theory behind the program may be accurate and the program itself may be appropriate, but the "dose" may be too small. This applies to many interventions designed to prevent and treat family and intimate violence and is not unique to intensive family preservation services. The National Academy of Sciences (National Research Council, 1998) concluded that the duration and intensity of the mental health and social support services needed to influence behaviors that result from or contribute to family violence may be greater than initially estimated. It is likely that more services are necessary or the length of the interventions should be increased. If this were true, however, it would partially negate the cost-effective claims for intensive family preservation services.

With regard to theory, there are other plausible explanations for the apparent ineffectiveness of intensive family preservation services. As noted earlier in this article, current child welfare programs, including intensive family preservation, assume that abuse and maltreatment are at one end of a continuum of parenting behavior. However, it is possible that this model of abusive behavior is inaccurate. It may be that there are distinct types of abusers (Gelles, 1991, 1996). Abuse may not arise out of a surplus of risk factors and a deficit of resources, but rather, there may be distinct psychological and social attributes of those caretakers who inflict serious and/or fatal injuries compared to caretakers who commit less severe acts of maltreatment. If there are different types of offenders and different underlying causes for different types of abuse, it is reasonable to assume that a "one size fits all" intervention or policy would not be effective across the board.

Another problem with the child welfare system and with intensive family preservation and family reunification is the crude way behavior change is conceptualized and measured. Behavior change is thought to be a one-step process; one simply changes from one form of behavior to another. For example, if one is an alcohol or substance abuser, then change involves stopping the use of alcohol or drugs. If one stops, but then begins again, then the change has not successfully occurred. A second assumption is that maltreating parents or caretakers all want to change–either to avoid legal and social sanctions or because they have an intrinsic motivation to be caring parents. As a result, those who design and implement child abuse and neglect interventions assume that all, or at least most, parents, caretakers and families are ready and able to change their maltreating behavior. However, research on behavior change clearly demonstrates that change is not a one-step process (Prochaska & DiClemente, 1982, 1983, 1984; Prochaska, Norcross, & DiClemente, 1994). Rather, changing behavior is a dynamic process in that one progresses through a number of stages in trying to modify behavior. There are also cognitive aspects to behavior change that can be measured.

One of the reasons why child welfare interventions in general, and intensive family preservation programs in particular, may have such modest success rates is that most interventions are "action" programs. These programs are often provided to individuals and families in what Prochaska and his colleagues call the precontemplator or contemplation stage of change (Prochaska & DiClemente, 1982, 1983, 1984). This is what others may refer to as denial or ambivalence about the need for change.

TOWARD A SAFER AND MORE EFFECTIVE
CHILD WELFARE SYSTEM

In response to criticisms leveled at intensive family preservation services, proponents of intensive family preservation have modified their unqualified support for the effectiveness and safety of programs like Homebuilders. Susan Notkin, Director of the Program for Children of the Edna McConnell Clark Foundation, stated that:

> even the staunchest proponents of such an approach (intensive family preservation) do not believe that every family can or should be "preserved." On the contrary, a balanced and well-functioning child welfare system needs a full toolbox of services–from early prevention to intensive family preservation to foster care and adoption. . . .

(Wall Street Journal, June 6, 1996)

The Edna McConnell Clark Foundation has been one of the strongest supporters of the Homebuilders model and intensive family preservation. An earlier report by the Edna McConnell Clark Foundation was a glowing testimony to the effectiveness of intensive family preservation that claimed few risks with such programs (Barthel, 1991). Susan Kelly, Director of Michigan's Family First program, is now quoted as saying that:

> Family preservation efforts were never intended to be a stand alone program or a program that is expected to fill all the needs of every at-risk family. It's a false dichotomy to say we should have foster care or family preservation. (Lawton, 1996)

The problem with these arguments is that the same individuals continue to also promote family preservation programs by stating that they are effective. Moreover, preserving families is still the preferred approach to dealing with child welfare. Thus, although there appears to be an effort to find a balance between preservation and safety, preservation remains the child welfare system's central goal. Taking Susan Notkin's toolbox metaphor one step further, the best promoted and most widely used tool in the box is still preservation and reunification. And, as the homily goes, "if the only tool you have is a hammer, the whole world tends to become a nail." The argument that we need a full tool box notwithstanding, the child welfare system still tends to reach for one tool, first and foremost, preservation and reunification.

An additional problem that continues to plague the child welfare system is that the system tends to swing back and forth between child protection and family preservation in what Lindsey (1994) refers to as a pendulum. Public outcry over sensational cases, such as children killed by biological caretakers, pushes the pendulum toward child protection; children injured or killed in foster care or false accusations of abuse, push the pendulum toward family preservation. Theory, informed research, and rigorous evaluations of interventions exert much less force on the movement of the pendulum.

One thing that is clear is that there is no "one size fits all" explanation for child maltreatment, and no "one size fits all" intervention or treatment. The National Academy of Sciences panel on assessing family violence prevention and treatment programs concluded that: "Intensive family preservation services represent an important part of the continuum of family support services, but they should not be required in every situation on which a child is recommended for out-of-home placement" (National Research Council, 1998: p.8). No side of the pendulum can or will be effective all the time. Nonetheless, striking an appropriate balance is extremely difficult. The most constructive approach is to examine under what conditions family preservation might or might not be effective and to better target services or intervention to individual families and children.

Schuerman et al. (1994) identified "targeting" as a key issue in their examination of "Families First" in Illinois. One reason why "Families First" was not found to be effective was that it was delivered to many families for whom it was not intended or appropriate, families in which there was not an "imminent risk of placement." A second targeting problem is when services are delivered to families or individuals that may not be ready or able to change and are the least likely to benefit from efforts to help. One means of improving targeting and matching interventions is to develop better risk assessment for use by the child welfare system. Child abuse investigators and assessment workers all engage in risk assessment. Some agencies and investigators use formal, written risk assessment devices; others rely on clinical judgment, clinical intuition, or just accumulated experience. A survey conducted in 1991 found that 42 of the 50 states have experimented with or implemented some form of systematic formal risk assessment (Berkowitz, 1991). The reliability and validity of risk assessment instruments are variable. Some risk assessment is merely formalized clinical judgment while other risk assessment is what I have called "olfactory risk assessment." Homes that smell of urine or feces, homes that are filthy, with trash and garbage not disposed of, and disorganized homes are typically rated as high risk; while homes that smell of "Lestoil," that are neat as a pin and structurally sound, are regarded as low risk, irrespective of the presence of other important risk factors. Some instruments are well grounded in the scientific study of the causes and correlates of maltreatment. One such instrument is the Child at Risk Field System (CARF) (Doueck, English, DePanfilis, & Moore, 1993). But even this risk assessment instrument only assesses proximate risk factors for maltreatment; it does not measure whether parents or caretakers are ready or willing to change their behavior.

A more sensitive and appropriate risk assessment model would assess recognized risk factors such as income, substance abuse, etc., as well as "stage of readiness to change" so that action-oriented interventions will be targeted for families ready to use them. More importantly, child welfare agencies will be able to move to protect children at high risk by identifying risk in terms of the presence of risk factors and reluctance, unwillingness, or inability to change. Agencies will not have to wait for a child to be seriously or permanently injured to suspend "reasonable efforts," because they will have the ability to identify families where "reasonable efforts" are unlikely to work, as with high-risk parents not ready to change (precontemplators). The grid in Figure 1 illustrates this kind of risk assessment.

Risk assessment, however, is not the entire solution to the problems that plague the child welfare system. The system still considers the preservation of families its highest priority. Thus, for the system to truly change and meet the needs of children, it should replace "reunification and preservation" with "child safety and the best interests of the child" as its main goals. Although it is admirable to try to balance the goals of preservation with child safety, social scientists who are familiar with statistics and the problem of Type I and Type II error know that one cannot simultaneously reduce both. A choice must be made; families can be preserved, but at the cost of injuries and harm to children; or children can be protected at the cost of inappropriate intrusion into some families. The child welfare system needs to give up the notion that

FIGURE 1. Two Dimensions of Risk Assessment for Child Abuse and Neglect

Severity of Risk

Stage of Change	High	Medium	Low
Precontemplator	No reunification High likelihood of terminating parental rights		Parent Education Classes
Contemplator			
Preparation			
Action			
Maintenance	Family Preservation only with close monitoring		Family Preservation Reunification recommended

it can have both preservation and protection all the time. A child-centered system using appropriate risk assessment, which matches interventions to stage of change, is the best promise for an effective and safe child welfare system.

REFERENCES

Barthel, J. (1991). *For children's sake: The promise of family preservation.* New York: Edna McConnell Clark Foundation.

Berkowitz, S. (1991). *Findings from the state survey component of the study of high risk child abuse and neglect groups.* Rockville, MD: Westat.

Bowlby, J. (1958). The nature of the child's tie to his mother. *International Journal of Psychoanalysis, 39,* 350-373.

Bowlby, J. (1969). *Attachment and loss. Vol. 1 Attachment.* New York: Basic Books.

Doueck, H. J., English, D. J., DePanfilis, D., & Moore, G.T. (1993). Decision-making in child protective services: A comparison of selected risk-assessment systems. *Child Welfare, 72,* 441-452.

Forsythe, P. (1992). Homebuilders and family preservation. *Children and Youth Services Review, 14,* 37-47.

Gelles, R. J. (1991). Physical violence, child abuse, and child homicide: A continuum of violence, or distinct behaviors? *Human Nature, 2*, 59-72.

Gelles, R. J. (1996). *The book of David: How preserving families can cost children's lives.* New York: Basic Books.

Harlow, H. (1958). The nature of love. *American Psychologist, 13*, 673-685.

Harlow, H. (1961). The development of affection patterns in infant monkeys. In B. M. Foss (ed.), *Determinants of infant behavior*, Vol. 1. London: Methuen.

Heneghan, A. M., Horwitz, S. M., & Leventhal, J. M. (1996). Evaluating intensive family preservation programs: A methodological review. *Pediatrics, 97*, 535-542.

Lawton, K. A. (1996). Controversial program tries to keep endangered kids out of foster homes. *The American News Service.*

Lindsey, D. (1994). *The welfare of children.* New York: Oxford University Press.

MacDonald, H. (1994). The ideology of "family preservation." *The Public Interest, 115*, 45-60.

National Research Council. (1998). *Violence in families: Assessing prevention and treatment programs.* Washington, DC: National Academy Press.

Pelton, L. (1989). *For reasons of poverty: A critical analysis of the public child welfare system in the United States.* New York: Praeger.

Prochaska, J. O. & DiClemente, C. C. (1982). Toward a more integrative model of change. *Psychotherapy: Theory, Research and Practice, 19*, 276-288.

Prochaska, J. O. & DiClemente, C. C. (1983). Stages and processes of self-change in smoking: Toward an integrative model of change. *Journal of Consulting and Clinical Psychology, 5*, 390-395.

Prochaska, J. O. & DiClemente, C. C. (1984). *The transtheoretical approach: Crossing traditional boundaries of change.* Homewood: Dow Jones/Irwin.

Prochaska, J. O, Norcross, J. C., & DiClemente, C. C. (1994). *Changing for good.* New York: Morrow.

Rossi, J. S. (1992, March). *Stages of change for 15 health risk behaviors in an HMO population.* Paper presented at the meeting of the Society of Behavioral Medicine, New York, NY.

Rossi, P. (1992). Assessing family preservation program. *Child and Youth Services Review, 14*, 77-97.

Schuerman, J., Rzepnicki, T. L., & Littell, J. H. (1994). *Putting families first: An experiment in family preservation.* New York: Aldine de Gruyter.

Tatara, T. (1993). *Characteristics of children in substitute and adoptive care.* Washington, DC: Voluntary Cooperative Information System, American Public Welfare Association.

Aligning with the Battered Woman
to Protect Both Mother and Child:
Direct Practice and Policy Implications

Colleen Friend

SUMMARY. The act of addressing domestic violence in the context of Children Protective Service (CPS) work has been inconsistent at best. Generally, battered women and CPS workers collude in avoiding the subject for reasons ranging from fear of children's removal to anticipation of an emotional response to increasing caseload time restrictions. Recently some innovative programs and training efforts have begun to help CPS workers navigate these very complex intersections and assessments. This paper explores the historic background to these efforts. It then describes a sample of innovative CPS programs and explores the components of a specific training program. The latter was a Department of Health and Human Service funded program which was designed at UCLA for the largest Public Child Welfare agency in the country. An assessment instrument was specifically developed for use in the training and agency; it is outlined here. The author examines the obstacles the training encountered as well as the resistance to the implementation of a comprehensive approach which follows the assessment instrument. This

---

The training team appreciates the contribution of our Advisory Council and the Los Angeles County Domestic Violence Council to the UCLA domestic violence/child abuse initiative. Without their support, the training would not have been successful. The author also acknowledges the willingness of the Los Angeles County DCFS and Orange County Social Services Agency to be receptive to this training.

Address correspondence to: Colleen Friend, LCSW, UCLA School of Public Policy and Social Research, Department of Social Welfare, 3250 Public Policy Building, Box 951656, Los Angeles, CA 90095-1656.

[Haworth co-indexing entry note]: "Aligning with the Battered Woman to Protect Both Mother and Child: Direct Practice and Policy Implications." Friend, Colleen. Co-published simultaneously in *Journal of Aggression, Maltreatment & Trauma* (The Haworth Maltreatment & Trauma Press, an imprint of The Haworth Press, Inc.) Vol. 3, No. 1 (#5), 2000, pp. 253-267; and: *Children Exposed to Domestic Violence: Current Issues in Research, Intervention, Prevention, and Policy Development* (ed: Robert A. Geffner, Peter G. Jaffe, and Marlies Sudermann) The Haworth Maltreatment & Trauma Press, an imprint of The Haworth Press, Inc., 2000, pp. 253-267. Single or multiple copies of this article are available for a fee from The Haworth Document Delivery Service [1-800-342-9678, 9:00 a.m. - 5:00 p.m. (EST). E-mail address: getinfo@haworthpressinc.com].

examination led to a consideration of policy issues that were addressed and those which require ongoing attention. *[Article copies available for a fee from The Haworth Document Delivery Service: 1-800-342-9678. E-mail address: getinfo@haworthpressinc.com <Website: http://www.haworthpressinc.com>]*

KEYWORDS. Domestic violence, child abuse, child neglect, child welfare, family violence, child welfare training, child welfare policy

Traditionally, Child Protective Services (CPS) workers have failed to address domestic violence in any deliberate and meaningful way. Although very closely related to child maltreatment, domestic violence often goes "undetected" by busy CPS workers who may either lack the skills to ask the right questions or do not have adequate resources to address the problem. Honest answers from battered women about their intimate violence are not always forthcoming as they fear the CPS workers' power to remove their children. These are only a few of the dilemmas faced by CPS workers in their effort to address domestic violence in their child welfare practices.

This article will review the tensions between how CPS treats domestic violence and how battered women's advocates address the problem. It will also cite some of the research documenting the overlap between the CPS and the domestic violence client. To place these issues in programmatic context, the article reviews several innovative programs which address this overlap. One of these, a training effort at UCLA which received U.S. Department of Health and Human Services (U.S. DHHS) funding, will be described. This program focuses on aligning with the battered woman to protect both the mother and the child. Obstacles to this approach will be identified. Several policy implications will be discussed which expose the tensions that are inherent when these two problems intersect.

BACKGROUND TO THE INTERSECTING PROBLEMS OF DOMESTIC VIOLENCE AND CHILD ABUSE

Initially, the tensions between the domestic violence and the child abuse "systems" came from their different concepts of what was in a child's best interest. Historically, domestic violence advocates focused on protecting the victim which they saw as the key reference point to providing safety to the children. Because of their proximity to the mother's (i.e., battered woman's) interests, domestic violence advocates recognized the mother's commitment to protect the children no matter how fragile, incremental or successful. No doubt domestic violence advocates had better access to information from the battered woman, because she did not fear that her shortcomings were being evaluated by those with the authority to remove her children.

This obstacle loomed large for CPS workers who, in a parallel fashion, focused on protecting children. At times, they stood accused of emphasizing children to the exclusion of other interests; they had the difficult task of removing children whose safety appeared to be or was certainly in jeopardy. If this were not complicated enough, the CPS system often pushed workers to include batterers in reunification plans, which domestic violence advocates rallied against. These general tensions often led to stereotypes. The camps remained fairly divided until a reconciliation forged by community coalitions and domestic violence councils began to emerge. Some attribute these new coalitions to the success of models developed in such cities as Duluth, Minnesota and Quincy, Massachusetts. These new alliances brought the promise of mutual systems accountability, in the service of holding batterers accountable for their actions. Innovative partnerships and trainings inside CPS agencies continue to contribute to this emerging coalition.

CPS workers and domestic violence advocates have now mostly come to believe that there is more that unites them than divides them. One compelling tie that binds them is the overlap in the statistical occurrence of the two problems: domestic violence and child abuse. Depending on the study referenced, from 45-70% of the cases of domestic violence where there are children in the home, the children are also being abused (American Humane Association, 1994). Conservatively, child abuse is 15 times more likely to occur in households where domestic violence is also present (American Humane Association, 1994). O'Keefe (1995) examined a shelter sample of 184 ethnically diverse children; in 47% of the families where there was domestic violence, physical child abuse was also present. O'Keefe (1995) also found that the children in her study were at high risk for externalized behavioral problems.

State and local officials now struggle to determine whether or not exposure to domestic violence should be considered a form of child maltreatment. In a recent California Court of Appeals case, the court ruled that children were aware of their parents' domestic violence (despite parental claims to the contrary) (*In re Heather A.*, 1997). Further, the court concluded that this exposure, even if only secondary, constituted neglect. Recently, the family violence field has looked to child trauma as an explanation for how witnessing domestic violence affects children. Children who witness violent acts against their mothers are likely to be at risk for exhibiting Post Traumatic Stress Disorder (PTSD) symptoms (Jaffe et al., 1990; Rossman & Rosenberg, 1997; Wolfe et al., 1986).

Early research describes boys as retaining a longer-term legacy. Boys who witness family violence are more likely, as adults, to batter their female partners (Hotaling & Sugarman, 1986). In a comparison of violent men with a control group of non-violent men, the sons of violent parents have a rate of wife beating 900 times greater than sons of non-violent parents (i.e., 20% versus 2%) (Straus & Gelles, 1986). There is mixed data on whether or not girls who grow up in homes where domestic violence exists are likely to experience it in their adult relationships (Fantuzzo & Lindquist, 1989).

PROGRAMMATIC RESPONSES TO THESE INTERSECTING PROBLEMS

Given these alarming statistics and a clear overlap of domestic violence and child abuse, this article examines the innovative and model programs that have been implemented to address the intersection of child abuse and domestic violence. Aron and Olson (1997) describe five programs that capture the variety of responses Child Protective Services (CPS) agencies have had to the problem of domestic violence; these strategies are described below.

- The Department of Social Services (DSS) in Massachusetts hired a domestic violence advocate in 1990. The domestic violence program has since evolved into a separate unit, staffed by eleven domestic violence advocates (a.k.a. specialists) and two full-time supervisors. The domestic violence CPS staff supervise interventions and find appropriate resources. They also developed a domestic violence protocol that has been adopted agency-wide.
- Oregon's State Office for Services to Children and Families used its U.S. DHHS Office of Community Services Grant to fund meetings for managers and supervisors in their own agency as well as domestic violence program directors. These meetings focused on developing collaborations. The remaining funds were used to hire part-time domestic violence workers to consult directly with workers. They are now using funding to locate those advocates directly in four CPS offices.
- San Diego County established a new unit that managed cases active in both CPS and Adult Probation Systems. This brought special expertise to high-risk cases involving their hardest-to-serve families and the most violent perpetrators. They have now embarked upon establishing training and protocols for all agency workers.
- Michigan's Families First worked with the Family Violence Prevention Fund in San Francisco to develop a domestic violence training curriculum specifically for family preservation workers. Funding is now available for some domestic violence shelters to hire their Families First staff. The emphasis here is on empowering families to use their strengths to make changes.

- In Hilo, Hawaii, there is a semi-unified family court that allows the same judge to oversee all cases involving temporary restraining orders, divorce, juvenile justice, and child protection. Child welfare workers are involved in every step of the proceedings to provide immediate feedback to the judge and to assure orders and criminal histories are considered in the development of protective case plans.

The author (and several co-authors) are just completing a summary article outlining the goals and accomplishments of four U.S. DHHS funded projects (1995-97) designed to train child welfare workers on domestic violence:

- Columbia University School of Social Work developed a two-day training curriculum for CPS workers in New York City. They trained over 400 CPS workers in a sophisticated method for intervening in cases involving both domestic violence and child abuse. They developed a World Wide Web site for dissemination of information about the project. Columbia University School of Social Work also developed a training manual that was widely disseminated.
- Simmons College worked with the Department of Social Services' (Boston's CPS Agency) Domestic Violence Unit. In addition, Simmons grantees worked with the DSS training department to facilitate collaboration between units within DSS and to provide on-site trainings in domestic violence. They focused on supervisors from varying units, hoping to intervene "at the top."
- Temple University developed the "Training Project on Collaborative Responses to Community and Domestic Violence." They provided two training sessions to 200 professionals total, the purpose of which was to bring together a diverse group of violence prevention and intervention workers, especially child welfare workers, to foster better understanding of the problems of family violence, to identify the roles and mandates of the different systems and to establish linkages between them, to recognize the interrelatedness of family violence, and to propose policy systems change.
- UCLA trained workers and supervisors on the intersections of domestic violence and child abuse, and developed an assessment instrument that would make their interventions more effective when domestic violence was suspected. They developed a one-day training program to train large groups of CPS workers and supervisors from Los Angeles County Department of Children and Family Services (DCFS) and Orange County Social Services Agency, and a six-day "fellows" program for a small select group of Los Angeles County DCFS workers and supervisors. These "fellows" were to become the domestic violence resource consultants utilized by the other workers and supervisors in their of-

fices. Policy change was essential to UCLA's goals; they wanted to ensure that their instrument, or some instrument like it, became an integral part of a child abuse assessment in Los Angeles.

UCLA TRAINING PROGRAM

The program in Los Angeles warrants further discussion because it traversed themes central to this article:

- It took a position controversial in Child Protective Service practice: it focused on aligning with the battered woman in order to protect both mother and child,
- It identified obstacles to the effective implementation of this approach,
- It analyzed both the "in process" and potential policy implications.

This program attempted to give trainees the skills to:

- Enhance self-awareness leading to more confident and effective use of the self in both clinical and protective service interventions with this population.
- Consider emotional, cultural and financial barriers to changing a relationship.
- Protect children through empowering their mothers.
- Know and utilize community resources to assist in safety planning.
- Empower the battered woman to design her own safety plan.

To date, over 900 workers, supervisors, and administrators were trained. Two small groups, of approximately 55 each, were given intensive (six sessions) training and deemed "fellows." As outlined before, the goal was to have the fellows become consultants on cases involving the two abuses and to ensure that there was effective case management of families where domestic violence and child abuse intersect. The remainder (approximately 790) were provided a one-day training addressing the identified areas in an abbreviated fashion. The goal was to provide these one-day trainees with a foundation of understanding and effectiveness that the fellows could build on.

The UCLA training team has taken the position that "domestic violence is child abuse," a position espoused by the management of the Los Angeles County Department of Children and Family Services. Although nationally there is no clear consensus on whether a child who witnesses violence in his/her own home is by definition a victim of child abuse and neglect, California case law, as stated earlier, has recently recognized witnessing as a form of neglect (*In re Heather A.*, 1997). *In re Heather A. et al. v. Harold A.* (1997), the court ruled that a child's exposure to domestic violence, even if only secondary (that is, the child is not actually being injured during fighting episodes), is child neglect. The court dramatically concluded that, "Domestic violence in the same household where children are living is neglect, it is failure to protect from the substantial risk of encountering the violence and suffering serious physical harm/illness from it. Such neglect causes the risk" (*In re Heather A. et al. v. Harold A.*, 52 Cal App 4th 183, 1997). Interestingly, this neglect finding was brought against the father, the alleged batterer. The woman in this case was not the children's natural or adoptive mother. In many cases, CPS charges battered women with "failure to protect" their children. Edleson (1997) suggests that this reflects a misunderstanding of the mother's concern for her children and her rational fear of the violent partner. The *Heather A.* case could have a profound effect on the CPS system in general, especially on those mothers or fathers who are perpetrators or victims of domestic violence.

In connection with this work, Mills (1997) has looked at all 58 California counties' CPS/Risk Assessment Instruments. She found that with the exception of the six counties using the Los Angeles Risk Assessment form, CPS workers statewide have not yet begun to formally factor domestic violence into their assessment of child abuse (Mills, 1998). Indeed, even the Los Angeles Risk Assessment form falls far short of adequately determining the extent to which domestic violence is present in a family, and does not require the worker to discuss with a battered woman her experience of intimate abuse.

This is why a comprehensive Assessment Instrument and Social Support Inventory form was developed to guide the worker through these sometimes difficult encounters (Mills & Friend, 1997). These cases are often difficult to assess because of the complexities in the domestic violence situation. Since these cases are especially difficult to manage, the CPS worker needs special tools and skills to better manage the multiple risks inherent in these situations. The instrument includes: interview strategies, research-based inventories, input from academic experts, content from focus groups of CPS and domestic violence practitioners, and comments from a sample of clients.

Organized into ten sections, the instrument begins with a one-page summary sheet. Note that the use of pronouns reflects what most often occurs and what is often reported to CPS agencies: her–an allegedly battered woman; him–the alleged batterer. Summarized briefly, and addressed to the worker, the instrument proposes the following:

I. *Initial Approach*: Be aware that your presence creates a crisis. Address the issue of potential child removal directly and up-front. Advise you will not ask her to make permanent changes, that is something for her to decide. Explain criteria upon which decisions are made. Ask her to enter a partnership with you. Tell her a lot of what happens after today, depends upon honest sharing between the two of you. Ask her to tell you if you are not reflecting back to her what her actual experience has been. Ask (directly/indirectly) if domestic violence is present. Keep in mind that this is a "critical connection" phase of the interview.

II. *Listen*: Use her terms, elicit her conceptualization. Try not to interrupt. Find out why she feels she must stay in the relationship. Get clues why she might go back, then determine what you can do together to address her needs. In this way, you are addressing her level of vulnerability on the continuum. For example, if safety is her reason for staying, what resources do you have to enhance safety (e.g., money to get locks changed, formal request to phone company for 911 service only, if phone service is turned off)?

III. *Discuss Her Perspective*: Comment on patterns, if appropriate. Give validating messages. Elicit what she has done so far to protect herself and her child. Ask about the positive qualities of the relationship. Refer to the partner by name. Search for and identify the woman's strengths.

IV. *Issues of Responsibility*: Ask about good things in the relationship. As noted, refer to the batterer by name, and do not label either party. This participates in a strategy to reduce defensiveness, and may free her to tell you the range of qualities the partner has. Avoid blaming the woman for the actions of the batterer. Ask yourself if you have provided all resources to allow her to move to a position of strength and safety. In the training, we called this moving to a higher safety plateau.

V. *Assessment of Threat*: Explain that you are very interested in what her experience was with her husband or partner. State that because her safety is critical for both her and the child, you hope that she can be as honest as possible in sharing information; it is helpful if she can see your relationship as a partnership in determining her and the child's safety. The reliability and validity limitations surrounding any threat assessment are particularly daunting for CPS workers; hence, your best strategy is to mobilize her to identify the level of "threat" herself.

VI. *Conducting the Social Support Inventory*: Helps you and the woman make a joint assessment of supports that may become resources and part of her safety plan. The Social Support Inventory facilitates your assessment of strengths, and her view of herself as having some assets. It identifies work to be done to reduce isolation, gain support, and move to a higher safety plateau. If she leaves and goes to a relative, consider: Will the relative be protective/allow access? What level of risk does the relative incur? Does the relative pose any risk to the child?

VII. *Interview the Children, Other People Living in the Household*: The guidelines help the CPS worker to interview children who may have been exposed to domestic violence using both a direct and indirect approach. The guidelines remind workers that in households with domestic violence, other forms of abuse (such as elder and sibling abuse) may be present.

VIII. *Worker Safety Planning and Interview with Alleged Batterer*: Although these clients may not be antagonistic and dangerous to the worker, it is always worthwhile to assess for risk and make a worker safety plan. Specific tips are provided for consideration. The issues to be covered in the batterer's interview (e.g., his expectations, sense of responsibility) are covered.

IX. *Case Planning Options*: This examines the real options in both a restrictive and non-restrictive environment. In most CPS agencies in California, the criteria for maintaining an open case with a voluntary family maintenance agreement contract reflects a lower level of concern about safety. This differs from cases where the safety concerns are so high that a juvenile court dependency petition is initiated to describe the need to remove the child immediately. Before removing the child, consider:
   ~ What other options exist?
   ~ What will constitute reasonable efforts to prevent placement before removal can be justified?
   ~ Have you consulted with your supervisor on the plan?

X. *Safety Plans for Clients*: This is divided into two plans: one focused on a woman who has decided to stay in the abusive relationship, and the other on her leaving. No matter what happens, it is critical for the CPS worker to attempt to devise a safety plan with a woman who may be in danger of being battered again. Closing the interaction on this note facilitates a mutual understanding that her and her child's safety are what is important.

OBSTACLES TO THIS APPROACH

A thorough domestic violence assessment encompasses, at a minimum, the ten domains previously outlined. The numerous obstacles to an appropriate response include the worker's ability to: navigate the necessary time constraints, build a relationship through effective interviewing, develop new resources, assess lethality, and receive administrative and community support.

The average DCFS worker in Los Angeles County carries approximately 60 cases; there is an explicit demand that they will manage all the tasks, crises, and interviews for all those clients. Our experience is that these interviews where there are allegations of both domestic violence and child abuse as well as the follow-up they require can considerably alter any worker's best laid plans. Ultimately, a comprehensive approach such as this has the potential to reduce overall agency time spent with the family but it is initially time consuming. By forming an alliance that facilitates the gathering of more accurate information, it is hoped that multiple case openings and/or closings without meaningful movement will be reduced. Paradoxically, the incorporation of these interview techniques into their approach yields much more information, and perhaps a demand to do more work. We asked workers to tell us how and why they would manage this disincentive to discovering information. Workers told us very poignantly that the importance of being true to their initial motivation for taking the job, i.e., helping families and children, requires involvement.

The training also addressed the worker's sense that they would be held accountable, if, despite their most careful efforts, a child ended up being injured. The training worked to broaden the concept of the child's safety as a priority by including the child's mother in this safety priority. This brought the trainers directly to the issue of relationship building. The training taught workers to present child safety and mother safety as a dual priority. Further, workers were encouraged to address the potential for removal of the children from the home in an up-front manner, in an effort to establish an honest partnership with the mother. Listening and inquiring about the range of all parties' behaviors became another cornerstone to relationship building.

All of this is greatly complicated by the worker's need to assess the mother and kinship care providers for their possible risk to the child. Specifically, some studies show that while women are being battered, they are at an increased risk to abuse their child (Giles-Sims, 1985; Ross, 1996; Walker, 1984). Although the good news is that the mother's abuse risk may lessen when the battering ends (Walker, 1984), workers must, nevertheless, assess for this possibility. When workers seek to use relatives for placement of mother and child, they must also assess any safety risk posed by kin and whether or not the location would be safe from a pursuing batterer.

The training clarified for workers that this prediction of dangerousness and lethality is still an emerging science. The trainers could find only one instrument that claimed some reliability and validity (Campbell, 1995). Parts of this instrument were incorporated into the instrument developed for the training and were then modified via consensus (Mills & Friend, 1997). Workers were encouraged to engage mothers in a mutual assessment of threat activity through the use of a calendar to facilitate recollection. Furthermore, workers were warned to be cautious about making pronouncements about danger; this was another reason why the involvement of the women in considering all dangerous elements is critical. The training also focused on the risk when women decide to leave.

It is well known that resources for women and children in abusive situations are anything but plentiful. This is complicated by the woman's reluctance to leave and the restrictions imposed by some shelters (i.e., some will not take "older" boys or admit women with substance abuse or complex mental health histories). Many women have had experiences with leaving that have been unsuccessful and even dangerous. We used content from research using social support inventories with advocates to help mothers and workers operate from a strengths perspective and explore all potential client resources (Tan, 1995).

The unifying obstacles to all this work tap into the relationship, resource, lethality, and reporting issues. Given that a woman's homicide risk increases dramatically when she leaves or separates from a battering relationship (Campbell, 1995), and given that she is privy to what the abuser is capable of doing with and without a monitor, she may come to the conclusion that staying in the relationship may be the most protective and safe option for herself and the children. We challenged workers (in consultation with the supervisor and chain of command) not to automatically exclude this as an option. The training developed a matrix to help workers make decisions in both a conservative and less conservative agency climate (Mills, 1997).

When workers are dealing with a large bureaucracy and geographic area, administrative and community support are always critical elements of success. Although line workers were the highest number of participants, the training team made several efforts to solicit administrative support. We felt strongly that all levels of agency personnel needed to be aware of the training's content. First, a conscious solicitation was made to include supervisors, mid-level managers and high-level managers as both one-day trainees and fellows. A deputy director accepted the initial chair of the Advisory Council and was succeeded by a bureau chief. Our training Advisory Council was made up of directors and managers of agencies that had a direct involvement in responding to domestic violence (law enforcement, district attorney, city attorney, shelters, drug treatment consortium, adult protective services, etc.). We strategically partnered in this effort with our Los Angeles County Domestic Violence Council. Many of our trainers were drawn from this partnership and advisory group, and they played a key role in curriculum development.

POLICY ISSUES

A project of this size has the potential to impact policy in substantial ways. The training team felt our policy accomplishments should be divided between the preliminary results and those that have been identified (yet remain) outstanding. In part, the elusiveness of these outstanding issues inspired us to apply for more U.S. DHHS funding.

The following preliminary policy "accomplishments" were acknowledged by the training team:

- This training helped mobilize CPS to consider domestic violence as a separate domain on their assessment instrument. This puts the issue "on the map" for all assessments, as a key issue in evaluating risk to children.
- All levels of staff (line, supervisor, and management) have been sensitized to the complexities that surface at the nexus between child abuse and domestic violence. Trainees now know about the problems associated with threat assessment, the myths widely held, why women stay and men batter, and the impact of domestic violence exposure on children.
- The fellows were challenged to develop innovative programs within DCFS to meet service gaps. Three projects were selected by the Advisory Council as "outstanding." All are in the development phase and will hopefully receive the necessary support to become pilot projects. Other fellows were so inspired, they initiated their projects independently.
- A network of existing fellows can access community resources and know how to work within the domestic violence system. Some have been more proactive in utilizing themselves as consultants for their colleagues than others. We are currently working on a campaign to give them a higher profile.
- Through the use of small groups and role plays the potential minefield for transference/countertransference issues were addressed. The new self-awareness will hopefully be used to facilitate better decision-making. We have seen this demonstrated in one follow-up focus group of trainees. Our intention is to do more focus groups. We are curious about how a training effort might instigate the need for more explicit policy in this area. Our belief is that once workers are trained, they will press for policies that support their work.
- This project facilitated the federal government's (U.S. DHHS) efforts to provide technical assistance and match its research with local concerns. A recent General Accounting Office (GAO) report (1997) cited the crisis state of CPS agencies across the country. U.S. DHHS was in general concurrence that: funding be targeted to community partnerships, information be disseminated to local agencies in a cost-effective method, and technical assistance be provided to promote community-based approaches.

The outstanding issues are made up of problems that may be remediated with continued effort; others are consistent with the overloaded and crisis state many CPS agencies find themselves in. We list them here in that order:

- Although domestic violence is listed as a domain/item in the Los Angeles County DCFS Risk Assessment Instrument, no further guidelines for exploring the issue are outlined. We will explore the possibility of getting some material from the Assessment Instrument (developed for this training) integrated into their standard instruments.
- The implications of the recent *Heather A.* (1997) decision, which holds that domestic violence is neglect, have yet to be fully explored. We are involved with a joint Advisory Council and Domestic Violence Council taskforce that will seek to explore the impact on protective service intake, dependency petitions, and criminal prosecution with all community systems.
- Although pre- and post-tests can measure attitude change and immediate learning, we seek to determine the impact of the training on worker decision-making, client safety and further policy development. We intend to devise an acceptable method to do so that will also help us modify the training.
- High worker caseload issues remain. This continues to limit the worker's ability to address domestic violence and child abuse problems and follow up consistently. The issue will continue to be a key area for negotiations between the DCFS worker's union and management.
- There is a need for ongoing strategies to encourage all CPS agencies and community-based agencies across the nation to take a more proactive stance in violence prevention outreach and early intervention. As Hubner and Wolfson (1996) have identified in their groundbreaking book on the juvenile dependency system, these children who are exposed to violence, abuse and neglect, are all of our children. Three of our outstanding innovative projects focused on prevention in schools and residential treatment agencies, as well as early intervention with first time reports of domestic violence and child abuse. We all have a future stake in providing a higher safety plateau for the next generation.

Lastly, we were successful in obtaining additional U.S. DHHS funding to continue the training, with an emphasis on the issues of substance abuse and mental health. We will extend the training to contract family preservation workers from community agencies in an effort to give those workers the skill to work with, rather than automatically exclude (as current policy dictates) families with domestic violence from their services. The UCLA training effort has both exposed our local CPS workers to the complexities of these cases and has had a profound impact on changing some aspects of CPS culture to recognize domestic violence as an intersecting problem with child abuse. Having trained a substantial number of Southern California's CPS workers and supervisors, this effort has helped resolve many of the conflicts that existed between the two communities. In addition, the training materials will provide a model for intervention nationwide.

BIBLIOGRAPHY

American Humane Association (1994). *Child protection leader: Domestic violence and child abuse.* Englewood: American Humane Association.

Aron, L., & Olson, K. (1997a). *Efforts by child welfare agencies to address domestic violence: The experiences of five communities.* Washington, DC: Urban Institute.

Campbell, J. (1995). *Assessing dangerousness: Violence by sexual offenders, batterers and child abusers.* Thousand Oaks: Sage Publications.

Digre, Peter. Personal communication, 1995.

Edleson, J. (1997). Charging the battered mothers with "failure to protect" is often wrong. *APSAC Advisor, 10*(2), 2-3.

Fantuzzo, J., & Lindquist, C. (1989). The effects of observing conjugal violence on children: A review & analysis of research methodology. *Journal of Family Violence, 4*(1): 77-94.

Geffner, R. (1997). Family violence: Current issues, interventions, and research. *Journal of Aggression, Maltreatment & Trauma, 1*(1), 1-25.

General Accounting Office. (1997, July 21). Child protective services: Complex challenges require new strategies. Report # HEHS-97-115, pp. 1-40.

Giles-Sims, J. (1985). A longitudinal study of battered children of battered wives. *Family Relations, 34*, 205-210.

Hotaling, G., & Sugarman, D. (1986). An analysis of risk markers in husband to wife violence: The current state of knowledge. *Violence and Victims, 1*, 101-124.

Hubner, J., & Wolfson, J. (1996). *Somebody else's children: The courts, the kids, and the struggle to save America's troubled families.* New York: Crown Publishers.

In re Heather A. et al. v. Harold A., 52 Cal App 4th 183 (1997).

Jaffe, P., Wolfe, D., & Wilson, S. (1990). *Children of battered women.* Newbury Park: Sage Publications.

Mills, L. (1998). Integrating domestic violence assessment into child protective services intervention: Policy and practice implications. In A.R. Roberts (Ed.), *Battered women and their families.*

Mills, L.G. (1997). Domestic violence in CPS cases: New legislative standards and suggestions for policy and practice responses (in press).

Mills, L., & Friend, C. (1997). *Assessment instrument and social support inventory.* Developed for U.S. Department of Health and Human Services Training Project (U.S. DHHS#: 09CT0206/01).

O'Keefe, M. (1995). Predictors of child abuse in maritally violent families. *Journal of Interpersonal Violence, 10*(1), 3-25.

Ross, S. (1996). Risk of physical abuse to children of spouse abusing parents. *Child Abuse and Neglect, 20*(7), 589-98.

Rossman, B.B.R., & Rosenberg, M.S. (1997). Psychological maltreatment: A needs analysis and application for children. *Violent Homes, 1*, 245-262.

Schechter, S., & Edelson, J. (1994). In the best interest of women and children: A call for collaboration between child welfare and domestic violence constituency. Briefing paper presented at the Conference on Domestic Violence and Child Welfare: Integrating Policy and Practice for Families, Wingspread, Racine, WI, June, 1994.

Straus, M., & Gelles, R.J. (1986). Societal change and family violence from 1975 to 1985 as revealed by two national surveys. *Journal of Marriage and the Family, 48*, 465-479.

Tan, C., Basta, J., Sullivan, C., & Davidson, W. (1995). The role of social support in the lives of women exiting domestic violence shelters. *Journal of Interpersonal Violence, 10*(4), 437-451.

Walker, L. (1984). *The battered women's syndrome.* New York, NY: Springer.

Wolfe, D.A., Jaffe, P., Wilson, S.K., & Zak, L. (1985). Children of battered women: The relation of child behavior to family violence and maternal issues. *Journal of Consulting and Clinical Psychology, 53*(5), 657-665.

Wolfe, D.A., Zak, L., Wilson, S.K., & Jaffe, P. (1986). Child witness to violence: Critical issues in behavioral social adjustment. *Journal of Abnormal Child Psychology, 14*(1), 95-104.

Innovative Approaches to Child Custody and Domestic Violence in New Zealand: The Effects of Law Reform on the Discourses of Battering

Ruth Busch
Neville Robertson

SUMMARY. In 1995, as part of a major review of domestic violence law, the New Zealand Parliament amended the legislation under which disputes about custody of and access to children are determined by the Court. Specifically, the amendment introduced a rebuttable presumption that a parent who had used violence against a child or against the other parent would not have custody of, or unsupervised access to the child unless the Court could be satisfied that the child would be safe during visitation arrangements. Three years after the implementation of this legislation, it is timely to reflect on the impact of this major domestic violence law reform initiative. Our findings indicate that there are indeed advances. Psychological violence is now clearly being considered when Courts are assessing the issue of children's safety. As well, the delineation of mandatory risk assessment factors has led many judges to see a continuum of power and control tactics as relevant in domestic violence related visitation proceedings; the previous emphasis on physical violence has given way to an analysis which more closely reflects accords with women's and children's realities of the abuse they are exposed to. Some of the old problems continue to exist despite the

---

Address correspondence to: Ruth Busch or Neville Robertson, University of Waikato, Private Bag 3105, Hamilton, New Zealand.

[Haworth co-indexing entry note]: "Innovative Approaches to Child Custody and Domestic Violence in New Zealand: The Effects of Law Reform on the Discourses of Battering." Busch, Ruth, and Neville Robertson. Co-published simultaneously in *Journal of Aggression, Maltreatment & Trauma* (The Haworth Maltreatment & Trauma Press, an imprint of The Haworth Press, Inc.) Vol. 3, No. 1 (#5), 2000, pp. 269-299; and: *Children Exposed to Domestic Violence: Current Issues in Research, Intervention, Prevention, and Policy Development* (ed: Robert A. Geffner, Peter G. Jaffe, and Marlies Sudermann) The Haworth Maltreatment & Trauma Press, an imprint of The Haworth Press, Inc., 2000, pp. 269-299. Single or multiple copies of this article are available for a fee from The Haworth Document Delivery Service [1-800-342-9678, 9:00 a.m. - 5:00 p.m. (EST). E-mail address: getinfo@haworthpressinc.com].

law changes. There are still recent cases where perpetrators of serious violence are awarded unsupervised access and where their violence continues to be construed as "out of character," arising because of the perpetrator's "despair" about the breakdown of his relationship. These and other issues are discussed. *[Article copies available for a fee from The Haworth Document Delivery Service: 1-800-342-9678. E-mail address: getinfo@ haworthpressinc.com <Website: http://www.haworthpressinc.com>]*

KEYWORDS. Visitation decision-making, supervised access, judicial discourses of domestic violence, child witnessing of spousal violence, perpetrators programs

INTRODUCTION

In 1990, the authors were commissioned by the New Zealand Victims Task Force to study repeated breaches of protection orders. The perspective of women victims of domestic violence shaped the project's research design. Our study looked at the circumstances which brought women to courts seeking protection and their experiences when they attempted to action those orders in an attempt to achieve their stated purposes (i.e., freedom from violence and molestation by the abusers).

Twenty detailed case studies of battered women who had experienced breaches of their protection orders (including two women who had obtained protection orders and were subsequently killed by their husbands) were made a central part of the resulting report. In addition, over 70 interviews were conducted with key informants connected with the justice system including Family and District Court judges (9), Family Court Counseling Coordinators and counselors (10), police officers (25), refuge (shelter) workers (10) and solicitors (8). Archival material from police files and log books, 46 published and unreported decisions of the courts and Justice Department statistics added to the data we collected.

While the stories of the women in the case studies varied, they had a common theme: there was a significant gap between the victims' experiences, a lived reality of violence and the ever-present threat of further violence, and the ways in which the justice system responded to their victimization. The case studies demonstrated how the justice system, through its minimization of domestic violence, colluded with the perpetrators of the violence.

Our findings showed a legal system in which violence against women and children was repeatedly trivialized, the victims' safety was regularly compromised, and women were held at least partly responsible for the violence directed against them. For example, police officers were often reluctant to arrest or charge batters, despite an official police policy favoring arrest and charging by police to shield victims. We found Family Court counselors who appeared to prioritize reconciliation above the safety of battered women. Counseling was often a point of exposure to further violence for women: in one of our case studies, a woman was murdered by her estranged husband as she left a Family Court-ordered counseling session. The emphasis on relationship counseling had masked the center's need for safety protocols concerning violent spouses' knowledge of their estranged partners' appointments. Other women reported being intimidated by their estranged partners in joint counseling. Maori women were particularly disadvantaged by the almost complete lack of culturally appropriate counselors.

However, it was the attitudes of certain judges and their decisions which seemed to be central to the justice system's failure to protect battered women and their children. Some women were denied protection orders because judges regarded such orders as an unjustified impediment to a husband's efforts to effect a reconciliation. Physical violence was viewed a-contextually, without any reference to the array of power and control tactics which were being utilized by perpetrators. Single acts, such as punches or kicks, were evaluated from the viewpoint of (typically) male judges as relatively trivial. Judges ignored or failed to understand the fear and intimidation which batterers could invoke by actions which, to outsiders, might seem trivial or even loving, but which were, in fact, carefully coded messages reminding women of their vulnerability to further attack. Judges characteristically imposed minimal sentences on men who assaulted their partners compared to men who used similar violence against strangers. There was little understanding of separation violence. Judges often assumed that women would be safe from further violence once they separated from their partners. The key issue for many judges was commonly "why doesn't she leave?"

Moreover, violence against one's spouse was typically regarded as irrelevant to custody and access determinations. There was a view among many judges that one could be a violent spouse (even a spouse killer) but still be a good parent.[1] Custody and access decisions were frequently made as if a parent's violence was irrelevant to his ability to provide a physically and psychologically safe environment for children; this despite repeated research findings concerning the statistical relationship between spouse and child abuse and the deleterious effect on children of witnessing domestic violence. In many cases, the children were further abused, either directly by the abuser or indirectly as the children witnessed assaults on their mothers at access change-over times.

Many women who gained protection orders found them to be ineffective ("just a piece of paper") as police inaction and judicial approaches commonly gave men who breached protection orders no meaningful consequences. Discourses of judges and other practitioners all too often adopted perpetrators' justifications for violence, with the violence itself characterized as relationship based. Social, historical, and cultural constructs which legitimized perpetrator violence were often unquestioned.

Our 300-page report contained 101 recommendations, including some 35 recommendations for statutory amendments. We called for protection orders to be available to cover a variety of family and domestic relationships, not just heterosexual marriages or defacto relationships. We recommended judges receive training in the dynamics of domestic violence. We suggested that the law be written in simple English, to help ensure both applicants and respondents knew clearly what was proscribed by protection orders. We proposed that respondents be automatically mandated to attend stopping violence programs (previously this was a matter of judicial discretion) and that parallel programs for applicants be made available free of charge to those women who wished to attend. We called for increased penalties for breaching protection orders and incremental penalties for repeated breaches.

In particular, we recommended amendments to the Guardianship Act governing custody and access decision-making. We suggested the law be amended to require judges to consider the effects of being exposed to violence when determining the best interests of the child (the sole criterion for determining custody and access in New Zealand until July 1996). We proposed that joint custody to parents was inappropriate where violence had characterized the spousal relationship. We also recommended that access to the abusive parent be supervised or denied if the child's or primary caregiver's physical or emotional health would be endangered by unsupervised visitation arrangements.

The report's publication was surrounded by controversy.[2] The government significantly "edited" the report. Missing from the published version were the analyses of all Family Court cases as well as the names of the 46 family and criminal court judges whose decisions were discussed. The words used by victims to describe their experiences of Family Court hearings and counseling sessions were in places deleted. We took our names off the expurgated version which was made available to the public and pointed out that the distortion of women's stories and the deletions of judges' identities and family court judgments (all but four of which were reported and readily available in libraries and journals) symbolized the silencing of victims and the reasons they often failed to gain protection from the justice system.

Ironically, publicity about the censorship of our report mobilized support for law changes in the area of domestic violence, popularized our findings about the gap and made judicial accountability a part of everyday New Zealand conversation. It also made domestic violence a political issue as the opposition Labor party repeatedly questioned the government about when our recommendations would be codified into law. Then in early February 1994, three Wanganui children, Tiffany, Holly and Claudia Bristol, were killed by their father who had been given interim custody of them three months earlier.[3] The custody order was made despite the fact that the Family Court had previously granted at least one protection order in favor of the children's mother, Christine Bristol, and that a current application for a further protection order was before the Court. That the custody order was made on an ex parte basis, despite the lengthy history of proceedings between the parties, the involvement of counsel for the child in the current proceedings and the fact that there was an existing shared custody arrangement, was a further surprising feature of the case.

In the aftermath of their deaths, Christine Bristol called for a ministerial inquiry into the actions of the Family Court in awarding custody of the children to her violent husband. Suddenly, an issue to which we had drawn attention, namely, a tendency by certain judges to see violence against one's spouse as irrelevant to the determination of one's suitability to be a custodial parent, came under public scrutiny. In June 1994, the findings of the Ministerial Inquiry galvanized the New Zealand public. In his report to the Minister of Justice, the former Chief Justice of New Zealand, Sir Ronald Davison, stated:

> My conclusion is that under the law as it presently is and with the current practices of the family court, the deaths in the circumstances of this case were not foreseeable and were not preventable. They were not preventable simply because the law and practices did not deal with a situation where a parent, although he had allegedly been violent to his spouse, was otherwise regarded by all who dealt with him, including counsel for the children, as being a proper person to have custody of his children . . .[4]

Sir Ronald Davison recommended that the Guardianship Act be amended to incorporate a rebuttable presumption that a parent who had been violent to a spouse and/or a child should not have custody of or unsupervised access to the child unless the Court could be satisfied that the child would be safe with the violent parent during these visitation arrangements. In a very tragic and powerful way, the Bristol Inquiry had shown that "the gap" had been a significant factor in the deaths of these three small children.

CLOSING THE GAP:
CHANGING THE STATUTORY DISCOURSES
ABOUT DOMESTIC VIOLENCE

The Domestic Violence Act 1995 and associated amendments to the Guardianship Act, the Family Proceedings Act and the Legal Services Act, go a long way to codifying a power and control analysis of domestic violence. For instance, the definition of "domestic violence" in the Domestic Violence Act includes not only physical abuse but also various tactics of power and control that perpetrators commonly employ. Sexual and psychological abuse (defined in the Act as including threats, intimidation, harassment, damage to property, and causing or allowing a child to witness physical, sexual, or psychological abuse of a family member) have been defined as acts of domestic violence.[5] To curtail the tactics of trivialization, minimization, and denial that decision-makers have at times employed to deny a victim legal protection, the Act specifies that acts which "when viewed in isolation can appear to be minor or trivial" may form "part of a pattern of behavior" against which a victim can claim protection.[6] Similarly, in order to curtail a victim blaming approach in respect to the issue of child witnessing, the Act provides that "the person who suffers the abuse is not regarded . . . as having allowed the child to see or hear the abuse."[7]

The scope of the Domestic Violence Act has been widened to include gay and lesbian couples, people who have had a child together but have not lived together, members of extended families and other culturally recognized family groupings, and others who have a "close personal relationship."[8] Importantly, in determining whether there is a close personal relationship between parties, the Act specifically states that "it is not necessary for there to be a sexual relationship between the persons."[9] This widening allows protection to be afforded to many categories of people (for example, elderly parents dependent upon their adult children and parents in need of protection from their teenage children) who previously could not obtain protection orders but were in fact being abused within a domestic context.

In an attempt to deal specifically with problems that can arise as a result of separation violence, new partners of previously victimized ex-spouses can also obtain protection under the Act.[10] The Court may also direct that a protection order apply against an associated respondent, that is, a person who is engaged or encouraged by a perpetrator to commit an act of violence against his victim.[11]

The effect of these amendments has resulted in shifting the focus of judges and other practitioners away from a concentration on physical violence in heterosexual marriage-like relationships to an emphasis on prohibiting the use of a myriad of tactics of power and control against a diverse range of domestic victims. As a result of the Domestic Violence Act, commonplace discourses of domestic violence have needed to be re-shaped. Providing legal protection for victims of violence in gay and lesbian relationships or of elder abuse has entailed recognition of previously unacknowledged power and control tactics. For instance, "outing" has been identified as an important tactic of power and control in same sex relationships.[12] Similarly, withholding medication may be a common tactic in elder abuse situations. Like the famous "categories of negligence" in *Donaghue v. Stevenson,*[13] the tactics of power and control are clearly not exhaustive. Because it has been developed as an analytical tool to deal with adult heterosexual relationships, the Power and Control Wheel itself may mask certain tactics used by perpetrators.[14]

Many sections of the Domestic Violence Act and the Guardianship Act focus on separation violence. The sentencing provisions for breaches of protection orders implicitly reject the previously common judicial discourse that an abuser's violence arises because of communication problems in his relationship. Under section 49 of the Domestic Protection Act, a respondent who has committed three protection order breaches within a three-year period will be liable for enhanced penalties (the maximum penalty increases from 6 months in jail and/or a $1000 fine to 2 years in prison).[15] A perpetrator's three convictions, however, need not involve breaches of the same protection order for the elevated penalties to apply. Serial abusers, those perpetrators who commit acts of domestic violence against two or more victims, also face the increased penalty provision. Moreover, it is now a standard condition of protection orders that firearms will be confiscated and firearm licenses suspended on the granting of interim protection orders. On the granting of final protection orders, firearm licenses are revoked.[16]

The Guardianship Act amendments now reflect a similar focus on separation violence issues by attempting to curtail the high incidence of violence on access changeovers.[17] Section 16B(4) of the Guardianship Act states that the Family Court *shall not* make any order giving custody or unsupervised access to a party who has used violence[18] against the child who is the subject of the proceedings, a child of the family, or against the other party to the proceedings *unless* the Court is satisfied that the child will be safe while the violent party has custody of or access to the child. In addition, Section 15(2B)(b) mandates that the Court consider imposing "any conditions for the purpose of protecting the safety of that other parent while the right of access conferred by the order is being exercised (including while the child is being collected from, or returned to, that other parent)."

The s.16B(4) presumption is a major improvement over the previous "welfare of the child" statutory formulation.[19] The presumption highlights Parliament's recognition of the ongoing nature of spousal violence even after separation and prioritizes safety of children as the primary consideration in custody/access decision-making. Had this provision been in effect in early 1994, the murders of the Bristol children might have been averted.

Section 16B(5) provides a list of statutory criteria to be used in deciding the child safety issue including the nature and seriousness of the child and/or spousal violence; how recently and frequently such violence has occurred; the likelihood of further violence; the physical or emotional harm caused to the child by the violence; the opinions of the other party as to safety; the wishes of the child (depending on his/her age and maturity); and steps taken by the violent party to prevent further violence from occurring.

Some two years after the implementation of this legislation, it is timely to reflect on its impact. The question is, to what extent have the Domestic Violence Act and the Guardianship Amendment Act been effective in closing "the gap"? In other words, has this major reform package of domestic violence related legislation resulted in the New Zealand legal system affording (greater) protection to women and children? Have discourses of domestic violence changed to reflect the intention of the drafters of the legislation? In what ways are previous victim-blaming discourses still apparent in the most recent decisions of New Zealand judges?

Our preliminary answers to these questions are based on an analysis of recent case law and reports from intervention agencies working "at the coal face" with victims and perpetrators. They indicate that there are indeed advances to celebrate. For instance, in terms of the Guardianship Act, case law developments have widened the forms of violence to be considered relevant beyond the narrow statutory definition of "violence" found in s.16A. Psychological violence is now clearly to be considered when judges are assessing children's safety under s.16B(4).[20] As well, the delineation of mandatory factors to be considered when assessing safety under s.16B(5), combined with the explicit inclusion of psychological violence under s.3 of the Domestic Violence Act, has led many judges to see a continuum of power and control tactics as relevant in domestic violence related proceedings; the previous emphasis on physical violence has given way to an analysis which more closely reflects women's realities.[21]

Our research also has shown that some old problems remain and, as batterers respond to the new statutory provisions, new problems are appearing. We have seen recently decided cases which continue to suggest that victims "provoke" domestic violence incidents.[22] We have seen judgments where the causes of violence within a relationship continue to be attributed to communication problems between the parties.[23] We have also seen judgments where women have been characterized as suffering from battered women's syndrome and this has been used to justify the removal of children from their custody.[24]

As well, there are still some issues to be worked out. One involves the parameters of the concept of "close personal relationships." Others arise in the interface between the Domestic Violence Act and the Guardianship Act. What approaches should be developed to determine when no access, rather than supervised access, should be awarded? Under what situations can relatives or friends be suitable access supervisors? How should perpetrators' attendance at stopping violence programs be assessed in terms of s.16B(5) risk assessment considerations?

DEALING WITH RESPONDENTS' TACTICS OF MINIMIZATION: RECENT CONSTRUCTIVE JUDICIAL APPROACHES

In our previous research we noted that "the gap" was sustained within the legal system when decision-makers (e.g., judges, police, counselors) adopted the perpetrator's analysis of events or saw specific incidents "a-contextually"; as if each act of physical, sexual and/or psychological violence was distinct and had no impact on the way victims and perpetrators alike viewed each subsequent incident.[25] We suggested that a Court's assessment of the causes of the violence would be critical in terms of the provision of protection.[26] If such violence were seen as the perpetrator's attempt to exercise power and control over his victim, the need for ongoing protection would be affirmed by the Court. If, however, the violence were characterized, and minimized, as arising from "the stress of a collapsing marriage" or of a dysfunctional family system to which each party at least somewhat contributed, protection would often be withheld.[27] The perceived "worthiness" of the victim as well as any apparent out-of-character nature of the perpetrator's violence were also critical.[28]

The statutory provisions of the Domestic Violence Act and the Guardianship Amendment Act outline the desired approach. As stated, the Court must now have regard to the victim's perception of the respondent's behavior and its effects. As well, specific acts must now be contextualized; the Court is mandated to regard whether even apparently minor or trivial acts may form "part of a pattern of behavior" of domestic violence.

However, even under the new legislation, gaps still remain. Do Courts adopt an interpretation of violent incidents which "understands" the respondent's actions? Are applicants seen as "reasonable" when they assert their need for ongoing protection, or as manipulative, provocative, and/or over-reactive if they continue to be frightened by their batterers? These questions become especially relevant in cases where respondents profess to having made changes in their behavior and to having gained "insight" or "empathy" with their victims through their participation in stopping-violence programs. The questions also arise in cases where perpetrators acknowledge that they may have "stepped over the line" as a result of their frustration or anger at having been left, but now assert that they have moved beyond caring for their estranged partners or wanting their relationships with them to resume.[29]

D v. D,[30] *Cocker v. Middleton,*[31] and *Gill v. Welsh*[32] are three recent cases in which judges reject what might be termed the typical "respondent's discourse" of domestic violence. In *D v. D,* an admittedly violent parent applied for supervised access to his two-year-old twins. In that case, the respondent minimized and trivialized his use of violence to his victim (the children's mother) and ultimately blamed her for the violence she sustained. By refusing any access to the respondent, the judge held the respondent accountable for his violence and clearly identified the respondent's responsibility to effectively stop his violence as the pre-condition for any future award of access. The case is also significant because of the judge's refusal to see the mere participation of the respondent in a stopping-violence program as indicating that he had begun to deal with his power and control issues.

Echoing an approach earlier taken in *V v. T*,[33] the judge stated that no access should occur because of the inevitable "emotional strain" that would be placed on the children and the applicant.[34] While conceding that in the long-term, access to the respondent by the children might be in their interests, the judge underscored the need to protect the applicant and therefore the children from further emotional harm. The posttraumatic stress disorder that the applicant was found to suffer from was not seen as an impediment to her caregiving role but rather as a factor which indicated that access should be denied. The possibility of face-to-face interactions with the respondent during access changeovers (the applicant had no private transportation) was likely to exacerbate her condition and therefore even supervised access was counterindicated.

In *Cocker v. Middleton*,[35] the Judge also followed the prescribed statutory approach and assumed a similar constructive approach to the minimization of violence by the respondent. In *Cocker,* the respondent father had had custody of the two children by agreement since separation. The mother was now applying for custody. The respondent admitted incidents of physical violence at the time of separation and subsequently. Some of these incidents occurred in the presence of the children at changeover times. While stating that "no good purpose is served by describing in detail the admitted incidents of physical violence to which the applicant mother was subjected,"[36] the judge found:

> From the time of separation, the father adopted a very hostile attitude towards the mother. Apart from the incidents of physical violence, he threatened and intimidated her. In the course of one extended incident, while she was driving the children, he followed her in his own car for some distance in what she correctly interpreted as an intimidating manner, stopped her for the purpose of collecting her key to the former home, followed her again and finally overtook her brandishing a gun.[37]

Clearly the children and their mother were both physically endangered and intimidated by the father's dangerous driving. The psychological impact of gun brandishing can only be speculated upon.

As in the case of *D v. D,* the respondent father "explained" those incidents by saying that he was upset at the separation and the reasons for it (in his mind, the mother's affair during the marriage was the sole cause) and "disappointed" by what he saw as "access hassles" created by her.[38]

The judge noted that the respondent had attended an anger management program for 10 weeks but that his abusive behavior continued. Commenting that the respondent had enrolled in a further anger management program, the Judge stated:

> That is commendable. But whether such a programme will assist with the father's real difficulty by addressing the real cause of his anger and the intensity of his feeling that he has been wronged and his right to retain control of the situation still remains to be seen.[39]

The judge correctly distinguished between attending a stopping violence program and choosing to stop being violent. As well, the judge recognized that the respondent not only had to stop physically abusing the applicant; he also had to stop intimidating and harassing her.

From *Cocker v. Middleton* and the other decisions referred to in this section, it would appear that the significant role that psychological abuse plays in maintaining power and control over victims is being more readily acknowledged since the passage of the Domestic Violence Act. As already mentioned, it may be that the explicit inclusion of psychological abuse in the s.3 definition of "domestic violence" has somewhat remedied a previous tendency among decision-makers to focus on the presence or absence of physical violence while allowing many varieties of psychological abuse to remain invisible. If this is a judicial trend, a major component of the gap will have been closed as a result of the newly enacted legislative reform package.

While analyzing the relevant s.16B(5) safety factors, the judge in *Cocker* made some significant comments about the nature and seriousness of domestic violence currently seen in New Zealand Family courts. He pinpointed the need to contextualize the physical violence within the continuum of power and control tactics utilized by the respondent in order to properly assess its seriousness. Moreover, he acknowledged that the "seriousness" of acts of psychological violence could only be understood within the context of prior physical violence.

Significantly, the judge utilized the approach outlined by s.3 of the Domestic Violence Act in his risk assessment under s.16B(5) of the Guardianship Act. He also tied the granting of unsupervised access to the respondent's acceptance of accountability for his violence.

Gill v. Welsh[40] provides another good example of how the approach laid out in the amendments to the Guardianship Act has positively impacted on child custody/access decision-making. The case concerned an application by the father to have access to his four-year-old son. The mother had had the care of the boy since she separated from the father some three years earlier. At the time of separation, the mother obtained interim (later final) non-violence, non-molestation, occupation and custody orders. The father had regular access, having the boy in his care for most weekends. Initially, access changeovers were organized by a third party but later changeovers occurred directly between the parties. After some two-and-a-half years, access was suspended by the mother and the father applied to the Court for its resumption.

As required by s.16B(2) of the Guardianship Act, the judge first turned her attention to the allegations of physical violence in order to determine whether they were true. She found that the father had a long history of physical violence, not only against the mother and the child, but also against his previous and subsequent partners, and against a person whom he erroneously believed was Ms. Gill's current partner. The judge also considered the fact that the father had several convictions for assaulting and intimidating the mother and had twice been convicted of breaching her protection order.

Several instances of violence against the mother had occurred after separation. In one incident, an argument developed during which, by his admission, the father grabbed the mother around the neck and pushed her. The mother gave evidence that he also threatened to kill her. The child, who was in her arms at the time, became very distressed. On another occasion, the father assaulted the mother when she visited his workplace in the course of her job.

As the judge noted, the assaults against the mother occurred during the relationship and during the first six months of separation. The father, however, had not physically assaulted the mother since then. While the judge allowed that this could possibly be seen as indicating a decreasing risk, she stated that any optimism needed to be tempered in the light of other factors. In particular, there was a recent incident in which the father had assaulted the mother's friend and (again) this assault had occurred in the presence of the child. The mother had stopped access after this incident.

The judge took the view that this "stranger" assault fell within the definition of psychological violence set out in section three of the Domestic Violence Act because the assault was clearly an act of intimidation towards the mother. As well, the child had witnessed the assault. While the mother's friend was clearly not in a domestic relationship with the child, the deleterious effects on the child of such witnessing were clear.

The Court also heard evidence that the father had been sexually abusive towards his son. He had pulled his son's penis, apparently on a number of occasions, always characterizing it as a joke. According to evidence before the Court, when the mother asked the father not to do this, he answered, "Get fucked, bitch, I'll touch my boy there if I want to."[41]

The judge carefully evaluated the allegations of physical and sexual violence and found them proved, thus triggering the presumption against custody and/or unsupervised access. The judge went on to assess the risk to the safety of the child of the father having unsupervised access, using the criteria specified in section 16B(5).[42] In what we consider a best practice model, for judges as well as psychologists preparing custody/access evaluations, the judge discussed every criterion set out in the provision individually prior to presenting her conclusions about the father's access. The newly enacted statutory language shaped her risk assessment analysis. Its prioritization of child safety over any other matters presented to the court provided the organizational structure of her decision.

In applying the section 16(B)(5) criteria, the judge considered the nature and seriousness of the violence used [c.f. subsection (5)(a)]. The judge considered how recently the violence had occurred and the frequency of the violence [c.f. sections 16B(5)(b) and (c)]. While the mother had not been physically assaulted in the previous two-and-a-half years, the judge reviewed evidence of frequent assaults on her up until that time. Further, the judge saw the father's ongoing intimidating behavior towards the mother, his sexual abuse of the boy, and the more recent assault on the friend as evidence of the continuing risk of his further violence.

The judge made explicit other criteria she used in assessing the likelihood of further violence [c.f. section 16(B)(5)(d)].

> Reviewing a history of violence is one of the important indicators to predicting future violence. Other important indicators are, in my view, the situation in which those incidents arose, both in terms of the victim and in terms of the perpetrator, the understanding evidenced now as to the cause and effect of the violence both on victim and perpetrator, and the ability displayed by the perpetrator to shield himself from involvement in a situation which has previously shown up his or her vulnerability to the unacceptable violent behaviour.[43]

In relation to each of these factors, the father was assessed negatively. His history of violence was reviewed in some detail. Secondly, the judge utilized what might be termed a contextualized approach, considering not only the violent incidents but also "the situation in which those incidents arose."[44] In this regard, as the judge noted, much of the father's violence occurred in circumstances similar to those he was likely to encounter in future access arrangements. Thirdly, the judge was unconvinced that the father showed any insight into his violence, citing the manner in which the father had minimized his violence, blamed others for it and shown no concern about the impact of his behavior on the child. To the contrary, the father's evidence "focused on the rights of a father in relation to the treatment of his son."[45]

The judge considered that she had limited evidence as to the emotional harm caused to the child by the violence [c.f. section 16(B)(5)(e)]. However, there was evidence from staff at the day care center the child attended to the effect that the boy was typically aggressive and threatening after access weekends but more settled as the week progressed. It was the center manager's view that the boy's behavior had improved in the period since access had ceased.[46]

The judge also considered the views of the mother [c.f. section 16(B)(5)(f)] who believed that the child would not be safe if unsupervised access was granted and who opposed access unless it was supervised. The judge did not formally ascertain the views of the child [c.f. section 16(B)(5)(g)]. There appeared to have been no section 29A investigation. Instead, the judge speculated:

> I accept that given how faithfully his father has exercised access, [the child] is likely, at least in part, to have had positive experiences with his father, and that he may wish to maintain contact with his father.[47]

This may or may not be the case. Perhaps the judge felt that given the preponderance of evidence which contraindicated unsupervised access, it was unnecessary to subject the child to a formal evaluation. However, if the judge's assumption as to the positive aspects of continued access between the boy and his father is wrong, then the supervised access which was ordered may be experienced by the child as an ordeal. As well, such an access evaluation may have led the judge to consider no access rather than supervised access, given the sexual abuse to which she found the child had recently been subjected on a regular basis.

The Court considered the steps taken by the father to prevent further violence [c.f. section 16(B)(5)(h)].

> Mr. Welsh has undertaken anger management counselling attending 12 group therapy sessions between August and November 1994. He stated in evidence that he has used the techniques he learned extensively in order to avoid physical confrontations. That physical confrontation with Ms. Gill has not occurred since then may be a result of his efforts. It may also be a result of the easing of tension simply as time passes after separation. However, whatever the impact of the anger management counselling on actual physical violence, it is plain to see that Mr. Welsh has not learned the techniques or has not chosen to use them in relation to controlling intimidation and the inappropriate expression of his anger.[48]

This appears to be a realistic assessment. As we have noted, there is little evidence that counseling or other batterer treatment programs are effective in stopping the violence in more than a minority of cases.[49] Program participation per se should not be taken as an indicator of reduced risk.

The judge concluded that any access the father had to the child had to be supervised. Unlike some other decisions, which have led to undefined and unsatisfactory supervision arrangements,[50] in *Gill v. Welsh,* the judge considered these carefully. The father had suggested three potential supervisors. As the judge noted, all were friends of the father. One of the potential supervisors was rejected because it was considered likely that she could be intimidated by the father. The other two potential supervisors, a married couple, were rejected after the husband gave evidence to the effect that he had not known about the father's violent offending and believed that any violence would be out of character and/or provoked by others. Instead, the judge made an order that access be at an independent supervised access center, on alternate Saturdays "on terms and conditions as to transport and contact as laid down by the Center supervisor."[51] The last point is important. Authorizing a professional access supervisor to determine such details contrasts with some other decisions in which the parties have been expected to negotiate these themselves. When there is a history of the custodial parent being intimidated by the access parent, any informal negotiation between them must be seen as placing the former at considerable risk. As well, if the custodial parent's safety strategy has involved placation of the abuser, it may well be that the arrangements made will not reflect the child's best interests.

RECENT EXAMPLES OF JUDICIAL ACCEPTANCE OF RESPONDENTS' MINIMIZATION TACTICS

If *D v. D, Cocker v. Middleton,* and *Gill v. Welsh* represent cases in which judges have given clear and unambiguous messages about perpetrators' violence and have refused to be lulled into "learned hopefulness" by respondents' participation in stopping-violence programs, other decisions have not been so successful in avoiding this pitfall.[52] In these cases, judges have failed to identify the impact of current power and control tactics on victims and instead have criticized victims for their inability to believe respondents' assertions of behavioral changes. Furthermore, in cases where the victim is characterized as "unworthy" (whether because of occupation, perceived culturally inappropriate behavior, or because her actions are seen as being detrimentally influenced by battered women's syndrome), the violent parent's actions have been characterized as either understandable or irrelevant. In these cases, unsupervised access or even custody has been awarded to the perpetrator. In these cases, the statutory presumption against custody and/or unsupervised access to violent parents has been displaced and instead the violence has been either legitimized or "understood."

In *Bayly v. Bayly,*[53] the judge adopted the respondent's perspective of his violence. The judge failed to view the nature and seriousness of the violence from the perspective of the applicants, as mandated under s.14(5) of the Domestic Violence Act. The judge conveyed the view that the applicant mother, although abused, was a victim unworthy of protection. One reason for this involved the applicant's occupation and the suggestion that she had gang associate friends. The judge commented that she was "a relief manageress of two massage parlors. She is generally in a management position although she did acknowledge that she has a couple of clients whom she sees on a regular basis."[54]

The primary issue of the case was whether Mrs. Bayly and her mother had ongoing needs for protection. They alleged one physical assault and also psychological abuse by stalking. They said, and the respondent admitted, that he followed them in his car, waited outside his estranged wife's workplace and drove up his mother-in-law's drive.[55] Despite this, the Court characterized Mrs. Bayly as provoking the psychological and physical abuse meted out to her by the respondent. It would appear that she deserved the abuse she received; she had "signaled" the sort of behavior that would most annoy her and the respondent obliged, just "to indicate his displeasure" at the alleged obstruction of his access to the couple's five-year-old daughter S.[56] What does it mean when a judge gives a message to a perpetrator that "getting back" at his estranged spouse through the use of harassment is understandable? It is clear that once this approach is adopted, statutory provisions aimed at affording protection to victims of violence are subverted.

There also were previous problems with the exercise of access to the parties' child S. In the most recent incident, Mrs. Bayly refused Christmas access until the 27th of December, because S was ill. She then arranged that access should be supervised by a friend who lived at a fortified gang house.[57] The respondent, feeling that he "had wrongfully been denied the access ordered to him by the Court,"[58] took the child from that house against the mother's will. He then called to say that S:

> was so upset he would be returning her. But in fact he did not return (S) that day. It was then negotiated that he would return her at 5 p.m. on (the next day). (S) had been ill and Mrs. Bayly did not have a contact address for her.[59]

The judge characterized the respondent's actions in the following way:

> He was enjoying the opportunity of further frustrating Mrs. Bayly in her attempts to get (S) back. He had been in contact with the police and knew that he must return (S) by 5 p.m. He had therefore arrived at the scene round about that time, in compliance with the order, but was just putting the knife in as he extracted (S) from the seat. This served to inflame Mrs. Bayly who began pushing and shoving at Mr. Bayly. In pushing her out of the way it appears that Mr. Bayly struck her in the face.[60]

The use of the phrase "putting the knife in" is bizarrely hyperbolic in this context. The judge seemed to suggest that the respondent was engaging in some form of understandable prank, not as having engaged in a day-long series of psychologically abusive actions. Given that the respondent's actions subsequently escalated into physical abuse of both applicants and further emotional abuse of the child S, the judge's vernacular reinforces the view that the applicant was "the dominant person" in the relationship against whom the respondent "acts out" in an understandable, if somewhat childish, manner. "[P]utting the knife in," with its humorous gloss, obscures the impact and seriousness of the respondent's psychologically abusive behavior, especially against the child.

S's grandmother, the second applicant, told Mrs. Bayly to get S out of the car from the driver's side.[61]

> When Mr. Bayly realised that this was about to happen, he took hold of (S's) legs in order to prevent Mrs. Bayly from removing her from the vehicle. This resulted in Mrs. Bayly holding (S) by the arms and Mr. Bayly holding her by the legs.[62]

S's grandmother tried to intervene and the respondent pushed her backwards. She fell and then got up and hit Mr. Bayly.

Finding that the incident had been precipitated by Mr. Bayly's attempt to "indicate his displeasure," the judge concluded that Mrs. Bayly was not in need of ongoing protection and she was denied a final protection order. The judge stated that "all her protection applications have been motivated by a desire to stop access."[63] That desire he saw as blameworthy despite the respondent's admissions of physical violence and repetitive stalking, despite S witnessing these incidents and being enmeshed in her parents' hostility, despite the fact that he absconded with S, and despite previous undetailed "breaches of trust" by him, involving a dog and visits with S to his own abusive father. And despite the fact that the court appointed psychologist found that S "had never essentially developed an ongoing substantive or positive access relationship with her father,"[64] did not want to see her father "because he took her away and she felt scared"[65] and appeared to be suffering from post-traumatic stress disorder. Despite the evidence, the judge concluded that S's relationship with the respondent needed to be strengthened.[66] Indeed, the judge searched for a reason for Mrs. Bayly's attitude toward Mr. Bayly specifically and men in general. Rather than seeing her as needing protection from Mr. Bayly's physical and psychological abuse, Mrs. Bayly was characterized as a man hater as are other massage parlor workers who, along with Mrs. Bayly's father, are blamed for her supposed "jaundiced views" of men.

Both Mr. and Mrs. Bayly were warned by the judge. If Mr. Bayly continued to engage in confrontations, a protection order could be made in Mrs. Bayly's favor in the future,[67] access could be stopped and an order for costs might be made against him. Mrs. Bayly was also cautioned:

> There will also be sanctions against her if she continues her confrontational attitude. She needs to be aware that under the Guardianship Act she can be prosecuted if she obstructs access. She must also be aware that orders for costs can be made against her.[68]

The Judge further commented:

> One way of reducing the potential for future conflict is to remove Mrs. Bayly's control by imposing expert observation and control in place of that exerted up until now by Mrs. Bayly.[69]

The judge explicitly pinpointed the blame for the conflict on Mrs. Bayly's "control" and concluded on a note of learned hopefulness that counseling and non-violence programs for both parties could see dramatic changes ensue:

> Counselling for Mr. Bayly and Mrs. Bayly is a priority. They both have the opportunity of non-violence programmes, an individual one for Mr. Bayly and a group programme for Mrs. Bayly. They will also need concurrent personal counselling from their own separate counsellors . . . Each of them have their own individual problems which they need to resolve. It seems to me that this is the most important thing and that it will take three or four months before it can be concluded or at least some dramatic improvements made.[70]

Will Mr. Bayly's stalking and other abusive behaviors alter in three or four months?[71] One can only hope that when access arrangements are ultimately decided, the judge will analyze the s.16B(5) safety factors from the child's perspective rather than attributing the access problem to a "meek" husband and a "dominating" wife/masseuse.

Simmons v. Foote[72] was a case which raised many of the same issues as *Bayly.* In *Simmons,* the applicant applied for a final protection order. The respondent filed a defense to the application and an objection to the direction to attend a stopping violence program. He also applied for custody of the children, ages two and one.

The judge indicated that the respondent engaged in instances of harassment and verbal abuse. Rather than seeing these behaviors as commonplace examples of the respondent's use of power and control tactics, the judge found that the respondent's psychologically abusive actions arose as a result of the parties' separation and their inability to communicate with one another. He concluded:

> It is inevitable in a case of this type, where the parties have had a volatile relationship and there have been confrontations that problems will arise over communication. Certainly, as 1996 progressed, it is my impression that the communication problems between the parties worsened. As a result of this non-communication, the perceptions of each of the parties differed. In this context, it is very easy to understand how certain events can be misinterpreted by either party.[73]

The judge commented on what he saw as "natural" within relationships.

> It is often the case in a relationship that one partner may be more dominant than the other and as a result the dominant partner's opinion may prevail. It is my view that the respondent was initially the dominant partner in this relationship. It seemed to me that the applicant was unable to state her views clearly to the respondent because she perceived that if she did he would react adversely to her. For his part the respondent impressed me as being a person who wanted to know where he stood. It seems clear throughout 1996 that the level of his frustration increased when he could not get clear answers from the respondent.[74]

He further concluded that:

> In making these observations I wish to stress to both the parties that I am not trying to apportion blame on either of them for the state of affairs they found themselves in, but what each must accept is they are responsible to resolve the issues between them. It was clear when there were problems of non-communication that they themselves had to do something about that. Inevitably matters worsened . . .[75]

The respondent's position was that the applicant was over-reactive and that his repetitive phone calling and dropping by was done simply to establish whether the parties' relationship was on or off. The judge, however, concluded that by the end of 1996 even the respondent knew that the relationship was over but the persistent phoning continued. In an ironic characterization, the judge commented:

> To his credit (the respondent) acknowledged that on occasions the phone calls would get out of hand and he knew this would happen but he still continued to ring the applicant. He stated he could not accept not raising issues about their relationship in December 1996.[76]

The judge minimized the continuance of the abuse and its effect on the applicant, who by the end of January described herself as being "constantly on edge, terrified that the respondent would be ringing and coming around."[77] The judge did make a final protection order in favor of the applicant but he reassured the respondent that his psychological violence would not have any impact on his custody application.

This case seems out of step with the intent of both the Domestic Violence Act and the Guardianship Act and clearly is situated in the judicial discourses about domestic violence which were prevalent before these statutes were enacted. While physical violence had not occurred, psychological violence had. The detrimental effects on the children of witnessing domestic violence, including psychological abuse, were not mentioned by the judge. Even though the rebuttable presumption of s.16B(4) might not be triggered because of the absence of physical violence, surely the respondent's psychological violence must be relevant in a future s.23 assessment of the welfare of the children. Does the utilization of power and control tactics have no relevance to custody/access outcomes, especially when they have clearly been demonstrated to undermine the physical and emotional health of the children's primary caregiver?

FURTHER EXAMPLES OF MINIMIZATION TACTICS: PLAYING THE CULTURE CARD

Another court decision, *L v. S*,[78] represents a startling departure from the intent of the amendments to the Guardianship Act. In *L v. S*, the mother unsuccessfully sought custody of her 11-year-old daughter J. Both J (and her 16-year-old brother) had been born in Taiwan. The family immigrated to New Zealand in June 1994. The parents effectively separated a month later when L returned to Taiwan leaving her children in the care of their father. Although the mother returned to New Zealand after a further six months, the relationship was not resumed. Thus, by the time of the hearing, both children had been in the care of their father for over two-and-a-half years.

The judge found that this was a case where Section 16(B)(4) applied. The mother's evidence of the father having assaulted her was supported by medical certificates obtained in Taiwan and the fact that the father had been convicted of an assault on her in New Zealand. This assault occurred when she returned from Taiwan and went to the family home, apparently wishing to reconcile. Although the father made allegations of violence against the mother, these were not supported by any collaborative evidence. In the judge's view the father "still [did] not accept his responsibility and guilt" for the assault of which he was convicted.[79] The judge found:

Overall where it is necessary I prefer the mother's evidence but also find that she played her part in the violence in the relationship.[80]

And later concluded:

I am not prepared to find that the mother was entirely blameless.[81]

The judge's perspective on the violence is problematic in at least two ways. Firstly, it is not at all clear what "part" the mother has been found to have "played" in the violence. The judge appears to be of the view that in certain circumstances, violence might be at least partly justified, a view diametrically opposed to the objects of the Domestic Violence Act.[82]

The judge then described what he saw as a paradox. While he preferred the mother's evidence about the violence, the children had expressed a clear preference to be with the father. In his analysis, the Judge assumed that:

one would have thought that the children would have taken the mother's side had her version been entirely correct.[83]

But why does he think that? Clearly under certain circumstances, some children may feel loyal to an abusive parent, particularly a parent of the same gender. This is even more likely after they have been in that parent's care for some time. In this case, for more than two-and-a-half years the 11-year-old girl had her view of her mother shaped by her father and, perhaps also, by her older brother.

Having made an equivocal finding on spousal violence, the judge moved on to consider the safety of the children in terms of the factors set out in section 16B(5). In respect of the likelihood of further violence criterion, the judge stated:

There is little likelihood of further violence between the parties provided they remain separated and apart. In relation to the violence in Taiwan, it is noteworthy that the mother was prepared to continue the relationship and was prepared to come out to New Zealand to start a new life which goes some way towards her acquiescing in whatever wrongs the husband had committed.[84]

The judge concluded that there is little likelihood of further violence if the parents "remain separated and apart." Given the father's lack of insight into his use of violence, won't the mother remain justifiably fearful? What are the implications of the judge's finding for access? After all, the mother was assaulted after she returned from Taiwan and that assault happened while the parties were living apart.

The violence the mother experienced in Taiwan was held to be relatively insignificant because she was prepared to come to New Zealand with her husband. One might speculate about whether she had a choice *not* to come to New Zealand, given that her husband had decided that he and the children were immigrating? What does it mean that her decision to accompany her family "goes some way towards her acquiescing in whatever wrongs the husband had committed"?[85] Where is such "acquiescence" relevant under the Guardianship Act?

Thirdly, the judge used the fact that the mother "was prepared to leave the children in the sole care of the father" as indicating her satisfaction with him as a custodial caregiver. This is ironic. By coming to New Zealand with her children, the mother had given the judge cause to discount the violence against her. Now, the fact that she had gone to Taiwan without her children is similarly used to discount the risk of violence.

Fourthly, the assault which occurred in New Zealand was described as an " 'on-off' situation." Yet it occurred immediately when the mother returned from Taiwan and followed a pattern of violence in Taiwan.

Finally, the judge concluded that "there is no evidence that violence continues in the home." The judge here was clearly limiting his discussion to physical violence. What about the safety of the children from psychological violence? Here, the judge took a contrasting position to that taken in *Fielder v. Hubbard*[86] and *Gill v. Welsh*[87] that psychological violence is relevant to the consideration of "further violence" in terms of Section 16B(5)(d) and (h) once physical violence by one parent to the other has been established. Significantly, in *L v. S,* the psychologist described the children as exhibiting parental alienation syndrome, which he felt was a form of psychological abuse of them by their father.

This psychological assessment is significant in at least two ways. Firstly, in a general sense, how can it be in the children's best interests to be in the care of such a pathologically dependent parent? Secondly, and more specifically, one would have thought that this assessment would have been relevant to the judge in terms of his analysis of the safety criteria under Section 16B(5)(d) and (e) of the Guardianship Act; the likelihood of further violence occurring and the emotional harm caused to the child by the violence.

But while the judge accepted the psychologist's assessment of parental alienation syndrome, he rejected the recommendation that the custody of the younger child be shifted from the father to the mother and that counseling be made available to ease the transition. Instead, he took a rather different view. The judge concluded that the mother had contributed to the alienation of the children from her. They were assumed to have been adversely affected by the loss of her company when she returned to Taiwan, especially so soon after their arrival in New Zealand. More importantly, the mother's actions were evaluated within the supposed context of Taiwanese culture. According to a doctor who had been counseling the children, Taiwanese culture is patriarchal; great value is placed on not losing face and there is strong disapproval of airing family matters in public. By initiating domestic violence, matrimonial and custody proceedings against her husband and by being the complainant in criminal proceedings against him, the judge found that the mother had violated important Chinese cultural norms. In effect, he blamed the mother for accessing legal remedies to protect herself and her children. This judicial approach appears to directly contradict the objects of the Domestic Violence Act as expressed in section 5,[88] objects which were enacted to challenge very similar values present in New Zealand culture.

The judge, while allowing that the mother was entitled to initiate the various legal proceedings, took the fact that she had done so as indicating a deep distrust of the father and a depth of feeling incompatible with "promot(ing) the whole family and being supportive of the father."[89] Is this what the Guardianship Act amendments are aimed at promoting? What is the implicit message to immigrant battered women who are seen as coming from patriarchal cultures? In this case, has the father made such an effective job of alienating the children from their mother that the new statutory approach is ignored? Whatever happened to the prioritization of the safety of children over all other factors? And finally, how can it possibly be in the best interests of children for the Court to collude with abusers?

DISCOURSES PATHOLOGIZING BATTERED WOMEN

Despite the new legislation's focus on child safety and exposure to spousal abuse as a form of psychological abuse to children, this approach may mean little if battered women are not afforded adequate protection by police and courts. Indeed, there can be ways in which well-intentioned concerns about the safety of children in the light of spousal violence may rebound on adult victims if the legal system's interventions are ineffective and/or non-existent. *E v. S*[90] is one case which vividly illustrates this issue.

E v. S involved a battered woman whose primary goal was clearly to keep custody of her children. There was well-documented evidence of the father's severe violence against the mother, of continuing threatening behavior (even within the courtroom), of physical and psychological violence against the children and of threats to abduct them. The perpetrator had "in excess of 60 charges" over the past four years including threatening to kill a police officer which the testifying officer said "that he regarded as a genuine threat at that time and that he still regarded it as genuine." The mother had, on numerous occasions, obtained non-molestation orders, which had lapsed upon resumption of cohabitation. More recently, she had consented to the father having unsupervised access. Immediately following this, counsel for the children sought, and was granted, an order placing them under the guardianship of the Family Court, with the Director General of Social Welfare being appointed the Court's agent. The children were then removed from the mother's care.

In a not uncommon pattern, the mother appears to have repeatedly sought protection from the police and the Courts but when that protection proved ineffective, to have reverted to the only other tactic available to her, that of placating her abuser. Unfortunately, the pattern was not seen as reflecting the inadequacy the legal protections afforded to her but as indicative of her incompetence as a mother. In the end, by losing the guardianship and the day-to-day care and control of her children, she is punished by the very system which she had approached repeatedly for protection for herself and her children.

The children were, at various times, exposed to the father's violence. A social worker gave evidence that, according to records held by the Children and Young Persons Service, the father had, on one occasion, broken all of the children's Christmas toys. There was evidence from a caregiver of one of the children that the child had been assaulted by the father. The mother told the Court of the father interrogating the children about her activities. The father's willingness to use the children in his campaign against their mother was illustrated by the fact that he had apparently intended to call one of them, then aged nine years, to give evidence in his defense on a charge of breaching a protection order.[91] The judge had direct evidence of the father's propensity for violence in the courtroom itself.

The father represented himself. This gave him opportunity to attempt to intimidate witnesses. For the mother's evidence in chief, the judge cleared the courtroom except for the mother, her lawyer and the court-taker.

Given his history of violent and threatening behavior, it is doubtful that the father's temporary removal from the courtroom provided the sort of safety the mother needed to speak frankly. The mother's response to questioning by counsel suggested that she was fully aware of the constraints she was under. When asked if she thought the children should have a final protection order made in their favor, the mother replied,

If the Court feels that it is in the kids' best interests, then yes.[92]

Her words appear carefully chosen in the face of a painful dilemma. On the one hand, if she unambivalently supported the granting of the protection order, she risked the retaliation of the father, retaliation she had already experienced many times over. On the other hand, if she opposed the protection order, she was likely to jeopardize her chances of regaining her children. After all, the Court had already removed them from her because her earlier consent to unsupervised access by the father was perceived as indicating her inability/unwillingness to adequately protect them.

Unfortunately, while the Court showed some limited understanding of the mother's position, it did not see the problems she faced as reflecting a failure of the legal system and the community to protect battered women. The Court preferred an individualized, psychological explanation, one which gave her no credit for having insight into her situation. That is, the Court found the mother to have been suffering from battered women's syndrome.

In coming to this conclusion, the judge reviewed expert testimony on the syndrome given in the recent Court of Appeal decision, *Ruka v. DSW*.[93] In that decision, reasons why battered women may stay in abusive relationships were reviewed. It is certainly true that the factors of the sort reviewed in *Ruka v. DSW* can serve to keep women in abusive relationships. Too often, however, these facts are not seen as representing woman's reality, one which reflects the community's lack of responsiveness to her needs and the justice system's failure to provide her with adequate protection. Instead, staying in the relationship is attributed to some internal psychological condition. The woman, we are told, "is inclined to genuinely believe these threats" as if it is her *belief* which is the problem, whereas, the problem is that threats can be made and carried out with impunity. Certainly, this had been the case in *E v. S*.

In *E v. S*, the mother had earlier given consent to the father having unsupervised access. Rather than considering the likely role that the father's terroristic tactics may have played in obtaining that "consent," the Court considered the mother's consent to be further evidence of her disability.

> She is just not able to escape the relationship with the father and I believe that she is quite unable to comprehend the probable consequences for her and the children if that relationship is to continue.[94]

We think otherwise. The mother's earlier affidavits and her carefully considered response to questioning by counsel for the children, suggest that she understood the risks she and her children faced quite well. In the face of inadequate protection, she had managed that risk in the only way possible.

The judge granted the protection order against the father sought by counsel for the children and deferred the father's application for access, pending a psychologist's report. It also deferred, until after that report, the mother's application for a variation of the guardianship order which would have allowed her children to reside with her at the home of their maternal grandparents. The Court's reasoning was interesting.

> [T]he Court will be concerned about the children's safety if they are to live with their grandparents, bearing in mind the history of the relationship between the parents and the fact that the mother will be living with them.[95]

In other words, while the children might otherwise be safe with their grandparents, their mother is such an unprotected target for the father that, in the judge's view, they may come to harm if the mother resides with them. It seems hard to avoid the conclusion, that in the end both mother and children pay the price for the lack of adequate protection afforded them.

This case is a reminder that law reform alone will not afford protection to battered women. It is especially problematic, however, given that the child witnessing section of the Domestic Violence Act specifically states that:

> the person who suffers [physical, sexual, or psychological abuse] is not regarded as having caused or allowed the child to see or hear the abuse, or, as the case may be, as having put the child, or allowed the child to be put, at risk of seeing or hearing the abuse.[96]

CONCLUSION

We welcomed the implementation of the Domestic Violence Act and the associated amendments to the Guardianship Act. Many of the decisions made under the new legislation reflect significant advances in the accuracy of the discourse on domestic violence over those we have analyzed in previous articles. In particular, we now more often see a sophisticated, contextualized analysis of violence within the domestic sphere by New Zealand judges. Violence against one's spouse is no longer seen as irrelevant to one's abilities to be a suitable custodial or access parent. With respondents being mandated to attend stopping-violence programs, they are, theoretically at least, being given less ambiguous messages about the unacceptability of violence.

Less positively, however, we have noted the persistence of some old discourses about violence reflecting a communication problem, about women acting provocatively, and about women who are deemed unworthy of protection. Moreover, we believe that certain judges are giving too much weight to the fact that a respondent has completed a stopping-violence program in determining the need for further protection or in custody and access decision-making. As the research literature clearly shows, a stopping-violence program is no magic bullet.[97]

We argue that there are no magic bullets. Single solutions, even law reform legislative packages, implemented in isolation are, at best, destined to achieve only modest gains, and may, in some cases, make things worse. What does it benefit battered women if they can obtain protection orders on expanded grounds but the orders are never served? Or if protection orders are served but those orders are not enforced by police? Or if there is police enforcement but respondents can represent themselves and are allowed to conduct abusive forms of cross-examination during custody/access hearings? Or if only supervised access is granted but there is a lack of secure supervised access centers? What does it benefit them if they can obtain protection orders and custody but lack housing and financial resources to live their lives independently of their batterers?

Effective action to end domestic violence requires nothing less than a comprehensive community-wide approach in which the courts, along with police, refuges, child-protection services, health services and social services share a common commitment to the safety and autonomy of women, to the welfare of children and to ensuring that batterers are held accountable for their actions. We believe that "the gap" we identified in our 1992 report and which we tried to close through legislative reform has narrowed somewhat. But that gap goes on.

NOTES

1. As an example, see *R v. Panoa-Masina, Unreported, Court of Appeal, 7 October 1991* (CA 309/91), at 5. In the High Court, Masina had been sentenced to 9 months periodic detention for killing his wife. The judge had stated that "The . . . most important special circumstance was that Masina had a son who was then only eight years of age who had lost his mother and who would if (Masina) was sentenced to imprisonment, temporarily lose the advantage of the guidance and companionship of his only surviving parent."

2. The research report that we submitted to the Victims Task Force was entitled Domestic Violence and the Justice System (Hamilton, University of Waikato, 1992). After considerable controversy, described later in this article, the report was published with a change of title in two versions, a full version for a restricted audience of (basically) lawyers and psychologists and an abridged version for the public. The full version is: Ruth Busch, Neville Robertson, and Hilary Lapsley, *Protection from Family Violence: A Study of Protection Orders Under the Domestic Protection Act* (Wellington: Victims Task Force, 1992). The abridged version is *Protection from Family Violence: A Study of Protection Orders Under the Domestic Protection Act 1982 (Abridged)* (Wellington: Victims Task Force, 1992). We insisted that our names be removed as authors from this "abridged" report.

3. For a full discussion of the Bristol case and the Ministerial Inquiry into the Family Court's handling of the matter, see Busch and Robertson, "I Didn't Know Just How Far You Could Fight: Contextualising the Bristol Inquiry" (1994) 2 *Waikato Law Review* 41.

4. Davison, R. *Report of Inquiry into Family Court Proceedings Involving Christine Madeleine Bristol and Alan Robert Bristol* (Department of Justice, Wellington, 1994, at 35.

5. Domestic Violence Act, section 3(2).

6. Ibid., section 3(4)(b).

7. Ibid., section 3(3).

8. Ibid., section 4(1)(a)-(d).

9. Ibid., section 4(4).

10. Under the recently evolving case law, the estranged partner has been characterised as a "family member" of the current partner. See, for instance, *A v. P* [1996]

NZFLR 878 (HC); cf *Dudley AKA Woodman v. Brooks,* unreported decision, High Court, Giles J., 28 October 1998.

11. Domestic Violence Act 1995, section 17.

12. See Christie, "Thinking About Domestic Violence in Gay Male Relationships" (1996) 2 *Waikato Law Review* 180.

13. [1932] A.C. 532. This landmark English torts case affirmed that there could be no exhaustive definition of negligence, i.e., there was an infinite variety of categories of negligence. We argue that the same is true of power and control tactics utilised by perpetrators, especially as law reform expands the categories of people entitled to protection orders.

14. Editorial (1996) *Waikato Law Review* 4.

15. Domestic Violence Act 1955, section 49(3).

16. Ibid., section 21(1) and (2). Pursuant to section 77(1), if a respondent does not apply for a discharge or variation of the protection order within 3 months of a temporary protection order being made, the order becomes final. Final orders can subsist indefinitely.

17. While there is no statistical data available on the incidence of violence on access changeovers, anecdotal evidence from police records and women's refuges support Melanie Shepard's findings in her study, "Child-Visiting and Domestic Violence" (1992) 71 Child Welfare League of America 357.

18. Under s.16A of the Guardianship Act "violence" is defined as physical and sexual violence. Despite its inclusion in section 3 of the Domestic Violence Act, psychological violence, therefore, does not automatically trigger the s.16B(4) presumption against custody and/or unsupervised access to violent parents.

19. The "welfare of the child as the first and paramount consideration" test still remains for guardianship, custody, and access determinations where there are no allegations of physical and/or sexual violence or where it is not satisfied on a balance of probabilities that such allegations have been proven by the applicant.

20. In *Fielder v. Hubbard* [1996] NZFLR 769, the very first case decided under s.16B(4) and (5), "further violence" was held to include the perpetrator's psychologically abusive behaviour. The judge's analysis of this term includes a very telling remark. He stated:

"It may be that this [is] the first such defended case in the Family Court requiring consideration of the provisions of this amendment and, if that is so, it would be appropriate, since it was in this Court that orders were made affecting the children of the Bristol family whose tragic fate subsequently gave rise to the Commission of Inquiry whose recommendations led to this significant legislative change."

Perhaps even more tellingly, the judge noted:

"It might have been expected that the significance of the event, and of the legislative change, would have made more impression on counsel in this case, some of whom were involved in that other."

21. See, discussion infra of *D v. D* [1997] NZFLR 673; *Cocker v. Middleton* [1997] NZFLR 113; and *Gill v. Welsh,* Family Court at Lower Hutt, FP 236/96, November 1996.

22. See, for example, discussion infra of *Bayly v. Bayly,* unreported decision, Family Court at Christchurch, FP009/1537/92, 23 May 1997.

23. See discussion infra of *Simmons v. Foote,* unreported decision, Family Court at Wanganui, FP083/280/95, 8 April 1997.

24. See discussion infra of *E v. S* {1997} FRNZ 550.

25. See, for example, discussion of how "de-contextualisation" undercut the Court's assessment of Alan Bristol's propensity for violence in Busch and Robertson, supra n.3.

26. See, for example, Busch, "Safeguarding the Welfare of Children" (1995) 4 Butterworths *Mental Health & the Law* 47; and Robertson and Busch, "Not in Front of the Children" (1994) 2 *Butterworths Family Law Journal* 107.

27. For a further discussion of these issues, see Robertson and Busch, "The Dynamics of Spousal Violence: Paradigms and Priorities" in M. Pipe and F. Seymour (eds), *Psychology and Family Law: A New Zealand Perspective* (University of Otago Press, Dunedin, 1998). The phrase "the stress of a collapsing marriage" is found in *N v. N* (1986) 2 FRNZ 534, 537. The full quotation reads:

"A parent's performance as a parent is not to be judged by that parent's behaviour in the stress of a collapsing marriage; now that it is accepted that the marriage is finished, the real question is the quality of parenting each of these people will be able to offer in the future. As I have already indicated, there has been no suggestion that the father's qualities as a parent should be judged by the events between the husband and wife which led to the recent crisis."

"The recent crisis" involved the husband's rape of his wife and his subsequent incarceration."

28. For a clear example of an "unworthy victim" case, see *Titter v. Titter* (1992) NZFLR 79 where the judge refuses to grant a battered woman a final protection order. She had left her husband and begun a relationship with their friend of 25 years. The judge characterised her as having "betrayed, abandoned, and humiliated" her husband and saw her as undeserving of protection as a result. For a general discussion of this issue, see Busch, "An Analysis of New Zealand Judges' Attitudes Towards Domestic Violence" in J. Stubbs (ed) *Women, Male Violence and the Law* (University of Sydney, 1994), 106-122.

29. See, for example, *M v. M,* Family Court at Gisborne, 20 June 1996, discussed in *M v. M* [1997] NZFLR 210. In *M v. M,* a wife was denied a final protection order against her estranged husband because the judge concluded that "things had settled down." This assessment was made despite the fact that the husband had been charged with assaulting the wife's new partner in May 1996. The judge had accepted the husband's statement that "he was getting on with his life and putting his negative feelings about her behind him" (at p. 10). Just 4 months after the wife was denied a protection order, her new partner, Mr. S, also sought a protection order against the husband. He related further incidents of physical violence and threats to kill made by the husband against him. The judge in *M v. M* had failed to see the husband's ongoing threats and violence against Mr. S as acts of psychological abuse against his estranged wife. One can only question whether Mrs. M was seen by that judge as an unworthy victim.

30. (1997) NZFLR 673.

31. (1997) NZFLR 113.

32. *Gill v. Welsh,* unreported, Family Court at Wellington, FP 236/96, 1 November 1996.

33. (1994) NZFLR 454.

34. *D v. D*, supra n. 29, at 682.

35. Supra, n. 30.

36. Ibid., 116.

37. Idem.

38. Idem.

39. Ibid, 119.

40. Supra n. 31.

41. Ibid., 9.

42. As mentioned supra, the criteria are: the nature, seriousness and frequency of the violence; the physical and emotional harm it has caused the child: the likelihood of further violence; the views of the other party; the wishes of the child; any steps taken by the violent party to prevent further violence; and other matters the Court considers relevant.

43. Ibid, 18.

44. Idem.

45. Ibid, p 19.

46. Ibid, p. 20. It was largely concerns about the boy's behaviour at the day care centre that led the mother, justifiably in the Court's view, to suspend access.

47. Ibid. p. 21.

48. Ibid., 21-22.

49. Busch and Robertson, "The Gap Goes On: An Analysis of Issues under the Domestic Violence Act" (1997) 17 NZULR 337, 363-367.

50. *Parker v. Reekie*, unreported decision, Family Court at Henderson, FP 476/94, 4 March 1997 and *Pancha v. Pancha*, unreported decision, Family Court at Lower Hutt, FP 381/96, 12 February 1997.

51. *Gill v. Welsh*, supra n. 31, at 23.

52. Claire Renzetti in *Violent Betrayal: Partner Abuse in Lesbian Relationships* (1992) has argued that "the concept of 'learned hopefulness' may be more applicable to the majority of battered women than the idea of 'learned helplessness'." The comment is meant to illustrate the unjustified optimism that many victims have when their batterers promise to change. We would posit that many decisionmakers, including judges, also have internalised this response in order to continue working in this highly stressful field.

53. Supra n. 21.

54. Ibid., 6.

55. Ibid., 25.

56. Idem.

57. Ibid, 11.

58. Ibid, 17.

59. Ibid, 11.

60. Ibid., 17, emphasis added.

61. Idem.

62. Idem.

63. Ibid., 21.

64. Ibid., 2.

65. Ibid., 3.

66. Ibid., 28.

67. Ibid., 26.

68. Ibid., 28.

69. Ibid., 26.

70. Ibid., 28.

71. The Court concluded that "It is probable that Mr. Bayly does not understand the impact that his actions have on (Mrs. Bayly and Mrs. Keith)." (at 25). He hadn't seemed to lack such "understanding" when his actions in late December were characterised by the judge as "putting the knife in."

72. Supra n. 22.

73. Ibid., 2, emphasis added.

74. Ibid, 4-5.

75. Ibid., 5.

76. Idem.

77. Ibid., 7.

78. [1997] NZFLR 481.

79. Ibid, 483.

80. Ibid., 484.

81. Idem.

82. Section 5(1) of the Act reads, "The object of this Act is to reduce and prevent violence in domestic relationships by (a) Recognising that domestic violence, in all its forms, is unacceptable behaviour; and (b) Ensuring that, where domestic violence occurs, there is effective protection for its victims."

83. *L v. S*, supra n. 98, at 484.

84. Idem.

85. Idem.

86. *Fielder v. Hubbard.* Supra n 19.

87. *Gill v. Welsh.* Supra n 31.

88. Supra n. 102.

89. *L v. S*, supra n. 98, at 489.

90. Supra n. 23.

91. It appears that the child did not, in the end, give such evidence, after a psychologist's report concluded that "it would be psychologically abusive to require that he give evidence regardless of any form of protection that could be offered," that the child was afraid of his father and that protecting the child while he gave evidence would not protect him in the longer term. Ibid, 561.

92. Idem.

93. *Ruka v. DSW.* [1997] 1 NZLR 154 (CA).

94. Idem, emphasis added.

95. Ibid, p. 569.

96. Domestic Violence Act, section 3(3).

97. The phrase "magic bullet" was used by Zlotnick to describe the tendency to see arrest of the batterer *the* answer for domestic violence. We think the term can be usefully applied to unrealistic expectations held of any single solution. (Zlotnick, D.M., "Empowering the Battered Woman: The Use of Criminal Contempt Sanctions to Enforce Civil Protection Orders" [1995] 56 Ohio State Law Journal 1153-71).

A Differentiated Legal Approach
to the Effects of Spousal Abuse
on Children:
A Canadian Context

Nicholas Bala

SUMMARY. In the past decade judges have started to recognize the destructive effects of spousal violence on children, but too many judges and justice system professionals still fail to take adequate account of spousal abuse when dealing with child related issues. Courts need to take a "differentiated" approach to spousal abuse, one that recognizes its different forms, nature and effects on adults and children, with a continuum of responses ranging from ordinary visitation, through supervision of exchanges or visitation, to termination of visitation. Canada should enact legislation that explicitly recognizes spousal abuse as a factor in child related disputes, increase education about domestic violence for judges and other justice system professionals, and provide more support for services such as supervised visitations programs. While this article focuses on Canadian developments and case law, there are similar issues in other countries. *[Article copies available for a fee from The Haworth Document Delivery Service: 1-800-342-9678. E-mail address: getinfo@haworthpressinc.com <Website: http://www.haworthpressinc.com>]*

This is a substantially revised version of a paper by Bala (1996), 13 *Canadian Journal of Family Law*, 215-285. A fuller discussion of the policy issues raised here is Bala et al., *Spousal Violence in Custody and Access Disputes: Recommendations for Reform* (Ottawa, Status of Women Canada, 1998).

Address correspondence to: Prof. Nicholas Bala, Faculty of Law, Queen's University, Kingston, Ontario, Canada K7L 3N6.

[Haworth co-indexing entry note]: "A Differentiated Legal Approach to the Effects of Spousal Abuse on Children: A Canadian Context." Bala, Nicholas. Co-published simultaneously in *Journal of Aggression, Maltreatment & Trauma* (The Haworth Maltreatment & Trauma Press, an imprint of The Haworth Press, Inc.) Vol. 3, No. 1 (#5), 2000, pp. 301-328; and: *Children Exposed to Domestic Violence: Current Issues in Research, Intervention, Prevention, and Policy Development* (ed: Robert A. Geffner, Peter G. Jaffe, and Marlies Sudermann) The Haworth Maltreatment & Trauma Preess, an imprint of The Haworth Press, Inc., 2000, pp. 301-328. Single or multiple copies of this article are available for a fee from The Haworth Document Delivery Service [1-800-342-9678, 9:00 a.m. - 5:00 p.m. (EST). E-mail address: getinfo@haworthpressinc.com].

KEYWORDS. Spousal abuse and family law, spousal abuse and courts, spousal abuse in Canada, spousal abuse and children

INTRODUCTION

Issues of spousal abuse may arise in some form in as many as half of all parental separations and present complex, challenging issues for lawyers, judges and other professionals involved in the justice system. There is a growing awareness of the nature and effects of spousal abuse, not only for the direct victims, most often women, but also of the potential harm for children who live in families where there has been spousal abuse. Some situations involve a high potential for violence, and a failure to take an appropriate protective response may place children and adults at grave risk. In other situations, however, there may have been some spousal abuse but there is little risk of future harm and professionals need to avoid taking an inappropriately aggressive response that can needlessly heighten tension and exacerbate relationships.

Spousal abuse poses many sensitive, complex and contentious issues. Spousal abuse cases are often emotionally charged cases and maintaining an appropriate perspective can be difficult for professionals. Some of the challenges arise out of the potentially tragic, life threatening consequences of some of the cases. Another dimension of both challenge and opportunity arises from the political aspects of spousal abuse issues, at least in terms of gender politics. In this article it will be argued that a gendered analysis of spousal abuse, one that emphasizes that women are victims and that gender inequality lies at the root of wife abuse,[1] is extremely important, and will often provide the best guide to the appropriate handling of a case. However, in other situations, an exclusively gendered analysis may not be appropriate.

There is a need for all professionals who work with families affected by separation and divorce to have knowledge, understanding and sensitivity about issues of spousal abuse. There must be awareness of the different forms, nature and effects of spousal abuse, and an ability to help develop appropriate, differentiated responses, particularly when working with children. As observed by Janet Johnston, a mental health professional with extensive experience with divorcing families: "All violence is unacceptable . . . however . . . not all violence is the same . . . domestic violence families need to be considered on an individual basis when helping them to develop post-divorce plans."[2]

This article describes the nature and range of conduct that may constitute spousal abuse, and the potential effects of spousal abuse on the children. It offers a review of some of the issues facing family lawyers and judges in cases involving spousal abuse, with a special emphasis on issues related to children. Canadian developments and case law are analysed, though there are similar issues in other countries. The article provides an analytical framework that recognizes the need for differentiated responses that meet the circumstances of the different situations, and considers the extent to which Canadian courts have adopted the approaches advocated. Many Canadian judges now understand issues of domestic violence in the context of disputes related to children, and they deal with cases in a relatively sophisticated fashion, but some judges continue to display insensitivity.

HISTORY AND POLITICS

Until the 1970s the issue of spousal abuse was largely ignored as a social and legal problem in Canada.[3] Justice system professionals, such as judges, lawyers and police, were virtually all men who displayed little sensitivity or understanding of various forms of violence arising in intimate contexts, such as wife abuse, sexual assault and child abuse. There was a tendency to view those cases of "domestic" violence that came to the attention of the police as "private" matters. Except in the most serious cases of wife assault, the police were unlikely to lay charges, and spousal abuse was only a factor in family law cases if it was "excessive."

The late 1960s saw the beginnings of the modern feminist movement and the beginnings of an awareness of the serious and extensive nature of abuse of women in intimate relationships. In 1968, as part of Canada's divorce law reform, physical and mental cruelty became grounds for dissolution of marriage. In the 1970s advocates for women and various professionals began to demand government action on the issue of spousal abuse and the first shelters for battered women were established.

By the early 1980s there was a growing concern about the inadequacy of the legal responses to spousal abuse. In particular, the police practice of expecting abused wives to bring their own "private prosecutions" in criminal court was criticized; these women often lacked the psychological and financial resources to carry forward their cases, or were easily intimidated or cajoled by their abusers into withdrawing charges. There was also a growing awareness of the "cycle of wife abuse," which often resulted in abused women repeatedly going through an emotionally destructive and physically dangerous pattern of abuse and reconciliation with their partners. In the early 1980s many police forces responded by increasing training for their officers, and introducing policies requiring mandatory police charging in response to all cases of domestic violence.

There continued to be many examples of judicial "insensitivity" to wife abuse in the 1980s.[4] However, by the early 1990s, judicial education programs in Canada were starting to deal with domestic violence, including presentations by advocates for battered women, and the civil and criminal courts were starting to display more understanding of the problems of domestic violence and wife battering. In 1990 in *R. v. Lavallee*[5] the Supreme Court of Canada ruled that a woman charged with murdering her common law partner could raise the "battered woman" defense. Her acts might be considered "self-defense" even though at the time she faced no immediate threat to her physical safety, if taking account of her mental state as an abused woman, she had a "reasonable apprehension of death or grievous bodily harm." The jury could hear expert evidence about the mental state of abused women to determine whether this particular victim of battering was acting reasonably, taking account of all of her circumstances and the context of the abusive relationship.[6]

By the mid 1990s, not only were highly publicized[7] criminal trials dealing with spousal abuse, but the media and popular culture had raised public and professional awareness of the existence of the phenomenon of the "battered woman." Some of the advocacy and analysis, however, may have focused too exclusively on the gender dimensions of the problem. *Some* of the feminist rhetoric about spousal abuse may have been excessive. By way of reaction, at 1998 Parliamentary Committee hearings on the reform of custody and access laws, representatives of men's groups erroneously claimed that *most* allegations of domestic violence that are made in the context of child related disputes are false, and heckled women who testified about their experiences as victims of abuse, turning the hearings into what one Committee member called a gender "war zone."[8]

THE NATURE AND INCIDENCE OF SPOUSAL ABUSE

Early research understandably focused exclusively on the problem of abuse of women, the most frequent victims of spousal abuse. These women often feel guilty and ashamed, and may blame themselves for the abuse. In many cases, especially during an ongoing relationship, victims and perpetrators of abuse minimize or deny that any abuse is occurring, making research and advocacy difficult. Abuse can take different forms, and may have physical, sexual, financial and emotional aspects. It can be a continuing feature of a relationship, or might begin or become worse at some point in time, such as during pregnancy, or when the spouses are separating.

One of the most complete studies about abuse of women by their partners was the 1994 Statistics Canada report, with 12,300 women surveyed by telephone.[9] Of those women who were or had ever lived in a married or common law relationship with a man, 29% reported at least one physical or sexual assault from a partner; one third of those women who were assaulted at some point feared for their lives. Fifteen percent of all women reported an assault by a current partner, but for prior relationships the rate was 48%, suggesting that almost half of all women who are separating or divorcing have experienced a spousal assault. About 20% of women who experienced abuse from a prior partner reported violence during or following separation, and in 35% of those cases the violence increased in severity after separation, but in only 8% of cases of violence did it begin after separation. Three percent of all women reported a physical assault in the 12 months prior to the survey, with the highest rates for women who were younger, less well educated and had a lower income, though women from all income and age groups reported abuse in the previous 12 months.

About one third of those women who reported physical abuse in a relationship indicated more than 10 violent incidents, while one third stated that there had been only one incident. The most common physical abuse reported was a slap, shove, or a threatened strike (which constitutes an assault under Canadian law), but 5% of those women who had been physically abused reported the threat or use of a knife or gun. About one third of all women (17% in a present relationship and 59% in previous relationships) reported serious emotional abuse in a marital relationship (e.g., denial of access to information about family finances, verbal denigration, or an excessively controlling husband). In a majority of cases, emotional abuse was accompanied by physical or sexual abuse. Emotional abuse is an important concept, and is used by judges dealing with family law disputes, though it is a nebulous concept, and in contrast to physical and sexual abuse, it is not a criminal offense (unless it involves post-separation harassment).[10]

In 39% of all relationships where there was violence, the women reported that children were observers, rising to 61% of those women who were injured (*i.e., a child was more likely to witness more serious violence*). Of those women whose children observed an assault, 60% left their abusive partner, versus only 34% of women whose children did not observe the abuse.

The Statistics Canada survey of women revealed a very broad spectrum of abusive conduct, ranging from a substantial number of cases where there was only one, relatively minor, assault over the course of an entire relationship, to situations where there was a pattern of serious repeated physical and emotional abuse.[11]

The psychological effects of wife assault can also be far-reaching. Victims of spousal abuse reported depression, anger, fear, drug and alcohol abuse, guilt and lowered self-esteem. While in general, a woman is more likely to experience drug or alcohol problems if there is both physical and emotional abuse, or if the physical abuse is more severe, for some women even a single act of physical abuse can create a very intimidating, emotionally destructive environment.

If there is a pattern of abuse or control while the parents are living together, the abuser will often resort to threats to seek custody of the children, either to keep his partner in the relationship, or to extract a favorable financial settlement. Many abusive spouses are highly controlled and present very well in public, while being highly abusive in intimate relationships.[12] Even if an abusive person may not be likely to succeed in legally obtaining custody, the threat may seem very credible to a spouse who has been constantly denigrated by her partner. Further, the threat of prolonged litigation can be a very worrying prospect. In some situations, the implicit or explicit threat may be that if the victim attempts to leave with the children, the abuser will abduct the children to obtain control of them. In some cases the abuser may threaten to kill a partner if she leaves, or may threaten suicide. Of particular concern, the risk of a woman and her children being killed by her abusive partner is significantly elevated in the period following separation.[13]

In 1993, Janet Johnston and Linda Campbell, two California-based mental health professionals, developed a differentiated set of "profiles" of relationships involving interspousal abuse, arguing that parent-child relationships also differ in each of these situations. This range of profiles provides a richer picture than Walker,[14] though it clearly builds on her work. The Johnston and Campbell profiles were based on a sample of their custody and access assessments, of which three-quarters involved cases where there was an issue of domestic violence.[15]

On-going or episodic male battering. This closely resembles Walker's "battered wife" scenario and made up under a fifth of the cases in the Johnston and Campbell sample; this type of situation may have been under-represented in their sample since these situations may be less likely to be litigated and assessed in custody and access disputes. In these cases the propensity for violence is produced by the psychological state of the man, who demonstrates low tolerance for frustration and poor impulse control, at least in the context of the spousal relationship, and is possessive, domineering and jealous about his partner. Physical abuse usually develops early in the relationship and is ongoing or intermittent. The potential for violence is high and has the potential to escalate after separation, often with harassment and threats alternated with pleas for the women to return to the relationship. While children sometimes have superficially good relationships with these fathers (especially girls who may be treated "princess like"), the children tend to be very afraid of their fathers. These fathers have a low tolerance for stress and tend to be very demanding. Johnston and Campbell recommend that visitation should be supervised or suspended, especially if the threat of violence continues after separation.

Male controlling interactive violence. The defining feature of these relationships is the man's attempt to control his partner, and maintain an authoritarian or dictatorial role. Physical aggression can be initiated by either spouse, as part of a struggle for control. There tends to be mutual blaming and anger in these cases, which were about 20% of the cases in their study. Once separated, there is a good prognosis for termination of violence. Both parents in this scenario tend to be abusive towards children, at least emotionally, and would benefit from help in developing parenting skills; access should be clearly structured to minimize possibilities of power struggles and abuse of the children.

Separation-engendered and post-divorce trauma. About one quarter of the cases in their study fit a pattern in which violence was notably absent during most of the relationship, but one or more acts of violence occurred around the time of separation, perhaps associated with the humiliating discovery of a lover. Because the violence is uncharacteristic, it casts a shadow of fear and distrust over the victim, but there is generally a good prognosis for a positive parent-child relationship, and after the incidents at the time of separation, there is likely to be a violence free relationship between the parents.

Female initiated violence. In these cases the woman initiates the acts of physical aggression, which has its source in her internal state of tension. These women are usually histrionic; emotionally labile, dependent and self-preoccupied. Their male partners are characteristically passive, sometimes depressed, obsessive and intellectualizing. The man usually retains his self-control in the face of aggression. These situations were 10%-15% of the cases in the Johnston and Campbell study. Relationships between the mother and children are erratic and unpredictable; boys are especially likely to be the victims of maternal abuse. Fathers, to the extent that they are passive and intimidated by their wives, are not considered good role models and contribute to the child's feelings of ambivalence towards the mother.

Psychotic and paranoid reactions. This type of situation often involves unpredictable attacks by either spouse, based on disordered thinking or drug induced state, and leaves the victims feeling traumatized, intimidated and fearful. About 5% of the cases in the sample were in this category; some of the children in this situation were badly traumatized while others identified with the psychotic parent and were themselves psychotic-like. Johnston and Campbell argued that visitation should be supervised or suspended in these situations, unless the psychotic parent has undergone effective treatment.

Although Canadian courts have not specifically referred to the Johnston and Campbell taxonomy, it is useful in trying to analyse and understand what judges have been doing. It is also consistent with the Statistics Canada study that found a broad range of situations of abusive conduct, from those where there may have been just one assault reported (about one-third of the cases of domestic violence reports) to those where there is a repeated cycle of violence with the potential for escalating risk after separation (also about one-third of the reports).

One controversial aspect of the Johnston and Campbell categories that is relevant to matrimonial litigation is *abuse by women in domestic relationships,* a question that the 1994 Statistics Canada survey did not address. The relative size of the Johnston and Campbell categories must be approached with real caution, due to the small size of the study (140 separated families). Further, as it was a sample drawn from litigation cases sent for assessment, it may have understated the proportion of serious abuse by males, since these are cases that would not get to the assessment stage of custody or access disputes because the father is unlikely to present as adequate as a parent.

A Canadian study by Jaffe and Austin found that in only 4% of a sample of contested custody and access cases involving domestic violence was there spousal abuse by the wife alone, and 9% involved mutual abuse.[16] One large-scale American study revealed that for 38% of couples where there was spousal violence, the woman initiated the violence.[17] While some feminists dismiss *all* female initiated violence in relationships as self defense,[18] there is substantial Canadian[19] and American[20] data that calls such blanket assertions into serious question.

Gender is a very important dimension for understanding issues of spousal abuse, but it is clearly not the only dimension. As Johnston concludes:[21]

> both men *and* women . . . are perpetrating a considerable amount of physical and verbal aggression in . . . separating/divorcing families. However . . . the consequences of male aggression are . . . more serious . . . Most men are physically stronger than women and can protect themselves better against female aggression. . . . aggressive males . . . are more likely to dominate, control, and physically injure their partners.

There are reported Canadian family law cases where the woman has clearly been the aggressor,[22] but these are relatively rare. There is a need to take violence against men by their partners seriously, and to recognize that for some of these men a feeling of humiliation may make disclosure more difficult. However, it is also important to recognize that, in general, abuse of husbands has a less serious consequence than abuse of wives, because of differences in social and economic power as well as strength. Further, women are more likely to be injured and intimidated by their partners' abuse, and to have the abuse affect their self-image and ability to effectively protect their interests and their children. In situations of mutual abuse, men are more likely to be the primary instigators, and women are more likely to be injured. A woman's use of force is often an act of self-defense.

Abused women are more likely to feel that their partners controlled the relationship; some research indicates more frequent post-separation disputes about visitation and other issues related to the children for abused than non-abused women.[23] It is also necessary to consider the social context of abuse. Some women, such as those who are members of immigrant communities, with language or cultural barriers, and possibly immigration concerns, may be especially vulnerable.

In each case where the issue of spousal abuse is raised, there is a need to consider the specific nature and context of the abuse. As Johnston points out:[24]

> domestic violence is not a unitary syndrome with a single underlying cause but rather a set of behaviors arising from multiple sources, which may follow different patterns for different individuals and families.

In order to assess what is the best response, it is necessary to consider a range of questions. Who is the primary aggressor? What is the frequency, nature, and intensity of the abuse? What is the effect of the abuse, since the same acts will affect different individuals in different ways? What is the prognosis for recurrence of abuse, given different possible interventions? And is there evidence about the effects of the above on the children?

EFFECTS OF SPOUSAL ABUSE ON CHILDREN

Children may have a special role in situations of spousal abuse. Sometimes an abused spouse, usually the mother, may decide to stay in an abusive relationship "for the sake of the children," though as noted above, Canadian research suggests that abused women whose children are witnesses to assaults are more likely to ultimately leave their partners than those women whose abuse "remains between the grown ups." As discussed in previous articles in this volume, there is now a substantial and growing body of research on the negative effects on children of growing up in a home where there is interparental abuse, even if the children are not direct observers of the abuse.

Direct effects–potential for child abuse. Research[25] indicates that at least one quarter of those spouses who physically abuse their partners also physically abuse their children. In some studies as many as three-quarters of abusive husbands also abused their children; at least some of the variation in rates depends on type of population studied, with higher degrees of spousal abuse making abuse of children more likely.[26] In situations of spousal abuse or conflict young infants may be dropped or accidentally injured, while older children may be injured trying to protect an abused parent.

There is also the possibility of abduction by an abusing spouse. Sometimes the abusive spouse will threaten abduction to intimidate or control a partner, and if separation occurs, the abusive parent may abduct the child. If there is a possibility of abduction, this may be grounds for supervising or denying access.[27] In the most serious cases, an abusive parent, usually the father, may kill both his spouse and his children, or may kill his children and commit suicide; such homicides are likely to occur in the context of marital breakdown or separation.[28]

Effect on abused parent. An abused spouse often suffers from lowered self-esteem, depression, drug or alcohol abuse or may take out feelings of powerlessness by mistreating his/her children. A history of physical aggression in the family is "strongly associated with mother's diminished parenting, in that mothers from violent relationships are less warm and more coercive with their children."[29] While it is clear that children suffer from the diminished parenting capacity of an abused parent, there may be difficulty in deciding how to take account of this in a custody dispute. One response may be for the abused parent to present evidence on the positive effects of therapy for victims of spousal abuse, in particular for improving parenting capacity. It may also be important to introduce evidence on the controlling possessive, nature of abusive spouses, and the negative effect that this can have on their parenting capacity.

Indirect effects of spousal abuse on children. There is a growing body of research on the negative effects on children who are exposed to one parent being abused by another. Children who observe interparental abuse are often terrified by the experience, and may not understand it. In some cases witnessing even a single serious incident of abuse can produce post-traumatic stress disorder in a child.[30] Even if a child does not directly observe spousal abuse, living in a home where there is spousal abuse can have serious negative effects. The worst outcomes for children are associated with both observing spousal abuse and being directly abused.

Fortunately, there is evidence that for most children,[31] there will be substantial improvements in behavior and emotional state when the child ceases to live with the abusive parent, and that therapy for the child is often helpful. There is a need for more research into long-term effects on children of spousal abuse, as well as on the effects of different types of legal arrangements (e.g., no access vs. supervised access vs. open access), and to research the effect of different patterns and types of spousal abuse on children.

PROVING ABUSE

In all family cases, and to some extent in all litigation, there are problems of proof associated with witnesses having selective memories and making interpretations of past events most favorable to themselves or to their friends or relatives, as well as deliberate manipulation and dishonesty. Problems of proof can be especially difficult in spousal abuse cases, as the abusive conduct often occurs in private, and the perpetrator will invariably have a psychological tendency to deny or minimize his conduct, as well as a tactical motivation for dishonesty.

Beyond the testimony of the parties, the spouse seeking to prove abuse may submit such evidence as letters from her partner admitting abuse or photographs that depict it. In some cases there will be relatives, neighbors or professionals such as doctors, police or social service workers who can testify as to having observed abusive conduct, or having seen injuries or other evidence of abuse. One of the difficulties in proving abuse is that at the time it occurs, victims often hide or deny their abuse. The 1994 Statistics Canada study of domestic violence against women revealed that only 26% of assaulted women called the police, but most told a friend or neighbor; only one-quarter told a doctor and 22% told no one.[32]

Sometimes children can testify about spousal abuse, though it will generally be preferable not to call them as witnesses and embroil them in parental disputes unless absolutely necessary. In some cases a child's disclosure of spousal abuse may be revealed in an assessor's report, or through a neighbor or relative who heard the child speak about the violence in the home. Often, however, children are very frightened in abusive families, and will be reluctant to disclose, especially in the context of ongoing litigation.[33] Sometimes an abused mother will know of other women involved in previous or subsequent relationships with the abuser, who may also have been victimized, and who can testify as to his abusive behavior. If they were involved in a relationship after the separation with the mother, they may be able to testify about the father's abuse towards children during access visits.

FALSE OR EXAGGERATED ALLEGATIONS

Judges and lawyers need to be aware of problems of false or exaggerated claims of spousal abuse, though false denial or minimization of domestic violence by abusers is a much more common problem than exaggeration by victims.

There are substantial conceptual problems in trying to do research about false claims (or false denials) of abuse. One interesting study by Johnston found very substantial disparities in descriptions of divorced partners about the extent and initiation of verbal and physical aggression during their relationship, with men and women most commonly each reporting that their partner was the aggressor and minimizing their own role. She concluded that it is, in general, more likely men are refusing to acknowledge their violence, since women were offering "more detailed and highly specific accounts, whereas men tended to be vague or dismissive of the event."[34]

The incidence of false allegations probably varies over time (and perhaps locality). Johnston and Campbell compared two samples they studied of divorcing parents who were contesting custody or visitation:[35] With respect to exaggeration and elaboration of incidents . . . in the first sample studied during the years 1982-84, only two women clearly did this. In the second sample, seen more recently during 1989-90, by which time some spouses and their attorneys had become very familiar with the feminist sociopolitical position with respect to domestic violence and the battered women's syndrome–through television, the press and women's shelters–seven women and one man (13%) were judged to have exaggerated the issue of violence as a ploy in the custody dispute.

With more awareness among the public, and a much higher degree of psychological validation and support than in the past, it is quite possible that there may now be more false or exaggerated claims of spousal abuse than in the past. However, many more genuine victims of spousal abuse are also coming forward.

The fact that access to or priority for some services, such as shelters and legal aid, is given to women who identify themselves as abused may also result in some exaggerated or fabricated claims. This is a justified prioritization, and should ensure that lawyers with legal aid clients canvas the issue of abuse, but it may also tend to promote the making of false or exaggerated allegations.

An example of a case where the judge concluded that exaggeration was an issue was in the 1995 Ontario case of *K.A.S. v. D.W.R.*[36] where the parents separated when the child was less than a year old; the father was seeking access more than a year later, while the mother sought to deny access. There was evidence that the father had been controlling and on occasion abusive of the mother; he pled guilty to criminal harassment of her as a consequence of post-separation phone calls, and was convicted of offenses relating to assaults of previous partners. However, Katarynych Prov. J. concluded that much of the mother's testimony had exaggerated incidents of abuse. She observed:

> according to her evidence, she was regularly assaulted by him in the course of their altercations. . . . Over the course of my deliberations, I remained wary, but not entirely disbelieving, of Ms. S's assertions that she was a typical battered woman. Conclusions drawn from stereotypes are . . . highly suspect and I felt that at times she was constructing her testimony to fit carefully the profile advanced by the literature. She was embellishing parts of her evidence on the issue of his assaultive behaviors towards her. . . . Her professed "fear" of contacting the police appeared contrived and significantly inconsistent with the evidence

showing that she was quite prepared to contact the police when it suited her purposes. . . . Overall, it was not fear. . . that I detected in her testimony. It was disdain, tinged with a few vindictive touches as it became important to excise him from her life.

The judge also considered the expert evidence of a "feminist marriage and family therapist" about the effect of spousal violence, but gave it little weight. There was substantial evidence from other individuals that the father had positive involvement with other children, including a child from a previous relationship. While rejecting some of the mother's allegations of spousal abuse, the judge had concerns about the father, and ordered that he should have supervised access, as well as requiring counselling for both parents, with an indication that unsupervised access should begin when the father demonstrated that he was ready.

From a societal perspective, the problem of male abusers denying or minimizing their acts is a more pervasive and serious problem than the problem of women exaggerating or falsifying claims of abuse. However, justice system professionals must approach each case on its own facts, and be prepared to deal with both types of problems.

CUSTODY AND ACCESS

Spousal Abuse as a Factor in Custody and Access Disputes

Until the late 1980s Canadian judges clearly downplayed the importance of domestic violence in all legal contexts, including custody and access proceedings.[37] More recently, however, Canadian judges have begun to place significant weight on spousal abuse as a factor in child related proceedings, though some judges display more understanding of spousal abuse than others. Judges consider the nature and effect of the spousal abuse on the children, as well as the individual circumstances of the case in making a determination.

While over 40 American states have legislation that explicitly mentions domestic violence as a factor in custody and access related cases, in Canada only Newfoundland's *Children's Law Act* s.31(3) makes specific reference to this factor. Canada's *Divorce Act* and legislation in most provinces specifies that in assessing a child's "best interests," the court shall not take account of a person's "past conduct unless that conduct is relevant to the ability of that person to act as a parent of a child."[38] While this statutory provision may exclude evidence of such marital "misconduct" as adultery, many judges have held that spousal abuse is relevant to custody and access and given it significant weight as a factor in deciding about these issues. In many of the "earlier" reported decisions (only from the late 1980s) expert testimony was essential to establish the effects of spousal abuse on children; while this type of expert evidence is still valuable, it is no longer essential in every case.

One of the first reported Canadian cases dealing with the effects of spousal violence on children was *Young v. Young,* decided in 1989. The parties separated after about 15 years of marriage. While the children, aged 11 and 13, expressed a wish to live with their father, Bolan L.J.S.C. was concerned that the father was trying to manipulate the children by showering them with lavishness during visits. There was significant emotional abuse of the wife by the husband throughout the marriage, several incidents of sexual abuse in the last two years of cohabitation, and two physical assaults after the separation. There was expert testimony from three mental health professionals. The judge remarked that "relevancy of this finding of abuse is that it goes to [the father's] ability to parent the children on a full time basis." She accepted the expert testimony based on the literature on the effect of spousal abuse on children, namely that:[39]

1. An abuser who goes without therapy will continue to abuse in another relationship;
2. Children who witness abuse can become abused even though the abuse is not intentionally directed at them;
3. Abused male children often become abusers and abused female children may become compliant to abusers.

The judge awarded custody to the mother with liberal, but structured, access to the father.

Since *Young* there have been many reported Canadian cases in which mothers who have been victims of emotional and physical abuse have called expert witnesses to testify about the negative effects of this abuse on the children, and hence explain why the father should not get custody.[40] These experts have also explained how the abuse has affected the adult victim, for example, causing loss of self-esteem and depression, and how counselling can (or has) helped the victim to recover and be an effective parent.

In some more recent cases, abused women have been able to obtain custody without calling expert evidence, even in the face of an assessor's report favorable to the father. At least some judges are now prepared to take "judicial notice" of the harmful effects of spousal abuse on children.

For example, in the 1995 British Columbia case of *Stewart v. Mix*[41] the parties cohabited for seven years, during which the man attempted to constantly control the woman, verbally abused her daily, and displayed a temper that could quickly be inflamed to violence, including assaulting his partner. The last assault occurred in the presence of their then two-year-old son at the start of an access visit, which was the only occasion on which charges were laid. An assessor recommended that the father should have custody, in large part because the mother had moved and formed a new relationship and had a young baby, and the assessor felt that the older boy had bonded to the father's extended family. The judge rejected the assessor's recommendation and observed that the "father has a history of a violent temper, was consistently jealous of his common law wife, used violence when aroused. . . . It is difficult to see how he can be considered a good role model." The judge awarded custody to the mother, with specified access to the father, including a provision for supervision of the exchange of the child.

While Canadian judges are generally starting to be aware of the effects of spousal abuse on parenting capacity, it is clear that this is not always the determinative factor in a custody dispute, and some judges still give this factor little weight. For example, in a 1995 Saskatchewan case the judge questioned "what relation might there be between the violence and the capacity to be a custodial parent. Custody is not a means of punishing a perpetrator."[42]

Children's Wishes

Children's wishes can be very problematic in spousal abuse situations because the abused parent may be seen by the children as weak and "ineffectual," and children may wish to align themselves with the "stronger," more powerful, abusive parent. An abusive spouse can be very manipulative and the denigration of the other parent may influence a child's relationship with the victim of abuse. It can be psychologically difficult for an abused parent to accept a situation where children are ambivalent or express a desire to live with a parent who has been an abusive spouse. At times the abusive parent may coerce or threaten the children to express views favorable to himself. In some cases, a man who is an abusive spouse will have a superficially good relationship with a child, especially a daughter who may be treated "princess like," and who will express a desire to live with him.

Perhaps the most infamous Canadian example of this was the *Thatcher*[43] tragedy, where the father was a former premier; as his relationship to his wife began to deteriorate he became increasingly demeaning and controlling towards her. His sons and eventually his daughter indicated a strong desire to live with him, and continued to express support for him even after he was convicted of the murder of their mother, which occurred after she had remarried.

Sometimes individuals who abuse their partners present very well, are highly manipulative, and are able to "con" assessors, especially those who may not be familiar with patterns of abuse, or who are impressed by children's wishes and their apparently close links to the abuser. This may be challenging for the counsel of an abused spouse to counteract, but it is possible to do so, in particular by introducing independent evidence of abuse as well as testimony of other mental health professionals on the effects of spousal abuse on children. The courts have stated that they are not bound by an assessor's recommendation or a child's wishes, especially in situations of spousal abuse.[44] On the other hand, a child's wishes can be an important factor favoring a parent who abused a partner but appears to pose no risk of direct abuse to a child. A child's wishes should have less weight in cases where there has been spousal abuse than in other contexts.

Joint Legal Custody

Joint custody is not appropriate if there has been a history of spousal abuse and the abused parent is unable to effectively negotiate issues without the involvement of an advocate. Indeed joint custody is not appropriate if there is a high level of parental conflict or serious power imbalances even without abuse;[45] there is all the more concern if there is a history of spousal violence. There are Canadian judgments which recognize that where there is a history of significant disagreement and argument, let alone abuse, joint custody is not likely to be appropriate.[46] It would, however, be preferable to follow the example of several American states and have a statutory prohibition against joint custody if there is a significant history of domestic violence,[47] as there are Canadian cases in which judges have imposed joint legal custody despite a history of spousal abuse.[48]

Interactive Spousal Abuse

In their analysis, Johnston and Campbell characterize some marital situations as ones of "interactive violence," where either party can initiate physical aggression as part of a struggle for control, with mutual blaming and anger. In general, these cases seem to have a relatively good prognosis for elimination of violence after separation. Some Canadian cases seem to fit this scenario. In *Derow v. Derow,*[49] Archambault J. concluded that both parents had been abusive towards one another in the presence of their children, though the husband had the more serious anger problem and a greater tendency to initiate violence. The court awarded the mother custody, but the father was to have "liberal access"; in view of conflict between the parents, at least initially access was not to be overnight and the judge indicated that the father would be "well advised to seek counselling" for his lack of anger management. There is serious doubt about whether it is appropriate to have "liberal" or "reasonable" access in high conflict situations. It is preferable to specify the terms of access in such cases, to avoid the possibility of altercations or exploitation around the arranging of access.[50]

Imposing a requirement of counselling is not a solution to all problems of spousal abuse, since not all individuals who take counselling or therapy overcome their problems, but it is a useful option for cases where a judge is determined to allow a parent with a history of spousal abuse to have custody, or even access. Indeed, it would also be appropriate for some parents with a history of violence to be required to take a course or receive counselling about the effects of their violence on children.

Separation Engendered Violence

Johnston and Campbell categorize some cases as ones in which abusive conduct is not a constant feature of the spousal relationship, but rather is confined to a few episodes around the time of separation. Such situations often have a better prognosis for future relations than relationships where violence has been more pervasive.

In *Hallett v. Hallett* the parents cohabited for 12 years, in a relationship that was apparently free of physical violence. During the process of separation, which went over several months, the man assaulted the woman on three occasions, in incidents involving shoving and some hitting; one of the two children saw one of these incidents and later told an assessor that he was frightened by it. The police were called and charges laid after the third assault, and the woman and her children went to live in a battered woman's shelter. While the man questioned whether the woman should have had the advantage of a support network and long-term housing for "battered women," a worker from the shelter testified on behalf of the mother at the custody trial. Schnall Prov. J. observed:[51]

> This does not justify his conduct by any means, but it does reflect that physical violence . . . was not the usual characteristic of the parties' 14-year relationship . . . these three incidents were apparently out of character for [the man].

The custody assessor did not consider the spousal abuse to be an important factor, and did not question the children about this issue to any extent. The judge concluded that the assaults were "not relevant" to issues of custody and access, though she criticized the assessor for not exploring the issue more fully. The mother was awarded sole custody, with specified access to the father on alternate week-ends and vacation periods.

Abusive Women

As discussed above, women are most commonly the victims of spousal abuse, and are more seriously affected if there is a mutually abusive relationship, but there are some cases in which the woman is the initiator of violence.

There have been a few recent Canadian cases in which it is apparent that the woman was the more aggressive partner. Sometimes this reflects the mother's emotional condition, while in others she may be psychotic. Even if the woman has initiated the spousal abuse, there is often a mitigating factor, such as the mother is clearly the child's primary caregiver, which supports her custody claim, and abusive spousal behavior by a wife is less decisive in a custody dispute than abuse by a husband.

In *D.M. v. L.M.*,[52] the court accepted that during the marriage the mother had behaved in an erratic and violent fashion towards the father and the contents of the house, and that the "child [had] been exposed to these outbursts in a totally unacceptable way." The mother had interim custody. A court appointed assessor recommended that the father should have custody, but the judge chose to rely on the opinion of the mother's doctor, to the effect that after the assessment but before the trial the mother's emotional condition substantially improved and was under control by drug treatment. The court ordered joint legal custody, with the principal residence with the mother and extensive access to the father.

Interim Orders

In cases involving spousal abuse, and in particular violence, there is often a need for quick action to protect the victim of abuse and ensure that she is not driven away from the children, which would allow the abuser to later make a continuity of care argument for custody. Arguably in a situation of potential for serious harm to a child from an abusive spouse, a parent has a duty to take immediate steps to protect a child and seek a court order later. As stated by L'Heureux-Dubé J. in the Supreme Court of Canada in *Young v. Young:*[53] "a custodial parent aware of sexual or other abuse by the noncustodial parent would be remiss in his or her duty to the child not to cut off access by the abuser immediately, with or without a court order." The same principle should apply if the parents are residing together and one parent believes that it is necessary to leave to protect the children. This view is reinforced by *Criminal Code s.*285, which creates a defense to a prosecution for parental child abduction if action is taken to protect a child from danger of "imminent harm."

Pending trial, victims of abuse should make an application to a court for interim custody, restrictions on or/and termination of access by the abuser and quite possibly interim exclusive possession of the matrimonial home.

Access

The so called "friendly parent" provision of the federal *Divorce Act* s.16(10) provides that:

> (10) . . . the court shall give effect to the principle that a child of the marriage should have as much contact with each spouse as is consistent

with the best interests of the child and, for that purpose, shall take into consideration the willingness of the person for whom custody is sought to facilitate such contact.

In practice s.16(10) creates a presumption that access with the non-custodial parent is in the best interests of a child. While this provision is used by advocates for abusive spouses to secure access rights, most judges accept that in cases where there is evidence of a significant risk of harm to a child, access will be restricted or even denied. Section s.16(10), however, may sometimes make those seeking custody reluctant to put forward a claim to restrict access for fear of appearing "unfriendly."

Supervised Access

Supervised access may be appropriate if there is a reasonable apprehension of a threat to the safety of a child during a visit, if the child is afraid of or refusing to visit, or if there is a reasonable apprehension that the non-custodial parent will abduct the child. Supervision can help reduce fears of a custodial parent if there has been a history of abuse. Some supervisors will keep records and are able to testify about the quality of parent-child interaction during a visit. In some cases there will be sufficient evidence of hostility or stress on the part of the child during supervised access to obtain an order terminating all access, though this will generally require that the supervisor is a person qualified to express an opinion about parent-child relationships.[54] In a number of localities, supervised access projects have been funded, at least in part by the government, and these are valuable services for helping to maintain parent-child relationships while protecting children. Unfortunately, some of these services are facing resource cutbacks, and they are becoming less available in Canada. In the absence of a suitable supervisor, access should be terminated if there is a risk to safety of a child.

A supervisor can be a professional, a volunteer or a relative (e.g., a member of the father's family chosen by the mother). It is important that the supervisor not be an inappropriate person, in particular not someone who may be controlled by the abuser and who may not actually protect the child.

While the legal precedents indicate that access should be ordered only if it will actually benefit a child, there may be a tendency for some judges to order supervised access as a "compromise" (or some might say a "cop out"), rather than take the hard decision of terminating all access. Given its intrusive, expensive and artificial nature, supervised access should not be seen as a permanent arrangement when a parent is too much of a risk to be alone with a child, but rather should be as a "temporary measure . . . to help resolve a parental impasse over access."[55] Preferably during the period of supervised access, the abuser will be taking steps, such as participation in counselling, that will reduce the risk to the child and permit unsupervised access at some future time.[56]

Some parents have such a high potential for unpredictable or uncontrollable violence or abuse towards the children, that a court should not order supervised access. A judge should also be concerned about subtle non-physical threats or psychological abuse that can occur during even supervised access and be a basis for rejecting this option. Ultimately, even if there is no immediate risk to the child, a court should deny any access if it is not satisfied that the child will receive some benefit from visits.

Exchange Supervision

In some situations where there is a concern about the potential for violence, or at least verbal abuse, between the separated parents but the risk of direct harm to the children seems low, it may be appropriate to have supervision of the process of exchanging care of the child for access visits. In high conflict situations, the process of exchange of the child has the potential for violence or abuse. Supervision may be especially appropriate during an initial period after separation when the risk of violence may be higher. Exchange supervision is less costly, intrusive and restrictive than access supervision, but should only be contemplated if there is no significant risk of direct harm to the children from the abusive spouse.

For example, in *Fullerton v. Fullerton*[57] the parents separated after five years of marriage, during which the husband assaulted the wife many times, including breaking her jaw and holding a knife to her throat. The three children observed many of these assaults. After several years of access that apparently occurred without incident, the man assaulted the mother on an occasion when she came to his residence to get the children at the end of an access visit. While even the father acknowledged that the violent nature of his relationship with his wife had an adverse effect on the children, the mother accepted that he did not pose a direct threat to the children when they were in his care. Citing the *Divorce Act* s.16(10) the judge felt that the children had a "right" to access to their father (though there was no evidence in the judgment about their views). The judge concluded that any "risk of harm to the children can . . . be substantially eliminated if the parties have no contact with each other." Accordingly the court ordered that arrangements should be made for a third person acceptable to both parents to pick up and return the children, with the judge to select someone if the parents could not agree. The father was also to abstain from consuming drugs or alcohol during access and 24 hours prior, and to "refrain from any displays of anger, violence or threats thereof in the presence of the children." While this last condition might appear desirable, one may question how it can be enforced in a way that would not unfortunately involve the children in "reporting on" their father. If there had not been several years of access with only the one assaultive incident, termination of access may have been more appropriate given the father's history of violence towards the mother, and its negative effects on the children.

Some American judges order that the access exchange should occur at a police station or in a court house, to limit any threat of violence at the time of exchange. While this may be a last resort, these locations may be frightening for a child as well as inconvenient.[58] Finding a suitable, willing exchange supervisor is preferable. It should be appreciated that if a man with a history of spousal abuse is awarded custody, the exercise of access rights by the mother may be occasions for continuing the abuse, intimidation or control, and a court order may be required to supervise the exchange of the child or otherwise prevent harassment.

Denial of Access

Although the legislation and case law create a presumption that continued contact between a noncustodial parent and child is in the child's best interests, a significant number of reported Canadian decisions have recognized that in situations where there has been a history of serious spousal abuse or violence, access may not be in the child's best interests and should not be permitted. One of the leading cases on denial of access to an abusive spouse is the 1992 Ontario Court of Appeal decision in *B.P.M. v. B.L.D.E.M.* The woman had a son from a previous relationship; the parties were married for two years, during which time the wife gave birth to a daughter. The father began to be abusive during the pregnancy, undermining the woman's relationship with her family and having "violent rages"; after the birth he became increasingly violent and threatened to kill her. In 1985 the woman left out of concern for the safety of herself and the children. After the separation, while the harassment and threats against the mother escalated, the father had access to his daughter. The man often followed the woman around, left her harassing notes, and was verbally abusive to her at the time of access. He sometimes threatened not to return the child after access. Despite this type of conduct, judges in 1986, 1988 and 1989 permitted unsupervised access; during this time the woman moved from Alberta, where the parties were married, to Ontario to be near her parents. The daughter was finding the visits stressful. Supervised access was ordered, but the child continued to experience stress related to the visits. Eventually in 1991, access rights were terminated, a decision affirmed by the Ontario Court of Appeal in 1992. The Court of Appeal characterized the man's post separation conduct as "incessant and obsessive," creating stress on both the child and mother.[59] Although the child continued to tell an assessor that she was not adverse to seeing her father, as long as it was infrequent and supervised, Abella J.A. observed that a court should also consider the effects of continued access on the custodial parent, especially when she has been the victim of continued harassment by the father:[60]

> The needs of children and their parents are obviously inextricable, particularly between children and the parent on whom they depend for their day-to-day care. . . . But the central figure in the assessment is the dependent child. . . . There is no evidence of any bond whatsoever between this child and her father. On the contrary, there is evidence that she was hostile towards him during supervised access visits, withdrawn before and after the visits, had nightmares and some bed wetting.

Abella J.A. rejected an application for supervised access; although Finlayson J.A. dissented and would have permitted supervised access, the majority position of Abella J.A. must be regarded as the dominant judicial view. It would seem that courts are becoming more willing to terminate access and one would hope that a mother and child would not now be expected to live through years of unsupervised access with such an abusive man, as occurred in the late 1980s in *B.P.M. v. B.L.D.E.M.* Although the situations will be "rare," there have been cases involving abusive spouses where the courts have refused access without any attempt to try access, even on a supervised basis.[61]

If a court has initial concerns about access and orders supervised access, the court may consider abusive conduct or a failure to regularly visit as a reason for terminating supervised access. Similarly if it is acknowledged at the time of the original access order that the man has been abusive and must take part in counselling, the failure to complete a program or the completion of a program but the continuation of harassment and threats against the mother, will justify termination of all access.

The unhappiness of a custodial parent about access, or her sense of anger or hatred towards the non-custodial parent, do not justify a termination of access. However, where there is a history of abuse of the custodial parent during, and especially after the end of the period of cohabitation, the feelings of the custodial parent may legitimately be an important factor in terminating access. In *Matheson v. Sabourin* the parties cohabited for one-and-a-half years during which they had a son. The father physically and verbally abused the mother during the period of cohabitation, and continued to harass and assault her after the separation. In terminating all access Hardman Prov. J. wrote:[62]

> There can be no question that it is dangerous to state as a principle of law that if access causes stress for the custodial parent then it should be terminated. However, it is clear that there are circumstances where the

impact on the custodial parent is such that extinguishing access must be considered. . . . .No one could put it more clearly than the [mother] . . . did in her evidence: "I'm trying to raise him and you're trying to destroy me and that affects him."

Again, it may be argued that even in this 1994 decision in *Matheson v. Sabourin,* the woman and child were subjected to abuse for far too long before access was terminated. In those situations where spousal abuse continues after separation, access should be terminated, or at very least the exchange of the child should be supervised. A parent with primary responsibility for the care of a child should not be subjected to abuse so that her former partner can continue to enjoy a relationship with the child.

While the wishes of a child are not determinative, they will be an important consideration in dealing with access issues, especially those involving a battering husband. When there has been a significant history of spousal abuse and the children have become fearful of their father and express a desire not to see him, this should be a very persuasive factor in denying access.[63] Conversely, a child's continued desire to have contact with a parent with a history of spousal abuse is likely to influence a court to permit access, at least where the court is satisfied that the abusive partner does not pose a direct risk to the child.[64]

CONCLUSION

All justice system professionals who work with divorcing couples, including lawyers, judges, police, assessors and mediators, need knowledge and training to deal most effectively with situations where spousal abuse is an issue, and in particular to be aware of the risks faced by victims of abuse and their children. These professionals must appreciate that spousal abuse covers a broad range of conduct. Given the wide range of abusive spousal conduct and the high proportion of separations and divorces that involve at least one incident of spousal abuse, it has been necessary for professionals to develop differentiated responses that take account of the specific situation of abuse, and its effect on the particular parents and children involved.

While there are clearly some judges who are less sensitive to the issue, Canadian jurisprudence now recognizes the importance of spousal abuse as a factor in custody and access disputes. Judges are starting to appreciate the need for differentiated responses, depending on the nature of the abuse, the effects of that abuse on the children and the prognosis for the future, as well as on the risk of immediate harm.

Newfoundland and most American states[65] have statutes that specifically acknowledge the significance of domestic violence for child related proceedings. The 1998 Report of the Parliamentary Special Joint Committee recommended the amendment of Canadian legislation so that any "proven history of family violence" should be a factor in any "best interests" decision about a child.[66] The enactment of this type of legislation is desirable, as it would clarify the law, and facilitate the education of lawyers, judges and other professionals as well as the public. However, the Committee's use of the term *"proven"* is unnecessary and reflects the bias of some members of the Committee that there are a large number of cases of false allegations of domestic violence. More important than changing legislation is improving the enforcement of present laws, in particular ensuring that the remedies afforded to victims of domestic violence, such as restraining orders, are effective. The protection of victims must be a priority. There is a need for more support for supervised access programs, and for appropriate services for victims of domestic violence, including counselling for victims and the children of these families, as well as counselling programs for abusive spouses.

There is also a need for further research, such as refinement of the work of Johnston and Campbell on different patterns and effects of spousal abuse, as well as research into the effects on children from abusive relationships of different patterns of access, supervised access and denial of access, and on the most effective short- and long-term strategies for reducing the incidence of spouse abuse.

NOTES

1. See, e.g., Hon. Bertha Wilson, "Family Violence" (1992), 5 Can. J.W.L. 137, at 140: "Violence against women in the home is an expression and manifestation of power and is perpetuated by the fact that men do and women do not have power in our society."

2. Janet Johnston, "Domestic Violence and Parent-Child Relationships in Families Disputing Custody" (1995), 9 Aust. J. Fam L.12-25, at 16.

3. For a history of the treatment of wife abuse in Canada, see N. Zoe Hilton, "One in Ten: The Struggle and Disempowerment of the Battered Women's Movement" (1989), 7 Can J. Fam L. 313-336.

4. See generally Canadian Panel on Violence Against Women, *Changing the Landscape: Ending Violence-Achieving Equality* (1993, Ottawa, Ministry of Supply and Services Canada); and Linda MacLeod, *Battered But Not Beaten: Preventing Wife Battering in Canada* (1987, Ottawa, Canadian Advisory Council on the Status of Women).

5. [1990] 1 S.C.R 852, 55 C.C.C. (3d) 97. These developments in the courts coincided with the appointment of more women judges, with *Lavallee* written by Bertha Wilson, the first woman appointed to the Supreme Court of Canada.

6. See *R. v. Malott* [1998]1 S.C.R. 123, 121 C.C.C. (3d) 456 which made clear that an abused woman does not have to establish that she is suffering from a "syndrome," but rather that her experiences of abuse and her psychological state are rele-

vant to the issue of whether she believed, on reasonable grounds, that she could not preserve herself from death or grievous bodily harm without taking the action that she did.

7. In Canada see, e.g., "Joudrie cleared in attack," *Globe and Mail,* 10 May 1996; and "Disorder, disorder in the court," *Globe and Mail,* 13 May, 1996. The most highly publicized trial in world history, the O.J. Simpson prosecution in California, also raised the issue of spousal violence.

8. "Women heckled, men grilled at federal hearings," *Canadian Press,* 31 March 1998. An example of an analysis that has important elements of insight that were lost in excessive rhetoric and exclusively gendered analysis is provided by The Canadian Panel on Violence Against Women, *Changing the Landscape: Ending Violence–Achieving Equality* (1993, Ottawa, Ministry of Supply and Services); critiqued in John Fekete, *Moral Panic: Biopolitics Rising* (1994, Montreal, Robert Davies Publishing).

9. Karen Rodgers, "Wife Assault: The Findings of a National Survey" (March, 1994), *Juristat* 14:9 (Ottawa, Statistics Canada).

10. *Criminal Code of Canada* s.264, criminal harassment, and s.372(3), harassing phone calls.

11. Another 1994 Statistics Canada report, this one on spousal homicide, revealed that women are more than three times as likely to be killed by their spouses than are men, and nine times as likely to be killed by a spouse as by a stranger. Wilson & Daly, *Spousal Homicide, Juristat* 14(8) (1994, Ottawa, Statistics Canada); see also Wilson, Johnson & Daly, "Lethal and Nonlethal Violence Against Wives" (1995), 37 Can. J. Crim. 305-330; and "Femicide increasing study shows," 29 April 1997, *Globe & Mail,* p. A6.

12. Donald Dutton, *The Batterer: A Psychological Profile* (1996, Basic Books).

13. Wilson & Daly (1994), *supra* n.11.

14. Lenore Walker, *The Battered Woman Syndrome* (1984, New York, Springer Publishing).

15. Janet Johnston & Linda Campbell, "Parent Child Relationships in Domestic Violence Families Disputing Custody" (1993), 312(3) Fam. & Con. Cts. Rev. 282-298. They studied 140 domestic violence cases.

16. Peter Jaffe and Gary Austin, "The impact of witnessing violence on children in custody and visitation disputes," presented at the International Family Violence Research Conference, Durham, New Hampshire, July 1995.

17. John Fekete, *Moral Panic: Biopolitics Rising* (1994, Montreal, Robert Davies Publishing), Chapter 2, reporting on a study by Schulman (Kentucky, 1979).

18. See Rhonda Lenton, "Power versus Feminist Theories of Wife Abuse" (1995), 37 Can. J. Crim. 305-330; and Lenton "Feminist versus Interpersonal Power Theories of Wife Abuse Revisited" (1995), 37 Can. J. Crim. 567-574, for a sociologist who takes this position, and reviews some of the feminist literature that takes a more strictly gender based approach.

19. See, Parliament of Canada, Report of The Special Joint Committee on Child Custody and Access, *For the Sake of the Children* (Ottawa, December 1998), p. 78-82.

20. See especially M.A. Straus, R.J. Gelles & S. Steintmetz, *Behind Closed Doors: Violence in the American Family* (1980, Sage Publishing); and M.A. Straus &

R.J. Gelles, "Has family violence decreased? A reassessment of the Straus and Gelles data" (1988), 50 J. Marr. & Fam. 281-291.

21. Johnston (1995) *supra* n.2, at 16.

22. See discussion below. See also, e.g., *MacDonald v. MacDonald* (Ont. Gen Div. 1991), *Lawyers Weekly* No. 1112-016 where the wife was alcoholic and violent towards her husband; the separation occurred after she stabbed him while he was driving. Flaningan J. reduced the amount of spousal support that she would have been entitled to on account of her "gross repudiation of the relationship."

23. L. Newmark et al., "Domestic Violence and Empowerment in Custody and Visitation Cases" (1995), 33 Fam & Council. Cts. Rev. 30, at 32.

24. Johnston (1995), *supra* n.2 at 24.

25. In general in this section, see P. Jaffe, D. Wolfe & S. Wilson, *Children of Battered Women* (1990, Newbury Park, CA, Sage); and E. Peled, P. Jaffe & J. Edelson (eds), *Ending the Cycle of Violence: Community Responses to Children of Battered Women* (1995, Newbury Park, CA. Sage).

26. Straus, Gelles & Steinmetz (1980), *supra* n. 20; 28% of children in couples classified as having high levels of violence were abused in year prior to the interview, and 77% had been abused at some time in the past. An American study based on a large population survey reveals that the greater the use of violence by a spouse against a partner, the more likely that person will also physically abuse children; the correlation was especially strong for male abusers: Ross, "Risk of Physical Abuse to Children of Spouse Abusing Parents" (1996), 26 Ch. Abuse & Neglect 589.

27. See, e.g., *Zahr v. Zahr* (1994), 24 Alta. L.R. (3d) 274 (Q.B.).

28. Wilson & Daly (1994), *supra* n. 11, report that 94% of "familicides" (killing of one's spouse and children) in Canada were committed by men, while 76% of spousal killings not also involving the killing of children were committed by men.

29. J. Johnston, "High-Conflict Divorce" (1994), 4(1) The Future of Children, 165-182, at 175.

30. Articles in this volume by King et al., and Rossman & Ho. See also D.G. Saunders, "Child Custody Decisions in Families Experiencing Woman Abuse" (1994), 39 Social Work 1; H.A.Davidson, "Child Abuse and Domestic Violence: Legal Connections and Controversies" (1995), 29 Fam. L. Q. 357-373.

31. P. Mertin, "A Follow Up Study of Children from Domestic Violence" (1995), 9 Aust J. Fam. L. 76-85.

32. Karen Rodgers (1994) *supra* n.9.

33. F. Lehrman, "Factoring Domestic Violence into Custody Cases" [Feb. 1996] *Trial*, 32 at 38.

34. Johnston (1995) *supra* n.2 at 16.

35. Johnston & Campbell (1993), *supra* n.15 at 286.

36. [1995] O.J. 1711 (Prov. Div.). For similar cases, see *Sekhri v. Mahli* (1993), 112 Sask.R. 253 (U.F.C.); *Lindsay v. Lindsay* (1985), 19 R.F.L. (4th) 163 (Ont. Gen. Div.); *Brigante v. Brigante* (1991), 32 R.F.L. (3d) 299 (Ont. U.F.C.).

37. See, e.g., *Peterson v. Peterson* (1988), 85 N.S.R. (2d) 107 (Co. Ct.) and more generally Canadian Panel on Violence Against Women, *Changing the Landscape: Ending Violence–Achieving Equality* (1993, Ottawa, Ministry of Supply and Services Canada) 229-231.

38. *Divorce Act,* R.S.C. 1985, c.3 (2nd Supp), s. 16(9).

39. (1989), 19 R.F.L (3d) 227, at 235 (Ont S.C.).

40. See, e.g., *Thind v Thind,* [1994] B.C.J. 1131 (S.C.), per Meredith J.; and *Blackburn v. Blackburn* [1995] O.J. 2321 (Prov. Div.), per Dunbar J.

41. [1995] B.C.J. 2414 (S.C.).

42. *Allen v. Allen,* [1995] S.J. 410 (Q.B., Fam Div.) per Armstrong J.

43. See, e.g. (1980), 16 R.F.L. (2d) 263 (Sask. Q.B.) & 20 R.F.L. (2d) 75 (Sask Q.B.). At least initially, the court did not rely on the children's expressed wishes, though eventually it did. See M. Siggins, *A Canadian Tragedy: JoAnn and Colin Thatcher: A Story of Love and Hate* (1985, Toronto, MacMillan).

44. See, e.g., *Young v. Young* (1989), 22 R.F.L. (3d) 227 (Ont. S.C.), discussed above. More recently see *A.J.M. v. T.D.M.* [1996] O.J. 1342 (Gen Div.).

45. See, e.g., J. Johnston (1994), *supra* n.29.

46. See, e.g., *D.E.C. v. D.T.G.* [1997] O.J. 1976 (Gen. Div.); and *T.N.L.* v. *B.C.M.* [1996] B.C.J. 2743 (Prov. Ct.).

47. Family Violence Project of the National Council of Juvenile and Family Court Judges, "Family Violence in Child Custody Statutes: An Analysis of State Codes and Legal Practice" (1995), 29 Fam. L. Q. 197, at 200.

48. See, e.g., *Boothby v. Boothby* [1996] O.J. 4346 (Prov. Div.) where the mother testified that the father was "controlling, demanding and . . . emotionally abusive" towards her during the period that the parties cohabited. He had interim custody after separation, and on occasion thwarted the mother's access visits; the court awarded joint legal custody, with primary residence to the mother.

49. [1996] S.J. 207 (Q.B. Fam. Div.).

50. J. Johnston (1994), *supra* n.29.

51. [1993] O.J. 3382 (Prov. Ct.) per Schnall J. (Quicklaw online).

52. [1993] O.J. 1973 (Ont. Prov. Ct.) per Pedlar Prov. J.

53. (1993), 49 R.F.L. (3d) 117, at 184 (S.C.C.).

54. *B.P.M.v. B.L.D.M.*(1992), 42 R.F.L. (3d) 349, at 360 (Ont. C.A.).

55. Judge Norris Weisman, "On Access After Parental Separation" (1992), 36 R.F.L. (3d) 35, at 74, quoted with approval by Abella J.A. in *B.P.M. v. B.L.D.M.* (1992), 42 R.F.L. (3d) 349, at 360 (Ont. C.A.).

56. See, e.g., *F.K.H.W. B. v. F.S.M.W.B.* [1995] N.S.J. 471 (Fam. Ct.) and *D.F.M. v. J.S.S.* (1995), 17 R.F.L. (4th) 283 (Alta, CA). The failure to comply with terms of supervised access, such as obtaining counselling for anger management, may result in the termination of even supervised access: *C.D. v. J.B.* [1996] A.Q. 181 (Sup. Ct.).

57. (1994), 7 R.F.L. (4th) 272 (N.B. Fam Div.).

58. R. B. Straus, "Supervised Visitation and Family Violence" (1995), 29 Fam. L. Q. 229-253.

59. Counsel may face a real dilemma in deciding how much to emphasize the negative effects of the stress and abuse on parenting capacity. This type of evidence may be important to terminate access, but it may also invite a claim for custody from the abuser based on the "incapacity" of the victim of abuse.

60. (1992), 42 R.F.L. (3d) 349, at 359-60 (Ont. C.A.). See also *Abdo v. Abdo* (1993), 50 R.F.L. (3d) 171 (N.S.C.A.); and *E.H. v. T.G.* (1995), 18 R.F.L. (4th) 21 (N.S.C.A.).

61. *Pereira v. Pereira* [1995] B.C.J. 2151 (S.C.) husband was violent towards wife during marriage, and after separation even attempted to arrange for her murder.

62. [1994] O.J. 991 (Prov. Ct.) (Quicklaw online).

63. See, e.g., *DiMeco v. DiMeco* [1995] O..J.3650 (U.F.C.) where father was violent and abusive to mother, including a threat made in the presence of the children to kill her; the children told an assessor that they feared him; access was denied.

64. See, e.g., *Brusselers v. Shirt* [1996] A.J. 333 (Q.B.).

65. In USA forty-four states have enacted custody and access legislation which contains specific provisions concerning domestic violence, many creating a presumption that it is not in a child's best interests to be placed in the custody of a parent who has abused a partner. See Family Violence Project of the National Council of Juvenile and Family Court Judges, "Family Violence in Child Custody Statutes: An Analysis of State Codes and Legal Practice" (1995), 29 Fam. L. Q. 197-227.

66. Parliament of Canada, Report of the Special Joint Committee on Child Custody and Access, *For the Sake of the Children* (Ottawa, 1998), Recommendation 16.11 on legislative changes, and Recommendations 34 & 35 on support service changes.

Custody and Visitation Trends
in the United States
in Domestic Violence Cases

Nancy K. D. Lemon

SUMMARY. This article addresses custody and visitation trends in domestic violence cases in the United States. It defines domestic violence behaviorally, looks briefly at its prevalence, and discusses national policy statements and studies. It also examines statutory trends concerning the role of domestic violence in custody and visitation cases, including the O. J. Simpson guardianship case. Practical suggestions for litigants and judges are included. The article concludes that the way domestic violence issues are treated in custody and visitation cases is often problematic, and calls for specific reforms. *[Article copies available for a fee from The Haworth Document Delivery Service: 1-800-342-9678. E-mail address: getinfo@haworthpressinc.com <Website: http://www.haworthpressinc.com>]*

KEYWORDS. Visitation, statutes, policy issues, family law recommendations, practice guides

INTRODUCTION

Custody and visitation cases are a very important area within the larger domestic violence arena. The deleterious effects of growing up in a domestic

This article is based in part on a presentation given June 5, 1997 at London, Ontario.

Address correspondence to: Nancy K. D. Lemon, JD, Boalt Hall School of Law, UC Berkeley, Berkeley, CA 94720.

[Haworth co-indexing entry note]: "Custody and Visitation Trends in the United States in Domestic Violence Cases." Lemon, Nancy K. D. Co-published simultaneously in *Journal of Aggression, Maltreatment & Trauma* (The Haworth Maltreatment & Trauma Press, an imprint of The Haworth Press, Inc.) Vol. 3, No. 1 (#5), 2000, pp. 329-343; and: *Children Exposed to Domestic Violence: Current Issues in Research, Intervention, Prevention, and Policy Development* (ed: Robert A. Geffner, Peter G. Jaffe, and Marlies Sudermann) The Haworth Maltreatment & Trauma Press, an imprint of The Haworth Press, Inc., 2000, pp. 329-343. Single or multiple copies of this article are available for a fee from The Haworth Document Delivery Service [1-800-342-9678, 9:00 a.m. - 5:00 p.m. (EST). E-mail address: getinfo@haworthpressinc.com].

329

violence setting can either be exacerbated or diminished by the court, depending on what the custody and visitation orders provide. Joint custody, liberal visitation, or sole custody awards to batterers provide the opportunity for ongoing and serious problems for years to come. On the other hand, orders which are adequately investigated and well crafted can provide contexts for ongoing contact between the perpetrator and the children, if appropriate under the circumstances of each case, while protecting both the children and the formerly battered partner.

This article, therefore, addresses policy statements concerning domestic violence and custody or visitation, legislative trends, and trends in case law. A high-profile custody decision in which domestic violence was a factor, the O. J. Simpson case in California, is also analyzed. The article concludes with recommendations for improving the family law system's response to domestic violence.

The working definition of domestic violence used in this article is the deliberate use of threats, violence, and other types of abuse in intimate teen or adult relationships in order to exert power and control over the victim. These mechanisms include: intimidation; emotional abuse; isolation; minimizing, denying, and blaming; using children; using male privilege; economic abuse; and coercion and threats.[1] This article focuses primarily on the mechanism of using children, as this is *a* type of power and control often seen in custody litigation between batterers and their former partners. Since the issue of the effects on children from living with batterers is developed more fully in prior articles of this volume, the reader is encouraged to apply all of that information when thinking about the response to this problem in family law courts.

U.S. National Policy Statements About Custody and Domestic Violence

What does all of this information mean in terms of custody cases involving domestic violence? First, many mainstream national US entities have issued strong policy statements regarding this issue. These include the US Congress, the American Bar Association, the National Council of Juvenile and Family Court Judges, and the American Psychological Association. The US Congress unanimously passed a resolution which declared in 1990, stating:

> It is the sense of Congress that, for purposes of determining child custody, credible evidence of physical abuse of a spouse should create a statutory presumption that it is detrimental to the child to be placed in the custody of the abusive spouse . . . There is an alarming bias against battered spouses in contemporary child custody trends such as joint custody . . . [J]oint custody guarantees the batterer continued access and control over the battered spouse's life through their children . . . [J]oint custody, forced upon hostile parents, can create a dangerous psychological environment for a child . . . [2]

Similarly, the American Bar Association has stated:

> Anyone who has committed severe or repetitive abuse to an intimate partner is presumptively not a fit sole or joint custodian for children. Where there is proof of abuse, batterers should be presumed by law to be unfit custodians for their children.[3]

The National Council of Juvenile and Family Court Judges (NCJFCJ) spent several years developing a Model Code on Domestic and Family Violence, which provides:

> In every proceeding in which there is at issue a dispute as to the custody of a child, a determination by the court that domestic or family violence has occurred raises a rebuttable presumption that it is detrimental to the child and not in the best interest of the child to be placed in sole custody, joint legal custody, or joint physical custody with the perpetrator of family violence.[4]

The Model Code continues:

In addition to other factors . . . [where] the court has made a finding of domestic or family violence:

a. The court shall consider as primary the safety and well-being of the child and of the parent who is the victim of domestic or family violence.
b. The court shall consider the perpetrator's history of causing physical harm, bodily injury, assault, or causing reasonable fear of physical harm, bodily injury, or assault, to another person.[5]

Finally, the American Psychological Association has also gone on record in this area:

> In matters of custody, preference should be given to the nonviolent parent whenever possible . . . [6]

Trends in U.S. State Statutes Pertaining to Custody Cases Involving Domestic Violence

The statutory trend requiring courts to take domestic violence into account when making a custody decision is very strong. As recently as 1990, less than 16 states had such statutes.[7] By 1995, 44 of the 50 states had enacted statutes which contained some provisions in this area.[8] In 35 of those states, courts were mandated to consider domestic violence when determining the best interest of the child.[9] In 1996, Hawaii adopted a presumption against custody to batterers, and four other states adopted language addressing domestic violence as a best interest factor.[10] In 1997, five more states required courts to consider domestic violence as part of the best interests of the child, while two others adopted a rebuttable presumption against custody to batterers.[11] Massachusetts adopted this presumption in 1998, bringing the total number of states with this policy to 14 as of January 1999.[12]

Domestic violence is also increasingly recognized as an important consideration in other types of cases involving children. These include Vermont's adoption law, in which the court is authorized to terminate parental rights if the court finds the parent to have committed an act of violence in violation of a protective order or a crime of domestic violence.[13] Idaho's statute provides that the court is authorized to terminate a parent-child relationship where the parent murders or intentionally kills the co-parent.[14] Finally, California requires that custody evaluators receive training on domestic violence before they can be appointed by the court.[15] Montana requires courts to take domestic violence into account in approving adoptions.[16] Minnesota mandates judicial training in the area of domestic violence and child custody.[17]

Along the same lines, California adopted language in 1997 stating that it is detrimental for children to reside in homes where child abuse or domestic violence is occurring.[18] The same bill also now requires courts to state reasons on the record or in writing if any type of custody is awarded to an alleged batterer, child abuser, or substance abuser,[19] and clarifies that the health, safety, and welfare of children is more important than the legislative policy favoring frequent and continuing contact with both parents.[20]

Trends in U.S. Case Law Regarding Custody and Domestic Violence

Some states are developing bodies of case law dealing with domestic violence provisions in custody statutes.[21] While the statutes described above represent a significant change in the ways domestic violence is considered in the custody arena, it is important to note that it is still very difficult for many individual battered women to find qualified attorneys who are willing to represent them at the fees the women can afford. It is also still a struggle in many jurisdictions to convince judges that domestic violence should be given much weight in the custody decision, even when they are statutorily mandated to consider such abuse.[22]

Furthermore, a leading expert in the field reports: "Despite men's claims that fathers are discriminated against in custody disputes, in actuality fathers who fight for custody in America win sole or at least joint custody in 70% of these contests."[23] The author attributes this outcome to mothers being held to a higher standard than fathers, and mothers being believed less often than fathers. She cites many gender bias studies which have found these two disparities. Additionally, financial factors are often key: men's greater earning capacity, ability to obtain free child care services from their mothers, new wives, or girlfriends, and low rates of paying child support frequently result in the mother being seen by the court as unstable.

In domestic violence cases, the trends unfortunately similarly privilege fathers over mothers, with a larger proportion of batterers than non-batterers actually winning custody.[24] In addition to the factors applying to custody cases in general discussed above, this phenomenon has been attributed to lack of training on domestic violence for judges and custody evaluators, as well as several incorrect stereotypes held by these professionals. These stereotypes include the seriousness of domestic violence, which person is responsible for it, that it ends when the parties separate, or that it does not adversely affect the children.[25]

VISITATION ISSUES

Domestic Violence Likely During Visitation

Since, of course, visitation is inextricably linked to custody, similar problems and trends are found in this area. As stated previously, the likelihood of domestic violence assaults increases at the time the battered woman leaves her partner.[26] The period of separation is also the time during which visitation is being determined and taking place. In one 1990 California study involving data from over 100,000 battered women from 37 shelters, researchers found that during court-ordered visitation, 24% of the batterers continued to verbally and emotionally abuse the victim; in 10% of these cases, the batterers continued their physical violence.[27] Another study by the same researchers conducted in 1988 and involving 94 battered women found that 20% of them had returned to the batterer at least once due to his threats to take or hurt the children.[28]

Given this dangerous nature of visitation cases in which domestic violence has occurred, it is imperative that courts note the distinctions between these types of cases and other cases. The following chart, Table 1, developed originally by Dr. Peter Jaffe, is useful in articulating these differences.

Policy Statements

The National Council of Juvenile and Family Court Judges advocates a presumption in favor of supervised visitation in domestic violence cases:

> Where one party to a custody dispute is protected by a restraining or protective order entered against the other party, there [should be] a

rebuttable presumption that any award of visitation should require participation in a supervised visitation center program or be supervised by a third party who is accountable to the court.[29]

The Model Code discussed previously also contains policy statements about visitation in domestic violence cases:

TABLE 1. Special Issues in Visitation Disputes with Allegations of Domestic Violence

ISSUES	NORMAL VISITATION DISPUTE	VISITATION DISPUTE WHEN ALLEGATIONS OF ABUSE
Central Issue	• Promoting children's relationship with visiting parent; co-parenting	• Safety for mother and children
Focus of Court Hearing	• Reducing hostilities; setting schedule	• Assessing lethality risk and level of violence; protection
Assessment Issues	• Children's stage of development, needs, preferences • Parenting abilities	• Impact of violence on mother and children; developmental needs • Father's level of acceptance of responsibility • Safety plan for mother and children • Parenting abilities
Planning for Future	• Visitation schedule that meets needs of children	• Consider no, suspended or supervised visitation
Resources Required	• Mediation services • Divorce counseling for parents and children • Independent assessment/evaluation	• Specialized services and assessment with knowledge and training about domestic violence • Supervised visitation center • Coordination of court and community services • Well-informed lawyers, judges, social service, & mental health professionals

(Adapted from Peter S. Jaffe, Ph.D., London Family Court Clinic, for Family Violence Prevention Fund, 1996.] P. Jaffe & R. Geffner (1998). Child custody disputes and domestic violence: Critical issues for mental health, social service, and legal professionals. In G. Holden, R. Geffner, & E. Jouriles (Eds.), *Children exposed to marital violence: Theory, research, and applied issues.* Washington, DC: American Psychological Association.

1. A court may award visitation by a parent who committed domestic or family violence only if the court finds that adequate provision for the safety of the child and the parent who is a victim of domestic or family violence can be made.
2. In a visitation order, a court may:
   a. Order an exchange of a child to occur in a protected setting.
   b. Order visitation supervised by another person or agency.
   c. Order the perpetrator of domestic or family violence to attend and complete, to the satisfaction of the court, a program of intervention for perpetrators or other designated counseling as a condition of the visitation.
   d. Order the perpetrator of domestic or family violence to abstain from possession or consumption of alcohol or controlled substances during the visitation and for 24 hours preceding the visitation.
   e. Order the perpetrator of domestic or family violence to pay a fee to defray the costs of supervised visitation.
   f. Prohibit overnight visitation.
   g. Require a bond from the perpetrator of domestic or family violence for the return and safety of the child.
   h. Impose any other condition that is deemed necessary to provide for the safety of child, the victim of domestic or family violence, or other family or household member.[30]

Similarly, the Model Code provides:

1. The [state agency] shall provide for visitation centers throughout the state . . . to allow court ordered visitation in a manner that protects the safety of all family members . . .
2. A visitation center must provide:
   a. A secure setting and specialized procedures for supervised visitation and the transfer of children for visitation; and
   b. Supervision by a person trained in security and the avoidance of domestic and family violence.[31]

The American Psychological Association issued a similar policy statement:

> . . . [U]nsupervised visitation should not be granted to the perpetrator until an offender-specific treatment program is successfully completed, or the offender proves that he is no longer a threat to the physical and emotional safety of the child and the other parent.[32]

Statutory Trends

Similar to the custody statutes discussed previously, many US state statutes address the issue of visitation in domestic violence cases. In some states, the court is authorized to deny visitation to an abusive parent when limits on visitation are inadequate to protect a child from abuse or harm.[33] Statutes may also require the court to order or at least consider supervised visitation in such cases, or to order that visitation may not occur unless other conditions are fulfilled.[34] These conditions include restrictions on the time, place, and manner of transfer of the child; counseling for the perpetrator; "no alcohol or drugs" provisions; a professional investigation before visitation is ordered; no visitation pending a hearing; and modification of orders if abuse reoccurs.[35]

> [C]ollectively, the codes appear to create a new legal principle; to wit, the existence of domestic violence in a family . . . militates against an award of . . . unsupervised visitation to the abusive parent.[36]

Legislatures continue to amend visitation statutes frequently to incorporate domestic violence issues. For example, in 1996 eight states passed such legislation.[37] These included a mandate that the California Judicial Council create standards for supervised visitation centers and providers,[38] the creation of a *new* clearinghouse and network for supervised visitation programs in Florida,[39] and a requirement that the Kansas Attorney General provide for child exchange and visitiation centers, to be funded by marriage license fees.[40] In 1997, Arkansas passed a law adding domestic violence as a visitation factor, South Carolina enacted the Model Code's provisions for supervised visitation (quoted above), and Massachusetts barred visitation where one parent is convicted of the death of the other by murder in the first degree.[41] In 1998, New York and California adopted the same provision regarding visitation with convicted murderers (with an exception where the defendant was abused by the victim), and West Virginia adopted most of the visitation provisions from the Model Code.[42]

Currently, California has a pending bill in the 1999 legislature, AB 673 (Honda), which would use a portion of that state's share of the parental access money in the federal welfare reform bill to subsidize supervised visitation for low-income families, with the state providing matching funds in the future. Kansas is also planning to use federal welfare reform funds for the same purpose.

Practical Difficulties

While supervised visitation centers and professional individual supervisors or monitors are more prevalent than they used to be, it is still very difficult in most jurisdictions to find a qualified supervisor whom the parties can afford. Unfortunately, in many cases where no trained person is available to supervise the visitation at the rate the parties can pay, judges often appoint untrained relatives as supervisors, or grant unsupervised visitation.

Recommended Practices

The following materials focus on the unique issues presented by visitation cases involving domestic violence, and contain suggested conditions and language for court orders. They are taken from a judicial curriculum developed by the author.[43]

- Considerations in Visitation Decisions: A Checklist (Table 2);
- Conditions of Visitation to Consider in Domestic Violence Cases (Table 3); and
- Examples of Specifically Worded Visitation Orders (Table 4)

O. J. SIMPSON CUSTODY CASE

The most prominent US custody case involving domestic violence in the last few years was the one between O. J. Simpson and his parents-in-law, Louis and Juditha Brown, in Orange County, California. The Browns had cared for the two young children during Mr. Simpson's time in custody when he was charged with killing their mother, Nicole Brown Simpson. This was based on an agreement with Mr. Simpson in which he consented to the Browns becoming temporary guardians of the children. When he was acquitted of the murder charge, Mr. Simpson filed a petition to terminate the guardianship, which the trial court ordered after a lengthy and closed trial. The trial court refused to consider any evidence regarding the circumstances of Nicole Simpson's murder. Nor was the trial court willing to postpone the guardianship decision until the results of a civil trial were known; that case resulted in a finding that Mr. Simpson was liable for killing Ms. Simpson and her friend, Ronald Goldman.

In early 1998, the Browns appealed the guardianship termination; the appellate decision was released late in 1998, reversing the trial court.[44] The appellate court gave several reasons for its decision, stressing the prime importance of the evidence concerning whether Mr. Simpson had murdered his ex-wife, and stating that failure to admit this evidence was reversible error. It pointed out that even though Mr. Simpson had been acquitted of the murder in the criminal case, that case used the highest standard of proof, beyond a reasonable doubt, while the standard used in a termination of a guardianship is the lowest, a preponderance of the evidence. Therefore, even though he was acquitted in the criminal case, Mr. Simpson could still be

TABLE 2. Considerations in Visitation Decisions:
A CHECKLIST

❑ Is the perpetrator likely to kill or commit life-endangering violence? (See lethality checklist)[1]

❑ Should the court order an evaluation by a domestic violence expert regarding the effect on the children of contact with the perpetrator? (See N.J. Stat. Ann. § 2C: 25-29(b)(3), supra; see also discussion of Evaluations in Chapter 8, infra.)

❑ Should the court order the perpetrator to satisfy certain conditions before permitting visitation (e.g., completion of batterer's counseling, alcohol or drug counseling, parenting counseling)? (See 23 Pa. Cons. Stat. Ann. § 5303(c), supra.).

❑ Are there criminal charges pending against the perpetrator? Is the court authorized to take judicial notice of these in making its determination? (See, e.g., Ariz. Rev. Stat. Ann. § 25-337, discussed supra).

❑ If the evidence suggests that the violence may have been mutual, is more investigation needed to determine whether a party acted in self-defense or to protect the children?

❑ Can the order be crafted in a manner that promotes the safety and well-being of the children and the abused party?

❑ Does the order ensure that contact between the parties is conducted in a manner such that the abused party feels and is safe?

❑ Does the order compromise or conflict with orders issued by another court?

❑ Does the order contain specific language that will enable law enforcement to properly enforce it?

❑ Is someone available to meet with the children and help them create a safety plan, in case the perpetrator becomes dangerous during visitation?

❑ Does the order keep the address of the abused party and the child confidential?

---

[1] If the court concludes that the perpetrator is likely to kill or commit life-endangering violence, visitation should be suspended or denied.

---

found to have killed his ex-wife for purposes of the guardianship matter. The court was very concerned about this issue, stating that it was the single most important and relevant issue in the case.

The decision also stated that the trial court had erred in assigning the burden of proof regarding termination of the guardianship to the Browns. In fact, when someone seeks to terminate a guardianship, the burden of proof is on the petitioner, in this case, Mr. Simpson. And the appellate court stated that Mr. Simpson must show his overall fitness sufficient to overcome the

TABLE 3. Conditions of Visitation to Consider in Domestic Violence Cases

The National Council of Juvenile and Family Court Judges recommends the following conditions of visitation in cases involving domestic and family violence (NCJFCJ. Family Violence: A Model State Code, 1994, pg 34).

- Do not require or encourage contact between the parties.

- Order visitation in a location physically separate from the abused party (whether supervised or unsupervised).

- Require transfer of children between the parents in the presence of a third party and in a protected setting (e.g., police station or visitation center).

- Start with short, daytime visits in a public place, and increase length only if things are going well.

- Include no alcohol or drug provisions for the visiting parent, and direction as to the immediate consequences of violation (e.g., other parent should call police).

- Place limits on overnight visitation.

- Require the perpetrator to successfully complete a batterer's intervention program, drug/alcohol program, or parenting education program before being allowed visitation.

- Require a bond from the batterer to ensure the child's safe return.

- Build in automatic return dates for court to review how order is working.

- Do not order the victim into counseling with the perpetrator as a precondition of custody or visitation.

inherent trauma of removing the successful caregivers (the Browns) as guardians. Because of the trial court's error, Mr. Simpson was not required to make this showing.

The appellate court also faulted the trial court for excluding Ms. Simpson's diaries, which contained passages that could be interpreted to mean Mr. Simpson had beaten her. Furthermore, the appellate court was concerned that Social Services had never been asked to file a dependency petition regarding the two children, noting that this agency is supposed to act in cases involving the rich and famous as well as the nonrich and nonfamous. Finally, the appellate court held that changing judges at the trial level from a commissioner to a judge without good cause was unconstitutional.

Overall, this case is notable not because it involved a celebrity, but because the appellate court placed such great importance on the history of domestic violence by Mr. Simpson toward the children's mother. While most domestic violence cases, fortunately, do not result in the batterer killing the

TABLE 4. Examples of Specifically Worded Visitation Orders

Specific language describing conditions of an order and how future disputes between the parties will be resolved prevents either party from taking advantage of any loopholes or ambiguities that may otherwise result. Law enforcement officers report that they have difficulty enforcing orders with ambiguous conditions.

Vague clauses such as "reasonable visitation" are not effective. Similarly, the court should not order that visitation be "as agreed upon by the parties," or "to be determined later." A subsequent negotiation process between the parties could lead to further violence, often in front of the children who may wrongfully see themselves as the cause of the turmoil.

Examples of specifically worded conditions include:

♦ Visitation shall take place every first and third Saturday from 6 a.m. to 3 p.m., at the home of and in the presence of Mary Smith, plaintiff's aunt, at 123 Main St., city. The plaintiff is responsible for dropping off the child by 9:45 a.m. and picking up the child at 3:15 p.m. In the event that visitation cannot take place, the party must telephone Mary Smith at (000) 123-4567 by 8:30 a.m., and visitation shall then take place the following Saturday with the same provisions.

♦ If respondent wishes to exercise visitation rights, he must call Mary Smith at (000) 123-4567 by 10 a. m. the day before a scheduled visitation. Mary Smith shall then call the plaintiff.

♦ Respondent shall consume no alcohol or illegal drugs during the 12 hours prior to and during visitation. If he appears to have violated this provision, Mary Smith is authorized to deny him visitation that week.

♦ Visitation is conditioned upon respondent receiving weekly batterer's counseling from X organization, for a certain period of time, e.g., 1 year.

♦ Visitation may be denied if the respondent is more than 30 minutes late and does not call by 8:30 a.m. to alert Mary Smith to this (to prevent custodial parent and child from waiting for the other parent).

♦ (If there is a third party available for pick-up and drop-off, or supervised visitation): Plaintiff must arrive at the drop-off location 20 minutes before respondent, and then leave before respondent arrives. At the end of visitation, respondent must remain at the location for 20 minutes while plaintiff leaves with the children. (This prevents respondent following plaintiff to harass her or ascertain the location of plaintiff's new residence.)

♦ (If there is no third party available, even for exchanging the children): Drop-off and pick-up of the children shall occur at the local police department, in the lobby. Respondent shall leave with the children immediately; plaintiff may request a police escort to her car or to public transportation. At the end of visitation, respondent shall wait in the lobby at least 20 minutes while plaintiff leaves with the children. (See above comment.)

victim, it appears that this appellate court would also have seen beatings short of homicide as relevant in a termination of a guardianship. The court makes very clear its concern about the children's future welfare due to Mr. Simpson's propensity for violence. Hopefully, the Orange County trial court on remand, and other courts around the US, will similarly give any history of domestic violence by one parent toward the other great weight in any decisions regarding the children.

CONCLUSION

Custody and visitation cases involving domestic violence represent an area of law where there is a lot of interest on the part of legislatures and of the public. However, a basic tension is apparent: while legislation and policy statements in this area increasingly stress the importance of considering domestic violence as an important part of the custody decision, trends in cases indicate that batterers are still being awarded custody at rates similar to nonbatterers.

The widespread interest in domestic violence as an issue has led to significant improvements in the response to domestic violence in the criminal justice system over the last two decades. However, ironically, the more we are successful in prosecuting and convicting batterers, and sentencing them appropriately, the more noticeable the problems are in the family law area. One reason for this is that in most family law cases (unlike most criminal cases), one or both parties cannot afford attorneys. Thus, battered women are quite likely to be representing themselves while they attempt to communicate to the court the ongoing dangers presented by the batterers in terms of long-term contact with the children. When this factor is combined with some courts' and evaluators' inaccurate beliefs about battered women, batterers and gender bias, along with financial disparities between mothers and fathers generally, it is clear that victims of domestic violence often face difficult challenges in family court.

Family law is the next major arena which the domestic violence movement needs to address. If even some of the key goals and changes can be put into place, we will be a step closer to an effective coordinated community response to domestic violence. These goals include:

1. mandatory education on the effects of domestic violence on children for attorneys, mediators, evaluators, and judges;
2. funding for family law attorneys who have received such education to represent victims of domestic violence and their children;
3. legislation creating rebuttable presumptions against custody to batterers; and
4. funding for high-quality supervised visitation programs, prepared to deal with domestic violence cases.

NOTES

1. These categories were developed by the Duluth Abuse Intervention Project in Duluth, Minnesota and are shown in a diagram called the Power and Control Wheel.

2. H.R. Con. Res. 172, Rep. Constance Morella, Vol. 136 Cong. Rec., page S 18252-04 (Oct. 25, 1990).

3. Howard Davidson, Reporter, "The Impact of Domestic Violence on Children, A Report to the President of the American Bar Association" (August 1994) at 13.

4. Section 401 (1994) at 33.

5. Section 402 (1994) at 33.

6. Violence and the Family (1996) at 99.

7. The Family Violence Project of NCJFCJ, "Family Violence in Child Custody Statutes: An Analysis of State Codes and Legal Practice," 29(2) Family Law Quarterly 197 (1995) at 199.

8. *Id.*

9. *Id.*

10. NCJFCJ, Family Violence Legislative Update (1997) at 8.

11. NCJFCJ, Family Violence Legislative Update (1998) at 7-8.

12. Phone conversation 3/8/99 with Family Violence Project staff, NCJFCJ.

13. NCJFCJ, Family Violence Legislative Update (1996) at 8.

14. *Id.* at 8-9.

15. *Id.* at 9.

16. NCJFCJ, Family Violence Legislative Update (1997) at 8.

17. *Id.*

18. Ca. Family Code section 3020.

19. Ca. Family Code section 3011.

20. Ca. Family Code section 3020.

21. See, e.g., North Dakota Supreme Court cases applying rebuttable presumption language, summarized in various issues of Domestic Violence Report, published by Civic Research Institute, New Jersey.

22. See Naomi Cahn, "Civil Images of Battered Women: The Impact of Domestic Violence on Child Custody Decisions," 44 Vanderbilt Law Review 1041 (1991).

23. Joan Zorza, "Protecting the Children in Custody Disputes when One Parent Abuses the Other," Clearinghouse Review, April 1996, at 1117, citing to Ruth Abrams and John Greaney, Report of the Gender Bias Study of the Supreme Judicial Court of Mass., 62-63 (1989), which also cites similar findings across the U.S.

24. Martha McMahon and Ellen Pence, "Doing More Harm than Good? Some Cautions on Visitation Centers," in Ending the Cycle of Violence, Einat Peled et al., editors (1995) at 187.

25. Zorza, op. cit., at 1119.

26. See Martha Mahoney, "Legal Images of Battered Women: Redefining the Issue of Separation," 90 Michigan Law Review 1 (1991).

27. Marsha B. Liss and Geraldine Butts Stahly, "Domestic Violence and Child Custody," in Battering and Family Therapy: A Feminist Perspective, edited by M. Hansen and M. Harway, Sage (1993).

28. *Id.*

29. State Codes on Domestic Violence: Analysis, Commentary, and Recommendations, 43(4) Juvenile & Family Court Journal (1992) at 35.

30. NCJFCJ, Model Code on Domestic and Family Violence, Section 405 (1994) at 34-35.

31. *Id.*, Section 406 at 35-36.

32. APA, Violence and the Family (1996) at 99.

33. See statutes cited in Nancy K. D. Lemon, Domestic Violence and Children: Resolving Custody and Visitation Disputes, Family Violence Prevention Fund (1995) at 60.

34. *Id.* at 60-61.

35. *Id.* at 61.

36. State Codes on Domestic Violence: Analysis, Commentary, and Recommendations, 43(4) Juvenile & Family Court Journal (1992) at 31.

37. NCJFCJ, Family Violence Legislative Update (1997) at 9.

38. *Id.;* see Ca. Family Code section 3200. The standards have been developed and adopted by the Council: Ca. Standard of Judicial Administration 26.2, effective 1/1/98.

39. NCJFCJ, Family Violence Legislative Update (1997) at 9.

40. *Id.*

41. NCJFCJ, Family Violence Legislative Update (1998) at 8.

42. Phone conversation 3/8/99 with Family Violence Project staff, NCJFCJ.

43. Nancy K. D. Lemon, op.cit.

44. Guardianship of Sydney Simpson et al. v. Louis Brown et al., 67 Cal.App.4th 914 (1998).

Collaborating on Family Safety: Challenges for Children's and Women's Advocates

Sandra K. Beeman
Jeffrey L. Edleson

SUMMARY. The problems of child maltreatment and violence against women have traditionally been viewed and treated as two distinct issues. In response to these two forms of family violence, two separate service systems with different approaches to prevention, treatment and intervention have developed. This article outlines sources of conflicts between child protection workers and battered women's advocates, and elaborates on these conflicts using child protection workers' and battered women's advocates' own words elicited in a series of focus groups. Models of cross-system collaboration in the United States are then described, and recommendations are made for practice and policy which support collaboration across systems. *[Article copies available for a fee from The Haworth Document Delivery Service: 1-800-342-9678. E-mail address: getinfo@haworthpressinc.com <Website: http://www.haworthpressinc.com>]*

KEYWORDS. Child maltreatment, violence against women, overlapping violence, collaboration, child protection, battered women's advocates

The problems of child maltreatment and violence against women have traditionally been viewed and treated as two distinct issues. In response to

---

Address correspondence to: Sandra K. Beeman, PhD, University of Minnesota School of Social Work, 400 Ford Hall, 224 Church Street, SE, Minneapolis, MN.

[Haworth co-indexing entry note]: "Collaborating on Family Safety: Challenges for Children's and Women's Advocates." Beeman, Sandra K., and Jeffrey L. Edleson. Co-published simultaneously in *Journal of Aggression, Maltreatment & Trauma* (The Haworth Maltreatment & Trauma Press, an imprint of The Haworth Press, Inc.) Vol. 3, No. 1 (#5), 2000, pp. 345-358; and: *Children Exposed to Domestic Violence: Current Issues in Research, Intervention, Prevention, and Policy Development* (ed: Robert A. Geffner, Peter G. Jaffe, and Marlies Sudermann) The Haworth Maltreatment & Trauma Press, an imprint of The Haworth Press, Inc., 2000, pp. 345-358. Single or multiple copies of this article are available for a fee from The Haworth Document Delivery Service [1-800-342-9678, 9:00 a.m. - 5:00 p.m. (EST). E-mail address: getinfo@haworthpressinc.com].

these two forms of family violence, two separate service systems with different approaches to prevention, treatment and intervention have developed. Services to maltreated children are provided by publicly-funded, child-focused agencies which protect "the best interests of the child," while services to battered women are most often provided by woman-focused, grass-roots advocacy organizations. Yet a growing body of research suggests that there is a large overlap between child maltreatment and woman battering in the same families, that children's and women's advocates share common ground.

Even with this common ground, child protection workers and battered women's advocates often operate in conflict. This article begins with a review of research on the overlap of child maltreatment and woman battering in the same families. The sources of conflicts between child protection workers and battered women's advocates within the context of their different histories and foci are then described and elaborated on using child protection workers' and battered women's advocates' own words elicited in a series of focus groups. Several models of cross-system collaboration in the United States are then described, and we end with practice and policy recommendations for collaboration.

OVERLAPPING VIOLENCE IN FAMILIES: COMMON GROUND FOR CHILDREN'S AND WOMEN'S ADVOCATES

A recent review examined research findings on the overlap between child maltreatment and woman battering in the same families (Edleson, 1999). Few studies have focused specifically on the extent to which both forms of violence occur in families; however, the examination of child maltreatment case records found that from 26% (Child Welfare Partnership, 1996) to 32.5% (Hangen, 1994) of cases included indications of adult domestic violence. A study of suspected child abuse and neglect cases at a major hospital found that in 45% of the cases, mothers' medical records indicated some evidence of battering (Stark & Flitcraft, 1988). Studies exploring the prevalence of child abuse among families with known battering, estimate that from 40% (Suh & Abel, 1990) to 50% (Straus & Gelles, 1990) of batterers also abuse their children. In a survey of 1000 women, Bowker, Arbitell and McFerron (1988) found that 70% of battered women with children reported that their children had also been abused.

In addition to children of battered women sometimes suffering physical abuse, children who witness woman battering but are not themselves abused are also thought to suffer ill effects. It has been estimated that up to one-third of American children have witnessed adult domestic violence (Straus, 1992).

Children witness adult domestic violence in a variety of ways, including seeing it, hearing it, being used as a tool of the perpetrator, or witnessing the aftermath of a violent event (Carter & Schechter, 1997). Many times, witnessing domestic violence has negative effects on children. A large number of studies have examined the problems associated with witnessing domestic violence on children's development, and have found negative associations with emotional and behavioral functioning, cognitive functioning and attitudes, physical functioning, and long-term effects on development (Edleson, in press). These effects often manifest themselves in behaviors or problems that bring the children to the attention of the public child welfare system. In fact, the growing evidence of harmful outcomes for children who witness adult domestic violence has led some professionals to view the witnessing of adult domestic violence by children as child abuse (Echlin & Marshall, 1995).

Thus, in a variety of ways children's and women's advocates share common ground. Child protection workers work with children whose mothers are battered, and battered women's advocates work with women whose children are abused. Yet a variety of differences prevent them from working together successfully toward family safety.

BACKGROUND AND HISTORY OF CHILD PROTECTIVE SERVICES AND DOMESTIC VIOLENCE PROGRAMS

One of the sources of differences and conflicts between child protection workers and battered women's advocates is their different histories and responses to family violence. Even though programs for the prevention of cruelty to children have long existed (Gordon, 1988), it was not until the 1960s when Dr. Henry Kempe "rediscovered" the battered child, that a new wave of public concern took hold (Helfer & Kempe, 1968). On the heels of this work and the public attention it drew, came legislation in every state to mandate the reporting of abuse and neglect and the protection of children. The protection of children became the responsibility of publicly funded child welfare bureaucracies with mandated services and case plans for parents. The prevailing philosophy within public child welfare systems currently is family preservation, a philosophy viewed suspiciously by many battered women's advocates, who fear that it encourages abused women to stay or reunite with their batterers. In addition, battered women's advocates often believe that child protection focuses exclusively on the safety of children, and in doing so will often revictimize women by alleging their "failure to protect" children from abuse by their batterers.

In the 1970s, the resurgent women's movement rediscovered another hidden form of abuse: wife beating (Schechter, 1982). In response, grass-roots organizations, in the form of battered women's shelters, developed to provide immediate safety to battered women and their children. In over 25 years since the founding of the first American battered women's shelters, public interest in the issue of woman battering has grown dramatically, recently expressed in the 1994 passage of the Violence Against Women Act. Services to battered women are still based mostly in non-profit, community-based organizations, are voluntary, and focus primarily on women. Although most battered women's shelters now provide at least minimal programming for children, child welfare agencies often believe that domestic violence agencies are exclusively woman-focused to the neglect of their children. They also believe that domestic violence agencies have been slow to acknowledge abuse and neglect perpetrated by women.

Child protection workers and battered women's advocates also use different professional terminologies and language. Findlater and Kelly (in press) point out that words used easily within each program, words such as family, victim, family preservation, protection, empowerment, choice, and perpetrator, become emotionally charged when child protection workers and battered women's advocates attempt to communicate. All of these aspects of child protection and battered women's services, their distinct histories, different types of funding, professional terminologies, and practice foci, contribute to differences and conflicts.

DIFFERENCES AND CONFLICTS:
RESEARCH FINDINGS FROM FOCUS GROUPS

Research findings also identify and elaborate some of the differences and conflicts between child protection workers and battered women's advocates. In a recent research project (Beeman, Hagemeister & Edleson, in press), we asked child protection workers and battered women's advocates to identify some of the barriers to successful collaboration with families experiencing both child maltreatment and violence against women. Some of the barriers identified were: conflicting philosophies of practice, different practice foci, lack of communication and cooperation across systems, and bias and lack of culturally appropriate services.

Philosophies of Practice: Child-Centered
vs. Woman-Centered Philosophy

One barrier identified was the tension between child protection's child-centered philosophy and battered women's advocates' women-centered philosophy (Beeman et al., in press). Child protection workers took a "child-centered" approach, reflecting the belief that they were the only ones "looking out for" the children. This focus on the best interests of the child stemmed from their legal mandate to protect children. As one child protection worker said:

> . . . from our level, we generally see ourselves as the only people fighting for the kids. And we see attorneys, and we see all kinds of public defenders, and all kinds of advocates for the mother. But often for the kids, it is child protection.

On the other hand, battered women's advocates took a "woman-centered" approach, working with women to set their own goals. One advocate said:

> We do not . . . do men bashing, and if a woman wants to go back into a situation, we emphasize that we are here to help women do what they want to do. It may not be what I would choose to do, but I am there to help them to do what they want to do. It is their life and it is not up to me. I can give them options, but they make their choices.

As a result of these different philosophies, child protection workers and battered women's advocates often viewed the same family in different ways. While a battered women's advocate may see a woman's decision to leave or stay as her own, a child protection worker may view her decision to stay as a danger to her children.

Practice Focus: Holding Mothers Responsible vs. Holding Male Batterers Responsible

Child protection workers and battered women's advocates in our focus groups also described a different practice focus. Child protection workers believed that their legal mandate to protect the child often meant they needed to focus case plans on mothers, even if she, herself, was also a victim of abuse. As one child protection worker described:

> Speaking a . . . company line . . . we are child protection and so we need to focus our attention on the child or the children and if the . . . partner is the one that is presenting the risk to the children, and the mother is the custodial parent, we do kind of turn to the mother and say, "what are you going to do about protecting your children? And if you are not going to protect them, well, then we may need to step in and protect them."

This often meant that cases were coded as a mother's "failure to protect," even if a child was physically abused by the father or the mother's male partner. This was particularly so when the child protection worker believed the mother was repeatedly "putting the child at risk." One worker described her strategy of developing case plans for mothers, knowing in advance that it may fail and that this failure would be used against the mother in an effort to find a safer situation for the children:

> We are very concrete and I am not saying that is the best approach . . . That you're laying out a plan that you know might very well fail and then you can document that it failed and you can justify whatever action you need to take to protect the kids.

Not surprisingly, battered women's advocates objected to the focus on holding mothers, rather than male batterers, responsible. As one advocate said, "And how much did anyone attempt to (hold) the perpetrator accountable? But I bet 190% of energy went into holding that woman accountable for what happened to her children." In fact, requiring a battered woman to obtain an order of protection against her better judgment was viewed by advocates as possibly further endangering her and her children.

Lack of Communication and Cooperation Between Systems

Both child protection workers and battered women's advocates described a lack of communication and cooperation between their two systems, and also with law enforcement and the courts. Child protection workers and battered women's advocates often described an adversarial working relationship between their two systems. As one advocate said:

> . . . child protection . . . they might have different priorities as to what the safe issues are and have certain procedures. But . . . I feel that sometimes child protection is anti-advocate. Child protection feels advocates are anti-child protection. So there is a huge barrier.

Furthermore, they weren't confident that this could change. As one child protection worker said:

> I don't think there necessarily is a solution. I think there is a built-in tension that is going to be there, because there is an element of what we end up doing from the child protection point of view that does, from a point of view, victimize the woman. But yet, I don't feel comfortable sacrificing children's safety to avoid that tension. I don't know how you resolve it.

Child protection workers and battered women's advocates also identified the lack of communication and cooperation with law enforcement and the courts as a barrier. One child protection worker said:

... the criminal justice system and the juvenile justice system are just more and more protracted, dragged out, non-responsive systems. It is the same type of thing that is part of the timing element. By the time the crisis passes, you are still waiting for something to happen in the court system.

Gender, Racial and Cultural Bias in Services

Finally, racism, sexism, cultural bias, and lack of culturally appropriate services for batterers, battered women, and their children were frequently mentioned as a barrier. One advocate said:

> They're (the police) not going to come to a neighborhood where the violence is always there . . . or they say "oh, we've been out here four times today" and not arrest anyone and leave this inebriated man there and then he goes and gets a weapon.

A child protection worker said:

> The other thing has to do with individualized and institutionalized racism. If the service is available that is culturally competent, there is a much better chance of success . . . so if the shelter is full, the woman can't get in to a shelter near where she lives or has staff of people like herself, she may not get the kind of help [she needs].

In addition, the child protection system often tracks child maltreatment cases through the mother's name. Consequently, the male abuser, especially if he does not have a biological or other legal relationship to the child, is often invisible in this system. Thus, as described above, efforts to protect children often focus on the mother, setting a foundation for what Susan Schechter calls "gender bias" in the system, one in which women are held to different standards than men (Schechter & Mihaly, 1992).

PRINCIPLES OF COLLABORATION

Based upon our research findings, we identified several principles of collaboration between systems that supported the best interest of family safety.

Best Interest of Mother and Child as Common Goal

Child protection workers and battered women's advocates envisioned working together with the best interest of the family–mother and child–as a common goal. As one child protection worker said:

I think that the two can find a common ground, if you're looking for what is safe for the woman, that will by default provide safety for the children. And maybe that is where the child protection and the domestic advocates can come together and say "OK, let's not just talk about the children, let's talk about what do we need to do to make the woman safe." Because, I have seen 9 times out of 10, if you can reach a safe resolution for the woman, it is also going to be a safe resolution for the children. And maybe you can avoid that tension by just focusing on what does the woman need to do to be in a safe environment.

Similarly, one battered women's advocate stated that she thought child protection agencies and battered women's advocates should share a common mission beginning with the child's safety:

What can we agree on and focus on? What can be the same mission that both agencies will share together? If it's for the safety of the child and therefore safety of the family to protect the child, then we know advocates and agencies can work on that collaboratively.

Holding Male Batterers Responsible

Our focus group participants emphasized the importance of holding the male perpetrator responsible and involving him in services and case plans. One child protection worker expressed the following vision for change:

. . . shift the focus in child protection as much as we can off the woman as the protector of the children and put the domestic abuser as the identified client . . . Try to keep the cases out of juvenile court as much as possible but try prosecution in criminal court . . . But [we] really need to shift the focus on to the party doing the abusing as responsible for what's happening to the children and try to move the mother out of that role as much as we can.

Another child protection worker emphasized that one way of accomplishing this was through a perpetrator tracking system within child protection:

That touches on another kind of controversial issue which has been kicking around for years . . . and that is we do not have a perpetrator tracking system . . . we track our clients, by the custodial parent of the child. And so if you've got a father that is fathering with a number of women, he may not be picked up on as a perpetrator because everything is tracked under the mother's name. If we had a perpetrator tracking system, that father would be identified and would be picked up on no matter how many different families he is connected with.

Collaboration with Courts and Other Systems

Most child protection workers and battered women's advocates emphasized that a focus on family safety and accountability for the batterer could only be accomplished in collaboration with the courts and law enforcement. One battered women's advocate said:

> ... the first thing that has to happen is the immediate identification that the mother is a battered woman, and that could be done through information sharing. That's a simple change that could be made to forms, to police reports, through emergency holds, through child protection intake, criminal courts, family courts and juvenile courts ... And then ... each court has to know what has happened with the children. Criminal court, if they get a misdemeanor case where there's a non-arrest situation, they file it away. You have tons of situations that are non-arrest where there's an open child protection case and nothing has happened to the perpetrator. So there has to be a means of insuring that there's accountability of the abuser.

Other focus group participants also commented on the role of the juvenile and criminal courts. As one child protection worker said:

> The other problem I see with juvenile court vs. criminal court is that the juvenile court only has jurisdiction in ... over the children. And so by definition of their statutory limitations they can only deal with the mother, with the custodial parent ... So right away that puts that mother into that role of we are revictimizing her and saying "if you don't do these things, then you are going to lose your children." Whereas in criminal court the focus may be more appropriately put on the guy who is doing the beating and saying, "You injured these children. You have to take the consequences of what you did to these children." That is one of the primary reasons I see the criminal court as the more appropriate court because it puts the onus of what happened on the appropriate person. Juvenile court by default shifts it off of the actual guy who did it.

As this focus group participant pointed out, child protection cases are more likely to be seen in juvenile than in criminal court. Within the juvenile court, the "stick" wielded by child protection is the threat of removing a child from the home which is not always a deterrent for the batterer. In fact, anecdotal evidence suggests that some batterers use the threat of CPS (child protection services) action as another way to intimidate and control their partners (Aron & Olson, 1997). To hold the perpetrator accountable, child protection workers and battered women's advocates must be able to depend on law enforcement and the criminal courts to respond consistently and effectively to the batterer's criminal behavior.

MODELS OF COLLABORATION

Several models of collaboration between child protection workers and battered women's advocates have been developed in the United States. Massachusetts developed a Domestic Violence Program within its Department of Social Services child protection agency. Staffed by 11 battered women's advocates, each advocate provides case consultation, direct advocacy and community networking to two or three area child protection offices. These advocates, or "domestic violence specialists" as they are called, may consult in a variety of ways: sitting in on case service plan conferences, providing training for staff, or developing connections to community-based services. In a three-month period in 1996, the 11 specialists received 1400 requests for consultation (Whitney & Davis, in press). In addition, all workers are trained in how to recognize domestic violence in their cases and how to work with these families (Aron & Olson, 1997). Recently, Oregon's State Office for Services to Children and Families worked with domestic violence advocates to develop and present a training curriculum throughout the state. Additional money is being spent to locate domestic violence advocates directly in several child welfare branch offices (Aron & Olson, 1997).

Michigan's Families First, the state family preservation program, and the Domestic Violence Prevention and Treatment Board have teamed up to develop extensive cross-training and a close working relationship between battered women's shelters and family preservation workers. Starting with five communities, the project has now expanded to include 11 communities with 18 family preservation workers who take referrals directly from battered women's programs and work with the mothers to provide safety to both them and their children. As of January 1997, 345 battered women and their children had received services, over 90% of whom were shelter residents (Findlater & Kelly, in press).

San Diego County is one of the few places in the country to formalize collaboration with the court system. The Family Violence Project within the county child welfare system bridges child protection services and adult probation. The unit serves only families served by both agencies. This model of collaboration between child protection and court takes advantage of the offending parent's probation status to hold him more accountable than would be possible under the traditional system. The child protection agency's only sanction is to remove the child from his or her home, whereas probation can put the offender in jail (Aron & Olson, 1997). While this particular program serves only those families who are already involved with both agencies, the Family Violence Project is expanding their focus by developing training curricula and protocols for all child protection agency caseworkers, along with acting as consultants with child protection on cases involving domestic violence.

A new effort is also underway in the Miami-Dade County Juvenile Courts to coordinate efforts by police, child protection, battered women's programs and the Juvenile court. Funded by the U.S. Department of Justice, the project has hired four battered women's advocates via a subcontract from the court. The advocates are working with battered women identified by child protection workers or through court-ordered assessments. This is one of the first efforts to attempt to coordinate so many systems in a response to multiple forms of violence in families.

RECOMMENDATIONS FOR PRACTICE AND POLICY CHANGES

To begin to overcome these barriers and unresolved issues and to move toward collaboration, we make the following recommendations for practice and policy addressing families with both child maltreatment and violence against women. Our recommendations focus primarily on the child protection services system, battered women's advocacy organizations, and the criminal and civil court systems; a critical triad of service systems encountered by batterers, battered women and their children. We believe that all three systems must come together to work for the safety of *all* family members who are victimized. First, each system must ask themselves difficult questions about their own role. What are the limits of the child protection system and the juvenile court to hold male perpetrators responsible and how can these limits be changed? What role does the criminal court play in keeping mothers and their children safe? What responsibility do advocacy organizations have in protecting children?

Second, each of these systems must recognize the unintended consequences of some of their current practices for the safety of battered women and their maltreated children. For example, child protection workers must understand that requiring a battered woman to obtain an order for protection, against her better judgment, may further endanger her and her children. On the other hand, battered women's advocates must understand that supporting a woman's decision to stay with a batterer may also endanger her children. Family and juvenile courts must be aware of other violence in the home before making decisions about custody and visitation. Third, these systems must work at eliminating their gender and cultural biases. Male abusers need to become more visible within the child protection system. The response of law enforcement and service systems must be appropriate and equitable for women of all races, ethnic backgrounds, and social classes.

We recommend the following mechanisms for overcoming the current fragmentation of the three systems, for identifying and working to eliminate gender bias, and for bringing together the expertise of these systems to better serve battered women and their maltreated children (Beeman et al., in press).

Cross-Training. We recommend that the expertise of each system be shared across the other systems through cross-training. Several excellent curricula for training child protection workers about domestic violence have recently been developed (Conroy & Magen, 1997; Ganley & Schechter, 1996). These curricula emphasize making shifts in traditional child protection practice including the following principles: (1) identifying domestic violence is critical to the safety of children; (2) helping battered women and providing services to them is necessary to keep children safe; and (3) holding perpetrators of domestic violence accountable for stopping the violence is essential to protecting children (Ganley & Schechter, 1996.) In addition, curricula for cross-training of battered women's advocates and child protection workers are being developed. The goals of these curricula are to increase the knowledge and skill levels of professionals in both child protection and battered women's agencies and to promote and plan for collaborative strategies to better serve all clients (Colorado Department of Human Services, 1995). Through cross-training, workers in both systems have the opportunity to come together to critically view their own systems and to build bridges toward collaborative relationships on behalf of battered women and their maltreated children.

Ongoing Communication and Consultation. We recommend that a structure for ongoing consultation, communication and collaboration across the three systems be established. This structure needs to be supported by agency policy which supports the sharing of information and case consultation across systems. By coming together, these programs can identify their common ground, the safety and protection of women and children. Juvenile and family courts must come together with the child protection system and battered women's advocacy organizations as a critical perspective in this communication and consultation. Only when these three systems come together to communicate and identify their common goals, will they be able to move to the next stage of working together, integration and coordination of services.

Integration and Coordination of Services. We recommend that states adopt some model of collaboration like those described earlier to coordinate and integrate services to battered women and their children across child protection and battered women's advocacy programs. In addition, we believe that collaborative efforts must include juvenile and family courts. Improved coordination should include an effort to revise management information systems in child welfare and the courts so that abusive males may be more easily identified and tracked, especially in cases of serial abuse across multiple family systems. Such a change should also include strategies to remove gender biases that currently leave non-abusive mothers as the only adult in records. Finally, child protection, courts, and domestic violence agencies must work together to aggressively intervene with abusive males, even when they have no legal relationship to the child. These efforts should include service plans that hold abusive males accountable, not just plans for abused mothers.

Child protection workers and battered women's advocates share a common commitment to ending violence in families. This commitment must serve as the basis for overcoming barriers and challenges and working together effectively and fairly on behalf of *all* victims of family violence.

REFERENCES

Aron, L.Y. & Olson, K.K. (1997). Efforts by child welfare agencies to address domestic violence. *Public Welfare*, 4-13.

Beeman, S.K., Hagemeister, A.K., & Edleson, J.L. (In press). Child protection and battered women's services: From conflict to collaboration. *Child Maltreatment*.

Bowker, L.H., Arbitell, M., & McFerron, J.R. (1988). On the relationship between wife beating and child abuse. In K. Yllo & M. Bograd (Eds.), *Feminist perspectives on wife abuse* (pp. 158-174). Newbury Park, CA: Sage Publications.

Carter, J. & Schechter, S. (1997). *Child abuse and domestic violence: Creating community partnerships for safe families.* Family Violence Prevention Fund.

Child Welfare Partnership. (1996). *Cohort Two: A study of families and children entering foster care 1991-1993.* Salem, OR: State Office for Services to Children and Families.

Colorado Department of Human Services (1995). *Crossing the bridge: A cross-training curriculum for domestic violence/child protection workers.*

Conroy, K. & Magen, R. (1997). *Training child welfare workers on domestic violence: Trainer's manual.* Columbia University School of Social Work.

Echlin, C. & Marshall, L. (1995). Child protection services for children of battered women. In E. Peled, P.G. Jaffe & J.L. Edleson (Eds.), *Ending the cycle of violence: Community responses to children of battered women* (pp. 170-183). Thousand Oaks: Sage.

Edleson, J.L. (1999). The overlap between child maltreatment and woman battering. *Violence Against Women*, 5(2), 134-154.

Edleson, J.L. (in press). Children's witnessing of adult domestic violence. *Journal of Interpersonal Violence.*

Findlater, J. & Kelly, S. (in press). Michigan's domestic violence/child welfare collaboration: Finding common ground by re-framing child safety. In J.L. Edleson & S. Schechter (Eds.), *In the best interests of women and children: Child welfare and domestic violence services working together.* Thousand Oaks, CA: Sage.

Ganley, A. & Schechter, S. (1996). *Domestic Violence: A national curriculum for child protective services.* San Francisco, CA: Family Violence Prevention Fund.

Gordon, L. (1988). *Heroes of their own lives–The politics and history of family violence–Boston 1880-1960*. New York: Viking Penguin.

Hangen, E. (1994). *D.S.S. Interagency Domestic Violence Team Pilot Project: Program data evaluation.* Boston: Massachusetts Department of Social Services.

Helfer, R.E. & Kempe, C.H. (Eds.). (1968). *The battered child.* Chicago, IL: University of Chicago Press.

Schechter, S. (1982). *Women and male violence: The visions and struggles of the battered women's movement.* Boston: South End.

Schechter, S. & Mihaly, L.K. (1992). *Ending violence against women and children in Massachusetts families.* Boston, MA: Massachusetts Coalition for Battered Women Service Groups.

Stark, E. & Flitcraft, A.H. (1988). Women and children at risk: A feminist perspective on child abuse. *International Journal of Health Services, 18,* 97-118.

Straus, M.A. (1992). Children as witnesses to marital violence: A risk factor for lifelong problems among a nationally representative sample of American men and women. *Report of the Twenty-Third Ross Roundtable.* Columbus, OH: Ross Laboratories.

Straus, M.A. & Gelles, R.J. (1990). *Physical violence in American families.* New Brunswick, NJ: Transaction Publishers.

Suh, E. & Abel, E.M. (1990). The impact of spousal violence on the children of the abused. *Journal of Independent Social Work, 4*(4), 27-34.

Whitney, P. & Davis, L. (in press). Child abuse and domestic violence: Can practice be integrated in a public child welfare setting? In J.L. Edleson & S. Schechter (Eds.), *In the best interests of women and children: Child welfare and domestic violence services working together.* Thousand Oaks, CA: Sage.

Index

LaVergne, TN USA
27 November 2010
206253LV00012B/17/P